In Sinu Jesu

When Heart Speaks to Heart—
The Journal of a Priest at Prayer

$\oplus$

In Sinu Jesu

When Heart Speaks to Heart—
The Journal of a Priest at Prayer

By
A Benedictine Monk

Introduction by
A Benedictine Oblate

 Angelico Press

First published in the USA
by Angelico Press
© Angelico Press 2016

NIHIL OBSTAT
Peter A. Kwasniewski, PhD
Censor Deputatus

IMPRIMATUR
+ Most Reverend Michael Smith, DCL
Bishop of Meath
Mullingar, October 11, 2016

For information, address:
Angelico Press
4709 Briar Knoll Dr.
Kettering, OH 45429
angelicopress.com

ISBN 978-1-62138-219-5 (pb)
ISBN 978-1-62138-220-1 (cloth)
ISBN 978-1-62138-221-8 (ebook)

Cover photograph of a stained glass window
from the Dahlgren Chapel of the Sacred Heart
at Georgetown University, by Fr. Lawrence Lew, O.P.
Cover design: Michael Schrauzer

Introduction

by a Benedictine Oblate

THIS BOOK is a remarkable testament of a friendship that transcends all earthly measures. In its pages, we see the Hound of Heaven pursuing a priest with the exquisite gentleness of one who would win his heart's love, the inexorable purpose of one who would show him mercy, and the compassion of one who would bring healing and peace.

It also resoundingly demonstrates the truth that when God chooses one out of many—when He chooses an Abraham or a Moses, the blessed Virgin Mary, or the founders of monastic movements and religious congregations—He always does so in order to bless a multitude, fashion a people, form a nation. He does something extraordinary for one, so that His word may radiate outward to countless souls and His grace be sought with renewed eagerness. He chooses the one not as an isolated exception or arbitrary preference, but as the humble centre around which a great circle will be drawn, a blazing hearth around which many can gather, be warmed, and find fellowship.

We could call it the principle of incarnation: God does not save us one-sidedly or generically, He does not speak vaguely or at random. He comes to us as a man, as *this* man, with His own voice, articulate words, clear doctrine, and commandments of life, to which we must respond with the very powers He placed within us for that response. He comes with the offer of His friendship, and invites us to reciprocate. In spite of our smallness, our weakness, and our unworthiness, He seeks us as His own, and grants us His precious and very great promises, that we may escape from the corruption that is in the world, and become partakers of His divine nature (cf. 2 Pet 1:4).

In 2007, Our Lord and Our Lady began to speak to the heart of a priest who was greatly in need of their intervention—something that could truthfully be said of all of us in our spiritual poverty. The priest was prompted to write down what he heard, first and most obviously for his own benefit, but increasingly, for the benefit of others who

would be touched by these words and find light and strength in them.[1]
Concerning the genesis of the manuscript reproduced in these pages, he
shared with me the following:

> Here is the text as I have transcribed it over the years from the
> notebooks that I started keeping in 2007. The vocabulary and the
> style are mine, but the substance of what I wrote came during
> prayer, without any effort or prior reflection on my part. There
> would be an inner movement to write, and I would write until the
> inspiration stopped. After writing, there would be a grace of quiet
> union with Our Lord or with Our Lady. On a few occasions, there
> were "words" from saints or from holy people.
>
> Although I have at times suffered from doubts over the authen-
> ticity of what was happening, my spiritual director throughout
> most of the period covered herein identified what was happening
> as a *gratia gratis data*. I can only say that the words came peacefully,
> rapidly, and effortlessly. By this, I do not mean that the words came
> from within myself, but rather, from what I experienced as an
> objective but intimate presence of Our Lord, immediately related
> to His real presence in the Most Holy Sacrament. It was precisely in
> His Eucharistic presence that these conversations with Our Lord
> unfolded, drawing me more and more into the light of His Face
> and the fire of His Heart.
>
> I am conscious of the length of some of the sentences. This does
> not reflect Our Lord's patterns of speech, for He does not commu-
> nicate in the form of literature. The words come rapidly, but they
> come as realities that impress themselves successively. I don't know
> how else to explain it.
>
> My own piety is essentially liturgical. Nonetheless, since the
> diagnosis of my serious illness, there has been a strong attraction
> to adoration of the Most Blessed Sacrament, to reparation for
> priests, and, in particular, to the mystery of Our Lord's Face hidden
> beneath the sacramental veils. This is something already present in
> the tradition, notably in the *Adoro te* of Saint Thomas.
>
> The texts have borne fruit in my own life and in the lives of oth-
> ers, especially of priests with whom I have been encouraged to
> share them, at the recommendation of my spiritual director. In
> spite of my reticence and desire for anonymity in regard to this

---

[1] If we look to the text, we find Our Lord speaking clearly and repeatedly about His purpose in giving these words. A collection of pertinent excerpts may be found in Appendix II.

journal, I have been repeatedly told by Our Lord Himself that His words are meant for the blessing, instruction, and comfort of many Christians today, above all, His beloved priests.

With a grateful and expectant heart, I gladly give this journal into the hands of all those readers whom Our Lord and Our Lady have already chosen for it, with my prayer that it shall bear abundant fruit, and with my priestly blessing.

Given the harmony of this book's content with the teaching of Sacred Scripture, Catholic Tradition, and well-known works of the mystics, it is eminently fitting that In Sinu Jesu be published in full at this time, in conformity with Our Lord's frequent insistence that these words are intended to reach many souls.

We know from the history of approved private revelations that Our Lord and Our Lady intervene in special ways in times of ecclesial crisis, worldliness, lukewarmness, infidelity, intellectual confusion, or spiritual anguish. They speak to us of truths that have become obscured, neglected, or contradicted; they instruct us in attitudes, virtues, and practices that are forgotten, despised, misunderstood, or poorly cultivated. They are gentle teachers and firm guides, unerring in their diagnosis, unambiguous in their counsels. Into the heart of our situation, our meanderings as pilgrims of the Infinite, and the dead-ends at which our society and culture have arrived, the Lord Jesus and His Blessed Mother bring their heavenly attentiveness, the purifying brightness of their gaze, the inexhaustible depth of their wisdom, and the ardor of their charity. Not wishing to leave us orphans in our age, they address to us a message that, while never adding to or taking away from the established content of public revelation, sheds new light and lustre on ancient truths and the path of holiness.

The pages of In Sinu Jesu shine with an intense luminosity and a heart-warming fervor, as they range across and plunge deeply into so many fundamental aspects of the spiritual life: loving and being loved by God; the practice of prayer in all its dimensions; the unique power of adoration; trustful surrender to divine providence; the homage of silence; the dignity of liturgical prayer and the sacraments; the mystery of the Holy Sacrifice of the Mass; priestly identity and apostolic fruitfulness; the role of the Blessed Virgin Mary and the saints in our lives; sin, woundedness, mercy, healing, and purification; the longing for heaven, the longed-for renewal of the Catholic Church on earth. So many consoling and challenging truths of which our age stands in dire need are brought forward, inviting the response of our hearts, summoning us to conversion, impelling us to a new way of life.

This book has changed my life as well as the lives of others who have read it. By its words, we have come to a greater knowledge and a dearer love of Our Lord Jesus Christ, His Blessed Mother, and His "eternal and universal kingdom—a kingdom of truth and life, a kingdom of holiness and grace, a kingdom of justice, love, and peace" (Preface for the Feast of the Kingship of Christ). May this publication of *In Sinu Jesu* bring such blessings to all of its readers.

Some Notes About This Edition

The few notes present in the original manuscript are distinguished by the addition of "—*Author*"; all the remaining footnotes are editorial. The manuscript abounds with direct quotations of and allusions to Scripture; these are indicated wherever it was thought helpful to the reader, particularly as material for *lectio divina* done in connection with the words herein. Certain more familiar scriptural references, partial allusions, and paraphrases are so numerous, however, that it would have been impossible to indicate them all without unduly cluttering up the text.

References to the Psalms are given first according to the Doauy-Rheims translation, which follows the numbering of the Vulgate, and then the Revised Standard Version, which follows the Hebrew text.

Many lesser-known friends of God, for example, Mother Yvonne-Aimée, are mentioned in these pages. At the first mention of their names, a short biography is provided in the notes. To locate these notes, consult the index of proper names in the back and look up the first page listed there.

The italicization of a paragraph indicates the words of the priest, while plain text indicates the words of another speaker. The text is given as written, but with proper names of certain individuals and locations replaced with "*N.*" or "———." Paragraphs referring in detail to a single person or set of circumstances have sometimes been omitted if they were judged too obscure or not sufficiently pertinent to a broader readership.

Appendix I gathers together all the prayers that are strewn throughout the journal, and explains how to pray the Chaplet of Reparation or "Offering of the Precious Blood for Priests." Appendix II contains excerpts from *In Sinu Jesu* about Our Lord's purpose in giving these words.

IN SINU JESU

When Heart Speaks to Heart—
The Journal of a Priest at Prayer

Erat ergo recumbens unus ex discipulis ejus
in sinu Jesu, quem diligebat Jesus.

Now there was leaning on Jesus' bosom
one of his disciples, whom Jesus loved.

GOSPEL OF JOHN xiii, 23

Wednesday, October 3, 2007
Blessed Columba Marmion, O.S.B.[1]

My Heart hath expected reproach and misery:
and I looked for one that would grieve together with Me,
but there was none: and for one that would comfort Me,
and I found none.[2]
   PSALM 68:21 [69:20]

Our Lord, in instituting the Eucharist, foresaw outrages and sufferings—
the sufferings, I mean, of a love that is wounded and spurned. He waits still
for some little compassion on the part of His priests. He is seeking, today
more than ever, priests who will console Him, priests who will adore and
make reparation.

Before leaving for the monastery, I opened the book by Dom Vandeur[3]
sent to me by Sister N., and I read: "Make me entirely Thy priest, as was
Saint John, Thy beloved disciple, standing at the foot of Thy Cross, the Tree
of Life."

This phrase describes perfectly the call that I received thirty years ago, a
call to which I did not know how to respond, or to which I found myself
unable to respond fully. There were too many obstacles in me, too many
infected wounds, still waiting for the healing that had to come through the
hands of Mary and by the precious Blood of Jesus.

---

[1] Dom Columba Marmion (April 1, 1858–January 30, 1923) was an Irish Benedictine monk and the third Abbot of Maredsous Abbey in Belgium. Beatified by Pope John Paul II on September 3, 2000, Bd. Columba wrote a number of classics well known for their grand and intimate scope, penetrating insights into the spiritual life, and poetic texture woven of Scripture and Tradition: *Christ, the Life of the Soul; Christ in His Mysteries; Christ, the Ideal of the Monk; Christ, the Ideal of the Priest; Union with God: Letters of Spiritual Direction.*

[2] Offertory of the Mass of the Sacred Heart of Jesus.—*Author.*

[3] Dom Eugène Vandeur (1875–1967) entered the Benedictine community of Maredsous in Belgium; he made his solemn profession in 1897 and was ordained a priest in 1899. He served as a teacher at the abbey school and preached countless conferences, particularly on the Mass and the liturgy; by the end of his life he had published dozens of books and written thousands of letters. He was responsible for numerous apostolic initiatives in France, involving especially the laity, whom he encouraged to drink deeply from the sources of monastic spirituality. He completed his earthly course as an "easily accessible hermit" (Dom Marc Melot).

I want priests who will adore for priests who do not adore, priests who will make reparation for priests who do not make reparation for themselves or for others. I want priest adorers and reparators.

That evening, before going to bed, I seemed to understand that the Lord desires that these priests should put on the stole for their time of adoration: a sign of their solidarity with all the priests of the Church. Then I asked the Lord, "Is this something that Thou wouldst have me begin tomorrow?" He answered me:

No, not right away, but it will come to pass soon.

Thursday, October 4, 2007
Saint Francis of Assisi

For some time already, Our Lord has made me desire to have adoration on Thursday in thanksgiving for the Holy Eucharist, and also in thanksgiving for the mystery of the priesthood.

After Mass, I made my confession to the chaplain of the monastery. He confirmed certain things having to do with the resistances to grace that I confessed. He directed me towards the saints, something that corresponds exactly to the strong attraction to the friendship of the saints that has always marked my life.

During my thanksgiving, I think, when I asked the Lord if this call to priestly adoration and reparation was for me alone or if I should live it with others, I believed that I heard Him say:

No, I shall give you brothers and sons.

I must add that the book by Dom Vandeur that was sent to me without my having requested it—to arrive precisely at the moment when I was preparing to begin this retreat—describes perfectly the Eucharistic-sacerdotal call that I believe I hear coming to me from Our Lord, Priest, Victim, and Altar. I do not know where, nor when, nor how this calling will be realised. I know only that it is urgent and that the time presses. I seem to see a little monastic nucleus with priest-adorer-reparators associated with it, and that these will be numerous.

I have known for some time that I was to do something for the sanctification and spiritual healing of priests. It would be a work of spiritual hospitality to priests in a place made radiant by Eucharistic adoration, and where the beauty of the sacred liturgy, including the choral Office, would be like a healing balm on the wounds of the priests who would be welcomed. I do not know if this will be done in collaboration with a community of nuns or not. I dare not advance this too far, nor can I exclude it altogether.

The place will have to be beautiful and welcoming, all in the radiance of the Blessed Sacrament exposed. I seemed to understand that there would be priests adoring and making reparation for priests, and among these there would be some penitent and rehabilitated priests. Charisms and graces will be given there in abundance. The Virgin Mary, my Mother of Perpetual Help, the Mediatrix of all graces, will look after all the details, even as she did in Saint John's home when she lived with him.

To hold myself before the Eucharistic Face of Jesus in the name of His priests, to offer them to His open Heart.

October 5, 2007
First Friday of the Month
Saint Faustina and Blessed Bartolo Longo

O Virgin Mary, my Mother of Perpetual Help, my hands are in thy hands, and my heart is in thy heart, and this forever.

> *Keep me in the truth. Consecrate me in truth.*[1]
> *Close to Him there is plentiful redemption.*
> "ET COPIOSA APUD EUM REDEMPTIO"
> PSALM 129 [130]:7

The spiritual redemption of priests in bondage to evil, the spiritual illumination of priests who live in darkness, the spiritual healing of wounded priests—and all of this by means of adoration of the Most Holy Sacrament, by the presentation of priests to the Eucharistic Face of Jesus, by the offering of priests to His open Heart in the Eucharist.

I feel, perhaps for the first time in my life, that I am fully in the truth. My whole life has prepared me for this mission, for this call to adoration and to reparation—by a priest or priests. All the evil that I experienced, and suffered, and inflicted on others, will be thus redeemed, not by me, but by Him who is always working in the Eucharist to redeem back from sin sinners and those who have been wounded by sin.

"ET COPIOSA APUD EUM REDEMPTIO"

"Apud," that is to say, close to Him in the Eucharist.

In the framework of a classic Benedictine life, but one warmed by the burning furnace of charity that is the Blessed Sacrament exposed.

I must make use of this passage in Europe to speak to those in authority

---

[1] Cf. John 17:19.

3

over me. All is already prepared in the paternal Heart of God, the bosom of the Father, and in the wounded Heart of the Son, and in the wisdom of the Holy Spirit enshrined in Mary. Keep Thou me in what is true; consecrate me in the truth.

The diagnosis of my illness was a portent of this calling. It was from that moment that Our Lord began to turn over my heart[1] in view of this design of His merciful goodness. It was Mary who obtained this grace for me; she wanted me to become for her another Saint John, living in her intimacy and in adoration of the Most Holy Eucharist. It was, in effect, Saint John, who, with the Virgin Mary, adored and made reparation for the other apostles. John and Mary, and in the middle between them the open Heart and the merciful Face of Christ, of Jesus the Host.

In the Eucharist, Christ, though He be all-glorious, remains eternally Priest and Victim. The offering that He makes of Himself to the Father is ceaseless. Mary and John are borne along after Him into this offering, and I must follow them in this movement, while bringing along with me a great number of priests who are adorers and reparators.

Keep me in the truth. Consecrate me in the truth.

Psalm 68 [69] was shown me as a re-reading of my life: my past, my present, and my future.

The Virgin Mary looks after the smallest details. Nothing escapes her attention. She is a mother.

Saturday, October 6, 2007
Saint Bruno

Last evening I asked Our Lord at length to "johanninise" my soul.

Monday, October 8, 2007

Before His Face.

Act with courage, with audacity, with confidence. Act as a man, a man of God, a man configured to Christ, a man anointed by the Holy Spirit. Act also as a father, a father to the poor, a father to little ones, a father to sinners, a father, also, to the priests whom I shall send you.

Act as a physician of souls. I will show you how to bind up the wounds of the heart, even the most delicate ones, and how to care for

---

[1] The idea was that of turning over my heart the way a farmer tills a field but I am not able to express it properly.—*Author.*

4

those whom I shall send you, so that you may heal them in My Name by loving them with My Heart.[1]

I shall speak to you, I shall speak to your heart, so that you may hear My voice for the joy of your heart. You will hear My voice especially when you will come before My Face, when you will adore My Eucharistic Face and draw near to My open Heart. I will speak to your heart as I spoke to the heart of My beloved disciple John, the friend of My Heart, the priest of My open Heart.

You did well to write to the archbishop. I will touch his heart. He will help you and you will have nothing to fear. He will be for you a friend, a father. I made you encounter the Father Chaplain here so that you might see a priest according to My Heart, a priest humble and gentle, a priest altogether marked by My merciful goodness.

I am speaking to you now because you need to hear My voice. You need to feel that I am close. It is My Heart that speaks to you. My Heart speaks to your heart so that you might live from My words, which are spirit and life.[2]

Mother Yvonne-Aimée is very close to you.[3] It is she who obtained for you great graces from My Heart. It is she who obtained that you should come back to France again. She will never forsake you. You are for her a beloved son.

Dom Marmion also intervenes on your behalf, as well as a multitude of saints whom you know and love.

Saint Peter Julian Eymard[4] recognizes you as one of his own. He will communicate to you a share in his spirit. You will live from this and you will cause others to live from it.

---

[1] Ps 146(147):3; Matt 10:8; Mark 3:15, 6:13, 16:17–18; Luke 9:1, 10:17, 13:32.

[2] John 6:64.

[3] Mother Yvonne-Aimée de Jésus (Yvonne Beauvais, July 16, 1901–February 3, 1951) was an Augustinian Canoness, Hospitaller of the Mercy of Jesus, of the Monastery of Malestroit in Brittany, France. Her life was indescribably rich in bitter sufferings (including having been assaulted and maltreated by three men) and in the most astonishing charisms, particularly in her lifelong outreach to discouraged, despairing, or derelict priests. An influential priest and writer, the Abbé Gaston Courtois, consulted her and entrusted priests in need of conversion to her. Dom Germain Cozien, Abbot of Solesmes 1921–1959, observed that Mother Yvonne-Aimée was marked by "the sense of prayer, of liturgical beauty, of praising God, in the school of the Church."

[4] Saint Peter Julian Eymard (February 4, 1811–August 1, 1868) was ordained a priest for the diocese of Grenoble in 1834 and later joined the Society of Mary. As his understanding of and devotion to the cult of the Blessed Sacrament grew, he eventually left the Marists and started the Congregation of the Blessed Sacrament and, with Marguerite Guillot, the Servants of the Blessed Sacrament. His writings on the real presence, Eucharistic adoration, frequent communion, and liturgical piety are much cherished.

Dom Vandeur will be for you an intercessor and a support. You will draw his writings out of obscurity for the greater joy of a multitude of souls.

I am speaking to you now because you need to hear My voice and to feel that I am near, very near to you.[1] I am the Friend of your heart, the best of friends, and I call you My friend, the friend of My Heart, as was John.

Beginning today I entrust you with a particular grace of intercession for the souls I will send to you. You will intercede also for all those whom I shall make you see in your prayer. Pray, pray with confidence and boldness, and I shall answer you each time.

Wednesday, October 10, 2007

O my Jesus, I place myself in spirit before Thy Eucharistic Face to adore Thee, to make reparation, to say to Thee all that Thy Spirit of Love will cause to rise in my heart. I come to look at Thee. I come to listen to Thee. I come to receive from Thee all that Thy open Heart desires to say to me and to give me today. I thank Thee for having made Thyself close to me. I praise Thy mercy. I confess the redeeming power of Thy Precious Blood. Amen.

O sweet Virgin Mary, I am thy child. Keep my hands in thy hands and my heart in thy heart all throughout this day and even during the night. So do I want to live and die. Amen.

One who desires to seek My Eucharist Face, one who desires to draw near to My open Heart, is never far from the tabernacle. I transport his spirit there where I am. I welcome his desire to abide in My presence. I give him the grace of My presence in the most secret part of his soul. There he will find Me, and there he will be able to adore Me.

Yesterday, the Lord told me that He was going to untie the latent powers of my priesthood for the good of souls and the glory of His Name. He told me to bless, to bless much, not to be afraid of giving people my blessing, and even to offer them my blessing. By the priestly blessing, the treasures of merciful goodness enclosed in His Heart are poured into the souls and about the persons of those who are blessed by the hands of the priest.

The blessing of the priest is a great means by which good is made to triumph over evil, love over hatred, and mercy over judgment. Similarly,

---

[1] Deut 30:14.

the blessing given with the relics of My saints pleases Me much. I am glorified in My saints, and I pass through them to distribute the riches of My Heart in the universe of souls.

O Jesus, I want to go in spirit to the tabernacle where Thou art most forsaken and most forgotten in the world. I want to go where no one adores Thee, where no one bows before Thee, where Thou hast only Thy Angels to adore Thee and to keep Thee company. And still, it is a human heart that Thou desirest, and above all, the heart of a priest. I give Thee mine in an offering of adoration and reparation.

I want you to speak to the faithful of the Holy Mass as a true sacrifice. They have forgotten this. No one thinks any more to tell them that the action of the Eucharist renews My sacrifice upon the Cross, and that I am present upon the altar as upon the Cross, as both Priest and Victim. It is the whole of My sacrifice of love that unfolds before their eyes. You must tell them this.

I want you to be another John for My Heart. I will fill your spirit with My words of love, so that you may communicate them to those who so much need to hear them.

I never wanted to leave you alone on earth; this is why I have always surrounded you with My saints. I wanted, and want still, that you should find in them a true friendship, a friendship that is all pure, a friendship that does not disappoint. Through the saints and by their ceaseless intercession for you before My Face, you will, at length, come to Me in glory. Do not cease invoking My saints and teach others to seek from them the help they need in the trials of this life on earth. In heaven, the saints will all be glad for having helped you make your way to Me in glory.

Thursday, October 11, 2007
Day of the Most Blessed Sacrament

Bless the Lord, O my soul, and let all that is within me bless His Holy Name. (Ps 102:1)

Lord Jesus, I present myself before Thy Eucharistic Face today, placing myself in spirit close to that tabernacle in the world, where Thou art most forsaken, most ignored, and most forgotten. Since Thou hast asked me for it, I offer Thee my heart, the heart of a priest, to keep company with Thy priestly and Eucharistic Sacred Heart. I adore Thee in a spirit of reparation for all the priests of the Church, but especially for those who never, or hardly ever, stop in Thy presence, there to put down their burdens, and to receive from Thee new strength, new lights, new capacities to love, to par-

don, and to bless. I do not want to leave this tabernacle today. I want, at every instant, to remain immersed in the adoration for which Thou waitest from Thy priests.

I unite myself to the most holy Virgin Mary, Mediatrix of all graces and first adorer of Thy Eucharistic Face. By her most pure Heart, may the prayers that rise from my heart reach Thy open Heart, hidden and, so often, left alone in the great Sacrament of Thy love. Amen.

The guardians of the sanctuary, that is, the priests, must also be adorers in spirit and in truth. They must abide at every moment—at least by desire and by the attraction that I shall place in them—in the presence of My Eucharistic Face, and very close to My Heart. This is what I ask of all My priests but, because not all will do it, I ask it of you. As for you: abide, at every moment, before My Eucharistic Face. Do not forsake My Heart that beats with love, that wants only to pour out torrents of mercy upon those who draw near to My real presence.

If I am speaking to you in this way now, it is because you need to hear My voice. For too long you have been far from Me, without being able to keep Me company, without being able to hear all that I wished to say to you. But now, the moment has come. Now and henceforth, I am speaking to you, and I shall speak to you, so that many may be brought back to Me and, in Me, find healing and peace.

And as I was saying to him, "Iesu, Iesu, Iesu, esto mihi Iesus,"[1] He answered me:

Nothing pleases Me more than this prayer said with confidence and from the depths of the heart.

Jesus Crucified: herein is all the mystery of My Face of suffering love; of My head bowed to say "yes" to the Father; of My pierced and open Heart, from which flows the gift of the Spirit in the Blood and in the Water. This is the mystery of Jesus Crucified. Contemplate this, and you will be in the way that I am opening before you.

You will find My suffering Face in the Eucharist. My head bowed to say "yes" to the Father: you will also find it in the Eucharist. And My

---

[1] "Jesus, Jesus, Jesus, be to me a Jesus [savior]." Known to be the last words of Saint Ralph Sherwin (October 25, 1550–December 1, 1581), ordained in Cambrai in 1577 with a view to being a missionary priest in England; he was arrested and imprisoned in November 1580, tortured on the rack, charged with high treason, and sentenced to death. St. Edmund Campion, St. Ralph Sherwin, and St. Alexander Briant were executed in succession at Tyburn on December 1, 1581. These three are among the Forty Martyrs of England and Wales canonised at St. Peter's, Rome, on October 25, 1970.

pierced and open Heart from which flows the gift of the Holy Spirit for the salvation of the whole world and the joy of the Church—it is in the Eucharist that you will find it.

As for yourself, do not fear. I am opening before you a path that leads to life in abundance, and no one will be able to contest this life. This will be the sign of My presence in your midst, because I, Jesus, am your Emmanuel.

While saying the joyful mysteries:

I received My human face from My Mother. When you contemplate My Face, it is her beauty that you are contemplating. I received My created beauty from My Mother. My uncreated beauty is the radiance of the glory of the Father on My humanity.

Evening

Today, I think it was during the glorious mysteries of the Rosary, the Lord spoke to me of a sacerdotal Pentecost, of a grace obtained by the intercession of the Virgin Mary for all the priests of the Church. To all [priests] will be offered the grace of a new outpouring of the Holy Spirit, to purify the priesthood of the impurities that have disfigured it, and to restore to the priesthood a brightness of holiness such as the Church has never had since the times of the Apostles.

This sacerdotal Pentecost is being prepared already in silence and in the adoration of the Blessed Sacrament. The priests who love Mary and who are faithful in praying her Rosary will be the first ones to benefit from it. Their priesthood will be wonderfully renewed and they will be given an abundance of charisms to vanquish evil and to heal those under the sway of the Evil One.

It was given me to understand that the intercession of Pope John Paul II will also have played a role in obtaining through Mary this grace of the sacerdotal Pentecost.

Certain priests will refuse this grace of the sacerdotal Pentecost, out of pride, or a lack of confidence, or an absence of faith in the real presence of Christ in the Blessed Sacrament. This sacerdotal Pentecost will begin from the tabernacle, the tabernacles of the world, as from a burning hearth of charity. Priests who will have been found faithful in keeping company with Jesus the Host will rejoice. They will understand straightaway the wonders that He will want to do in them and through them. The sacerdotal Pentecost will affect first of all the priests who are true sons of Mary, living, like Saint John, in her intimacy, very close to her Immaculate Heart.

Friday, October 12, 2007

O my beloved Jesus, each time that I am not able to pray before the taber-
nacle, close to Thy real presence, I would wish to transport myself in spirit
to the tabernacle in the world where Thou art most forsaken, most forgot-
ten, and most ignored. I want to console Thee there in offering Thee the
praises of the whole Church, and in saying to Thee all that the Holy Spirit
will cause to rise in my heart. I wish—according to the desire that Thou
hast made known to me—to adore and to make reparation for priests who
do not adore Thee and who make reparation neither for themselves nor for
the souls who count on their sacerdotal prayer.

Beginning the holy Rosary, I asked the Blessed Virgin for whom I ought
to pray in the first joyful mystery. It was N. The Virgin made me under-
stand that I had to pray for him, because the prayer of a priest must make
itself felt even in the depths of purgatory where souls are waiting for it,
waiting for it in patience and in suffering.

I want him close to Me in My light. I want him to see the splendour of
My Face and to exult together with his mother and all the saints. You, by
offering the Holy Sacrifice for him, will help him to leave purgatory and
to come to the light for which he waits, and which he desires. Do not
put this off. I want to deliver him.

The Vigil of October 13th,
Anniversary of the Great Miracle of Fatima

Always the Blessed Virgin asks me for the prayer of the Rosary, the prayer
that binds all her children to her immaculate and maternal Heart. The
Blessed Virgin asks all her priest sons to take up again the Rosary, to pray it
often, with attention and love. It is by the humble prayer of the Rosary that
priests will be delivered from the temptations that harry them. It is by the
Rosary that they will undo the machinations of the Evil One who seeks to
divide, to destroy, and to bring about the downfall of those whom God has
chosen for Himself.

At the right time the path will open before you, and you will have a
great joy in following it. Everything will be clear, because all will have
been prepared in advance by the foresight of My merciful love and by
the interventions of My most holy Mother. On that day you will have
nothing to fear. Live these days in a pressing, constant prayer. Draw
closer to My Sacred Heart. Drink from the refreshing streams of My
love. Allow yourselves to be prepared by My secret but so efficacious

action in you. Great graces are in store for you, but to receive them you must be very little, like children who have a limitless confidence in the love of their papa. When you seek to reason out everything, to know everything ahead of time, to control everything by human means, you keep Me from acting as the God of love that I am. I ask neither for ability nor for great preparations on your part; I ask only for confidence, your confidence in Me, in the love of My open Heart for each one of you.

You do well to say the little invocation, "O Jesus, King of Love," that I inspired My servant Yvonne-Aimée to say in analogous circumstances.[1] When nothing is clear, when nothing is foreseeable, it is the moment to make many acts of confidence. You will repeat them as often as necessary and, in them, you will find peace and joy in the Holy Spirit.

Father will take the path that I have always wanted for him. It was for this work that everything served as a preparation, including his own sins. But I, I shall draw out of this great spiritual benefit for the souls of My priests and for the glory of My open Heart. They shall come, they shall come towards Me, and I, I shall refashion them in My image, and they shall become the priest adorers desired of My Father.

My design is one, but each person will have a part in its realisation. For this, you must all be humble, little, and suspended on My word. I will not fail you, I will not leave you without light. You will always have before your eyes the wound in My open Heart, the source of all grace and of great mercy.

When I speak, you need not think; you have only to write, and all will become clearer for you and so much easier. I shall keep you in the truth, and in this truth you will find joy.

---

[1] Yvonne Beauvais (see p. 5, note 3) was sojourning at the Augustinian Monastery of Malestroit when Our Lord manifested Himself to her on August 17, 1922, and told her to say, morning and evening: *"O Jésus, Roi d'Amour, j'ai confiance en votre miséricordieuse bonté"* (O Jesus, King of Love, I put my trust in Thy merciful goodness). At Yvonne's request, the Superioress of the Monastery of Malestroit introduced the practice of reciting the little invocation every morning and evening, starting on August 28, 1922, the feast of Saint Augustine, the Doctor of Charity. She did this without revealing the origin of the prayer and without mentioning Yvonne. At first, the little invocation spread by word of mouth. In 1927, modest bookmarks bearing an image of the Sacred Heart were printed to promote the recitation of the prayer. In 1932, the Bishop of Vannes, France, approved the invocation for his diocese. The following year, Pope Pius XI indulgenced the prayer for the Augustinian Canonesses of the Mercy of Jesus, for their sick and for those hospitalized in their institutions. Pope Pius XII renewed the favour and, on December 6, 1958, Blessed John XXIII extended it to the universal Church.

Saturday, October 13, 2007
Ninetieth Anniversary of the Great Miracle of Fatima

O my beloved Jesus, I suffer that I cannot abide close to Thy tabernacle. I feel deprived of Thy real presence and, nonetheless, I rejoice because this shows me well how much Thou hast attached me to the adorable Mystery of Thy Body and Blood. Thou willest that I should be a priest adorer and reparator for Thy Eucharistic Heart, an adorer of Thy Face that, through the Host, shines for us. Let this be done according to all the desires of Thy Heart. Amen.

Sunday, October 28, 2007

This morning, before Lauds, the Father spoke to me for the first time:

Faith in My fatherhood will be the path of healing for many, who, like you, were kept from growing up in freedom and joy beneath the gaze of their father. I want to banish fear from your life. I want you to feel loved and surrounded by My presence as FATHER—a presence that supports you, that will not hold you back from becoming the man that I have always wanted you to be; a presence that will allow you, in turn, to become a father, a father in My image, a father as My Jesus was fully a father in the midst of His disciples. They discovered My fatherhood in His countenance.[1] They sensed it in drawing close to His Heart, they saw it at work in the signs of mercy and of power that He worked in My Name.[2]

It must be so for you. Be the image of My fatherhood. By means of the fatherly love that I shall place in your heart, be My instrument for the healing of many who did not know what it is to be loved by a father. The fatherhood of the priest is a grace that I shall renew in the Church now. It is when a priest is father that he corresponds to My designs of love upon him. The Church, the beloved spouse of My only-begotten Son, suffers in that so many priests do not know how to live the grace of their fatherhood. Souls ask for fathers, and too often they are sent away, abandoned to live like spiritual orphans.

You, be a father. Receive the graces and energies of My fatherhood in your soul. The more a priest lives his fatherly mission, the more will he resemble My Son, who said, "He who sees Me, sees the Father."[3] I bless

---

[1] John 12:40, 14:9.
[2] John 10:25, 10:37–38, 14:11.
[3] John 14:9.

you, My son. I bless you to be a father for the praise of My glory[1] and for the joy of the Church of My Son.

Monday, October 29, 2007

O Holy Spirit, Soul of my soul, I adore Thee.
Enlighten me, guide me, strengthen me, console me.
Establish my soul in Truth.
Today, Monday, is Thy day,
O Thou who proceedest from the Father and the Son.
I consecrate this day to Thee, O Divine Paraclete,
and all the Mondays for the rest of my life.
Today, I desire to live in Thy presence,
attentive to Thy inspirations, and obedient to Thy voice.
O Holy Spirit, come into my life through Mary.
Renew and invigorate my priesthood.
Sanctify me and all priests.

Before Vespers

Here I am, Lord Jesus! I heard Thy call and I have come to find Thee in the Sacrament of Thy love.

You could have come sooner. I was waiting for you. I am always waiting for you: I wait for all My priests in the Sacrament of My love, but they make little of Me, and of the fact that I wait for them day and night. If only they knew what awaits them in My presence: the plenitude of mercy, rivers of living water[2] to cleanse them, to reinvigorate their priesthood, to sanctify them.

This was the secret of My saints, of the holy friends whom I have made known to you: Dom Marmion, the Curé of Ars, Saint Peter Julian Eymard, Saint Gaetano Catanoso,[3] Dom Vandeur, Father Marie-Joseph

---

[1] Eph 1:12–14.

[2] John 4:10–14, 7:38; Rev 21:6; Num 20:6 (Vul.); Song 4:15; Jer 17:13–14; Zech 14:8.

[3] Saint Gaetano Catanoso (February 14, 1879–April 4, 1963) was an Italian parish priest canonized by Pope Benedict XVI in 2005. One of eight children, Gaetano was ordained in 1902 and served as a parish priest his entire career, giving himself wholeheartedly to pastoral ministry, including strenuous visits to remote places. Reflecting Catanoso's profound devotion to the Holy Face of Jesus, he established the Confraternity of the Holy Face in 1920, and founded an order of nuns, the Veronican Sisters of the Holy Face, in 1934.

Cassant[1]—all of these, priests according to My Heart. And there are so many others also who knew how to live between the altar and the tabernacle.

This is what I am asking of you. You are a priest adorer now. Do not forget it. This is the call that I addressed to you, and, with the call, I always give the grace to correspond to it. Accustom yourself to giving Me the best of your time. Your first duty now is to abide before Me for those of My priests who pass before Me without stopping, without even bowing to adore Me, without taking the time to make the genuflection that bespeaks the faith of the Church and the love of every believing soul.

Here in My presence I will fill you, not only for yourself, but also for all those to whom it will be given you to transmit My messages of love and of mercy. I want also that you should speak to them of My solitude in the tabernacle. Certain sophisticated minds will laugh at this. They forget that I am not there like some inanimate object. It is My Heart that waits for you in the tabernacle; it is My gaze that, full of tenderness, fixes itself, from the tabernacle, on those who draw near to it. I am not there for My own sake. I am there to feed you and to fill you with the joys of My presence.

I am He who understands every man's loneliness, especially the loneliness of My priests. I want to share their loneliness so that they will not be alone with themselves, but alone with Me. There I shall speak to their hearts as I am speaking to you. I am ablaze to be for each one of My priests the Friend whom they seek, the Friend with whom they can share everything, the Friend to whom they can tell everything, the Friend who will weep over their sins without, for a moment, ceasing to love them.

It is in the Eucharist that I wait for them as physician and as remedy. If they are sick in their body or in their soul, let them seek Me out, and I will heal them of the evil that afflicts them.

Many priests do not have a real and practical faith in My Eucharistic presence. Do they not know that the Eucharist encloses within itself all the merits of My Passion? Let them recover the faith of their childhood. Let them come to find Me there where I am waiting for them and I, for My part, shall work miracles of grace and holiness in them.

What I want above all else is that My priests be saints, and for this, I

---

[1] During his novitiate with the Trappists, Pierre-Joseph Cassant (March 6, 1878–June 17, 1903) received the name Marie-Joseph and was known for his strong determination to fulfil his lifelong wish of being ordained to the priesthood, in spite of his suffering from the tuberculosis of which he died not long after his ordination on October 12, 1902. Cassant said: "When I can no longer say Mass, Jesus can take me from this world." He was a member of the Association of Victim Souls dedicated to the Sacred Heart.

offer them My presence in the Eucharist. Yes, this is the great secret of priestly holiness. You must tell them this, you must repeat what I am saying to you, so that souls may be comforted by it and stimulated to seek holiness.

My Heart thirsts for the love of the saints. To those who come to Me, I will give love and holiness. And in this shall My Father be glorified.[1] And this shall come to pass through the intimate action of My Spirit. Where I am present in the Sacrament of My love, there also is the Spirit of the Father and of the Son. It is by the Holy Spirit that My Eucharistic presence is My glorious presence to the Father in heaven, and it is by the Holy Spirit that My Eucharistic presence touches the souls who adore Me to unite them to Me, and to bear them up even before My Father's face.

For now, this is enough. You did well to consecrate this Monday and all Mondays to the Holy Spirit. This was not a useless thing. I welcome such gestures and I ratify them in heaven. As for you, be faithful to this, and you will see great things.

Afterwards, it was the silence of the love that unites. Nothing casts me into the silence of the love that unites like the words received from the Lord.

Friday, December 7, 2007

You gave joy to My Heart by remaining this time in My presence. The light of My Eucharistic Face is shining in your soul and I have drawn you close to the wound in My side. You are always welcome in My presence. I long to receive you and to keep you close to Me. This is your vocation, priest adorer.

Respond to the call of My Heart. Adore Me for your brother priests who forget that I wait for them in the Sacrament of My love. Seek Me out for them and in their name and I will bless both you and them.

My Eucharistic Heart overflows with love for My priests. I would give to each of them the grace I gave Saint John, My beloved disciple: that of intimacy with My Heart and with the Sorrowful and Immaculate Heart of My Mother. I would renew the priesthood of My Church in this way. I would make My priests resplendent with holiness. I would impart to their tongues and to their hands the very graces that I poured out upon My Apostles in the beginnings of My Church. The reticence is not Mine. It is they, My priests, who flee My company. It is they who turn away from My Eucharistic Face and leave My Eucharistic Heart without the

[1] John 14:13.

15

consolation of their friendship. I look for consolers among My priests, and I find so few among them.

You, say "yes" to Me. Be the priest adorer of My Eucharistic Face and of My Sacred Heart present in the Sacrament of My love and waiting for the company of even one priest who loves Me and will offer himself with Me to the Father as a victim of reparation.

My Father, too, is grieved by the coldness and indifference with which I, who am His Beloved Son, His eternal Priest, His immaculate Victim ceaselessly offered in the sanctuary of heaven, am treated on earth. This comes not from strangers, but from My very own, from those whom I chose, out of love, to share in My priesthood, to abide in My presence, to nourish My people with the mysteries of My Body and Blood. All heaven weeps over the sins of My priests. For every sin there is mercy in the Blood and Water that flow from My wounded side, but the sins of My priests call for reparation.

Make reparation for your brother priests by adoring Me, by remaining before My Eucharistic Face, by offering the love of your heart purified by My great mercy. I bless you now. Be My priest adorer.

Saturday, December 8, 2007

This is how I would have you pray for the time being. Take the time to come before Me. Seek My Face. When you pray in this way I will draw you close to My Heart. Pray using My Mother's Rosary, even when you feel that your prayer is empty or mechanical, or when you are beset by distractions. The decision to pray pleases My Sacred Heart and the Immaculate Heart of My Mother.

The time you offer to us, when you pray as you did tonight, becomes precious in our eyes and is of immense benefit to your soul and to the souls for whom you pray. I see all of those for whom you prayed tonight—those whom you named and those whom you did not name— and I bless each one as I bless you now, My priest, My friend, My beloved brother.

I have chosen you and My designs on your life will be fulfilled. The time is coming when you will praise and thank Me for doing for you according to the promises I have made you. Trust Me and let nothing keep you from seeking My Face and My Heart in prayer. I bless you.

Sunday, December 9, 2007

Your prayer pleases Me. It is inspired by the Holy Spirit in you. The Holy Spirit facilitates the conversation with Me that is the expression of our friendship. Those who draw near to Me with confidence and simplicity, seeking My Face and longing for the warmth of the fire that blazes in My Heart—they are led and moved by the Holy Spirit.

Friendship with Me is not difficult. It is the gift that I offer freely and gladly to all souls, but in the first place, to the souls of My priests. If priests lived in My friendship, how different My Church would be! She would be a place of warmth, of light, of peace, and of holiness. Many of the sufferings and hardships experienced within My Church at the hands of her ministers, My priests, would not exist, were priests, My priests, living daily in the grace of friendship with Me that I offer them and long to give them.

The solution to the hardships and trials of priests, the answer to the problems that beset so many of them, causing them to fall into patterns of sin, is the friendship that I offer them. The Holy Spirit is poured out on every priest on the day of his ordination, and in that outpouring is given a marvellous capacity to live in My friendship and in the intimacy of My most holy Mother. So few of My priests accept this gift and use this capacity for holiness that I bestow upon them. This is the Johannine grace of which I have already spoken to you: friendship with Me, with My Sacred Heart, and a pure intimacy with the Heart of My Mother, like that of Saint John, and even of Saint Joseph.

The Immaculate Heart of My Mother loves all My priests. She accepts each one as her own son, and in each one she sees a friend of My Heart, a friend chosen by Me, and one in whom I want to find all the qualities of friendship that I found in Saint John. This is part of My Mother's role in the sanctification of priests. She will lead every priest who consecrates himself to her, as you did, into the deepest joys of friendship with My Sacred Heart.

As for you, this has already begun, even though you may not always feel that you are living in My friendship and in the intimacy of My most holy Mother. Our eyes never leave you, not even for a moment, and our Hearts are united in loving affection for you, even as they were for My beloved disciple and friend, Saint John. Live in this grace. Do not refuse what we would give you in abundance. Remain confident. We bless you, My Mother's hand in Mine.[1] We bless you, and those for whom you have asked our blessing.

---

[1] I thought this a strange expression until I looked up, right after having written it, and saw in the icon of Our Lady of Perpetual Help the hand of Jesus in that of His Mother.—*Author*.

IN SINU JESU

Monday, December 10, 2007

I am your Mother of Perpetual Help and I am the Mediatrix of all graces for my dear children. My eyes of mercy are turned toward you. My Heart is open to you. My hands are ever raised in prayer for you, or open over you to shower abundant graces upon you and upon those for whom you pray.

I am pleased that you want to imitate my son Saint John in making your home with me, in opening to me every part of your life. In this way, you allow me to act upon you, but you also allow me to act with you and through you. My presence and my action are revealed in gentleness, in sweetness, and in mercy. I want you to resemble me spiritually, just as my Jesus resembled me physically. Jesus, looking at me, saw the perfect reflection of all the dispositions and virtues of His adorable Heart. I, looking at you, want to see my own Immaculate Heart mirrored in yours. I want to communicate to you and to all my priest sons the virtues of my Heart. By consecrating yourself to me, you have made this possible, and already my transformation of you has begun.

My Son has given me sway over the hearts of His priests. I will transform and purify and sanctify the heart of every priest consecrated to me. Mine it is to change the souls of priests, to wash them, to lift them up into the heavenly places, so that their conversation may be with my Son, and through Him with the Father and the Holy Spirit.[1] For this reason am I rightly called PORTA CAELI, the Gate of Heaven. It is the will of my Son that His priests should live, while they are yet on earth, in the heavenly places. He would have them enter with Him into the sanctuary of heaven, beyond the veil where, as eternal High Priest, He offers Himself ceaselessly as a Victim of praise and propitiation to His Father.[2]

The Holy Spirit is the living flame of this heavenly holocaust. All of heaven glows with the fire of love that burns in the Heart of the Son who stands before His Father as eternal High Priest. I am for all my priest sons the Gate of Heaven. If any priest would ascend, even in this earthly life, into the glory of the heavenly liturgy ceaselessly celebrated by my Son before the Father's Face, he need only approach me. I will open the way into the mysteries of heaven for him. I will teach him the reverence, the silence, the profound adoration that befits one called to serve at the altars of my Son and in His place.

Let me be for you the Gate of Heaven. Come to me at every opportunity. Pray my Rosary. I will make you share in all that I hold in my

---

[1] Eph 1:3, 1:20; Eph 2:6; Phil 3:20.
[2] Inter alia, Heb 6:19–20, 9:24, 12:22–24.

Heart. I bless you now and I bless those for whom you have prayed to me. I bless my priest sons. I love them with all my Heart and I follow them in their comings and goings. When they fall I weep over them, and all my desire is to lift them up, to cleanse them, to heal their wounds, and to see them restored to the grace of friendship with my Son.

Tuesday, December 11, 2007

Our Lady:

I am with you tonight. I am present to you and I hear the prayers you address to me. I will open my hands, full of graces and blessings, over the souls whom you recommended to me. I am ever willing to come quickly to the aid of my poor children. I am ever ready to help them, to lift them when they fall, to bind up their wounds, and even to intervene in such a way as to repair the effects of their wrongdoing.

I am not distant. I hear every prayer addressed to me. My maternal Heart is moved to pity when my children, and especially my priest sons, have recourse to me in their needs. I am the Mother of Mercy, MATER MISERICORDIAE, honoured by the Church in her chant to me.[1] I do turn towards you my eyes of mercy, and I am ever willing to help poor sinners. Let sinners come to me; I will never turn them away. Let them appeal to my Sorrowful and Immaculate Heart; they will never be disappointed.

As for you, dear son of mine, persevere in praying to me. Hold fast to my Rosary and beware of every ploy of the Evil One to separate you from it. My Rosary is your safeguard and your weapon in the fight against the forces of evil. At the same time, for you it is a remedy and a comfort. Do you not see how the Rosary has stabilized you? Do you not experience its healing and all its benefits? Pray my Rosary and teach others to do the same.

I will bless your preaching and your writing. I will give you the gift of touching hearts and of winning them for me, especially those of my priests. Trust me for the unfolding of the plan of my Son. I will see to every detail. It is I who obtained this calling for you. You will be the priest adorer obtained by my Heart for this work so desired by my Son. Your part is to persevere in prayer. Trust, too, in the guidance of Father N. I am pleased that you wrote to him candidly. I have chosen him to help you that you, in turn, by my gifts, may help him and be to him a comfort and a friend.

I thank you for the *Ave Maris Stella* that you offer me. It touches my

---

[1] In the Marian antiphon *Salve Regina*.

Heart and I answer each one of its petitions in your favour. This is why I inspired you to begin praying it. I ask little of souls and I give much. Such is my way. Such, too, is the way of my Son. Yes, our Hearts are moved even by the smallest tokens of love, and our response to them surpasses what you can imagine. We bless you and those whom you have recommended to our Hearts.

Wednesday, December 19, 2007

Our Lord:

I remain your Friend, the Friend of your heart. I am always present to you and My eyes are upon you at every moment.[1] I desire your company. I long for the attention of your heart and for the consolation of your adoration, your reparation, and your love.

Tomorrow is Thursday. Do what I have asked you to do. Live tomorrow in adoration and reparation for all your brother priests, and in thanksgiving for the inestimable gifts of the Sacrament of My love and of the priesthood. Seek Me out and remain before My Eucharistic Face, close, very close to My open Heart. I will do all the rest. Adore Me. Make reparation. Approach Me and remain with Me in the name of all My priests who never approach Me and never remain in My presence.

My Sacred Heart is divinely sensitive to the coldness and indifference of My priests. I ask you to make reparation to Me for them. Allow Me to love you as I would love each of them. Allow Me to heal you, to comfort you, to sanctify you, just as I would heal, comfort, and sanctify any one of My priests. I love My priests—but few of them believe in My love for them. You, believe in My love for you. I am your Friend. I have chosen you to be in life and in death the privileged friend of My Sacred Heart.

I bless you and I bless those whom you entrust to the mercy of My open Heart. The light of My Face shines upon you. Believe in My love for you. I will never abandon you, never disappoint you. My plans are for your happiness, for your holiness, for your peace. Have no fear. I will do for you all that I have promised, and your heart will rejoice, and you will praise and glorify Me forever.

My Mother, too, is attentive to you. Her mantle surrounds you and protects you. Her Immaculate Heart is touched by the prayers you offer her. Love My Mother and pray to her ceaselessly. My Mother also blesses you and My Mother's blessing bestows upon the one who receives it heaven's sweetest graces and favours.

[1] Ps 32(33):18–19.

✛

Thursday, January 3, 2008
The Holy Name of Jesus

Listen to Me. Open to Me the ear of your heart and I will speak to you as I promised.[1] My Heart has so much to tell you. I will instruct you. I will teach you. I will show you the way in which you are to go. My Heart yearns for yours. I so desire your company.

I long for the company of every one of My priests. I wait for you in this the Sacrament of My love. So few priests respond to My desire. When I choose a man to be My priest, I choose him at the same time to be a privileged friend of My Sacred Heart. I desire the friendship of My priests and I offer them Mine.

I have called you to experience the grace of My friendship. I want you to be for My Heart another Saint John, loving Me, seeking Me, listening to Me, abiding in My presence.

My Mother, too, desires this for you, and I have entrusted you in a special way to her Sorrowful and Immaculate Heart. Turn to My Mother in every need of yours. I have made her the Immaculate Mediatrix of all My graces. All that I would give you, I want you to have through her.

Speak often of My Immaculate Mother's mediation. For you and for many souls, this doctrine is the secret of holiness. Trust in the goodness of My Mother's Heart. Know that her gaze is ever upon you. Her mantle surrounds you like a protecting shield. She is attentive to every detail of your life. Nothing of what you need or suffer is insignificant to her, and this because I have given her a Heart capable of mothering My entire Mystical Body and each of its members from the greatest to the least.

Listen to her voice as you listen to Mine. She too will speak to you. She too will instruct you, and counsel you, and guide your steps into the path of holiness that I have laid out for you. My Mother is intimately present to you. Honour her presence in your life. Do not forsake the prayer of her Rosary; it binds you to her. Do not neglect the *Ave Maris Stella* and the other acts of love for her that she has asked of you or that the Holy Spirit has inspired you to offer her. Such little means are of immense, incalculable value in My eyes and in hers.

I want you to love My Mother as John loved her—in obedience to My word from the Cross, "Behold your Mother."[2] All the graces that you have received over the past few years, and especially over these past

---

[1] Cf. St. Benedict, *The Holy Rule*, Prologue.
[2] John 19:27.

months, were obtained for you by her intercession and given you by her hands.

Your own mother was right when she told you today to be kind to the Sisters. I want you to have for them a gentle and fatherly compassion. Understand their limitations and their needs, and be for them a kind father, a father ever ready to show them goodness and loving attention. This patient kindness is a virtue that I want to see in all My priests, and because I want to see it in them, I will give it to them. When they stand at the altar to receive My Body and My Blood, all the kindness of My pierced Heart flows into them to make them priests and fathers according to My own desires for them.

Draw from My Body and Blood given to you all the graces of which you stand in need. Priests receive little from their daily communion at My altars because they expect so little. Ask and you shall receive.[1] Consult the saints. Learn from them what it is to ask great things of Me, to ask boldly, confidently, and joyfully. And thank Me for the effects of My Body and Blood in your body and blood, in your soul, in your mind, in your heart of hearts. The Eucharist is transforming for all who receive Me with faith and with confident devotion, but it is especially so for My priests. It is by the reception of My Body and Blood that you will grow in My friendship and in the shining priestly holiness by which I want to be glorified in you and in all My priests.

Then I recommended to Our Lord a number of souls. He answered:

I bless all those whom you bring to Me here, those whom you expose to the light of My Eucharistic Face and offer to the love of My open Heart. I am attentive to your prayer for Father *N.*, as is My Immaculate Mother. We love him and will deliver him. Let him trust us to do in him what he cannot do of himself. My grace is made perfect in weakness,[2] and My Mother is the Mediatrix of My grace. And I bless you and thank you for seeking Me out here. I call you My friend, the friend of My Heart.

Tuesday, January 8, 2008

Listen to Me and I will speak to you.

My Heart overflows with love for you, and when one loves, one has much to say—and then there is a communion in love deeper than all words, in the silence that unites souls to Me. I will give you that silence too.

---

[1] Matt 21:22; Mark 11:24; John 16:24.
[2] 2 Cor 12:9.

I have chosen you to live in My friendship. Let Me respond, as I see fit, to all your heart's desires. In what I will give you, there is no bitterness, no poison, no deception—I will give you only My light, My truth, My sweetness, My love, and a participation in all My states and in all My mysteries. I will take you into the innermost sanctuary of My Heart where I adore My Father as His eternal priest, and offer myself to Him as a perpetual victim of love.

This is what I desire to give all My priests, but first, they must consent to the gift of My friendship and live, as John lived, in the intimacy of My Heart and of the Immaculate Heart of My Mother.

I will renew the holiness of the priesthood in My Church. I will pour out the Holy Spirit upon all priests in the form of a purifying fire.[1] Those who welcome that fire will emerge from it like gold from the furnace, shining with holiness and with a wonderful purity for all to see. Those who refuse My fire will be consumed by it. They will be like the sterile branches that are cut away and then cast aside to be burned.[2]

The fire of My Heart is the Living Flame of Love, the Holy Spirit. Yield to that fire, and ask Me to enkindle it in you and in the souls of all My priests. The flame of purifying and sanctifying love blazes from My Body in the Most Holy Eucharist. Those who adore Me in My Sacrament of love will be the first to experience the sacerdotal Pentecost by which I intend to renew the priesthood of My Church. The sons of My Mother's Immaculate Heart will be prepared by her for this work of Mine.

If you desire to receive the fire of My purifying and sanctifying love, live in the presence of My Immaculate Mother as did My beloved disciple and friend, Saint John. She who was present in the cenacle at the Pentecost by which I sent My Church into the world is also at the heart of this Pentecost of holiness by which I will renew My priests and cause the priesthood once again to shine in My Church.

I bless those whom you present to Me, lifting them into the light of My Face. I will give to each one according to his need, but also according to his readiness to receive My gifts. Those who are poor in spirit are those most ready to receive what I would give them.

Those who are close to My most pure Mother and invoke her as Mediatrix of all graces will not be disappointed in their hopes. How it pleases Me to bestow graces and blessings in abundance through the pure hands of My holy Mother! She is the treasurer and dispenser of all the riches that are laid up for souls within My Sacred Heart. Souls that appeal to her will not go away empty. Souls that refuse to acknowledge

[1] Mal 3:3.
[2] Matt 3:12; Matt 13:40–42; Luke 3:17; John 15:6; Heb 6:8.

her unique place in My Father's great plan of mercy for the world will not receive in the same measure as those souls who look to My Mother and call upon her name with confidence. Insist on this when you are called to preach or teach.

The riches of My kingdom are for all whom I have redeemed with My own Blood, but it pleases Me to bestow them through My Mother, the Queen and Mediatrix who stood at the foot of My Cross, offering Me and offering herself with Me. Today she reigns with Me in paradise.[1] All that I won for souls from My Father on the altar of the Cross, with My Mother at My side, I will now pour out on souls through her Heart and through her hands. This, too, is the secret of a fruitful priesthood. In every priestly act and in all of life, place your hands in the hands of My Mother and your heart in her Heart.

Now I bless you and I leave you with the kiss of My peace.

January 10, 2008
Thursday Hour of Adoration and Reparation

Come to Me and I will speak to you heart to heart, as one friend converses with another. This dialogue of love is essential to our friendship. Remember, I have chosen you to be My dearest friend, the friend of My Heart. I want to share with you all that I hear in the bosom of My Father.[2] I want to communicate to you the desires of My Heart, My plans for the purification and renewal of the priesthood, and also the things that grieve My Heart.

I ask you to console Me by remaining before My Face. I ask you to console Me by staying close to My Heart, pierced for love of you and for all sinners. Be My priest adorer. Console Me and make reparation for those who spurn My love, for those who mock My wounds, My Blood, My sacrifice.

Soon I will give you time in My Eucharistic presence. I want you to learn to remain before My Eucharistic Face, silent, adoring, listening to Me, and loving Me for those who do not adore Me, those who do not listen to Me, those who never express their love for Me in this way.

If only My priests would spend time before My Eucharistic Face, I should heal them, purify them, sanctify them, and change them into apostles set all ablaze with the living flame that consumes My Heart in the Blessed Sacrament. But they stay away. They prefer so many other

---

[1] Ps 44:10 (45:9).
[2] John 1:18, 15:15.

things, vain pursuits and things that leave them empty, bitter, and weary. They forget My words, "Come to Me ... and I will refresh you."[1] My priests will be renewed in holiness and in purity when they begin to seek Me out in the Sacrament of My love.

The great renewal of the priesthood in My Church will begin when priests understand that I want them to live in the company of My Immaculate Mother. When they turn to her and acknowledge her as the Mediatrix of all graces, I will give wondrous signs of My favour to them. Priests will be transformed. They will discover, as for the first time, all the powers bestowed upon them on the day of their ordination. In so many priests of Mine, the full virtue of My priesthood in them is constrained and bound. I desire to release the full power of My priesthood in those whom I have called and chosen to represent Me—to *be* Me—at the altar where My sacrifice is renewed, and in all the works of the sacred ministry.

Bishops must begin to set an example of holiness for their priests. Look at the holy bishops celebrated by My Church in her calendar. How I desire to raise up holy bishops today! The means to holiness for bishops and priests are the same. Let them seek Me out in the Sacrament of My love. Let them learn to abide in adoring stillness before My Eucharistic Face. Let them beg to be set ablaze with the living flame of love that consumes My Eucharistic Heart. And let them turn to My Mother, the Mediatrix of all graces, entrusting themselves, and the flocks that I have entrusted to them, to her loving care. My bishops, too, must give the example of a personal devotion to My Mother's Rosary. Let them look at the example given, in this regard, by My servant Pope John Paul II. The desire of My Heart is that every bishop should live in the intimacy of My most pure Mother, and learn the meaning of belonging entirely to her, *Totus tuus.*[2]

But as for you, do what I ask of you humbly and quietly. Obey My words. Respond to My requests. Review My words to you and I will give you further light on what they mean for you and for others, especially for those whom you hold in your prayer. My Mother will give you the direction you need to order your life wisely and joyfully. She will rectify the things that are not as they should be, and show you how to use your

---

[1] Matt 11:28.

[2] The papal motto of Pope John Paul II, "totally thine," taken from a prayer of consecration to Our Lady given in St. Louis Marie de Montfort's *True Devotion to Mary*. The full text of the prayer is: *Totus tuus ego sum, et omnia mea tua sunt. Accipio te in mea omnia. Praebe mihi cor tuum, Maria* (I belong entirely to thee, and all that I have is thine. I take thee for my all. O Mary, give me thy heart).

energy, your time, and the talents I have given you. Take her as your Mother and Teacher, and do not be afraid to consult her even in little things. Nothing escapes the loving attention of her Heart. Trust her with all the details of your life and you will see that she is present to you, as she was to Saint John, and that nothing of what you live, or suffer, or fear, is foreign to her.

Continue to pray the *Ave Maris Stella* for yourself and for the priests whom I entrust to your prayer. My Mother will show herself a Mother to you and to those of her priest sons who accept the solicitude and unfailing tenderness of her Heart.

I am pleased, so pleased, by the time your father offers Me on Thursdays for My priests. Know that you are the first to benefit from his humble and confident prayer.

I have bound you closely to a network of souls. Each one has a role to play. Each one has a mission. In paradise you will see what I have done and with whom I have done it, and you will sing the praise of My mercy eternally.[1] Now I bless you and those whom you bring before Me. Receive My blessing and the kiss of My peace.

Thursday, January 17, 2008
Saint Antony, Abbot

I began my holy hour of adoration and reparation after Mass, and almost immediately Our Lord began to speak to my heart:

Put Me first. Put My friendship before all else. You cannot live without My friendship. It is not good that you should be alone.[2] Seek My Face at all times and in all things.[3] Seek My open Heart present in the Sacrament of My love. I have called you to be My friend. I have revealed Myself to you as the Friend whom you have always desired, the Friend who will never mislead you, never disappoint you, never abandon you. Open your heart to My friendship. Seek My Face. Converse with Me. Listen to Me. Remain in My presence. Know that at every moment My eyes rest upon you. My Heart is, at every moment, ready to welcome you. I desire your presence. I want the attention of your heart. I want your friendship in response to the friendship I have offered you.

My Heart has a particular love for you, a love that My Father destined for you alone and for no other from all eternity. How it grieves My

---

[1] Ps 88:2 (89:1); Ps 135(136):2–3.
[2] Gen 2:18; Eccles 4:10.
[3] 1 Chron 16:11; Ps 26(27):8; Ps 104(105):4.

Heart when the unique love I offer a soul is spurned, or ignored, or regarded with indifference! I tell you this so that you may make reparation to My Heart by accepting the love I have for you and by living in My friendship. Receive My gifts, My kindnesses, My attention, My mercies for the sake of those who refuse what I so desire to give them. Do this especially for My priests, your brothers.

I would fill each one of My priests with My merciful love, I would take each one into the shelter of My wounded side, I would give to each one the delights of My divine friendship, but so few of My priests accept what I desire to give them. They flee from before My Face. They remain at a distance from My open Heart. They keep themselves apart from Me. Their lives are compartmentalized. They treat with Me only when duty obliges them to do so. There is no gratuitous love, no desire to be with Me for My own sake, simply because I am there in the Sacrament of My love, waiting for the companionship and friendship of those whom I have chosen and called from among millions of souls to be My priests and to be the special friends of My Sacred Heart. Would that priests understood that they are called not only to minister to souls in My Name, but even more to cling to Me, to abide in Me, to live in Me and for Me, to live by Me and no other!

I want you to tell priests of the desires of My Heart. I will give you many opportunities to do this. Make known to them these things that I have made known to you. So many of My priests have never really heard and understood the invitation to an exclusive and all-fulfilling friendship with Me. And so, they feel alone in life. They are driven to seek out in other places and in creatures unworthy of the undivided love of their consecrated hearts, the fullness of happiness and hope and peace that only I can give them. So many go forward in bitterness and disappointment. They seek to fill the emptiness within with vain pursuits, with lust, with possessions, with food and drink. They have Me, very often, near to them in the Sacrament of My love, and they leave Me there alone, day after day and night after night.

Oh, how My Heart longs to raise up a company of priest adorers who will make reparation for their brother priests by abiding before My Eucharistic Face! I will pour out the treasures of My Eucharistic Heart upon them. I want to renew the priesthood in My Church, and I will do it beginning with a few priests touched to the quick by My friendship, and drawn into the radiance of My Eucharistic Face.

The graces stored up in My Heart for priests are inexhaustible, but so few open themselves to receive them. You, My friend, My chosen priest, remain in My presence and open your soul to all that I desire to give you. Open the ear of your heart to all that I have to say to you. Listen to

Me. Write what you hear. Soon I will let you share with others the things that I will have spoken to you in silence.

I love you with an undying love. Nothing can separate you now from the burning love of My Eucharistic Heart.[1] I have set you apart to be the priest adorer I have always desired you to be. Continue to listen to Me. Continue to obey Me. You will not be disappointed in your hope.[2]

I have many things to tell you.[3] I have only just begun to tell you the things that are stored up in My Heart for you, and this from all eternity.[4] Yes, I would speak to all souls in this way, but there are so few who know how to be still before My Face, so few who know how to rest, like Saint John, upon My Heart. My Heart is full of words of light and love and comfort for My priests. How I long to converse with the priests whom I have chosen as the friends of My Heart! Speak to My priests of the gift of divine friendship that I hold in reserve for each of them. This is the secret of priestly holiness: a life of friendship with Me, a "yes" renewed each day to the gift of divine friendship that I offer each priest in My Word and in the Sacrament and Sacrifice of My Body and Blood.

I want you to begin reading every Thursday chapters 13–17 of the Gospel of Saint John. Nourish your soul on this reading. I will make it a brightness shining in your soul. I will make it a nourishment for your spirit. I will make it a healing medicine, the antidote to all your spiritual ills and weaknesses. I spoke those words recorded there for all My disciples to the end of time, but I spoke them first of all for those whom I knew ahead of time and chose to be My priests, priests called to live in My friendship and, through Me, in the intimacy of My Father and in the light of the Holy Spirit. Begin today to read these chapters and make it a weekly practice, a way of further sanctifying Thursdays, all the Thursdays of your life, that I have asked you to consecrate to Me for the sake of all My priests, your brothers. Do this and I will enlighten you. Do this and I will instruct you. Do this and I will comfort you with a comfort that no creature can offer you.

And love My Immaculate Mother. Continue to honour her with the prayer of her Rosary and with the other prayers that I have inspired you to take up. To enter into My friendship is to enjoy a privileged and sweet relationship with My Mother. By becoming My friend, you become a son to her. Her Immaculate Heart overflows with tenderness for My priests. When you will speak to priests, never omit speaking of My

---

[1] Rom 8:35–39; Jer 31:3.
[2] Ps 21:6 (22:5); Rom 5:5.
[3] John 16:12.
[4] Eph 3:8–12.

Mother, your Mother, their Mother. Make her known in her privileges and in her mysteries, and she will pour forth graces upon you and upon those who receive your words.

Here I asked Our Lord about my daily routine. So often I am tired and need to rest. I feel guilty about not being able to keep up what I would see as a more normal daily round of prayer and activities. Sometimes I cannot say all of the Office. This weighs on me. So I asked Our Lord what I should be doing.

For now, your daily routine is what you can do. I will help you and My Mother will help you, gently and little by little, to make the changes that are necessary. Do not give in to the feelings of guilt that assail you because you are not living up to the ideal you have set for yourself. I do not ask you to be faithful to an ideal. I ask you only to be My friend and to live at every moment in the grace of My divine friendship. All the rest follows. Perfection is the fruit of friendship with Me, not a precondition for it. You, and many souls like you, are confused about this. My friendship is not earned, it is not something acquired by measuring up to the standards of perfection that you have set for yourself. My friendship is pure gift.[1] It is the gift of My Sacred Heart and I offer it freely. So few souls understand this. You are sanctified by living in My friendship. All the rest is secondary. Love Me and believe in My unconditional love for you. Trust Me. Show Me that you have confidence in My merciful goodness, especially when you experience weakness, or shame, or fear, and I will renew the grace of My love in your heart. I will uphold you with the gift of My unfailing presence. I am the Friend who will never forsake you. Let that be enough for you.

Then I offered a number of souls to His open Heart.

I bless them all and My Immaculate Mother blesses them. We give to each one according to his desire and his readiness to receive the graces made ready for him in our Sacred Hearts.[2]

---

[1] Matt 10:8; 2 Cor 9:15; Eph 2:8; Rev 21:6.

[2] Although not customary in English, the expression "the Sacred Hearts of Jesus and Mary" was popularized by St. John Eudes (November 14, 1601–August 19, 1680) and expresses the truth that our Lady's heart, just like her Son's, is a temple of the Holy Spirit, a consecrated place set apart for God alone. The traditional *Roman Martyrology* (1956 ed.) describes St. John Eudes on August 19 as "the promoter of the liturgical cult of the Most Sacred Hearts of Christ and his Mother."

Thursday, January 24, 2008
Saint Francis de Sales

Things happened differently today. I began by reading John 13, as Our Lord asked me to do on Thursdays. I understood that:

Had Judas but looked at Jesus,[1] grace would have washed the temptation out of his heart. "O my Jesus, hide me in the secret of Thy Face, far from the plotting of demons and of men."

Even now Our Lord washes the feet of His priests and wipes them with a towel. Even now, He would wash the feet of His chosen ones to teach them the humility of His love for them. If I want companionship with Him, I must let Him do for me all that His humble love seeks to do.

He is ever ready to wash and purify His priests—feet and hands, head and heart, body and soul. He desires that a clean priesthood should serve in His Church. He is ready at every moment to wash away the filth that disfigures so many priestly souls. No longer does He pour water out of a basin; the water that purifies His priests flows out of His open side and is mingled with His precious Blood.

Purification, cleansing, is the condition of friendship with Him. He cleanses every soul that accepts the offer of His divine friendship, and he who abides in His friendship abides at the wellspring of purity.

The "stains of the feet" are those sins committed by thought, word, deed, or omission in daily life. Our Lord is always disposed to wash away the "stains from our feet." One who abides in the friendship of Jesus is, according to His own word, "clean already." He desires nonetheless even to remove from our feet the traces of any connivance with evil.[2]

"You, in turn, ought to wash one another's feet."[3] This is the sacred ministry of the Sacrament of Penance: the restoration of purity to souls contaminated and stained by sin. For this reason the confessor must be profoundly humble. His is a service of humble love.

Then, Our Lord spoke to my heart directly:

Today [while you were reading], I did not speak to you directly, but I spoke to you through My word, enlightening your heart as you read it, listening to Me. This is the way I would have you read the Scriptures always. Read what is written but incline the ear of your heart to My voice, which speaks to souls inwardly and gives light and understanding to those who seek it. I am present to you when you open the Scriptures

---

[1] Luke 22:61–62.

[2] John 13:10. Translations vary in their rendering of *katharos holos*—e.g., "clean wholly," "completely clean," "clean all over."

[3] John 13:14.

and I want to enlighten you and instruct you. When you read My word, seek My Heart. When you read the Scriptures, seek My Face. You will find My Heart hidden in My word like the treasure hidden in the field, and you will discover My Face shining through the text and illuminating the eyes of your soul.

I want My priests to approach the Scriptures in this way: seeking Me and yearning for the grace of My divine friendship, a grace that can be deepened at every moment, a grace that I never tire of giving in greater measure.

Thursday, January 31, 2008
Saint John Bosco, Priest

Do you think that I am not faithful to you? Do you think that I have in any way distanced myself from you because you have not been able to spend time in My presence and draw near to My open Heart? Not at all. I am all the more happy to see you, to welcome you into My presence, to keep you close to Me in this the Sacrament of My love.

You and so many of your brother priests do not know Me as I would have you know Me. Many of you are strangers to My Heart. Come close to Me.[1] Remain in My presence. Seek My Eucharistic Face. Learn of My love for you, and you will begin to trust in it. I am not harsh. I am not a taskmaster. I am your divine friend. I am your advocate, your comforter, your refuge in every trial. Those who persevere in seeking My Eucharistic Face will begin to read there all the secrets of My Heart, that is, the unsearchable depths of My love for souls and, in the first place, for My priests.

This is the root of the evil that eats away at the priesthood from within: a lack of experiential knowledge of My friendship and love. My priests are not mere functionaries; they are My chosen ones, the friends whom I chose for myself to live in such communion of mind and heart with Me that they prolong My presence in the world. Each priest is called to love My Church with all the tender passion of a bridegroom, but to do this, he must spend time in My presence. He must experience Me personally as the Bridegroom of his soul.

I want you to call priests to the experience of My friendship. Show them how to remain before My Eucharistic Face by giving them an example of adoration and reparation. Draw near to My open side in the Sacrament of My love for them and in their place, and they will begin to follow you there. Reach out to My priests, not so much by speaking to them, but rather by reaching out to Me for their sake.

---

[1] Jas 4:8; Sir 51:23; Tob 13:6; Zech 1:3.

I tell you again: I want you to be My priest adorer, the priest adorer of My Eucharistic Face and of My Heart hidden in the Sacrament of My love. My Heart is wounded even in My glory.[1] It is My wounded Heart that you find when you approach Me in the Most Holy Eucharist. And from My wounded Heart there flows a ceaseless torrent of merciful love to purify souls, to strengthen, heal, sanctify, and glorify them. The mystery of My Sacred Heart hidden in the Sacrament of My love is still so little known. I want all My priests to know that in the Most Holy Sacrament of the Altar there beats for them a living Heart, a Heart all aflame with the most tender love.

There is no need for My priests to go through life isolated, lonely, and friendless. I want to be the faithful companion of their days and of their nights. I want to be their solace and their rest. I want to be their Friend, ever ready to listen to them, to welcome them, to heal them, and renew their hope. Oh, if only they would seek Me out in those tabernacles where I wait for them, in those tabernacles where no one joins Me in My ceaseless prayer to the Father!

Never miss an opportunity to greet Me, to adore Me, to remain with Me, even if only for a moment, in the Sacrament of My love. In eternity you will see the inestimable value of every moment spent in My Eucharistic presence.

I renew for you the gift of the protection and intercession of Saint Peter Julian. I renew for you the companionship and intercession of Abbot Marmion, of Father Vandeur, and of those saints whom, at different moments in your journey, I have sent into your life to minister to you.

Above all, I renew for you the words I uttered for Saint John from the Cross: "Behold your Mother."[2] Live in her presence. Honour her at every occasion and in every way possible. Every time you show love and devotion to My most holy Mother, you honour the words I spoke from the Cross, and you put them into practice. "Behold your Mother." She desires nothing more than to look after you, just as if you were her only son. Her attention for you is not divided, nor is it in any way impaired by the attention she gives to the vast multitude of her children through the ages. Trust in her care for you. Pray her Rosary. Honour her as you have been doing.

The presence of My Mother in the life of a priest is the supreme grace, because she is, by the will of My Father and by the operation of the Holy Spirit, the Mediatrix of all graces. How it pleases Me when you have recourse to her by this title! When you glorify My Mother, you glorify

[1] John 20:25–28; Rev 1:7, 5:6; 1 Cor 2:2; Gal 2:20, 3:1; Heb 10:19–20.
[2] John 19:27.

Me. And when you glorify Me, you glorify My Father and the Holy Spirit, the Advocate sent in My Name to complete My work and to bring to perfection the kingdom which I established by My death and resurrection.

Mary, My Mother, is Queen in the kingdom for which I died, and rose, and ascended to My Father. She is with Me in glory. She participates in My sovereign lordship over all space, all times, and all creatures visible and invisible. Nothing is too difficult for My Mother, nothing is beyond her means, for all that I have, I have made over to her. When she commands, it is in the power of My Name, and when she accomplishes marvels of grace in souls, it redounds to My glory and to the glory of the Father and the Holy Spirit.

Love My Mother as your Mother and submit to her as your Queen. Have recourse to her in every necessity of body or soul. Nothing is too small for her. Nothing is too great for her. Her eyes are upon you and her Heart is, at every moment, disposed to help you. She is your Mother of Perpetual Help.

I thank you for returning to My presence today. These Thursdays of adoration and reparation that I have asked you to offer Me are the means of your own growth in holiness and the means of healing and reconciliation for many priests. Remain faithful to what I have asked of you. I bless you and My Immaculate Mother smiles upon you, blessing you in My Name. Remain confident and grateful. We will not forsake you. We bless those whom you present to us. Our favour rests upon them. Go now, and remain in peace. I mark you with the seal, the kiss of My divine friendship.

Friday, February 1, 2008

Make no mistake about this: the renewal of My priesthood in the Church will proceed from a great return to the adoration of My real presence in this the Sacrament of My love. I will purify, heal, and mightily renew the priests who seek Me out in the Sacrament of My love. To them I will show My Face. I will speak to their hearts and I will make known to them the secrets of love that I hold within My Heart, and that I have reserved for them in these last days.

This is why I ask you to be My priest adorer. You will be one among many, for I am gathering My priests to My Eucharistic Heart. Those who belong to Me know My voice and they will come to Me and remain in My presence.[1]

[1] John 10:27.

This is the remedy for the evil that has so disfigured My holy priest-hood in the Church. I am calling priests into My Eucharistic presence that they may experience there the gift of divine friendship that I have longed to give them from the beginning. I will raise up a movement of priests who will seek My Eucharistic Face and remain close to My Eucharistic Heart, not for themselves alone, but for the sake of those priests who never adore Me, who never linger in My presence, or who flee from before My Face. My Heart is ablaze with desire for the holiness of My friends, My priests. I Myself will sanctify those who come to Me, and for their sake I will reach out to the others and draw them gently and powerfully to My Heart. This is a sign of My advent in glory: when priests will have returned to Me in the Sacrament of My love, adoring Me, seeking My Face, remaining close to My open Heart, then will the world begin to be ready to welcome My return in glory.

In all of this, have a boundless confidence in My Immaculate Mother. Her hands are open over the Church to dispense graces in abundance, first of all to My priests, and then through My priests to souls every-where. Call upon My Mother as Mediatrix of all graces, for you and all My priests are called to share in her mediation, as you participate sacra-mentally in Mine. My Mother is assembling a company of priests to be for her other Saint Johns. These will live in her presence and receive from her Sorrowful and Immaculate Heart an abundance of knowledge and of graces for the days that lie ahead.

As for you, dear brother, beloved friend, and priest of My Heart, attach yourself firmly to My Mother by means of her Rosary, and she will never forsake you. Call upon her in every need of yours, great or small, of soul or of body, and you will understand that she is in truth your Mother of Perpetual Help.

Love Me and return to Me often in the Sacrament of My love. Receive the kiss of My friendship. I bless you with all the love of My pierced Heart.

Tuesday, February 5, 2008
At the Shrine of Our Lady of Knock, Ireland

Our Lady spoke thus:

I desire, my dear son, that Knock should become a place of pilgrimage for priests.[1] I will make of Knock a place of healing for my priest sons. I

---

[1] This Marian apparition began on August 21, 1879, when fifteen people (men, women, and children, ranging in age from 5 to 74 years old) from the village of Knock and surrounding areas in County Mayo, Ireland, beheld Our Lady, St. Joseph, St. John

will restore them to purity and to holiness of life. I will draw them into my company. I will give them a share in the sacred intimacy with me that was the allotted portion of Saint Joseph, my most chaste spouse, and of Saint John, my adopted son. Here at Knock I want to reveal myself to priests as Virgin Bride and Mother. This is a secret that I have held in my heart for this time of trial for the Church. To every priest who desires it and asks me for it, I will give the grace of living in my presence as Virgin Bride—this was the vocation given to Saint Joseph—and of living in my presence as Mother—this was the vocation given to Saint John when, from the Cross, my Son entrusted me to him, and him to me.

I want priests to begin to come to Knock. I want them to come with their bishops. The desire of my merciful and Immaculate Heart is that Knock should become a wellspring of purity, holiness, and renewal for all priests, beginning with those of Ireland. I have waited until now to reveal this project of my Heart. The time is short. Let priests come to me here at Knock. I wait for them as Virgin Bride and as Mother. Let them come to wash themselves in the Blood of the Lamb, my Son, and to be united to Him, Priest and Victim, in the Mystery of His Sacrifice.[1] Knock is for all my people, but it was, from the beginning, destined to be a place of healing and of abundant graces for priests. Let this be made known to the bishops and priests of my Church. I long to be the Virgin Bride and Mother of all priests. In sacred intimacy with me they will find the holiness that my Son desires to give each of them: a radiant holiness, a holiness that will illumine the Church in these last days with the brightness of the Lamb.[2]

Let them come here to remain in adoration before my Son, the Lamb Who was slain. Let them wash themselves in His precious Blood by seeking absolution from all their sins. Let them entrust and consecrate themselves to me as Virgin Bride and Mother. Almighty God will do great things in them and through them. I so desire that Knock should become for all priests a fountain of living water, a place of healing, of comfort, and of renewal.[3] My hands are ever raised in supplication for my priest sons, and my Heart is ready to receive them here.

the Evangelist, and a Lamb and cross on an altar at the gable wall of the parish church. The witnesses watched the apparition in the pouring rain for two hours, reciting the Rosary. Inquiry was made into the witnesses' testimonies and the apparition was declared worthy of acceptance. Among the approved Marian apparitions, Knock is most unusual for the ensemble of figures and signs.

[1] Rev 7:14, 22:14.

[2] Rev 21:23; John 8:12 and 9:5; 2 Cor 4:2; Isa 62:1.

[3] Num 20:6; Isa 58:11; Jer 2:13; John 4:14; Rev 21:6.

Let them come to me and I will manifest myself to each one as the Mediatrix of all graces and as the helper given them by God in their priestly ministry.[1] I am the New Eve given to the New Adam—and given by Him from the Cross to all His priests, to those called by Him to continue His mission of salvation in the world. I, the Lady of Knock, am the Virgin Bride and Mother of all priests. Let them come to me and, in the company of Saint Joseph and Saint John, taste of my sweetness.

It is for this reason that I brought you here. I want you to be the first to consecrate yourself to me as Virgin Bride and Mother. I want you to model your own life after that of Saint Joseph and Saint John. Live in my sacred intimacy. Share all things with me.[2] There is no need for you or any priest to remain alone. My Heart is open to all my priest sons, and to those who ask for it, I will not refuse the grace of a special intimacy with me, a participation in the unique grace given Saint Joseph and Saint John in the beginning. This was the grace that I gave Archdeacon Cavanagh in this very place.[3] From his place with me in heaven, he intercedes for the priests of Ireland and for all priests. And now we bless you, in the Name of the Father, and of the Son, and of the Holy Spirit. Amen.

Wednesday, February 6, 2008
At the Shrine of Our Lady of Knock, Ireland

Our Lady:

You are here, my son, by my doing. It is I who brought you here, that, in the presence of my Son, the divine Lamb Who takes away the sins of the world,[4] you might be inwardly healed and refreshed. My maternal Heart yearns to lead all my priest sons into the presence of my Jesus, the Lamb by Whose Blood the world is saved and purified of sin.[5] My priest sons must be the first to experience the healing power of the Blood of the Lamb of God. I ask all my priest sons to bear witness to the precious

---

[1] Gen 2:18; Tob 8:8; Sir 15:1–6, 17:5, 36:26–27.

[2] Matt 1:20; John 19:27; Acts 1:14, 2:44, 4:32; 2 Cor 7:3.

[3] Bartholomew Cavanagh (1821–1897), one of thirteen children, was ordained in 1846 for the Archdiocese of Tuam and was appointed Parish Priest of Knock-Aghamore in 1867. He was parish priest there at the time of the apparition and remained in this post until his death. Famed for his devotion to Our Lady, he worked tirelessly to serve the ever-growing number of pilgrims, particularly in the ministry of hearing their confessions.

[4] John 1:29; 1 Pet 1:18–19; Lev 14:13.

[5] Inter alia, Rom 5:9; Heb 9:13–14; 1 John 1:7; Rev 1:5, 7:14, 22:14.

Blood of Jesus. They are the ministers of His Blood. His Blood is in their hands to purify and refresh the living and the dead.[1]

I desire that all priests should become aware of the infinite value and power of but a single drop of the Blood of my Son.[2] You whom He has called to be His priest adorer and reparator, adore His precious Blood in the Sacrament of His love. His Blood mixed with water flows ceaselessly from His Eucharistic Heart, His Heart pierced by the soldier's lance to purify and vivify the whole Church,[3] but in the first place, to purify and vivify His priests. When you come into His Eucharistic presence, be aware of His precious Blood streaming from His open Heart. Adore His Blood and apply it to your wounds and to the wounds of souls.

The Blood of my Son brings purity and healing and new life wherever it flows. Implore the power of the precious Blood over yourself and over all priests. Whenever you are asked to intercede for souls, invoke the power of the precious Blood over them, and present them to the Father covered with the Blood of the Lamb.

I am here at Knock for you and for all priests. Knock bears witness to the gift and mystery of the priesthood. I came to Knock to reveal myself in a special way as the Mother of priests. I want my priests to come here. Here I will comfort them. Here I will heal them. Here I will restore them to purity and to holiness of life.

Bear witness to what I will have done for you at Knock. I will arrange for you to return here. For you, my dear son, this is and will be a place of healing and of hope. Here you are surrounded by Saint Joseph, my beloved and most chaste spouse, by Saint John, my adopted son so dear to my Sorrowful and Immaculate Heart, and by the Archdeacon Cavanagh, a priest devoted to me, who intercedes in heaven for all who come to Knock.

Learn to trust me. I speak to you simply and with a mother's love.

---

[1] Our Lady speaks here in a manner reminiscent of how Jesus spoke to St. Catherine of Siena, e.g.: "This the divine charity provided in the Sacrament of Holy Confession, the soul receiving the Baptism of Blood, with contrition of heart, confessing, when able, to My ministers, who hold the keys of the Blood, sprinkling It, in absolution, upon the face of the soul" (*The Dialogue*, A Treatise of Prayer, ch. 5); and again, "This greatness is given in general to all rational creatures, but, among these I have especially chosen My ministers for the sake of your salvation, so that, through them, the Blood of the humble and immaculate Lamb, My only-begotten Son, may be administered to you" (*The Dialogue*, A Treatise of Prayer, ch. 24).

[2] Cf. St. Thomas Aquinas, *Adoro te devote*: "Pie pelicane, Jesu Domine, me immundum munda tuo sanguine: Cujus una stilla salvum facere totum mundum quit ab omni scelere" (Lord Jesus, merciful pelican, wash my filthiness and cleanse me with Thy Blood, one drop of which can free the entire world of all its sins).

[3] John 19:34; 1 John 5:6.

You are not deceived. I want you to know all that my Heart holds for you and for my priest sons. I am about to draw many priests into a relationship of sacred intimacy with me like that enjoyed by Saint Joseph and Saint John. Begin now to live in this grace. Turn to me in every need, great and small. Trust me to arrange all things to your advantage and to the glory of my divine Son.[1] Share your life with me. Entrust to me your concerns, your worries, and your fears. When you are in need of anything, be it spiritual or temporal, turn to me. I am your Mother of Perpetual Help. I am the Mediatrix of all graces. All good things are mine to bestow on whomsoever I will. This is my Son's gift to me, and the will of the Father.

Having stood with my Son as He hung upon the Cross, I stand with Him now in glory. Mine it is to dispense to all souls the fruits of His redemption. To me, His Heart is ever open, and I draw out from the wound in His side an infinity of graces and mercies for souls. The Heart of my Son is an inexhaustible treasury and I am its keeper. Those who desire anything from the Heart of my Son can come to me, and I will obtain it for them and give it to them with my own hands.

Consecrate yourself to me as I asked. Do it tomorrow on Thursday, the day of your adoration and reparation for priests. I thank you for listening to me this evening and for taking my words to heart. I bless you together with my adorable Son in the Sacrament of His love.

Friday, February 8, 2008
At D., Ireland

It is I who brought you here to this place made holy by the adoration and faith of so many souls. It is I who want you in My presence, to gaze upon My Eucharistic Face and to remain close to My Eucharistic Heart. I love you. I cherish your response to My gift of divine friendship. You need not fear that I will withdraw Myself from you or fall silent. It is I who initiated our conversations and I want them to continue so that you may grow in My friendship and become for Me more and more like My beloved friend, Saint John.

In this place My Eucharistic Heart is not forsaken nor is it forgotten. Here I am surrounded by grateful love. Here I find the adorers whom I seek. I take comfort in their presence close to My altar, and I rejoice to see each one arrive with his burden of cares, with thanksgiving, with sorrow for sin, or with a desire to offer Me the love that so many refuse Me in this world grown cold.

---

[1] John 2:1–11.

Tell the Sisters of My love for them. They do not forsake Me in the Sacrament of My love and I will not forsake them, nor will I disappoint them in their hope. This is a place blessed by My presence in a special way. It is a beacon in the dark night of faithlessness where so many are tempted to forget Me or to doubt of My love, and even of My existence. Here I answer prayers and I will continue to do so, for this house is founded upon a great love and rooted in a profound faith. It is My desire that hope, too, should flourish within these sacred walls. My Eucharistic Heart has a special love for this house and for the souls who dwell within it, loving Me, serving Me, living to be so many living flames of adoration before My Eucharistic Face. Comfort them with My words.

I desire to rekindle here an immense fire of Eucharistic charity. All those who suffer from the cold of the world will be drawn to the warmth of this house as to a radiant hearth. I desire to be loved and adored here, and I place My own desire in the hearts of My spouses, My little handmaids, that they may participate in the accomplishment of My designs. I do not want them to lose hope. I will renew their youth at the wellspring of My Sacrifice and in the light of My abiding presence. I want you to encourage and comfort them in My Name. I bless them continually from My place on the altar in the midst of them. Where My blessing prevails, all things are possible. Let them continue in faithfulness to the grace of adoration given them, and I will do the rest. My Heart is moved to pity for this little flock and My love is stirred to help them according to the desires that I have placed deep within them.

As for you, adore Me here as much as you can this week. I have brought you here to school you in adoration, to fill you with those graces that I have held for so long in My Heart for you and for no other. Seek Me out. Remain before My Face. Stay close to My wounded Heart in the Sacrament of My love, and I will do for you what I, and no one else, can do. Trust Me.

I bless you and with My most tender love I bless each of the Sisters here. My Heart is open to them and I delight in their presence to Me in the Sacrament of My love.

Be at peace. Continue the retreat as you began it, by speaking from your heart. Trust Me to inspire you, to help you, to give you the words that will comfort and sustain these souls so dear to Me.

Saturday, February 9, 2008

Learn to listen to Me and I will speak to you heart to heart, as a man converses with his friend. I long to hold conversation with you. I want to speak to you, to instruct you, to guide you, to comfort you, just as I instructed, guided, and comforted Saint John and My other disciples.

My Heart's desire is that all priests should enter into the gift of My divine friendship. I desire that My priests, My chosen ones, should turn to Me in their doubts, their fears, their perplexities, and their weaknesses. I desire that they should learn to share all things with Me. It is not enough to seek Me at certain times only, nor is it enough to share with Me only a part of what they live, or pieces of their existence. To live in My friendship is to share all things with Me, to keep no secrets, to reserve nothing for oneself alone. It is not good for man to be alone.[1] For this reason have I made Myself ever present and available in the Sacrament of My love. The soul who spends time in My presence, close to My open Heart, will learn all that My Heart contains, and will come to share in all My sentiments and desires.

Remain in My presence whenever and for as long as you can. Being with Me is the great means to healing and to holiness. It is enough to remain with Me if you *be* like Me. Come to Me, full of expectant hope, and I will do all the rest. To adore Me is to seek My Face and to approach My Heart, full of wonder and of holy fear, and above all, full of love. Adoration is the wordless confession of My divinity. Adoration proclaims that I am all and that all else is nought.[2]

When Saint Francis repeated during the hours of the night, "my God and my all!," he was offering Me the adoration in spirit and in truth that My Father desires.[3] His prayer ascended through Me even into the presence of the Father. So it is with every prayer addressed to Me. All who would reach the Father must pass through Me.[4] For this reason was My side opened by the soldier's lance. It is the way to My Father. If you would speak to My Father, speak to Me. If you would see My Father, fix your gaze upon My Eucharistic Face.[5] If you would serve My Father, serve Me, especially in the weakest and poorest members of My Mystical Body. Whatsoever you do unto them, you do unto Me,[6] and what is done unto Me becomes an offering pleasing in My Father's sight.

It is enough to begin by seeking Me out in the Sacrament of My love as often as possible. That is how every true friendship begins—by seeking out the presence and the company of the loved one. Then, allow Me

[1] Gen 2:18.

[2] Inter alia, 1 Cor 15:28; Eph 3:14–19, 4:6; Ps 94(95); Ps 38:6 (39:5); Isa 40:17; Dan 4:32 (4:35).

[3] John 4:23–24.

[4] John 14:6.

[5] John 12:45, 14:9.

[6] Matt 10:42, 25:40.

to love you in return, to speak to your heart, to touch you by means of the operations of My Holy Spirit in your soul.

The way to holiness is the path of My friendship. There are many who complicate the way to holiness and who make it seem forbidding and unattainable to others. It is enough to accept My gift of friendship. It is this that leaves Me free to act upon you, and with you, and through you. Let Me love you as a friend. That is enough.

I bless you and I bless the Sisters to whom you are preaching. My Eucharistic Face shines upon them. They are the cherished little flock of My Eucharistic Heart.

Sunday, February 10, 2008

Whenever a special need or intention is entrusted to you, appeal to My Eucharistic Heart. I am moved to pity so often as you appeal to My Eucharistic Heart, for it is the living organ of My merciful love and the means by which you will obtain from Me all that you ask. My Heart beats with love in the Sacrament of the Altar, and My Heart is wounded, ever open to receive your petitions, your pleas, your desires. Appeal then to My Heart, wounded by love and present in this Most Holy Sacrament. Be bold and confident in what you ask of Me. My Heart is open to receive all your petitions, and I will bless abundantly all those for whom you pray in My Eucharistic presence.

There are particular graces reserved for souls who keep watch before My Eucharistic Face during the night. Those who pray by night imitate My own night watches of prayer to My Father.[1] How often would I keep vigil in the presence of My Father, conversing with Him in the silence of the night, and taking up into My prayer the secret cares of a sleeping world, and even the groans of creation. You will discover that there is a clarity and a peace in nocturnal prayer that I do not give to souls at other times. Those who have discovered this return to Me by night and seek to remain close to My Eucharistic Heart. The light of My Eucharistic Face illumines them, and the night, though it be dark, shines for them inwardly.[2]

Learn to adore Me by night. I especially desire that priests should come to Me at night. They will lose nothing of their repose, for I will be their refreshment and their rest.

The day will come, and it is not far off, when you will have an opportunity to speak to My chosen ones, My friends, of the value of remaining

---

[1] Matt 14:23; Mark 4:46–47; Luke 6:12, 21:37.
[2] Ps 138(139):12.

close to Me during the hours of the night. I prayed to My Father in this way and, in so doing, I gave My priests and all My friends an example to follow. Make the most of the opportunity you are given here. I will bless you and My Heart will instruct you as you keep watch before My Face.

Thursday, February 14, 2008

I will not abandon or forsake you. I am faithful. I have chosen you and you are Mine.[1] Why do you doubt My love for you? Have I not given you signs of My favour? Have I not shown you that My mercy has prepared for you a future full of hope? Did I not promise you years of happiness, of holiness, and of peace? My blessing is upon you and the designs of My Heart are about to unfold for you. You have only to trust Me. Believe that I will keep you as the apple of My eye.[2] You are safe under My Mother's mantle. I hold you close to My wounded Heart. Trust that I will bring about all that I have promised you.

These days at D. are part of My plan for you. They are part of My preparation of you. I am preparing you for the work I have asked of you, and I am preparing the way for My plans to be carried out. You have only to trust Me. Obey the indications that I will give you. Test the thoughts that may come to you,[3] submitting them to Father N. He will tell you whether or not these things are of My inspiration. Be open and transparent.

Above all, remain close to Me. Seek Me out in the Sacrament of My love. Come to Me and remain in My presence. Be My priest adorer, My reparator. Be My friend, the friend of My Eucharistic Heart, as was Saint John. He will help you to follow him in the way of a strong and tender love for Me and for My Immaculate Mother. I have given him to you, among so many other saints, as a friend, a protector, and a guide. Ask for his intercession. I am pleased that you so often refer to him in your preaching and in what you write. He is the Apostle of these last days. He holds the key to the secrets of My Sacred Heart, and these secrets he shares with those whom I have entrusted to him.

The disciples of My beloved disciple will be known by their burning love for Me in the Sacrament of the Altar, by their tender and true devotion to My Immaculate Mother, by the charity that animates them in ministering to souls, and by their willingness to remain close to Me in My bitter Passion.

---

[1] Isa 41:8–9, 43:1–10, 44:1–2; John 15:16.
[2] Deut 32:10; Ps 16:8 (17:7); Zech 2:8.
[3] 1 Thes 5:19–22.

You are among these disciples of My beloved disciple. Be faithful to this grace obtained for you by My own Mother. It was she who intervened to save you from the evil that threatened to destroy you and your priesthood. It was she who obtained that you should be numbered among her dearest children: the disciples of John, her first priest son after Me.

Thank My Mother for all that she has obtained for you by remaining faithful to the humble prayer that she so loves, her Rosary. The Rosary will preserve you in purity, in humility, and in all the virtues pleasing to My Mother's Immaculate Heart and My own Heart.

I ask you to be grateful and full of confidence. I have given you every reason to hope that I will carry out all that I have promised and that I will fulfil all that I have made you desire. Now rest in My presence and be at peace. I bless you from My throne upon the altar. I draw you to My open Heart.

Thursday, February 21, 2008
In Connecticut

I was waiting for you to come and you did not fail Me. You came to seek My Eucharistic Face and to draw near to My Eucharistic Heart, just as I have asked you to do so many times. You will have the reward of your obedience to My Heart's desires. I am about to open to you the delights of an intimate friendship with Me. Trust Me with everything, and I will make you share in the experience of My beloved disciple John. He is your model in your friendship with Me and in your relationship with My Blessed Mother. John will guide you into the mysteries of My Eucharistic Heart. He will teach you how to live with My Mother, how to share with her every moment of your day, your joys, your sorrows, your disappointments, and your fears.

My Mother's Sorrowful and Immaculate Heart is to be your refuge and your place of solace. Go to My Mother in all your needs. She is your Mother of Perpetual Help, that is, of unfailing help. My Mother is at the service of all My priests. She is their Mother, but she is also the humble handmaid of the Lord. In every priest of Mine she recognizes Me, and she places herself wholly at My service in My priests. For all of that, she remains the Immaculate Queen of heaven and of earth. All the riches of My Sacred Heart are hers to give away as she sees fit. She administers the treasury of My kingdom, and all that is Mine is hers to bestow freely and lavishly according to the desires of her maternal and merciful Heart.

If all My priests knew this—not merely with their minds, but in their daily experience—the priesthood would be transformed. My most pure Mother is the faithful and indispensable collaborator of the priest who represents Me and pursues My work in the Church. My Mother is attentive to the ministry of the priest and to his personal spiritual needs, as she was attentive to My ministry and to all My needs during My life on earth.[1]

Priests who do not collaborate with My Immaculate Mother will be stifled in the exercise of their priesthood. I Myself chose to have My Mother at My side at the Hour of My Supreme Sacrifice. I gave her to My beloved disciple John so that all My priests would understand that My Mother's place is at the side of every priest of Mine, especially when he stands at the altar to offer My Sacrifice to the Father, and to speak and act in My Name.

Never fail to recognize the mystical presence of My Mother in the Mass. She is there at your side. She rejoices in your distribution of the fruits of My redemption, and participates in it. The hands of every priest are, in some way, held in My Mother's hands. She acts with the priest. Her participation in the Holy Sacrifice renewed upon the altar is silent but efficacious. Her presence at the altar, though invisible, is real. My Church has long acknowledged the presence of My Mother at every offering of My Holy Sacrifice, but it is now more than ever necessary that priests should deepen their awareness of this most precious gift. She is the Coredemptrix.[2] Just as My Sacrifice is renewed mystically in every Mass, her offering, her participation in My offering, is also renewed. The priest who knows this and allows it to penetrate his heart will be graced with a holy fervour in every Mass he celebrates.

---

[1] For indications, see Matt 12:46–50; Mark 3:31–35; Luke 2:7, 2:41–52, 8:19–21; John 2:1–12, 19:25–27; Acts 1:14.

[2] Our Lady's dignity as Coredemptrix is well explained in the Second Vatican Council's Dogmatic Constitution on the Church *Lumen Gentium* (November 21, 1964): "Embracing God's salvific will with a full heart and impeded by no sin, she devoted herself totally as a handmaid of the Lord to the person and work of her Son, under Him and with Him, by the grace of almighty God, serving the mystery of redemption. Rightly therefore the holy Fathers see her as used by God not merely in a passive way, but as freely cooperating in the work of human salvation through faith and obedience.... [T]he Blessed Virgin advanced in her pilgrimage of faith, and faithfully persevered in her union with her Son unto the cross, where she stood, in keeping with the divine plan, grieving exceedingly with her only begotten Son, uniting herself with a maternal heart with His sacrifice, and lovingly consenting to the immolation of this Victim which she herself had brought forth.... She conceived, brought forth and nourished Christ, she presented Him to the Father in the temple, and was united with Him by compassion as He died on the Cross. In this singular way she cooperated by her obedience, faith, hope, and burning charity in the work of the Saviour in giving back supernatural life to souls. Wherefore she is our mother in the order of grace" (§§56, 58, 61).

I grieve over the carelessness with which some priests approach My Holy Mysteries. The remedy for this lack of reverence, attention, and devotion is a filial recourse to My Mother. Hers it is to prepare the heart of the priest to offer the Holy Sacrifice worthily. My Mother is full of solicitude for all her priest sons. She wants to see them go to the altar clothed in humility, in purity, in innocence of heart, and in profound adoration. She accompanies every priest in the sacred actions of his ministry. She sustains every priest by means of her all-powerful intercession.

My Mother is the guardian of all priests and it is My desire that she be recognized as such. The priest who knows this will have a refuge in temptation; he will be safe under her protecting mantle. If he should fall out of weakness or negligence, she will be there to raise him up and to direct his steps into the way of penitence and of holiness.

Live these things and you will understand why I insist on them. Now be at peace. I bless you, and My Immaculate Mother blesses you and those for whom you desire to pray.

In the same week, one night just before going to bed:

I am not far from you. I hold you close to My wounded Heart and keep you at every moment, waking and sleeping, beneath My gaze of mercy and of love. Do not doubt of My love for you. I have chosen you to be My friend. I want you to trust in My gift of divine friendship. I do not withdraw it when I have given it. On the contrary, My love grows in the soul of one who accepts My friendship, and it is a fruitful love. I have called you to holiness. Believe in My love for you. Seek My Face and My Heart in the Sacrament of My love. Be the priest adorer I have called you to be. I bless you, and My Mother blesses you too. Trust in our care for you.

Thursday, March 6, 2008
Hour of Adoration and Reparation

Before I began praying the Office of Lauds, Our Lord said that He would speak to Me through the psalm of the Office. This was the text:

For us thy timely mercies,
for us abiding happiness and content;
happiness that shall atone for the time when thou didst afflict us,
for the long years of ill fortune.
Let these eyes see thy purpose accomplished,
to our own sons reveal thy glory;

the favour of the Lord our God smile on us!
Prosper our doings, Lord, prosper our doings yet.
PSALM 89[90]:14–17

Did I not tell you that I would speak to you through the psalm of the Office? And so I have. These words confirm My promise to you, My promise of a new beginning and of years of holiness, blessing, and peace. Cling to these words and hold them in your heart. My plan is unfolding before your eyes. Trust Me in all things. Allow Me to do for you what you cannot do, and what you would not know how to do. When a soul is abandoned to Me in obedience and in trust, I am free to carry out in her and around her all that I desire to do to satisfy the yearnings of My Heart and for the glory of My Father. Be that soul, abandoned to Me in obedience and in trust, and you will not be disappointed in your hope.

> *I thank thee, Lord, who wast once so angry with Me; now the storm has passed over, and thou hast brought Me consolation instead. God is here to deliver Me; I will go forward confidently, and not be afraid; source of My strength, tower of My defence, the Lord has made himself My protector. So, rejoicing, you will drink deep from the fountain of deliverance; singing when that day comes.*
> ISAIAH 12:1–3

There, I speak to you again. Hold fast to My words and store them up in your heart. They will bring you comfort and hope in the day of weariness and doubt.

After I prayed Psalm 148, Our Lord said:

Listen now to My word.

And I read 2 Thessalonians 2:12–16.

> *We must always give thanks in your name, brethren whom the Lord has so favoured. God has picked you out as the first fruits in the harvest of salvation, by sanctifying your spirits and convincing you of his truth; he has called you through our preaching, to attain the glory of our Lord Jesus Christ. Stand firm, then, brethren, and hold by the traditions you have learned, in word or in writing, from us. So may our Lord Jesus Christ himself, so may God, our Father, who has shown such love to us, giving us unfailing comfort and welcome hope through his grace, encourage your hearts, and confirm you in every right habit of action and speech.*

March 7, 2008
First Friday

I thank you for remaining in My presence this afternoon to keep Me company in My bitter Passion. I looked upon you from the Sacrament of My love as I looked upon John, My beloved disciple. Learn to remain thus in My company. It is enough for Me that you should seek Me out and remain quiet in My presence and content to be with Me. I have no need of your thoughts, no need of your words. It is enough for Me that you should offer Me an adoring heart full of love and grateful for My abiding presence in the Most Holy Sacrament.

It pleases Me that at the beginning of your adoration you renewed your offering for priests in a spirit of thanksgiving and reparation. I am pleased that you appealed to My Eucharistic Heart to obtain the grace you were seeking for Father N. I give audience willingly to all who come into My Eucharistic presence, and like the most gracious of kings, I grant favours to those who ask them of Me. When you appeal to My Eucharistic Heart, I cannot refuse what you ask of Me. At times My Heart will give a better gift than the one for which you ask, because you ask with the shortsightedness and limitations of your mortal nature, and I give according to the wisdom and infinite benevolence of My Heart. I bless those whom you present to Me. The light of My Eucharistic Face will shine upon all of them, and I bless you out of the depths of My pierced Heart.

Thursday, March 13, 2008

As long as you live on in Me, and My words live on in you, you will be able to make what request you will, and have it granted.
JOHN 15:7

I have been speaking to you over the past week by means of circumstances and events. Continue to listen for Me in the encounters and events of daily life. I am making My plan of love known to you and I will continue to make it known, not only by speaking to your heart in this way, as one friend speaks to another, but also by guiding the course of events and by revealing to you the wonders of My providence for those whom I have chosen and set apart for the designs of My Heart.

Do not doubt of My friendship. I understand that, for the moment, you are not able to spend in My Eucharistic presence all the time that you would wish to offer Me, but the day is coming, and it is coming soon, when we will live under one roof, when you will live in the radiance of My Eucharistic Face and draw other souls, especially those of

My priests, into that same radiance to be healed, and purified, and sanctified. I am about to open doors before you. I will touch the hearts of many to participate in this work of My Heart for My priests.

Your part is to be My priest adorer and reparator. Your part is to seek My Eucharistic Face and to remain close, very close, to My open Heart in the Sacrament of My love. Do these things and all else will be given you besides in full measure, pressed down, and running over.[1] Trust Me to direct the work that I desire to see in My Church. Give Me yourself in adoration, in reparation, in love for priests, and I will pour the fiery love of My own Eucharistic Heart into your priestly heart. That fire will purify your heart; it will heal the old wounds of sin that were for so long infected, and it will sanctify you for the sake of your brother priests, and for the sake of those wounded or scandalized by their sins. There is more that I would say to you, but for now, this is enough. Present to Me those whom you would have Me bless. I bless each one and shine upon them the radiance of My Eucharistic Face. My Mother too blesses you and those whom you present to My Heart.

Maundy Thursday Night
March 20, 2008

Watching at the altar of repose.

I am close to you now, and you are close to Me in the Sacrament of My love. I accept your presence here tonight as an offering of friendship and reparation for the sake of all My priests, your brothers. Tonight I look for them. I wait for each one to seek Me out. I continue to yearn that My chosen ones, even those who have allowed their hearts to grow hard against Me, will be converted tonight and find their way to My tabernacles where I wait for them.

There are graces destined for My priests in this the night of My agony and of My betrayal that are not given at any other time. I am bound tonight. I have already been taken, and My captors led Me away as a lamb to the slaughter.[2] I am silent but My Heart watches and waits for My priests. If only they would come to Me, I would undo the bonds that hold them in slavery. I would give them light in the spiritual darknesses that oppress them. I would speak to them words of comfort and of compassion.[3]

---

[1] Luke 6:38.
[2] Isa 53:7; Acts 8:32.
[3] Ps 84:9 (85:8); Hos 2:14; 2 Cor 1:3–4.

Your being with Me tonight allows Me to touch the souls of many priests who have stayed away from Me. You are here only because My grace has worked within you, changing your heart, and drawing you into the grace of My abiding friendship.[1] What I have done in My infinite mercy for you, I would do for every one of My priests.

I am about to renew the priesthood of My Church in holiness. I am very close to cleansing My priests of the impurities that defile them. Soon, very soon, I will pour out graces of spiritual healing upon all My priests. I will separate those who will accept the gift of My divine friendship from those who will harden their hearts against Me. To the first I will give a radiant holiness like that of John and of My apostles in the beginning. From the others I will take away even what they think they have.[2] It must be so. I want the priests of My Church clean in heart and faithful in responding to the immense love with which I have loved each one of them and chosen each one for Myself and for the realization of the designs of My Heart. Those who do not live in My friendship betray Me and impede My work. They detract from the beauty of holiness that I would see shine in My Church.[3] I weep over their hardness of heart, and My Immaculate Mother, their sorrowing Mother, weeps with Me over them.

The renewal of My priesthood in the Church will begin from the fire of love that blazes in the Sacrament of My Body and Blood. I call all priests to seek My Eucharistic Face and to abide in My presence. I want all My priests to discover My open Heart, My living Heart beating with love for them, and pouring forth a purifying stream of Blood and of Water for their holiness, and for the life of the world. I summon all My priests into My Eucharistic presence. They must learn that in My company is the fullness of joy.[4] They must discover in the Sacrament of My love the sweetness and strength of My divine friendship.

Many, so many, have forsaken Me in the Sacrament of My love, but I will not forsake a single priest who comes to Me in the Sacrament of My love. There I wait for My priests. There I offer them My divine embrace. There I would draw them to My open side, and through the wound in My side, into the sanctuary of My Sacred Heart.

Adore Me for the sake of your brother priests who do not adore Me. Let Me give you what I would give each of them. Accept My love. Receive

---

[1] John 6:44, 15:16; Matt 9:9; Luke 22:61; 1 Cor 15:10; Gal 1:15–16.

[2] Matt 13:12, 25:29; Mark 4:25; Luke 8:18.

[3] 1 Chron 16:29; 2 Chron 20:21; Ps 28(29):2; Ps 95(96):9. In the KJV, each of these verses uses the expression "beauty of holiness."

[4] Ps 15(16):11.

the gift of My divine friendship. Make My Eucharistic presence the very heart of your life and the centre to which you return for warmth, for healing, for comfort, and for light. Seek My Eucharistic Face, and invite others to do the same.

In the light of My Eucharistic Face great things take place in souls. You have only to present yourself before Me, and the light of My Countenance, veiled in the Sacrament of My love, begins at once to work in your soul. This is a secret that I would have you share with all souls, beginning with the priests whom I will send you.

Now, receive My blessing and present to the light of My Eucharistic Face those whom you would have Me touch, and heal, and comfort, and sanctify.

Thursday, March 27, 2008

The first of four days of adoration from the end of Mass until 3:00 p.m., using a monstrance blessed by Pope John Paul II.

Every priest of Mine is in passage from this world to the Father.[1] Know this and let it direct the course of your life.

Those who are My own, those whom I leave in the world, those whom I love and to whom I give the uttermost proof of My love, are My priests. It is into their hands that I entrust the mysteries of My Body and Blood for the life of the world. Never doubt of My love for you, My priests. You hold the proof, the testimony of My love for you in your hands each day: My very Self given to you, given for you and given by your hands to My Bride, the Church. You who hold Me in your hands, how can you doubt of My love for you?

Let Me wash you, and wash you frequently, that you may live in My companionship and grow in the gift of My divine friendship. Come to Me that I may wash you in the Blood and in the Water that ever flow from My open Heart. Come to the inexhaustible torrent that gushes from My side. Come, and other souls will follow you there.

I wait to purify My priests, to heal their wounds, and to wash away every trace of uncleanness from their souls. He who remains in the torrent that ever flows from My Heart will be pure as I am pure, for such is the power of My precious Blood. My precious Blood is offered to My Father and given to souls for their refreshment and for their life in the mystery of the Eucharist. It is applied most efficaciously to souls in all the sacraments, but in Eucharistic adoration the soul remains plunged, as it were, in My Blood. The effects of this, though ordinarily invisible,

---

[1] John 13:1, 16:28.

are lasting and they are deep. Seek to remain immersed in the inexhaustible torrent of My Blood when you approach My open Heart in the Sacrament of My love.

I know who are the men I have chosen.[1] Do you think that there are things hidden from My eyes? Do you think that there are things I do not see? I know My priests. I know them through and through. As deep and searching as is My knowledge of them, so too is My merciful love. I see all things, and nothing of what I see escapes the reach of My mercy, save that which is deliberately withdrawn and wilfully hidden from Me. Even that I see, and in seeing it, I grieve, because the desire of My Heart is to extend My mercy to every weakness, to take away every shame, to wash clean every soul defiled by sin. Submit to My all-seeing grace, and present to My mercy all that I see in you.

Believe Me when I tell you this: the man who welcomes one whom I send—My priest—welcomes Me; and the man who welcomes Me, welcomes him who sent Me.[2] Let this be your rule: always present yourself as My priest. Always and everywhere be My priest. Thus will you carry My presence and that of My Father and our blessing, that is, the anointing of the Holy Spirit, the sweet fragrance of our charity, wheresoever you go. The priest is the sacrament of My presence. I do not want this sacrament of Mine to be concealed. Display your priesthood. Let your first and only identification be with Me—and I will bless you in all your goings and comings. The world needs now more than ever the visible presence of My priests. The world must know that I have not abandoned My little flock, nor have I forsaken those who trust in My love.

Be My priest in all circumstances and I will fill your heart to overflowing with the sweetness of My own Sacred Heart. It is the fragrance of this sweetness that will draw souls to Me through you who are but the vessel containing it, the vessel by means of which I desire to spread it in every place.[3] My priests do well to honour the poverty and discipline of the ecclesiastical dress. It is at once a protection for them and a sign of hope given to the world. Enough vanity. Enough extravagance. Be instead pure mirrors of My Holy Face in the world.

Friday, March 28, 2008

Trust in the guidance of the One whom I have sent to befriend you, the Holy Spirit, your Advocate. Learn to listen to His gentle leading. The

---

[1] John 13:18.
[2] Matt 10:40; John 13:20.
[3] 2 Cor 2:14–16, 4:7; Eph 5:1–2; 2 Tim 2:20–21; Sir 24:20–23, 39:18–21.

more you follow Him, the more will you understand where and how He is leading you. This is the secret of holiness: to be led by the Holy Spirit in all things. Seek the guidance of the Holy Spirit actively. Call upon Him, for He is, at every moment, available to you. He dwells with Me and with My Father in the sanctuary of your soul. He is your Advocate against the world, the flesh, and the Evil One, the accuser. He is your Advocate with My Father.

It is the Holy Spirit who unites your soul to Mine, your heart to My Heart in such wise that when you pray, it is My own prayer that ascends to the Father as a fragrant incense. The Holy Spirit comes to the aid of your infirmity, for, it is true, you do not know how to pray as you ought.[1] The unseen work of the Holy Spirit is to bring souls into accord with My priestly intercession before the Father in the sanctuary of heaven and in the Most Holy Sacrament of the Altar.

When you come to adoration, put aside every anxiety and care of yours, and allow the Holy Spirit gently to unite you to the prayer that rises from My Eucharistic Heart to the Father. Every need of yours is contained in the prayer I offer to My Father. Be at peace. You may want to pray for this thing or for that, and such prayer is good and is pleasing to My Father, but there is another way, a higher way, and that is to yield to the prayer of My Sacred Heart present in the Most Holy Eucharist and in the glory of heaven. I send the Holy Spirit upon you and upon all My priests that they may enter into this priestly intercession of Mine, without forsaking that other form of intercession, which is, as I said, also pleasing to My Father when it is childlike and full of confidence in His loving providence.

Intercession is not incompatible with adoration. The soul who adores Me present in the Sacrament of My love will be united to Me in My everlasting intercession before the Face of My Father. My intercession is everlasting even in the glory of eternity because I chose to keep the wounds in My hands and in My feet and in My side. They constitute an uninterrupted pleading for the sake of all: for those in glory that they may go from light to light and from sweetness to sweetness; for those on earth that they may find in My wounds healing, purity, and holiness; and for the souls in purgatory that by the merits of My holy wounds they may be refreshed and delivered.

I want to impress the marks of My wounds deep in the soul of every priest. My wounds reproduced in the souls of My priests authenticate their intercession at the altar. This is the spiritual stigmata that is the perfection of priestly holiness. The indelible character of My priesthood

---

[1] Rom 8:26–27.

in your soul renders you capable of this perfect identification with Me in My crucified priesthood and victimhood, and in My glorious priesthood in heaven where I remain for all eternity an offering to My Father.

You have not yet begun to grasp the potential of priestly holiness. This is what I have wanted to teach you for so long, but the time is now. Accept what I will show you and allow Me to configure you entirely to Myself. Only in this way will you become capable of the work for which I have destined you.

Now, be silent. Adore Me. Trust Me. I have only begun to show you the path of holiness that I am opening before you. And give thanks to Me, for I have saved you, through a particular intervention of My most holy Mother, from the fate that the Evil One was preparing for you for so long a time.

Saturday, March 29, 2008

You see, I am also directing your prayer to Me by the movements of the Holy Spirit in your soul. Thus will you pray as I would have you pray. Thus will you ask of Me the things that I myself desire to give you.[1] Trust in the Holy Spirit to animate and form your prayer when you come into My Eucharistic presence. Even as you pray to Me, I am instructing you and teaching you the secrets of My merciful love.

The desires of My Sacred Heart are immense and I so long to share them, above all, with My priests. I have chosen you to be the intimate friend of My Heart. Your model is Saint John, and he is your faithful intercessor. Come to Me in the Sacrament of My love and allow Me to speak to you freely. I want to unburden My Heart to you and to all My priests. Understand this, that you are My other selves. All that touches Me, all that relates to Me, all that offends Me, also pertains to you.

This is where reparation begins: in the identification of your soul with all My interests, with all My sorrows, with all that offends Me; and in the union of your soul with My burning zeal for the glory of My Father and for the holiness of all people. Let Me share with you the things that I hold within My Eucharistic Heart. I want to unite your priestly heart to Mine, and this I have already begun to do.

Obey Me. Remain faithful to what I ask of you and all the rest will unfold *mirabiliter*—wonderfully—because it is, all of it, the work of My merciful love.

---

[1] Cf. Collect, Ninth Sunday after Pentecost: "Let Thy merciful ears, O Lord, be open to the prayers of Thy suppliant people; and that Thou mayest grant them their petitions, make them to ask such things as shall please Thee."

March 30, 2008
Sunday of Divine Mercy

I will not leave you friendless; I am coming to you. It is only a little while now before the world is to see Me no more, but you can see Me because I live on, and you too will have life. When that day comes, you will learn for yourselves that I am in My Father, and you are in Me, and I am in you.
JOHN 14:18–21

Yes, here I was speaking of the Eucharist, the gift of My abiding presence to My Bride, the Church, and this until the end of time. Not one soul who belongs to Me is left friendless in this world so long as the Church continues to do what I commanded on the night before I suffered, in memory of Me. The Most Holy Eucharist is not only My Sacrifice offered to the Father, although in a bloodless manner; it is not only the sustenance of souls, nourishing them with My very Body and Blood; it is also the Sacrament of My divine friendship, the pledge of My burning desire to remain close to all who seek Me, to all who need Me, to all who would spend time in My company.

This is why it so grieves Me that churches are locked and that I am left for days on end alone in the tabernacle. I would draw souls to My open Heart, I would have them experience what it is to abide in the radiance of My Eucharistic Face, I would give Myself in intimate friendship to souls drawn to Me in the Sacrament of My love, but you priests, shepherds of souls, have forgotten that keeping open your churches is integral to your sacred ministry. I would pasture souls in My Eucharistic presence, but you, by continuing to close My churches to souls, frustrate and contradict the desires of My Eucharistic Heart. There is sorrow in heaven over this. It is not difficult to keep My churches open and to provide for the spiritual needs of those who would readily enter them in search of My friendship. The obstacles are not those of which you think; the obstacle is a lack of faith, a loss of belief in My real presence. My priests will be held responsible for the coldness and isolation that has come to surround Me in the Sacrament of My love. How I desire to see My churches open! Open the doors of My consecrated houses and trust Me to fill them with adorers in spirit and in truth!

Come to Me in the Sacrament of My love and I will fill you with the sweetness of My friendship. Know that there is no companionship on earth that can be compared with Mine. For this too did I institute the Sacrament and Sacrifice of My Body and Blood: so that souls might find Me present in My churches and, by remaining in My presence, learn from Me all that I have heard from My Father. For this reason do I call you friends. You are My friends because, from the tabernacle where I am present, and from the monstrance that exposes Me to your gaze, I will share with you the secrets of My Heart.[1]

I am your Priest. I am your Victim, the Lamb offered in sacrifice for the sins of the world. I am your food and drink in this Sacrament of My love, but I am also your companion. The Eucharist is the Sacrament of My divine friendship. I desire that My priests should be the first to experience this for themselves. Let them come to Me and keep watch before My Eucharistic Face, close to My open Heart; then they will understand how grave an offense it is to lock My churches, placing a distance between Me and My people, those in whose midst I have chosen to dwell. I want the visit to the Blessed Sacrament to become once again a part of ordinary Catholic life, an instinct of the believing heart, an expression of gratitude and reparation to Me who am forsaken and spurned in so many places. Let My priests set the example and the faithful will follow it. Do not the sheep follow the shepherd? Where are the green pastures prophesied by the psalmist king, if not in My Eucharistic presence?[2]

I want My priests to learn to rest in My presence. There I promise to refresh them in a way that no entertainment, no diversion, no other means can do. Let them come to Me when they are weary and lonely. I will be their rest and their dearest companion. They will leave My Eucharistic presence restored and with their joy renewed. This I promise.

I want My priests actively to encourage souls to seek Me out in the Sacrament of My love and to spend time close to My Eucharistic Heart. Nothing will bring this about more effectively than the example of My priests. There are priests who go into My church only when they have a function to perform there. The hearts of these have already grown cold and I am grieved by their indifference towards My abiding presence, often very close to them. Priests must begin to frequent their churches, not only at the hours of divine service, but at other times during the day and even during the hours of the night. Thus will they begin to allow Me to restore My priests to a shining holiness. Let them begin, one or two, here and there. The great fire will begin with these few sparks and will spread until the whole Church is set ablaze with the Eucharistic holiness of My friends, My priests.

If there are so few priests in certain places, it is above all because those that are there have forsaken Me in the Sacrament of My love and

---

[1] John 15:15.
[2] Ps 22 (23):2.

no longer live in My friendship. Let every priest present himself as a friend of Jesus, and his ministry will soon take on the efficacy and fruitfulness that characterized that of Saint John, of Saint Paul, and of My first apostles. The friend speaks with the authority that only experience can confer.

To you I say that I am pleased with these days marked by adoration. I am touching souls and pouring forth blessings here. I will reward all who have come here seeking to remain in My presence and offering Me the adoration that I desire. And you, your place is to adore Me. Your place is and will be that of Saint John, My beloved disciple and the cherished adoptive son of My Immaculate Mother. Trust in My love for you. Remain close to Me. Obey what I ask of you. And I will do wonders of mercy in your soul and in the souls of those who will be touched by your priesthood.

Thursday, April 3, 2008
In the Chapel of Bishop N.

Tonight I have spoken to you in yet another way. I have communicated to your heart something of what I hold in My Eucharistic Heart: towards My Father, that in Me and with Me and through Me, you may love Him and glorify Him; and towards My priests, that all My desires for their purity, their holiness, and their fruitfulness may become the desires of your own heart and the burden you lift up in ceaseless prayer.

Fear not. I will help you every step of the way. This work is Mine. Ask Me for guidance and light in all things, even in the details of what is to be done. I will direct and inspire the work from beginning to end. It is a work born of the love of My Pierced Heart for My priests, and for you. My Mother considers this work her own and she will care for it and for those who labour in making it a reality with all the solicitude of her merciful Heart. Trust in the intercession and protection of My Mother. She is your Perpetual Help and the Mediatrix of the graces that I have destined for those who will participate in this work of Mine.

Thursday, April 10, 2008

I told Our Lord that I felt tired. I said: "O my beloved Jesus, the efficacy and fruitfulness of this time of adoration comes not from me but from Thee. It is all Thy doing. I place myself before Thee as a vessel to be filled." Then I asked Our Blessed Mother, Mediatrix of All Grace, to open her hands over me and to bestow on me what she knows to be best for me and for the priests whom I represent in the presence of her Son.

My dear one, beloved priest of My Heart, know that I am here for you in the Sacrament of My love, independently of what your feelings may be. It is enough for you to come into My presence. Did I not say, "Come to Me, all you who are burdened and heavily laden, and I will refresh you"?[1]

I said to you, "Come," and you obeyed Me by coming to Me and by remaining in the radiance of My Eucharistic Face. For you, there is nothing more beneficial. You need to spend time close to My Eucharistic Heart. In My presence I communicate to your soul all that I want you to have, and all that I want you to know. You may not be aware of this as it is happening, but later you will experience the fruit and the efficacy of this time spent in My presence.

When I choose a soul for a work of Mine, I begin always by drawing that soul very close to Me with the leading bands of My most sweet love.[2] I have given you the gift of My divine friendship, just as I gave it to John and to the other apostles in view of the great work that I entrusted to them: the foundation and growth of My Mystical Body, the Church on earth. Every work of Mine begins in this way.

Those who think that they can succeed by planning and by calculating and by making use of human means as the world makes use of them, these I cannot use for the upbuilding of My Church. I want the little and the poor, those who have nothing apart from an immense trust in My merciful love; I want them to come to Me and to offer themselves to My Eucharistic Heart for My own designs and purposes.

I am preparing you now for a work that will manifestly be all My doing. Trust in My love for you and for all My priests. Seek My Eucharistic presence at every opportunity and remain before Me that I may fill you and make you fit to be My instrument and the representative of My pierced Heart.

I am pleased that you came to Me this afternoon. I bless you and I bless those for whom you have promised to pray. My Immaculate Mother opens her hands over you. A shower of blessings falls from her pure hands into your soul. Now, give thanks to Me.

Thursday, April 17, 2008

It is not enough that you come before Me like this on Thursdays only. The desire of My Heart is to see you in My presence daily, and soon I will make this happen, for this belongs to the unfolding of My plan for you and to the mission I have given you in My mercy.

---

[1] Matt 11:18.
[2] Hos 11:4.

I will make you, even as I promised, the priest of My Eucharistic Face. I will be the radiant Sun of your life. The light of My Face will illumine your days and even your nights. I will draw you into My Eucharistic presence for the sake of those priests of Mine who flee from before My Face, for the sake of those priests of Mine who refuse the gift of My divine friendship and never linger in My Eucharistic presence. I will fill you with an abundance of graces. I will give you the graces that they refuse. I will use you as My instrument and channel to redistribute among My priests the choicest gifts of My Eucharistic Heart. Do not be afraid. Be faithful to what I will ask of you. Seek My Eucharistic Face and abide close to My Eucharistic Heart.

Thursday, April 24, 2008

Never think that your imperfections and failures are, in any way, an impediment to the work of My merciful love in your soul. You have only to give them to Me with confidence and they are consumed in the blaze of My Heart's love for you. When I ask certain things of you, it is not to burden you, but to offer you a sure way of obtaining the support of My grace. This is why I asked you to read every Thursday chapters 13 through 17 of Saint John's Gospel. This contact with My word is a real contact with My Heart. There are many things that I give you in this way. You are not aware of them now, but at the proper time you will experience the graces that, by obedience to this request of Mine, you will have stored up.

I am simple and tender with you. I am the Friend of your heart, the most faithful and the most compassionate of friends. Never doubt of My friendship for you; it is unfailing and I want you to rest secure in My love for you. I will give you the experience of My divine friendship whenever you come into My Eucharistic presence. Seek My Eucharistic Face and teach others, especially My priests, to do the same. One who seeks My Eucharistic Face will discover too the secrets of My Eucharistic Heart, the tabernacle of My friendship for you.

When I instituted the Sacrament of My Body and Blood, I did so not only to unite all the members of My Body more intimately to Me who am their Head; I did it not only to feed them and to give them to drink for life everlasting; I did it also so as to remain present, close, and ever available to those who would seek My divine friendship by adoring Me truly present in the Sacrament of My love. I instituted the Sacrament of My Body and Blood thinking first of all of all My priests. I saw them, every one of them down through the ages until the end of time. I saw those who would approach Me in the Sacrament of My love, and for them I rejoiced. I saw, too, those who would stay away from Me in the Sacrament of My love, and I grieved over them.

My priests are the men whom I chose to live in the intimacy of My Eucharistic presence. It was, first of all, for them that I hid My Face and My Heart in the Sacrament of My love. I want all priests to experience the mystery of the Most Holy Eucharist as the Sacrament par excellence of My divine friendship. The priest who approaches Me and who remains with Me in the Sacrament of My love is not losing his time; he is at the very source of every good thing, and I will bless his priesthood with a wonderful apostolic fruitfulness. This was the secret of so many of My saints. I have made them known to you and given them to you and to those whom I will send to you, as intercessors and protectors.

Above all there is My Holy Mother, My all-beautiful and Immaculate Mother Mary. She is where I am. She is close to the priest who is close to Me in the Sacrament of My love. Nothing gives so much joy to her Immaculate Heart as seeing one of her priest sons in adoration before My Eucharistic Face. She opens her hands over him—as she is doing over you at this very moment—and causes a shower of graces to fall into his soul. Love My Mother, love My Mother more and more. You will never approach the love of My own Heart for her by yourself, but I, by My free gift, can and will unite you to the love of My Sacred Heart for her. Thus will you come to experience the ineffable union of our two Hearts in your own heart.

Be faithful to her Rosary. It is the shield and sword of spiritual combat. It assures your victory over the powers of darkness. Why? Because it is a humble prayer, a prayer that binds the soul who prays it to the victory of My Mother over the ancient serpent.[1]

And yes, pray the *Ave Maris Stella* for all your brother priests, daily if you can. My Mother loves that hymn and responds to it as often as she hears it, with an abundance of graces poured out on those for whom it is offered.

I bless those whom you present to Me. Do not fear. I prepare the way before you. You glorify Me by trusting in My merciful love and by remaining secure in the gift of My divine friendship.

May 1, 2008
Ascension Thursday

Let Me speak to your heart. Do you think that I have nothing more to say to you? I have much to tell you. I want to pour the secrets of My Heart

---

[1] Gen 3:15; Rev 12:9, 20:2.

into your own heart. Is this not what happens between two friends? Trust in My divine friendship. I love you, and nothing on earth can separate you from My love.[1] I do not love you because you have done anything to deserve My love.[2] I love you because I am all love and because Mine is a merciful love, a love drawn to those most in need of redemption.

What drew Me to you was your profound misery, your brokenness, your utter need of My redeeming and sanctifying grace.[3] And I was drawn to you because you bear in your soul the indelible sign of My own priesthood. I was drawn to you to save My priesthood in you from dishonour. I want you to live in the fullness of the graces imparted to you on the day you became My priest.

Yours will be a priestly holiness, a victimal holiness, a holiness worthy of the altar and of My own sacrifice that is renewed upon it sacramentally. When I choose a man to receive the imprint of My own priesthood in his soul, our destinies are forever linked. He is bound to Me and I to him, and this bond lasts into eternity. This is why I am reaching out now to you and to all My priests. I want to be glorified in them and in them I want My Father to be glorified.

Prepare yourself intensely for the outpouring of My Holy Spirit at Pentecost. Withdraw into the cenacle with My Mother. Pray her Rosary ceaselessly during these days. Live in her company. Choose silence. Seek Me out in the Sacrament of My love. Spurn all that will distract you from desiring the Gift of the Holy Spirit. I want you to receive the fire of the Holy Spirit with a heart made pure by prayer and by confession. I promise you a fresh outpouring of the Holy Spirit and of His seven gifts. These gifts you will need in the days that lie ahead. You will need them for the work that I have asked you to undertake: the work of adoration and reparation for all My priests.

Call upon the Holy Spirit with a great desire. Keep your heart clean. Pray always. My Mother is with you. The prayer of her Immaculate Heart will sustain your prayer during these days, and it is through her that the Holy Spirit will descend upon you with a fullness that you have not known before. Call upon the Holy Spirit using My own Mother's sweet name. There is no more effective way to draw into your soul the graces of the Holy Spirit.

---

[1] Rom 8:35–39.

[2] Rom 5:8–9; 1 John 4:10, 4:19; 2 Tim 1:8–9; Tit 3:4–7.

[3] Ps 11:6 (12:5), 69:6 (70:5), 71(72):12–13, 112(113):5–9; Isa 41:17.

I bless you with all the tenderness of My divine Heart, and My Mother opens her hands over you and over those whom you have presented to us.

Thursday, May 8, 2008

Receive My teaching and put it into practice. I have begun to form you for the work for which I chose you and have set you apart. You will enter into the secrets of My Eucharistic Heart and help your brother priests to discover them for themselves by remaining in adoration before My Eucharistic Face. I have so much to tell you and, at the same time, all that you need to know for this work is already given to you in the Gospel of Saint John, the friend of My Heart.

Yes, I have called you to become another John. I want you to gaze upon My Face with all the tenderness and adoration that the Holy Spirit gave him during the years he spent in My company. Even after My Ascension he discerned My abiding presence in the Sacrament of My love and learned to contemplate there the glory of My Eucharistic Face.

John was the friend of My Heart. When he saw My Heart pierced on Calvary, his own heart was pierced too. This created between him and My most holy Mother the deepest of bonds. This it was that sealed the covenant of filial and maternal love that I established between them by virtue of My words from the Cross. This it was that made their life together after the birth of My Church at Pentecost a model of perfect unity and of burning charity. John and Mary together graced the Church by living in fidelity to the words I spoke from the Cross and by abiding in the mystery of My pierced Heart. Their own hearts—the Immaculate Heart of the Mother and the pure heart of the son—were a single channel of mercy and of light for souls. I want it to be the same for you and for all My priests in their relationship to My most holy Mother. Allow your heart to be pierced as was hers on Calvary. Thus will your heart be united to Mine through hers.

John's heart was mystically pierced when he saw blood and water gush forth from My side. Your heart will be pierced in the mystery of the Most Holy Eucharist, not only when you stand at the altar to offer Me to My Father, but also when you remain in My presence, seeking My Eucharistic Face, eager to receive My instructions, and allowing Me to reshape you into the priest I have, from the beginning, wanted you to be.

The piercing of your own heart will not be in a single thrust. It will be a work of My grace and an intimate, even hidden, action of the Holy Spirit. You will know that your own heart has been pierced when you begin to experience a continual and sweet union with the Heart of My

Mother and with My own Sacred Heart. This I will do for you, but I desire to work the same grace in the souls of all My priests. Even in the beginning, I wanted My friendship with John to serve as a model for the other apostles. I will not refuse the intimate friendship of My Heart to the priests I have chosen for myself. This is the secret of priestly holiness: union with My Eucharistic Heart through the pierced Heart of My Mother and yours, the Blessed Virgin Mary.

All of this I want you to share with Father N. It will comfort him and renew in his soul the desire for holiness that long ago I planted deep within him. I bless those whom you bring before Me today, and My Mother, the Queen of the Holy Rosary and Mediatrix of all graces, opens her hands over each one.

When I asked Our Lord about my daily life and my inability to achieve the balance I want with regard to sleep, food, and other things, He answered:

I am not displeased with what you are doing for the moment. Offer everything to Me.

Thursday, May 15, 2008

My beloved friend, priest of My Heart, I want you to review the words that I have spoken to you. I ask you to keep them fresh in your mind and to store them up in your heart, for the day is coming, and it is coming soon, when I will ask you to share with your brothers the things that I will have made known to you.

Trust Me to speak to your heart. Know that My desire and My delight is to converse with you as a man converses with his dearest friend. There is so much more that I want to tell you. Be faithful in seeking My Eucharistic Face; let Me draw you more deeply into My open Heart.

I wait for you in the Sacrament of My love. I want you to come before Me as much and as often as you can. Do this in reparation for those priests who flee from before My Face. There are so many who have no time for Me, and yet I have given them their lives and I will give them their eternity.

My priests are to form a company of friends surrounding Me with their fidelity, with their adoration, and with their grateful love. My Heart grieves over those who live as if I were not the very Centre and King of their priesthood, of their affections, and of their lives.

I will give you the gift of ministering to My priests. Even those hardened in sin will be touched by your words and their hearts will be softened by your adoration before My Face. I receive the time you give Me for them as if they themselves were offering it to Me and, in exchange, I will draw them to Myself.

Trust Me, for I will do all that I have promised. Soon you and I will live under one roof and your delight by day and by night will be to remain in adoration before My Eucharistic Face. I have prepared you for this. To this work and to this form of life I have called you. Review what I have already spoken to you, and you will understand the plan of My merciful love for you and for My priests.

Thursday, May 22, 2008
In Connecticut

I wanted you to come here to console Me and to be for Me a living flame of love. I was waiting for you here. My Heart was yearning for your presence. I am here, silent and still, waiting for at least one soul to recognize My real presence and offer Me the consolation of a visit, of an expression of adoration and of love. Who knows about the friendship I offer to all from the tabernacles where I dwell hidden and, for the most part, forgotten? My Eucharistic love is unknown because so few of My priests have experienced it for themselves and because so few of them dare to make it known.

This is the immense sorrow of My Heart: that this Sacrament, which I instituted in order to remain among My own until the end of time, meets with indifference, with coldness, and with a cruel insensitivity even on the part of My chosen friends, My anointed ones, My priests. Many receive My Body and Blood; few discern the mystery of My burning love concealed beneath the sacramental veils. Holy Communion has become, in so many places, a routine act, a mere custom.[1] This is why I ask for adoration of My Eucharistic Face and for reparation to My Eucharistic Heart. Adoration, especially adoration made by My priests —and by priests for priests—will hasten the change that I desire and that I will bring about in My Church.

For this have I chosen you to be My priest adorer. Seek My Eucharistic Face, approach My Eucharistic Heart. When I welcome you into My presence, I will welcome the priests, your brothers, whom you represent and in whose name you come before Me. I will cause a fountain of liv-

---

[1] Cf. 1 Cor 11:27–30; St. Pius X, *Sacra Tridentina* (1905), §2: "A right intention consists in this: that he who approaches the Holy Table should do so, not out of routine, or vain glory, or human respect, but that he wish to please God, to be more closely united with Him by charity, and to have recourse to this divine remedy for his weakness and defects."

ing water to spring up within your soul for their sake,[1] and I will renew, and purify, and sanctify My priests, for on them have I set My Heart. I bless you and those whom you have recommended to My Eucharistic Heart. The light of My Eucharistic Face will reach them. The intercession of My Holy Mother will bring them comfort and hope. Trust in the designs of My merciful love for you, and be at peace.

Thursday, May 29, 2008
Vigil of the Solemnity of the Sacred Heart of Jesus

Yes, My beloved friend, priest of My Sacred Heart, I intend to speak to you for your own sake and for the sake of the priests I will send to you. The time draws near. I am about to begin this work of My love for priests and I have chosen you, out of your weakness and your sin, to bear witness to My mercy, to adore My Eucharistic Face, and to make known to your brother priests My own burning desire that they should be saints.

There has never been in all of history a single priest whom I have not destined for a great holiness. My Heart has suffered much because so many of My chosen ones have refused My gifts and, preferring their own ways to Mine, gone into the outer darkness where it is night.[2]

My Heart burns to see My priests all ablaze with Eucharistic holiness. The altar is the source of priestly holiness. The kiss given to the altar at the beginning and end of Holy Mass means that the priest recognizes this. By kissing the altar, he makes himself vulnerable to My piercing love. By kissing the altar he opens himself unreservedly to all that I would give him and to all that I hold in the designs of My Heart for his life. The kiss to the altar signifies total abandonment to the priestly holiness that I desire and to the fulfilment of My desires in the soul of My priest.

The holiness to which I call My priests, the holiness to which I am calling you, consists in a total configuration to Me as I stand before My Father in the heavenly sanctuary, beyond the veil. Every priest of Mine is to be with Me both priest and victim in the presence of My Father. Every priest is called to stand before the altar with pierced hands and feet, with his side wounded, and with his head crowned as My head was crowned in My Passion. You need not fear this configuration to Me; it will bring you only peace of heart, joy in the presence of My Father, and

---

[1] John 4:10–14, 7:38; Rev 21:6; Num 20:6 (Vul.); Song 4:15; Jer 17:13–14; Zech 14:8.
[2] Matt 8:12, 22:1–14, 25:30; Prov 14:12; John 13:30.

that unique intimacy with Me that I have, from the night before I suffered, reserved for My priests, My chosen ones, the friends of My Heart.

Say "yes" to Me. Tell Me that you want for yourself only what I want for you. Tell Me that you desire what I desire for your life, and nothing else. This will give Me the freedom to sanctify you wholly—body, mind, and spirit.[1] This will allow Me to fashion you and to wound you into a living representation of Myself before My Father, and in the midst of the Church. Yes, it is in wounding you that I will make you another Me. It is by wounding you with a love that is indescribable in earthly terms that I will heal all the wounds of your sins, and cause you to shine like the sun in My kingdom.[2] This should not shock you. I desire that all who belong to Me should shine with uncreated light.[3] This will display My holiness in you. This will show to the eyes of all, of angels and of men, that there is no holiness in souls that is not My holiness communicated to them.[4]

I have chosen to communicate My light to your soul by making it pass through the pure and sinless Heart and hands of My Immaculate Mother. The more you turn to her, the more you remain confident and childlike beneath her gaze of maternal love, the more will you be changed from one degree of glory to another.[5] This is My Mother's work in the souls of priests, and the work of the Holy Spirit who touches souls by means of her hands.

I do not want you to doubt that it is I who am speaking to your heart. Have I not given you enough signs of My favour? And there will be more because I know your neediness and your fears, and because I have a burning love for you and a tenderness that moves Me to act with you in all things as the best of friends would act with the friend upon whom he has set his heart. I have set My Heart upon you. This I did many years ago, and I have been faithful to you even when you were so grievously unfaithful to Me. But now all that is past is forgotten. I have turned the page and given you the grace of a new beginning.[6]

Respond to Me with a childlike trust. Accept the gift of My divine friendship. Know that nothing can come between us. You are safe beneath the protecting mantle of My Immaculate Mother. I have given you My saints to stand guard about you, to comfort and counsel and

---

[1] 1 Thess 5:23.

[2] Job 5:18; Matt 13:43.

[3] Matt 17:2; Mark 9:2; Luke 9:29; Acts 9:3.

[4] John 1:16; 2 Pet 1:2–4; Eph 3:19, 4:13, 4:24; Col 1:12; Heb 3:14.

[5] 2 Cor 3:18.

[6] Isa 1:18, 38:17, 43:25, 44:22; Song 2:11; Eph 2:1–10.

assist you. You have nothing to fear. Only believe in My love for you, beloved of My Heart, My priest, My friend, My precious one.

Then I presented some souls to Our Lord, some by name, others indistinctly.

I bless them all as I bless you, and My Mother joins with Me in blessing you with all the tenderness of her Immaculate Heart.

Before leaving, almost as an afterthought, Our Lord said:

There is nothing in your life that escapes My attention.

Friday, May 30, 2008
Solemnity of the Sacred Heart of Jesus

In response to what Our Lord asked of me:

O my beloved Jesus, I come before Thy Eucharistic Face, and I draw near to Thy open Heart in this the Sacrament of Thy love, to respond today to what Thou hast asked of me. With trust in Thy infinite goodness, and fearing nothing apart from sin and the peril of separation from Thee, I say "yes" to all that Thy Sacred Heart desireth for me. I want for myself only what Thou wantest for me. I desire what Thou desirest for my life, and nothing else.

Making use of the free will that Thou hast given me, I give Thee, my Sovereign and all-powerful God, the freedom to sanctify me wholly in body, mind, and spirit. I allow Thee, as of this feast of Thy Sacred Heart, to fashion and wound me into a living representation of Thyself before Thy Father and in the midst of Thy Church. Wound me, that I may be another Thyself at the altar of Thy sacrifice. Wound me with that love that is indescribable in earthly terms so as to heal all the wounds of my sins. Penetrate my soul with Thy divine light. Let no vestige of darkness remain within me.

I renew my total consecration to the pure and sinless Heart of Thy Immaculate Mother, and await from her maternal hands all that Thou willest to bestow upon me. I thank Thee for Thy Mother's incomparable work in my soul and in the souls of all Thy priests. Through her, I am entirely Thine.

Accomplish all the designs of Thy Sacred Heart upon my life. Glory be to Thy Eucharistic Heart from my own heart and from the heart of every priest of Thine. Amen.

Wednesday, June 11, 2008

After Holy Mass.

You need not fear. Have I not been faithful to My promises to you? Am I not doing for you and through you all that I said I would do? Trust Me. Seek Me out in the Sacrament of My love as often as you can. I have chosen you to be, above all else and before all else, My priest adorer. Your place is close to My open Heart. Your place is before My Eucharistic Face. This is the year during which I will begin to fulfil all that I have prepared for you from the time I set My Heart upon you and chose you to be My priest adorer and the friend of My Sacred Heart, another Saint John for Me and for My all-pure Mother.

I will teach you how to abide in My presence: silent, adoring, trusting, and making reparation, first of all for your brother priests—and they are so many—who never linger in My presence. I tell you again that when I instituted this Sacrament and Sacrifice of My Body and Blood, I had in view, not only the renewal of My one Sacrifice through the ages, and the souls of all whom I would nourish with My Body and Blood, but also the need of My priests to find Me close at hand, and to discover in this Sacrament the gift of My divine friendship for them.

I tell you this because so many priests have forgotten or have never known that I wait for them in the Sacrament of My love. Priests are not mere functionaries dispensing the Sacraments; they are not mere presiders over the gatherings of My people; My priests are the friends that I have chosen to be the consolation of My Eucharistic Heart down through the ages.

Every priest is called to be a priest adorer. Every priest is invited to experience the most fruitful hours of his ministry in the radiance of My Eucharistic Face. For every priest My Heart remains open, a refuge ready to welcome him, in the Sacrament of My love. This is part of the message that I am giving you for My priests. It is time for My priests to return to the Sacrament of My divine friendship for them, and through them, for all believers. The priestly Pentecost of which I have already spoken to you will begin when priests return to My Eucharistic presence, when they return to the cenacle wherein I will bless them with a holy intimacy with My Sacred Heart, and with a chaste and fruitful union among themselves.

This is My word for you today. Be at peace. Trust in My love for you. Go now to your father with the Sacrament of My Body and Blood. I rejoice to go with you. I am with you always.[1] My love surrounds you at

---

[1] Matt 28:20.

every moment. I bless you now, and My most sweet Mother blesses you and opens over you and over your father and mother her maternal hands from which graces flow for you, for them, and for all her children.

Thursday, June 12, 2008
In Connecticut

It is enough for Me that you are here. I do not ask anything else of you. It is your adoring, loving presence that My Heart wants from you. In this way, you will console Me and make reparation for so much coldness, ingratitude, and indifference. I am here for you. Be here for Me. Seek My Eucharistic Face. Know that My Eucharistic Heart is open to receive you, to comfort you, to strengthen you, and to purify you in the Blood and in the Water that ever flow from My pierced side.

I long for the adoration of My priests. I see other adorers before My Face and I rejoice in their presence, and I bless them with all the tenderness of My Eucharistic Heart. But I look for My priests. Where are they? Why are they not the first to seek Me out in the Sacrament of My love and the last to leave Me at the close of the day? Even in the night I wait for them. In the night hours it is possible to have an intimacy with Me that one cannot experience at other times. I wait for My priests. I look for the friends chosen by My Sacred Heart and anointed to continue My victimal priesthood in the world. I want My priests to come to Me, and I will draw them, one by one, into the radiance of My Eucharistic Face. There I will refresh them. There I will heal them. There I will restore them and give them the choicest gifts of My Heart.

Your part is to begin humbly, silently, but with a great fidelity. I call you to go before your brothers, My priests, and to open for them a path in the wilderness leading directly to the temple wherein I wait for them, full of compassion and love.[1] You, do your part, and I promise you that I will do Mine.

Entrust all things, great and small, to My Immaculate Mother. She will provide for you even as she provided for John, My beloved disciple, by drawing out of her Heart the graces reserved there for you and for her priest sons. Live your consecration to My Mother in the practical details of your life. Allow her to form you and instruct you. You will begin to experience the peace and joy of the Holy Spirit in ways that you have never known before. Where My Mother is welcomed and allowed to do her work, the Holy Spirit is poured out in the greatest abundance, and the graces and charisms of the Holy Spirit flourish for the upbuilding of the Church.

---

[1] Ex 23:20–26; Ps 77(78):52–54.

This is enough for today. Thank Me for My presence here. Do what I have asked you to do. Be faithful in little things. I bless you. I bless your father, your mother, your brother, and all whom you desire to set before My Eucharistic Face. My Mother will be your Perpetual Help. I have made her the Mediatrix of all My graces. She is all-powerful over My Heart.[1] She too blesses you.

Tuesday, June 17, 2008

Trust Me with all the events of your life. I will not abandon you. You are Mine and I will not forsake you. The decisions of men are all in My hands. Nothing will befall you that I do not permit. I will give you My grace to accept the changing circumstances of your life. It is I who am behind all that happens to you. Nothing escapes My wisdom; nothing escapes My love; nothing escapes My omnipotence. Trust Me, and be at peace. I bless you with all the love of My Sacred Heart. Do not be afraid. Tell Me again and again that you trust in My merciful love for you.

Thursday, June 19, 2008

I was unable to go before the Blessed Sacrament for my holy hour of adoration and reparation today, so I did it at home.

I would have you kneel before your brother priests to wash their feet. I would have you minister to them in their weaknesses, in their brokenness, and in the shame that, too often, weighs upon their shoulders, causing them to stoop towards earthly things. I would have you speak to them words of comfort. Encourage them, bless them, assist them with the gifts that I have placed in you for their sakes. Let no priest leave you without receiving a word of consolation and a blessing. Through you I will give them a new heart and a new spirit; that is to say, I will infuse in them a desire for holiness, a new and fresh love for Me and for My Church. None of this will be your doing; I will act through you.

Humble yourself in My presence. Give Me your sins. Tell Me that you trust in My merciful love for you, and I will make you the instrument of My love for them. Despise not one of them.[2] See in each and every

---

[1] This is the Mother of God's *omnipotentia supplex*, the "omnipotence of intercession," spoken of by many Marian theologians (St. Louis de Montfort mentions, among others, St. Bernard, St. Bernardine, and St. Bonaventure: see *True Devotion to Mary*, pt. 1, ch. 1, §2, n. 27). Pope John Paul II uses this phrase in his general audience of May 2, 1979.

[2] Matt 18:10; Sir 3:15, 8:6–9.

priest My own features traced in his soul by the Holy Spirit on the day of his ordination. Express reverence for your brother priests. Avoid the familiarity that will impede My ability to work through you. When a priest is too familiar in ministering to souls, he takes the place that belongs to Me and to no other. He makes himself the point of attraction and steals My glory for his own satisfaction.

Do not look for personal comfort or the satisfaction of your own needs in serving My priests. Seek only My Face and love with My wounded Heart. I will give you a profound reverence for your brother priests. This, of itself, will touch their vulnerability in such a way as to give them a sense of their own supernatural dignity.

Consecrate each priest who comes to you to My Immaculate Mother. Allow her to use you as she worked through Saint John in her ministry to the other Apostles and to the early Church. Continue to pray to My Mother for your brother priests. Your daily *Ave Maris Stella* is pleasing to My Mother and obtains many graces for priests. It is she who inspired you to take up this prayer each day.

I accept this time from you as if you were in My Eucharistic presence. Tomorrow, come to Me in the tabernacle. Blessings await you in My sacramental presence. I bless you and I draw you to My wounded Heart. Be the priest of My Eucharistic Face and of My open Heart, which is ready to receive all priests as in a refuge, a place of healing, of refreshment, and of boundless mercy.

I had some questions in my heart about friendships. Our Lord answered them, saying:

I will give you the friends, fathers, and brothers whom I have chosen for you. These will be the friendships sanctified in My Heart. The others will be for you as sons. Your love for them will be that of a father. It is I who will infuse this spiritual paternity into you, and it will never be lacking.

Thursday, June 26, 2008

I said to Him: "O my beloved and ever-merciful Jesus, I adore Thee and I offer Thee all the love and desire of my heart. The desire I offer Thee is the very one Thou Thyself hast given me: the desire for holiness, that is, for union with Thee."

Is this not why Thou has taught me to pray, saying,

> *O my beloved Jesus, unite me to Thyself:*
> *my heart to Thy Heart,*

my soul to Thy Soul,
all that I am to all that Thou art.

I find it wonderful and amazing that Thou—God from God, Light from Light, very God from very God—shouldst call me to such a union with Thyself. Thou hast offered me the sublime gift of Thy divine friendship, but this union to which Thou callest me is something more yet. It is "all that Thou art in all that I am." It is, I think, like a kind of incarnation.[1] It is the communication of Thy divine filiation and of Thine eternal priesthood to me and to every part of my being. It is the communication of all the sentiments of Thy Eucharistic Heart to my own heart.

Priestly ordination disposed my heart to this communication. The heart of every priest is sacramentally disposed to receive the ineffable communication of all the sentiments of Thy Eucharistic Heart. Some offer themselves to Thee for this; a great number do not.

It is in the adoration of Thy Eucharistic Face that, little by little, the sentiments, desires, and sufferings of Thy Eucharistic Heart pass into the heart of Thy priest adorer. Let me be that priest adorer of Thy Eucharistic Face. Communicate to me all that Thou holdest in Thy Eucharistic Heart: Thy filial love and priestly adoration of the Father, and Thy merciful love for sinners, together with Thy spousal love for the Church.

My beloved Jesus, I ask Thee to give me the form of life Thou desirest for me. Yes, Thou hast already given it to me in so many ways. Help me to formulate it clearly and simply for the sake of those who will want to understand it.

In obedience to Thee, I entrust all the material details to Thy Immaculate Mother, my own Mother of Perpetual Help. I know that she is all-powerful over the treasures of Thy Sacred Heart. I know that she is the MINISTRA GRATIARUM appointed by the Father. I know that she is the necessary human agent of the works of the Holy Spirit in the world, in the Church, and in souls.[2] I trust her absolutely and in all things. I ask Thee to give me a boundless and childlike confidence in the goodness of her merciful and Immaculate Heart.

---

[1] As Bd. Elizabeth of the Trinity (July 18, 1880–November 9, 1906) wrote in her prayer "Ô mon Dieu, Trinité que j'adore" of November 21, 1904: "O Feu consumant, Esprit d'amour, 'survenez en moi' afin qu'il se fasse en mon âme comme une incarnation du Verbe: que je Lui sois une humanité de surcroît en laquelle Il renouvelle tout son Mystère" (O Consuming Fire, Spirit of Love, 'come upon me' and create in my soul a kind of incarnation of the Word, that I may be for Him another humanity in which He can renew His whole mystery).

[2] 'Necessary' not in the nature of things but by God's design and decree, and because it is most fittingly so—a truth we know from reflecting on God's choosing Mary as the immaculate Theotokos, the New Eve, and the mother of the beloved disciple.

Our Lord said to me:

Continue to trust Me in all things. I will not abandon or forsake you. I am directing every turn of events and all the circumstances that mark this moment in your life: the beginning of My work for the sanctification of My beloved priests and for the revelation of My Eucharistic Face and of My open Heart hidden in the Sacrament of My love.

From the very beginning—from that night in the cenacle when I handed over the mysteries of My Body and Blood—My Face and My Heart have been present in the Most Holy Eucharist. But this is a true revelation in the sense that now, I desire to draw back the veil, and to do this I will use you. There is nothing new in what I am saying to you, but there is much that has been forgotten, cast aside, or even refused out of hardness of heart. I will use you to draw back the veil on what *is*, wheresoever I am sacramentally present: My Face shining with all the splendour of My divinity, and My pierced Heart, eternally open, a wellspring of healing mercy and of inexhaustible life for souls.

For now, this is all that I will say to you. My Heart speaks to your heart. It is My joy to speak to you in this way. Trust Me with everything. Be at peace. Allow Me now to bless you from the tabernacle before you, in which I am hidden, but living and full of mercy for all who approach Me here.

Thursday, July 3, 2008

My beloved Jesus, I thank Thee for having called me to a life of adoration. I thank Thee that Thou wantest Me, unworthy as I am, to abide before Thy Eucharistic Face and to approach Thy open Heart in the Sacrament of Thy love.

I thank Thee that Thou hast called me to offer Thee reparation, first of all for my own sins, too many to be counted, and for all those offences by which I have grieved Thy most loving Heart and offended souls dear to Thee and purchased by Thy most precious Blood.

Thou callest me also to make reparation for all the sins of my brother priests, poor sinners like me, often caught in the snares of the Evil One, and insensible to the delights and peace that Thou desirest to give them in Thy presence.

I thank Thee that Thou hast chosen me to make reparation for the coldness, indifference, irreverence, and isolation that Thou receivest in the Sacrament of Thy love.

To Thy presence, let me offer my presence;
to Thy pierced Heart, let me offer my heart;
to Thy divine friendship, let me offer all the yearnings of my soul

for that companionship of Thine,
which surpasses every passing earthly love
and satisfies the deepest needs and desires of my heart.

I pray to Thee for the cenacle that is Thy own work. In obedience to Thee, I entrust it to Thy most holy Mother, confident that she will attend to every detail, for it will be her home, the place chosen by her Sorrowful and Immaculate Heart to welcome her priest sons, to heal them, to sanctify them, to refashion them in the image of Thy beloved disciple, her adopted son, Saint John.

I renounce every impulse of mine to control the course of events, and place myself, and this work, in the wound in Thy sacred side, to be purified there in the torrent of Blood and Water that flows out at every moment from Thy Eucharistic Heart. I ask Thee to purify me of the desire to please, to win approval, to solicit affection, and to manipulate the emotions of others in such a way as to feed my self-love and numb my insecurities. I renounce every desire to seek personal satisfaction in the relationships that will necessarily be a part of this new life of mine. I ask Thee to deliver me of possessiveness, vanity, fear, lust, and timidity.

I beg Thee to keep me pure, transparent, humble, and free, that I may fulfil with integrity, detachment, and joy the spiritual paternity to which Thou hast called me. I ask moreover for the grace to relate to all who will come to me as a father to a son, as a brother to a brother. I beg Thee to purify and strengthen every bond of friendship in the fire of Thy Eucharistic Heart.

I surrender to Thee my humanity with its wounds, its brokenness, and its scars. I give Thee my past in its entirety. I beg Thee for the grace to walk in the newness of life that I know Thou desirest for me.

And that all of this may come to pass in the most efficacious and fruitful way,

I abandon into the most pure hands of Thy Mother, my Mother,
all that I am, all that I have been, and all that Thou,
in the boundless mercy of Thy Eucharistic Heart,
wouldst have me be for Thee, O my beloved Jesus,
for Thy Mystical Body, Thy Bride, the Church,
and for the glory of Thy Father. Amen.

See, you have prayed according to the inspiration I gave you through My Holy Spirit. There is no better way to pray. One who listens to My Eucharistic Heart will pray rightly. His petition will be heard by My Father. It is I who will tell you how to pray.[1] I will make known to you

[1] Luke 11:1–4.

those things for which I want you to ask. And I will grant the graces that I will have caused you to desire and for which I will have inspired you to pray. This is what My Apostle meant when he wrote that "the Spirit comes to the aid of our weakness, for we know not how to pray as we ought."[1] The Spirit knows all that is in My Father's Heart and the Spirit knows all the desires of My own Sacred Heart for you.[2]

When you pray, there is no need to worry about what you will say or for what things you ought to ask.[3] It is enough to come humbly into My presence and to pray as My Holy Spirit gives you to pray. Such prayer will always be fruitful. Such prayer is always efficacious because it springs not from you, but from Me, not from what you may desire, but from what I desire to give you.

All of this I explained to My Apostles on the night before I suffered. I wanted them to begin to pray with confidence, with boldness, with the assurance that I would grant them the things for which I prompted them to ask. Thus does My Bride, the Church, pray in her sacred liturgy. You do well to love the liturgy of My Church. It is the work of the Holy Spirit who, making use of human instruments, created a prayer pleasing to My Father and worthy of My eternal priesthood. Enter humbly and wholeheartedly into the liturgy of My Church, and teach others to do the same.

I have given you a special gift that will allow you to instruct others in the prayer of My Bride, the Church. You will help your brothers, priests and deacons alike, to enter with Me into the hidden sanctuary beyond the veil where I stand as eternal Priest before the glory of My Father, with My Face transfigured and all-glorious in the brightness of the Holy Spirit.[4] Teach souls to enter with Me into the ceaseless liturgy of heaven and into the hidden liturgy of every tabernacle where I am present and active as eternal Victim and High Priest.

When you come to adore Me, allow Me to unite you to My victimal priesthood. Allow Me to pray in you. Present your heart to Me as a thurible made ready for the sweet incense of My prayer to the Father.

I am working now and will continue to work in this cenacle that is all My work and all My desire. Resist the temptation to control persons and things. Continually place all things and every person involved in this work in the hands of My Immaculate Mother. Be free and be at peace.

---

[1] Rom 8:26.

[2] 1 Cor 2:9–16.

[3] Matt 6:7–8, 10:19; Mark 13:11; Luke 12:11; Rom 8:26.

[4] Heb 6:19-20, 9:24, 10:19-21; Phil 2:11; 1 Pet 4:14, 5:10; John 1:14, 17:24; 2 Cor 4:6; 2 Pet 1:17; Matt 17:2; Mark 9:1.

This is My work, and I will do it. I bless you from My tabernacle and My Immaculate Mother blesses you and covers you with the mantle of her protection. Now, give thanks to Me.

Thursday, July 10, 2008

Listen to Me.

This will be your life: a vigil of adoration before My Eucharistic Face. Let nothing distract you from this, the one thing necessary. Measure the value of all other things against this one thing to which I have called you and set you apart.[1] I do not ask you to engage in a multitude of works; I ask you to engage in a ceaseless exchange of love with My open Heart present and waiting for you at every moment in the Sacrament of My love. You will be asked [by other people] to accept other works and to spend yourself in other ways, but this is not the way I have chosen for you. I want you for Myself alone.

Seeing you before My Eucharistic Face, I will see in you all your brother priests and deacons, those whom you represent before Me. I will speak to you heart to heart just as I am doing now, and I will give you the words that I want you to give them when you are asked to do so.[2] I have set you apart as a vessel to be filled with the unfathomable graces of My divine friendship.[3] Hold yourself still and open in My presence.[4] Receive all that I will pour into you and let My graces overflow to reach the souls of those whom you represent before My Eucharistic Face.

When you come before Me, be prepared to hear My voice. Let My words take effect in you; My words will sanctify you and, as you receive them, they will unite you to Myself. Put aside all else at the time of your adoration. Speak to Me as I give you to speak, and accept My words to you with gratitude and humility.

I am speaking to you in this way because you have fallen so low. Sin has humbled you, and now My grace descends to raise you up, even to union with Myself. You will experience the attraction of My Eucharistic Heart to your heart. Do not resist Me. Allow Me to draw you through the wound in My side into a communion of love with My Heart. I want you to be with Me where I am, in that hidden sanctuary beyond the veil of My Flesh wherein I adore My Father in the sweetness of the Holy Spirit and stand before him as his eternal Priest. My desire is to invite all

---

[1] Luke 10:42; Matt 13:46; 1 Chron 23:13; Acts 13:2; Gal 1:15.
[2] Mark 13:11; Num 22:38; Judith 9:18; 2 Cor 2:17.
[3] Acts 9:15; 2 Tim 2:21.
[4] Ps 80:11 (81:10); Ps 36(37):7; Ps 45:11 (46:10).

My priests to this eternal exercise of My priesthood here in the Sacrament of My real presence, as in the sanctuary of heaven where I am living and making intercession for you.

I will mark you with My own wounds. My wounds, now glorious, are the authentication of your priesthood. Every priest of Mine is called to bear in his own person the mystical imprint of My wounds, for they are the glory of My eternal priesthood.

Do not doubt My words to you. Do not fear. I am with you and My work is about to unfold in a wonderful way. Give Me every preoccupation and care. Entrust every care involved in the building of My cenacle to the hands of My most pure Mother. I have charged her with every detail of this work. I want you to be free, free of worry and anxiety, free to respond to My love for you with a love that is joyful and serene.

There will be obstacles, but you will see them melt like ice in the sunlight of My merciful love. Do not linger over obstacles and difficulties; instead surrender them all to Me as they appear. The longer you hold on to them, seeking to resolve them on your own, the more complicated and difficult to solve they will become. Develop the habit of giving Me every obstacle in your path. I am all-loving, all-merciful, and all-powerful, and this is My own work. You are but My instrument. I ask you only to take your place faithfully and peacefully before My Eucharistic Face. I will do all the rest. Believe in My promises, and go forward full of thanksgiving and hope.

I will teach you all that you need to know as you go forward. I will not give you My words ahead of time, but I will give them to you as you need them, at the moment chosen by My loving providence. Renounce the desire to control and arrange things ahead of the time that I have decreed. Each thing has its own moment, and that moment alone and no other brings with it the grace sufficient to your need, to your weakness, and to the task at hand. I am proceeding this way with you because I want you to trust Me completely, to trust Me in all things, great and small.

When you feel the onset of anxiety or fear, turn to My Immaculate Mother, the Mediatrix of all graces and your Mother of Perpetual Help. It is enough to call upon her sweet name. She will understand and she will do what is necessary for My work to go forward.

Again I give you Saint Benedict to be a father and a master to you. He is interceding for you even now. The bond that unites you to him is one that I created and it will lead you into eternity. I will give light to your understanding and, when the time comes, you will discover new lights in the *Rule* of Saint Benedict, and these you will share with those whom I will send to you. For now, rely on Saint Benedict's intercession. He is a powerful ally against the snares of the Evil One. You do well to wear his medal, for it wards off the Evil One and protects you from his attacks.

Enter into this feast of Saint Benedict with humility and with gratitude. I will not forsake you. I am doing all that I promised you. Trust in My merciful love. Turn often to My most holy Mother. Come before My Face in this the Sacrament of My love; this will be your resting place, and My Eucharistic Heart will be the anchoring place of your soul.[1]

I bless you now with a powerful blessing that will renew in your soul the grace of your priesthood. My Mother blesses you and holds you beneath her protecting mantle.

Thursday, July 17, 2008

You do well to give Me everything. Once you have given Me a thing, leave it with Me, and know that I will dispose of it for the greater glory of My Father and for the salvation of your soul and of the souls of many others. I want you to live in an interior freedom born of trust in My loving mercy. I will never abandon you. I have set My Heart upon you. Love Me, and show that you love Me by giving Me all things. Nothing is too small for Me and nothing is too great.

Live in the grace of My divine friendship. Consult Me whenever you want and about anything at all. I take a lively interest in all that touches you. You are the apple of My eye.[2] Mine it is to protect you, to shield you from all harm, and to preserve you from all dangers of body and soul, by day and by night.

All of these matters that you have given Me will be resolved in due time, and you will be filled with thanksgiving and with joy. It will be evident to you and to many others that I have intervened and that I have acted to protect and prosper the work of My own Eucharistic Heart.

The indult that came yesterday on the feast of My Immaculate Mother, the Queen of Carmel, was a sign that she has taken you, her priest son, and this work of adoration to her own Heart. She who intervened to save you from a life of sin and unhappiness will intervene again and again to sanctify you and to bring about what I intend to do.

You did well to tell N. to consecrate himself to My Immaculate Mother. He needs to do this in order to escape the sorrow and weariness that plague him. Tell him to entrust himself without fear to the Heart of My Immaculate Mother. She will intervene in his life and he will recover his joy and the fervour of his first love through her.

---

[1] 2 Chron 6:41; Ps 131(132):8; Heb 6:19.
[2] Deut 32:10; Ps 16:8 (17:7); Zech 2:8.

I bless you now and those whom you have placed before My Eucharistic Face. My Mother too stretches out her hands; receive the graces that fall from them in abundance. Let not one of them be lost. She has choice graces for you, her beloved priest son. She would have you be another John for her Sorrowful and Immaculate Heart. Open your soul to the gifts and graces she wants to lavish upon you. And thank and praise Me who love you with an everlasting love.

Earlier in the day, I heard Our Lord say to me:

Give Me priest adorers.

At 10 o'clock in the evening, after celebrating a Votive Mass of Christ, Eternal High Priest:

I am speaking to you. Take note of what I have to say. On Thursday evenings I want My cenacle open to all My priests and deacons. Begin with Vespers. Then, offer time for confessions. Confess your sins to one another. Be to one another the ministers of My pardon and the channels of My mercy. Holy Mass will follow; at the end of Mass, expose My Body so that all may remain in adoration before My Eucharistic Face. Read a few verses of My final discourse in the cenacle. After an hour of adoration, share a simple meal together.

I will bless these Thursday evening gatherings. I will be present in your midst to instruct and to heal, to console and to refresh. This will be integral to the work I am asking of you. Begin with a small group. Let the invitations go forth by word of mouth. I will do all the rest.

My Mother will be present. She is ever attentive to the needs of her priest sons. All the resources of her Immaculate Heart are yours. Call upon her with confidence. Entrust all things to her care. She is the Mother and Queen of My cenacle.

This will be a school of prayer for My priests. I will give you the grace of touching hearts. Your part is to remain simple and pure, humble and trusting, merciful and kind. And pray much. Remain before My Eucharistic Face and there I will teach you the secrets of My priestly Heart, secrets both sorrowful and glorious.

Give Me priest adorers! Yes, it was I who said that to you. You will begin to give Me priest adorers by these Thursday evenings in the cenacle. You will see what I will do. And you will sing hymns of thanksgiving and praise to My most loving Heart.

Thursday, July 24, 2008
Saint Charbel Makhlouf

Do not give in to feelings of discouragement. They cause you to focus even more on yourself and on your limitations. Rather, look to Me. Seek My Face and rely on the faithful love of My Heart for you. I chose you for this work, knowing full well your history and your incapacity to persevere in the pursuit of an ideal. None of this matters to Me. What I ask of you is to trust in My merciful love. You will find the wellspring of My merciful love in My Eucharistic Heart. I want you to live a fully Eucharistic life; thus will I do for you all that I desire to see in you. Thus will I deliver you from the paralysis of your inadequacies and make you a sign of My triumphant grace.

Continue to tell Me that you trust in My merciful love for you. Let the little invocation[1] inhabit your heart like a soft murmur by day and by night. My Heart is touched by every expression of confidence in My merciful love.

As soon as something causes you anxiety or fear, give it to Me. Present all your cares to My Immaculate Mother. She is your Mother, and there is nothing that she will not do for you, to bring you to holiness and to glorify Me in the Sacrament of My love. Continue to ask for the help of the saints whom I have given you as friends and companions for the journey. Do not fear about tomorrow. Trust Me in all things great and small.

Celebrate My Holy Sacrifice tonight with a tranquil heart. I have made you My priest for all eternity. With every Holy Mass, you enter more deeply into My designs for you. Now thank Me, adore Me, and wait for My blessing and that of My most pure Mother.

Thursday, July 31, 2008
Saint Ignatius of Loyola

I want you to go to confession weekly. This is necessary for the health of your soul and even of your body. You will experience the benefits of My merciful pardon and the saving power of My precious Blood. Prepare your confessions well. Listen to the voice of the Holy Spirit and repent of the sins that He will show you. The work to which I have called you requires a great delicacy of conscience and an uncompromising purity of heart.

So many of My priests have fallen into indifference and hardness of

---

[1] Namely, the invocation of Mother Yvonne-Aimée de Jésus: "O Jesus, King of Love, I put my trust in Thy merciful goodness."

heart because they fail to avail themselves of this sacrament of My mercy. If only they would come to Me often with their sins, I would be able to work miracles of healing and of holiness in their souls!

My priests should be the first to seek Me out in the Sacrament of Reconciliation. They should be the first to run to Me as soon as they experience the pangs of an uneasy conscience and the regret of their sinful weaknesses. The single greatest service My priests can offer one another is the readiness to hear each other's confessions and to pronounce over each other the healing words of absolution. In this way, they carry out the example I gave you when, at the Last Supper, I washed the feet of My disciples.[1] Frequent confession, weekly confession is, more than ever, *necessary* to My priests.

Thursday, August 7, 2008

You, My priest adorer, will live in silence and humility, attentive to the sound of My voice and obedient to whatsoever I will say to you. Submit to the discernment of those whom I have set over you, and in all things prefer the mind and sentiments of the Church to your own thoughts and attractions.

The work for which I have set you apart, in My infinite mercy and love for the men I have chosen, requires of you a lowliness of heart born of self-knowledge, boundless trust in My divine mercy, confidence in My divine friendship, and, in serving your brothers, a transparent purity of intention, serenity, and benignity. These virtues I will give you through your consecration to the Immaculate Heart of My Mother, the Blessed and ever-Virgin Mary.

You will order your days around the three hours that I ask you to consecrate to keeping watch before My Eucharistic Face. You will offer Me the daily round of praise that Saint Benedict calls the work of God.[2] And you will make the Holy Sacrifice of the Mass the sun of your existence, illumining each day with its brightness and suffusing your life with the warmth of the Holy Spirit.

You will turn to My Immaculate Mother, the Advocate of priests and Mediatrix of all graces, by offering her each day the humble homage of

---

[1] John 13:1–15.

[2] The phrase *opus Dei*, referring to the communal "work" of offering the sacrifice of praise to God in the sacred liturgy, appears several times in *The Holy Rule*: see chs. 7 (twelfth degree of humility), 19, 22, 43 (where Benedict famously writes: "Let nothing be put before the work of God"), 44, 47, 50, 52, 58, 67. Of course, other chapters delve into aspects of the Divine Office, which, together with the Mass, forms the substance of the *opus Dei*.

her Rosary and the singing of the *Ave Maris Stella* for all the clergy of My Church.

Each week you will relive My Paschal Mystery by passing with Me to the Father.

On Thursday evening you will offer the Holy Sacrifice and keep watch in adoration before My Eucharistic Face. Every Thursday you will meditate My final discourse in the Gospel of John, chapters 13 through 17. Thus will you commemorate the gifts and mysteries of the cenacle: the Sacrament of My Body and Blood, and that of Holy Orders. You will, whenever possible, share these Thursdays in the cenacle with your brothers in the clergy.

On Friday, you will offer Me a suitable act of penance in reparation for your sins and for the sins of all My priests. I will look for you from My Cross. I want to find you there on Calvary with My sorrowing Mother and with John, My beloved disciple. Each Friday take into your heart, as if for the first time, the words I uttered from the Cross. Contemplate My side pierced by the soldier's lance; enter into the sanctuary of My open Heart and adore My precious Blood. Receive the outpouring of My Holy Spirit, and withdraw into silence and recollection, as did John with Mary, My Mother, when all is accomplished.

Saturday is the day that, by a special title, belongs to My Mother in her solitude and hope. You will live every Saturday in her company, celebrating whenever possible her Mass and the Divine Office in her honour,[1] and offering her a token of special filial affection.

Sunday is the day of My holy and glorious resurrection. I will open your eyes to the vision of My Father and draw you with Me into His embrace. Be mindful on Sundays of the labours of your brothers in the sacred ministry. Seek for them spiritual refreshment and energy in My Eucharistic presence. Sunday evening through Monday, you will do well to recall the outpouring of the Holy Spirit, for that is the third gift and mystery of the cenacle.[2]

The time that remains after prayer, you will devote to the work of serving your brothers, to rest, and to the ordinary necessities of life, trusting in Me always to provide you with all that is necessary. Thus will you avoid the reproach addressed to Martha when I said, "You are busy about many things, but one thing alone is necessary."[3]

---

[1] A long-standing custom reflected in both the *Missale Romanum* and the *Antiphonale Monasticum* used by the Benedictines.

[2] The first two gifts are mentioned just above: "the Sacrament of My Body and Blood, and that of Holy Orders."

[3] Luke 10:41–42.

You will rise and retire at a fixed time and, when authorized to do so, you may come before My Eucharistic Face to adore Me in the hours of the night.

It will be enough in the beginning to follow these little rules that I have given you. You will find all the rest in the *Rule* of Saint Benedict, your father, and in the writings of those saints to whom I have entrusted you and this work of Mine. I will uphold you according to My promise and you will live, and I will not disappoint you in your hope.[1]

Then later:

I have consecrated thee the priest adorer of My Eucharistic Face.

Sunday, August 24, 2008

I have much to say to you. Why do you hesitate? Why do you not take up your pen and write the words of My Heart to yours? I am faithful to you. I will not forsake you, nor will I go back on any of the promises I have made to you.[2] See, the time of their fulfilment has already begun, just as I said it would. Soon, very soon, we will live together under one roof and My Eucharistic Face will be the joy and light of your existence.

I have given you this bishop. He understands My call to you; he will allow the desires of My Eucharistic Heart to be realized and he will hasten their realization. Show him respect and gratitude. I chose him for you, and this is the place I have prepared for you.

My most holy Mother accompanies you; she will provide for all your needs. She is, in all truth, your own Mother of Perpetual Help. She is your advocate and the advocate of every priest, no matter what the circumstances of his life may be.

Be faithful to all that I have asked of you. Trust Me to do for you and in you those things that, of yourself, you cannot do.[3] I will give you strength and energy, not only for your soul, but also for your body. Thus will you be able to correspond actively to My designs on your life.

Now I bless you. I make the light of My Eucharistic Face shine upon you. My Immaculate Mother too opens her hands over you. A shower of graces falls from them into your soul and over those whom you recommend to her merciful Heart.

---

[1] Cf. Ps 118(119):116, which is the verse said by a monk when making his profession: "Uphold me according to Thy word, and I shall live: and let me not be confounded in my expectation."

[2] Deut 34:12; Heb 13:5.

[3] Eph 3:20; Jer 1:6–7; John 3:27, 15:5.

Monday, August 25, 2008

Make it your first care to find the kingdom of God.
MATTHEW 6:33

The kingdom of God is present in all its fullness, though in a hidden manner, in the Most Holy Sacrament of the Altar. He who seeks out My Eucharistic presence is seeking the kingdom of God. He who approaches Me in the Sacrament of My love will find the kingdom and therein all that he desires according to My Spirit.

Come first to Me in the Sacrament of My love. Let this become the supernatural instinct of your soul: always to come to Me, always to seek My Eucharistic Face.

You did well to come into My presence this evening. This will be the first of many such evenings spent together. You will begin to taste the sweetness of My company and you will open yourself more and more to the gift of My divine friendship.

Adoration must become a need of your soul, just as food and drink and rest are needs of your body. Come to Me often and remain in the light of My Eucharistic Face, that I may sanctify you and do in you all that I desire to find in you. Come to Me for the sake of your brother priests who flee from My presence as soon as they have carried out their sacramental duties. I want all My priests to discover the sweetness of lingering before My Eucharistic Face. I want to draw them all to My open Heart.

Let this work of Mine begin with you. The next generation of priests will be wholly Eucharistic. There will be among them many adorers of My Eucharistic Face, many consolers of My Eucharistic Heart. They will have been schooled in intimacy with Me by My Virgin Mother and by John, My virgin disciple.

I so desire a priesthood transformed by the mysteries of My Body and Blood, a priesthood purified in My precious Blood and sanctified in the light of My Eucharistic Face. Offer Me your adoration so that this desire of Mine will find a response in the hearts of all My priests.

Thursday, October 17, 2008
Saint Margaret Mary Alacoque

Allow Me to speak words of peace to your soul. Trust Me in all things. Trust that I will not abandon you, nor will I deprive you of My friendship. My desire is to hold conversation with you, to speak to you, as I have often said, heart to heart, as a man converses with his best friend. Why do you doubt? Believe in My friendship for you. It is My gift to you, and I will not withdraw what I have given you out of the love of My Heart.

This is the underlying problem of so many souls, especially of so many of My priests. They allow doubt to take hold. Doubt is the narrow end of the wedge that separates from Me. I do not refer to a doubt of My teachings or of those of My Church, but to another doubt, one that is more fundamental: the doubt of My personal love for the soul upon whom I have set My Heart. So many begin to think, "He cannot possibly love me in this way or take a real interest in me"—and so they begin to withdraw from My friendship, to flee My presence, and to greet Me only from a distance as one would a passing acquaintance.

You must never let this happen. Know that My Heart is set upon you with an everlasting and most tender love, that I look upon you at every moment with all the delicacy of My divine friendship, and with an inexhaustible mercy.[1] Respond to My love for you by coming to Me as often as you can, by remaining in My presence, by seeking My Face, by resting upon My Eucharistic Heart. For this have I made myself so close to you in the Sacrament of My love, the Sacrament of My divine friendship for you and for all My priests.

My Immaculate Mother feels the same way towards you. She too follows you day by day. Everything you do and say interests her maternal Heart. She too is ready to converse with you. You have only to approach her as a trusting son approaches the most loving of mothers.

Dialogue with Me, with My most holy Mother, and with My saints belongs, even in this passing world, to those whose hearts are already fixed there where true joys are to be found.[2] For now, these joys are yours in My Eucharistic presence. The Sacrament of My love is your heaven on earth. Become the adorer that I want you to be, and you will see the heavens open within your soul; there you will enjoy conversations with Me, with My Mother, and with My saints and angels. This is the remedy for every solitude and the secret of a heavenly joy while yet on this earth.

Sunday, October 19, 2008
Saint Paul of the Cross

You did the right thing in coming to Me with your feelings of aloneness.

---

[1] Jer 31:3; Isa 54:8.

[2] Cf. the Collect for the Fourth Sunday after Easter: "O God, Who makest the minds of the faithful to be of one will, grant to Thy people to love that which Thou dost command and desire that which Thou dost promise, so that among the changing things of this world our hearts may be fixed where true joys are to be found."

I am here for you, and you, you are here for Me, only for Me, and for no other. Do you think that I will not honour the sacrifice you made in coming to live here for Me, with Me, close to Me by day and by night?

Understand just a little the sorrow of My Eucharistic Heart that is utterly forsaken in countless tabernacles all over the world. Why do I multiply My glorious presence in so real and miraculous a way, if not to be close to the souls whom I love with a burning passion and with a consummate tenderness? And I am left alone. Often I am forgotten from one week to the next or, worse yet, I am treated like a thing, like a commodity kept in reserve in case of need. This was not My intention in instituting this Sacrament of My redeeming love.

My intention was threefold.[1] It was first to perpetuate My one Sacrifice through all ages and even to the close of the age. It was to nourish souls with My Body and Blood for their healing, their sanctification, their union with Me and with all the members of My Mystical Body, in view of My return in glory when all will be one in Me, and I will be in them, and the sacrifice of our praise to the Father in the Holy Spirit will be unending. But I had a third reason as well: it was to offer souls—and especially My priests—the companionship and light and warmth of My REAL PRESENCE. It was to be present in such a way as to take My delights in conversing with the children of men. It was to extend the graces of My Incarnation and earthly life to *all* of My disciples, to My chosen friends, until the end of time.

So much of what I held in My Heart when I instituted this Sacrament has now been forgotten, or obscured, or deliberately contradicted. This is what causes the sorrow of My Eucharistic Heart. This is why I turned to you and asked you to give Me your life, the rest of your life, in adoration and reparation. I want the free response of your adoring love to My Eucharistic love.

Why do you think I have spoken to you so often of My Eucharistic Face? It is because "face" signifies "presence." The devotion to My Eucharistic Face is the remedy to the loss of faith in My real presence that has swept through My Church at every level, extinguishing the fire of Eucharistic charity and causing even My elect, My priests, to grow cold and distant from Me.[2]

This is My word to you tonight and this is why I brought you to this

---

[1] Concerning this threefold intention, cf. Matt 26:26–28, 28:20; Mark 14:22–24; Luke 22:19–20, 24:35; John 6:51–58; Acts 2:42; 1 Cor 10:16–21, 11:23–26; Eph 1:3–23, 5:2; Heb 9:26, 10:12, 13:15; Prov 8:30–36.

[2] Matt 24:7.

place. Any loneliness you may feel is an invitation to seek Me out in the Sacrament of My divine friendship and to console My Eucharistic Heart.

Saturday, October 25, 2008

Give Me N., and I will take care of him, just as I have taken care of you and, in My merciful love, provided for all your needs. He too has been prepared by suffering for this life of adoration and reparation, and now I would have him begin a new life as the cherished friend of My Sacred Heart and the beloved son of My Immaculate Mother. As for you, be a father to him. Begin to live the strong and tender fatherhood that is My gift to you in view of what is to come.

There will be difficulties, but you have nothing to fear. This is the work of My Eucharistic Heart; it is the work by means of which I will sanctify and heal My priests by drawing them into the light of My Eucharistic Face.

If you had a greater trust in Me, I would teach you more and speak to you as I promised I would: heart to heart, revealing to you those mysteries that I have held in reserve for My friends, those who walk in the path traced for them by John, My beloved disciple. Learn to expect more from Me, and I will give you more. Place no limits on My merciful love for you, and you will discover that it has no limits.

Trust Me with all things, even the most insignificant. I am like a mother to the souls who believe in My merciful love; whatsoever touches them, touches Me.[1] If only My priests knew this from personal experience, they would be compelled then to preach it, and many souls would discover through them just how deep and all-encompassing is the tenderness of My Sacred Heart for those who trust in My merciful love.

You cannot see from where you are in this life now the power and value of sufferings united to My own. Anything given to Me, anything placed in My priestly hands, I lift up and offer to the Father, covered with My precious Blood. It is this that makes your sufferings, even the smallest ones, precious to Me, and precious in the sight of My Father.

After I wrote a description of the life to be led:

Go forward, and know that I am with you.

When I asked Our Lord to show me how better to order my life so as to have sufficient time before His Eucharistic Face, He answered me:

---

[1] Ps 26(27):10; 130(131):2; Isa 46:3–4, 49:14–15, 66:13; Matt 23:37.

Where are you wasting time? What things are you putting before coming to Me in the Sacrament of My love? Are you relying on My grace to make possible what, of yourself and by yourself, you cannot do? Prepare each day more carefully and you will see that it will flow more peacefully, and you will find ample time to remain before My Eucharistic Face.

What I have asked of you is not difficult nor is it beyond your strength. It will bring you happiness, and will console My grieving Heart, My Eucharistic Heart that is so afflicted by the neglect and coldness of souls and by the loss of faith that affects even My priests.

Faith in this mystery of the Most Holy Eucharist grows *in proportion* to the time one gives Me in adoration. It is not enough that My priests should celebrate Holy Mass daily, even correctly and devoutly, if they do not approach Me and remain with Me, who wait for them in the Sacrament of My love. Nothing can replace the intimate experience of My Eucharistic friendship—and this is the experience that I offer to you and to all who seek My Eucharistic Face, all who offer a sacrifice of time to My Eucharistic Heart.

The loss of faith that afflicts so many souls is incompatible with a life of adoration. Souls do not stop adoring because they have lost their faith; they lose their faith because they have stopped adoring Me. This is why I would have you hold fast even to the outward forms of adoration.[1] When even these things are cast aside, there is nothing left to invite the soul to the inward adoration in spirit and in truth by which I am glorified. I speak here of the genuflection, the prostration, the profound bow and all the other marks of attention to My presence that provide the soul with a language in which she can express her faith and her desire to adore Me.

Again, it is for this reason that I call My priests to learn and to practice faithfully the humble rubrics of the sacred liturgy. They are not important in themselves, but they are important in that they contain and express all the sentiments towards Me and towards My sacrifice with which I have endowed My Bride, the Church. One who dispenses himself easily from such practices is guilty of a sin of pride that opens the door of the soul to the cold and hostile winds that would extinguish the flame of faith within.

Show yourself humble and obedient to My Church, and invite your

---

[1] As the text goes on to say, "outward forms" refer to such pious customs as exposition of the Blessed Sacrament in a monstrance, mounted on a tabor, and surrounded by lit candles; the double genuflection of the adorer before the Sacrament exposed; and the use of cope, humeral veil, incense, and bells for Benediction.

brother priests to the same joyful fidelity, even in little things.[1] I will reward them with an increase of faith, of hope, and of charity, and reveal to them the mysteries that My Father and I hide from those who think themselves learned and clever according to the world.[2]

I asked Our Lord about the distractions that plague me during Holy Mass and the Divine Office:

You experience distractions at Holy Mass and during your prayer because you have not yet allowed My order to reign over your heart and in your life. This is My desire: that your whole life should reflect, even now, the order and beauty that characterize My kingdom.

This is also My Mother's desire for you, and she will help you to attain it. Listen for her guidance and her inspirations and follow her wise direction. In this, she is the pure instrument of the Holy Spirit, who at every moment brings order out of chaos, peace out of dissension, and unity out of multiplicity.[3] There is dissension in your life when two interests compete for your time, your attention, and your energy. Allow My Mother to re-order your life, and you will discover the joy of living in a holy simplicity, in an order that anticipates the glorious order prepared for all My saints in heaven.

Monday, November 10, 2008
Pope Saint Leo the Great

Know that I have brought you here for one thing and one thing alone: to be the priest adorer and reparator of My Eucharistic Face. All other things are secondary, and you must keep yourself free of anything that risks burdening your soul or drawing you away from the heart of your mission here.

In all circumstances be humble; never insist on your own way. Present your desires and opinions simply and confidently, and then leave all things in My hands. The outcome will be according to My designs and I will not be thwarted by the resistance or shortsightedness of My human agents.

You are learning, at last, not to force events and not to manipulate people so as to have your own way. I want you to trust Me absolutely

---

[1] Matt 25:21–23; Luke 16:10, 19:17.

[2] Luke 10:21–24; Matt 13:10–17; Wis 6:24; John 7:14–17; 1 Cor 1:25–29; 2:12–16.

[3] Gen 1:2; Ex 31:2–5; Acts 2:1–11; Rom 8:5–9; Eph 4:1–16; 1 Cor 12:4–13; 1 John 4:1–3.

and in all things. Nothing escapes My attention. You are close to My Heart. My Mother watches over you. She is your advocate and your perpetual help. Go to her confidently with your doubts, your worries, and your fears. Trust in her maternal Heart is never misplaced, and she will never disappoint you.

What happened to Father N. is in answer to your prayer for him. It is an intervention of My loving mercy. Continue to pray for him. He will emerge from this trial purified and strengthened in My grace.

You do well to pray for My good servant, your father, Pope Benedict XVI. He has great need of your prayer for him. He is not entirely free to follow through on certain decisions that he has already taken in his heart. Pray, pray that the obstacles that surround him may be moved and that he may find collaborators who are loyal, pure, and true.

Yes, I have placed in your heart the desire for a more hidden life, withdrawn from the tumult and activities of the world, in order to give yourself over to Me in adoration and reparation for your brother priests. The essential thing is to come before Me bearing the sins and betrayals of your brother priests, and to expose them to the light of My Face and to the fire of My Sacred Heart. Come before Me with sorrow for your sins and for the sins of your brother priests and, at the same time, with an immense confidence in My love for each one of you. I call each priest to holiness, even the most indifferent and negligent among them, even the most perverted and broken. I want to heal them all. I desire that they should become saints, shining trophies of My loving mercy, worthy of being presented to My Father. There is no priest whom I have not called to holiness.[1]

Come before Me, bearing every degradation of the priestly state, every betrayal, every dark and wicked secret, and I will lift up the light of My Eucharistic Face upon you for the sake of My poor priests, sinners in need of My mercy, My healing love, and My friendship. Represent them before Me, and I will represent them before My Father.

My Mother is at your side in this work of reparation for her priest sons. Constantly she pleads on their behalf; she is the great Mediatrix who stands with uplifted hands, appealing to My pierced Heart for her sons. She has chosen you to share in this work of hers, to intercede together with her, and, in union with her Sorrowful and Immaculate Heart, to obtain abundant graces for those poor priests who are most in need of them.

---

[1] Deut 7:6–8; Ps 131(132):9, 16; Isa 40:26–31, 43:1–7, 62:11–12; Rom 1:7; 1 Cor 1:2; Eph 4:11–13; Col 1:11–14; 1 Thess 4:3; 1 Tim 3–6; 1 Pet 2:9.

Then, when I asked Our Lord to give me a prayer for this purpose:

Lord Jesus Christ, Priest and Victim,
Lamb without stain or blemish,
I come before Thy Face,
laden with the sins and betrayals of my brother priests
and with the burden of my own sins and infidelities.
Allow me to represent those priests
   who are most in need of Thy mercy.
For them, let me abide before Thy Eucharistic Face,
   close to Thy open Heart.
Through the Sorrowful and Immaculate Heart of Thy Mother,
Advocate and Mediatrix of all graces,
pour forth upon all the priests of Thy Church
that torrent of mercy that ever flows from Thy Heart,
to purify and heal them,
to sanctify and refresh them,
and, at the hour of their death,
to make them worthy of joining Thee before the Father
in the heavenly Holy Place beyond the veil.
Amen.

Wednesday, November 12, 2008

Know that I brought you here to detach you from many things that were an obstacle to the fulfilment of My plan for you. You had to be set free of the context of your life in —— in order to make a new beginning here. This was My will for you, and see, I have carried it out.

Continue to trust Me in all circumstances and with all things great and small. I will not forsake you. I have given you the friendship of My Eucharistic Heart, and in that Heart you will want for nothing. Live then in the cavern of My wounded side as in a tabernacle, and seek to enter My Heart of hearts. There the Father waits for you. There the Holy Spirit will transform you and configure you entirely to Me, Firstborn Son of the Father, His Victim and His Priest.

Why do I speak to you so often of My *open* Heart? It is because for you, My priest, it is the secret of union with Me. The wound in My side is the Holy Place of My Body, the Temple.[1] The Holy of Holies is My Sacred Heart, and that Holy of Holies you have before you in the Sacrament of

---

[1] John 2:19–22; Rev 21:22.

90

My love. Like the psalmist, yearn to abide in that secret innermost part of My Temple.[1] Hide yourself in Me, that I may manifest My Face through you.[2]

The movement of persecution that is about to break out against My Church will focus on three objects. In fact, this has already begun. I will be attacked in My priests; they represent My Eucharistic Face. The face of the priesthood is My Face, once again mocked and covered with mud, spittle, and blood. I will be dishonoured in the Sacrament of My Body and Blood. You will see an increase of sins against the mysteries of My Body and Blood: sacrileges, desecrations, and mockeries. I will be attacked in the weakest and most vulnerable members of My Mystical Body. This too has already begun, but it will increase until it reaches proportions that will oblige My Father to avenge the blood of His beloved innocents.

For all of this you must make reparation, serving Me in My priests and interceding for them; adoring Me in the Sacrament of My Body and Blood; and praying for an end to the persecution of the weak, the little, and the poor, those who have no one to defend them apart from Me.

The day is coming, and it is not far off, when I will intervene to show My Face in a priesthood completely renewed and sanctified; when I will intervene to triumph in My Eucharistic Heart by the conquering power of sacrificial love alone; when I will intervene to defend the poor and vindicate the innocents whose blood has marked this nation[3] and so many others as did the blood of Abel in the beginning.

Now kneel and adore Me in silence.

Thursday, November 13, 2008

At my morning adoration:

Nobody can come to the Father except through Me.
JOHN 14:6

And so I remain with you always, even until the end of time, in the Sacrament of My Body and Blood. I give *Myself* in the Most Holy Eucharist as your living bridge into the presence of the Father. This too is the work of every priest of Mine: to throw himself across the great chasm that separates sinful man from the holiness of My Father. Thus does he *replace*

---

[1] Ps 26(27):4–5; Ps 83(84):2.

[2] Ps 26(27):5; Ps 30:21 (31:20).

[3] Namely, the United States of America.

Me[1]—take My place and represent it—in every Mass as mediator and bridge.

Of himself, the priest cannot attain to this work of mediation. It is only because he bears within him the indelible mark of My priesthood that he can become the mediator between My Father and His sinful children. He is authorized to do so by the Holy Spirit who marks him for this essential priestly work at the moment of ordination. The representation of My Father, of His interests and His desires, is the task of My priests. One who sees My priest sees My Father because I have set apart My priests to be the images of My Holy Face in the world until the end of time.[2] The more closely a priest is united to Me, the more vividly will he reveal My Face and, therefore, My Father, to souls.

> It is to My Father I am going, and whatever request you make of the Father in My name, I will grant, so that through the Son the Father may be glorified; every request you make of Me in My own name, I myself will grant it to you.
> JOHN 14:13

I do not stand before My Father alone; every priest of Mine participates in My heavenly intercession before the Father's face, and I authorize and ratify the intercession of every priest at the altars of My Church. It is this that gives such efficacy to the prayer of the priest at the altar in the action of the Holy Sacrifice.

I desire that My priests should live in constant conversation with, and dependence on, the Holy Spirit. They should undertake nothing without first consulting the Holy Spirit. Once they have invoked the Holy Spirit and discerned what it is I am asking of them, they should go forward with courage and determination, free from fear and full of confidence in the power of My grace to accomplish through their weakness all that I have asked of them.

> You can see Me because I live on, and you too will have life. When that day comes you will learn for yourselves that I am in My Father, and you in Me, and I in you.
> JOHN 14:20–21

I live on in the Sacrament of the Most Holy Eucharist, but few understand that this Sacrament is the fulfilment of My promise on the night

---

[1] Not in the sense of eliminating the mediation of Christ, but rather as a sacramental representation of that mediation. Again, not as a mere image of that mediation or as something that points to it, but rather by way of effective participation in it.—*Author*.

[2] The implied premise is John 14:9: "He who sees me, sees the Father."

before I suffered. You have only to raise your eyes to the Sacred Host to *see Me*. There, in the Most Blessed Sacrament, I live on. There I am present to you and present before My Father in the glory of the heavenly sanctuary. Lift up your eyes to Me. Seek My Eucharistic Face and you will understand that My priesthood is one of ceaseless offering in heaven and on earth.

It is through My silent life in the Most Holy Sacrament of the Altar that I teach My priests how to be priests at every moment and not only when, vested in the insignia of their sacerdotal dignity, they stand before the altar to celebrate the Holy Mysteries. The life of the priest *is* My life in heaven: ceaseless attention to the Father and uninterrupted intercession, thanksgiving, reparation, and praise on behalf of all men.

There is not a moment when the priest cannot be united to Me in praising My Father for his great glory,[1] in mediating the praises of the saints and of the angels, in carrying forward every offering to the Father made on earth, from the rising of the sun to its setting.[2] The life of the priest is not only his Mass; it is every Mass that is being offered on earth, that has been or will be offered, and all of this in union with Me who stand in the presence of My Father as eternal Priest, as perpetual Victim, and as Altar covered with the outpouring of My own Blood. The service of My priests in the sanctuaries of My Church on earth is but a part of their day, a passing moment in time. My desire is that each priest should unite himself to My eternal service of the Father in the sanctuary not made by human hands that is in heaven.[3]

> *When that day comes you will learn for yourselves that I am in My Father, and you in Me, and I in you.*
>
> JOHN 14:20

Oh, that every priest of Mine would say with Me at the beginning of his day:

> *The world must know that I love the Father and act only as the Father has commanded Me to act. Rise up, we must be on our way.*
>
> JOHN 14:31

---

[1] Cf. the Gloria of the Mass: "Laudamus te, benedicimus te, adoramus te, glorificamus te, gratias agimus tibi propter magnam gloriam tuam."

[2] Mal 1:11; Ps 112(113):3.

[3] Mark 14:58; Heb 8:5, 9:11; Acts 7:48; 2 Cor 5:1.

IN SINU JESU

November 29, 2008
After First Vespers of the First Sunday of Advent

Begin this Advent season full of confidence and hope in My unfailing mercy. Although I am coming, and coming soon, I am already present.[1] Look at My Eucharistic Face: know that I am here for you in this the Sacrament of My love. I am here to console you, to comfort and instruct you, to give you an experience of My divine friendship already here in this life so as to prepare you for the glories of friendship in the next.

In this Sacrament I wait for you. So many emphasize that they must wait for Me, and yet I am already present, close to them, and disposed to reveal to them the secrets of My Heart. They forget that it is *I* who wait for *them* to come to Me. How often did I say to My disciples, "Come to Me."[2] They understood, at least most of them did, the intensity of My longing for the company of souls.[3] I would have all souls come to Me and remain with Me.

This is the secret of priestly holiness. Once a priest begins to come to Me, seeking My Eucharistic Face and longing for the company of My pierced Heart, I will come to him and make My home in him, and with Me will come My Father and the Holy Spirit.[4] Thus will his priesthood be forever consecrated and sanctified and rendered divinely fruitful.

Spend this Advent, My beloved friend, My priest, close to Me in the Sacrament of My love. Be My priest adorer. Offer Me yourself, and I will offer you with Me to our Father. Seek out the company of My Immaculate Mother and of the saints. Learn to live with them now so that you will live with them in eternity. Honour My Mother in the mystery of her Immaculate Conception. This is a mystery full of grace and of light for those who ponder it. It is the remedy for many of the ills that afflict My priests and poison their souls. Invoke My Mother conceived without sin and she will communicate to you something of the purity and brightness of her all-holy and immaculate Heart.

I asked Our Lord for help in preaching to the priests of the diocese.

Do not be fearful of preaching. Know that I will be with you to speak through you and to touch even the most hardened hearts. Abandon yourself to Me in complete confidence and I will abandon Myself to you so that your words will be My words and your presence My presence.

[1] Rev 3:11, 22:7, 22:12, 22:20; Isa 56:1; Bar 4:22–25.
[2] Matt 11:28; John 7:37; Sir 24:19–21.
[3] Luke 22:15.
[4] John 14:23.

This is what I long to do with every priest of Mine. If only My priests would allow Me to speak and to act through them, what miracles of grace they would see!

A holy priest is quite simply one who allows Me to live in him as in a supplementary humanity.[1] In every priest I would speak and act, delivering souls from the powers of darkness and healing the sick[2]—but most of all, I desire to offer myself in every priest and to assume every priest into My own offering to the Father. This I would do at the altar in the celebration of My Holy Sacrifice, but not only there; the life of a priest united to Me is a ceaseless oblation and he, like Me, is a *hostia perpetua*.[3] You cannot imagine the fruitfulness of such a union, and this is the fruitfulness that I desire for My Father's glory and for the joy of My Bride, the Church.

Do not stop transcribing My words to you. I speak to you to comfort and enlighten you, to show you how much I love you and want you at every moment close to My open Heart, but I speak to you also for your brother priests and for those souls who would pray for them and who would offer themselves, that priests might be sanctified in truth.[4] My word to you this evening is the cry of the prophet to Israel that you sang a few moments ago. "Be ye comforted, be ye comforted, for behold, I am coming very soon."[5] Desire My coming and prepare for it by living in communion with the most pure Heart of My Mother. I have confided to her the preparation of souls for My advent in glory.

Tuesday, December 9, 2008

Our Lady:

It was I who protected you last night and preserved your life from the plans laid by the Evil One who seeks nothing more than to stop you from persevering in this work that my Son has asked of you. Be on your guard, then, and be prudent, but without fear, because I am your Mother and, just as I said to my beloved little son Juan Diego, I hold you beneath my protecting mantle, in the crossing of my arms, close, very close to my Immaculate Heart. Trust in my protection. Yes, I am your Mother of Perpetual Help, ever ready to come to your rescue, ever ready

---

[1] See p. 71, note 1.
[2] Matt 10:8; Mark 3:15, 6:13, 16:17–18; Luke 9:1, 10:17, 13:32.
[3] A perpetual victim.
[4] John 17:19.
[5] Isa 40:1; Rev 22:7, 22:12.

to provide for your needs, to deliver you from danger, and to console you in sorrow. Approach me with childlike confidence and you will never be disappointed.

I have much to say to you. Please stop—remain quiet in my presence. Come before my image. Give me your time and give me a listening ear and an attentive heart, and I will instruct you in the way you should go.[1] There is no need for you to be afraid, because my Son has entrusted you to me and I will always keep you safe.

The Rosary is the means by which I attach souls to myself. The Rosary assures souls of my presence and of my protection. How could I not have come to save you last night whilst you were calling upon me by praying my Rosary? Speak of the Rosary to my beloved priests. They will find healing for their heart and a comfort for their souls in this prayer that I so love.

After the adorable and Most Holy Name of my Son, JESUS, there is no name in heaven or on earth that holds the power and sweetness of my name. I am but the humble servant of the Lord, but He who is mighty has exalted me, making me Queen of the Universe.[2] All things are subject to me and there is nothing that I ask of my Son that He will refuse me.[3] Pray in my name, that is, through my most pure Heart and trusting in my intercession, as you have already done, as you did yesterday in your prayer of consecration, and you will see wonders, miracles of grace, and signs of the power of my Son who is Lord of lords and King of kings,[4] my Son who is all-merciful and who hears the cry of the poor and grants their petition.

When you pray the Rosary, you are effectively praying in my name and in the sweet and adorable Name of my Son, Jesus. To pray in my name means to pray in union and in harmony with my Immaculate Heart. To pray in the Name of Jesus means to pray in communion with all the sentiments, desires, and plans of His Sacred Heart.

Then Our Lady asked me to close my prayer with the Litany of Saint Joseph.

⊕

---

[1] Ps 31(32):8; Isa 48:7; Prov 2:2.
[2] Luke 1:46–49; Ps 44:10 (45:9); Judith 13:22–25, 15:10; Rev 12.
[3] John 2:1–11.
[4] 1 Tim 6:15; Rev 17:14, 19:16.

IN SINU JESU

Thursday, January 8, 2009

Give Me the full attention of your heart—the ear of your heart—and I will speak to you.[1] I will show you the way in which you are to walk and I will give you My light about the things that weigh upon you, or sadden you, or perplex you.[2] Bring everything to Me and I will give you in exchange My grace and My love. It is fear more than anything else that prevents you from coming into My presence with confidence, with hope, and with a quiet heart.

With Me and from Me you have nothing to fear. I am here, in the Sacrament of My love, to be your comfort, your peace, your light, your refreshment, and your joy. Know this! Take it to heart. Believe it and act upon it. If souls believed this of Me, nothing would be able to keep them from seeking Me out in the Sacrament of My love and from remaining in My presence.

Even after two thousand years of Eucharistic presence in My Church, I remain unknown, I am forgotten, forsaken, and treated like a thing to be kept here or there, with little regard for My own burning desire to be present to My people in a visible way and to see them approach Me and remain, silent and adoring, in the light of My Eucharistic Face. Who can change this sad state of things if not My priests, My chosen friends—those into whose hands I give over My own Body and Blood, just as I did on the night before I died, with the apostles in the Upper Room? I want My priests to be the first to seek Me out in the Sacrament of My love. Let them begin, let them set the example: then others will follow.

As for you, My friend, My priest adorer, make more time for Me and I will give you time and energy for all the rest. You are here, first of all, to keep Me company. Everything else is secondary. I brought you here for Myself: to be the priest adorer of My Eucharistic Face and the consoling friend of My Eucharistic Heart. The more time you dedicate to Me alone in the Sacrament of My love, the more will I bless you in all that you are called to do. Resist every temptation to cut short the time dedicated to adoration. You are set apart for that work of reparation and of love, and nothing can take its place in your life. Do you hear Me? Then do as I am telling you. Follow My inspiration. Remain with Me and I

---

[1] Cf. the opening lines of the Prologue to St. Benedict's *Rule*: "Listen, O my son, to the precepts of thy master, and incline the ear of thy heart, and cheerfully receive and faithfully execute the admonitions of thy loving Father, that by the toil of obedience thou mayest return to Him from whom by the sloth of disobedience thou hast gone away" (Verheyen trans.).

[2] Isa 30:20–21.

will continue to instruct you and lead you into the future full of hope that I have promised you.

Monday, January 26, 2009

It is not by your works that you will be pleasing to Me, but by your confidence in My merciful love.

Tuesday, January 27, 2009

Faithfulness and constancy in good works and in the practice of your rule is the fruit of confidence in My merciful love for you. The more you trust My merciful love, the more will I give you the strength and energy necessary to fulfil what you have promised Me. Trust My mercy, especially in moments of weakness. When you cannot live up to the ideal you have set for yourself, live up to the one thing I ask of you before all else: trust in My merciful love. In this way you will always be pleasing to Me: in your moments of weakness as much as in your times of regularity and generous fidelity to your rule. Accept your weaknesses of body and those of your spirit as well; they are no obstacle to the work of My grace in your soul. The only obstacle to My work in souls is the lack of trust in My merciful love.

Thursday, January 29, 2009

I was praying over John 17 as I do every Thursday, in the presence of the Blessed Sacrament exposed. I understood that Satan could not break up the (physical) Body of Christ in His Passion: "You shall not break a single bone of His" (John 19:37). He has taken his revenge by seeking to break apart His Church. I understood that the fragmented Body of Christ can be healed by the ministrations of the Holy Spirit and of the Blessed Virgin Mary. The Mystical Body of Christ needs the gentle and perfect ministrations of the most pure hands of Mary. She is sent from heaven—without leaving her glorious heavenly throne—to nurse the ailing members of the Mystical Body and to restore health to the Church wheresoever she is weakened by sin or poisoned by evil. There cannot be—and there will not be—a full restoration of unity until the divinely appointed role of the Mother of Jesus is recognized and confessed. The same is true when it comes to the healing of broken lives and of souls poisoned by sin.
Then Our Lord continued:

My Mother is the agent of all healing, the chosen instrument of the Holy Spirit for the restoration of life, of light, and of unity in every place or instance where these are lacking. Not until this sovereign disposition of My Father is recognized and confessed will there be the healing, purification, and sanctification of the priesthood and of the Church for which so many souls labour and offer themselves. None of these objectives can be obtained by human means, or even by spiritual ones, apart from the role that belongs to My Mother and to none other, because she alone is the Immaculate and, so, is alone the human instrument fit for the workings of the Holy Spirit.

Now you see a little better why consecration to My Mother is not only desirable and praiseworthy; it is necessary.[1] It is the condition apart from which the realization of My promises in souls and in the Church—and especially in the priesthood of the Church—will continue to be thwarted and delayed. By consecration, I mean more than a simple act of devotion by which a person or group or nation is entrusted to My Mother's love; I mean a clear recognition of her role in My work of salvation and, then, a deliberate and conscious surrender to that role in all its implications.

Friday, January 30, 2009

One whom I call to a life of reparation must not fall into lukewarmness and the lack of generosity. These things are the very opposite of what a call to reparation signifies. I have called you and set you apart to live day after day in My presence and to adore My Eucharistic Face. For this have I brought us together in one house. I desire to be the centre and entire motive of all that you do. Live your life for Me, and construct your days around My desire to have you and to keep you before My Eucharistic Face, close to My open Heart.

I have called you to this life of adoration to make up for the coldness and indifference of so many priests who, while living close to My sacramental presence, rarely if ever come before My Face and approach My Eucharistic Heart. This is one of My great sorrows: that the men whom I have chosen and set apart to be My friends and My priests show so little interest in remaining in My company, in listening to what I have to say to them, and in pouring out their hearts to Me. I wait for them. I look for their arrival. And I remain disappointed because so few of My priests understand that My desire in instituting the Sacrament of love

---

[1] At least implicitly—that is, one could not be saved if one were to reject any of the truths concerning Our Lady or if one were to refuse to receive all grace through her hands and heart. If one is to be saved, it is necessary to belong to Mary, for those who do not belong to her do not belong to the Church or to Christ.

was that the priests who offer My sacrifice and nourish My people with My Body and Blood should also find in My Eucharistic presence the remedy for every loneliness, every fear, and every need for love—for the love that I cause them to crave. They suffer emptiness of heart without the love for which they were created. I am close to them. I wait for them. Why do they not come to Me?

I want you to come to Me and to remain before My Face for them and in their place. This is the reparation I ask of you. This is why I have brought you here. Do not disappoint Me. Come to Me. Remain with Me. I will speak to you heart to heart, and you will rejoice to recognize My voice.

You comfort Me by coming to Me, and I will give you all the consolation of My Eucharistic friendship, just as I gave it to My beloved disciple John. John learned very quickly, illumined by the Holy Spirit, to discern My presence in the breaking of the Bread, and so he prolonged his time before Me and found in My sacramental presence the fullest expression of that "love until the end" of which he wrote.[1] Be to Me another John. Be the friend and consoler of My Eucharistic Heart. Through you, if you are faithful to this, I will draw many priests back to Myself.

Sunday, February 1, 2009

I am here—really present—available to you at any hour of the day or night. I wait for you. I want to listen to the cares and preoccupations that you carry like a heavy burden. Give them all to Me. Trust in Me and I will act. I have told you this before: for Me nothing is insignificant. No detail of your life is too small and no sin of yours too shameful to be brought to Me and to be abandoned at My feet. Yes, this is how My saints acted. They were certain that any difficulty entrusted to My Heart would find there the best of all possible solutions. Tell Me that you trust in My merciful love by letting go of the things that burden and oppress you. I am the Lord of all things in heaven and on earth, and to Me nothing is impossible.[2]

Tuesday, February 3, 2009

Give Me the first place in your heart and in your life, and I will provide for you in every circumstance. I will not allow you or those with whom

---

[1] John 13:1; Luke 24:30–35; Acts 2:42, 2:46.
[2] Job 42:2; Ps 118(119):91; Wis 7:27, 11:23; John 15:5; Matt 17:20, 19:26; Mark 9:23, 10:27, 14:36; Luke 1:37.

you share this life to want for anything. My providence is wholly at the disposal of My merciful love. Trust then in My merciful love and you will see the wonders that I will accomplish for you.

So much time and energy is wasted in futile worrying and in endless discussions about what is needed and how to go about getting it. Simply present your needs to Me with a trusting heart and I will show you that I am a lavish provider for those who let Me take charge of their needs. The obstinate desire to control all things and to obtain by purely human means the things necessary to My work is an affront both to My merciful love and to My infinite generosity. Has this not been My message all through sacred history: "Trust Me, and you shall see wonders"?[1]

And thank Me. Thank Me always with a pure and humble heart. Come to Me as a child delighted with a gift goes to his father or mother, and tell Me how happy I have made you. This is the thanksgiving I seek from you and from all who experience the providence of My merciful love.

You are remembering M. Yvonne-Aimée today.[2] She had this simple childlike confidence in My merciful love that allowed Me to do for her and through her very great things, wonderful things, all because her trust in My merciful love was boundless and unshakable.

How does one come to that degree of trust? By entrusting to Me very little things, day by day, as they arise, and by leaving them to Me. This was also the wisdom of My priest Don Dolindo.[3] "Jesus," he used to say to Me, "you take care of this." And then he went his way lighthearted and confident that I would honour the confidence he placed in Me.

My apostles wanted for nothing so long as I was with them.[4] In having Me in their midst, they had the very Source and Creator of all that is, that was, and that ever will be. You have Me close to you. I am here before you in the Sacrament of My love. Remain with Me for My sake; I will provide for you.

---

[1] Cf., inter alia, Ex 15:11–13; Josh 3:5; 1 Chron 16:8–13; 2 Chron 20:17; Ps 76(77); Isa 66:14–16; John 1:50.

[2] Mother Yvonne-Aimée de Jésus.

[3] Don Dolindo Ruotolo (October 6, 1882–November 19, 1970) was an Italian priest and Franciscan tertiary from Naples, whose cause for canonization is presently under way. His biographer Luca Sorrentino portrayed him thus: "A scribe of the Holy Spirit, Wisdom infused from above, a wonder-worker of no lesser significance than Padre Pio of Pietrelcina, a stigmatic of Christ already in his name ['Dolindo' from 'dolore'], a favoured son of the Virgin, initiated in Wisdom by the Scriptures, a faithful servant who wanted to be the nothing of all nothings in God, and the everything of God in men."

[4] Luke 22:35.

It is My desire that priests should come to adore Me, keeping watch before My Eucharistic Face, close to My open Heart. Because I want this, I will provide all that is needed. Reassure N. of My fidelity and of My generosity. Do what I inspire you to do with simplicity and complete detachment, and then allow Me to act.

I will allow you to experience disappointment and failure only so that it may be clear to all that this is My work, and that I am doing it for the sake of My Bride the Church, and for the sake of My priests, those whom I have called to love My Church even as I love her.

Come to Me in the Sacrament of My love, and I will continue to instruct you. When you are bewildered or at a loss, have recourse to Me and I will send forth My light and My truth to bring you to My holy mountain,[1] that is, to the place where I will dwell in the midst of My priests, loved by them, adored by them—even as I heal, refresh, and sanctify them from the Sacrament of the Altar.

This is what I want of you: time "wasted," spent in My presence. Time given to Me for My sake. I want all My priests to recover a sense of gratuitousness in their prayer. I want them to come to Me, and to remain with Me, for Me alone and for My sake, because I alone am worthy of all their love.

Do you think that I was always meeting with My disciples to plan events, to organize and strategize and plot our course of action? All of this is the world's way of achieving what it sees as results. When I walked with My disciples, when I rested with them, our delight was in being together. They remained with Me for Me alone, and I remained with them out of My love for them, just as I remain in the Sacrament of the Altar out of the love I bear My whole Church, but especially, and first of all, My priests. Why do My priests not yet understand this? All of their priestly activity must flow out of their "being with Me," and thus, the fruit they bear will be abundant and vigorous—that is the fruit that will last.[2]

In saying these things I am not suggesting that My priests should lapse into a kind of indolent quietism, doing nothing and ceasing to demonstrate pastoral zeal. I am saying that they must make Me the principle, the fountainhead of all they do and say, and that everything they do should be redirected back to Me and placed in My hands, that I might give *all* back to My Father.

I promised the gift of My Holy Spirit, the Paraclete, to direct and

---

[1] Ps 42(43):3–4.
[2] Luke 8:15; John 12:25(24), 15:2–16; Rom 7:4.

inspire the work of My apostles.[1] He comes with His seven gifts. One who is led by the Holy Spirit will act, but he will act out of an entire confidence in My merciful love, and in a spirit of absolute reliance on My grace. He will not seek to bring about results; he will leave that to Me.[2]

I am the source of all fruitfulness in the vineyard that is My Church. Apart from Me, you can do nothing. Come to Me, then. Remain with Me.[3] Act for Me, guided by My Holy Spirit, and return to Me with thanksgiving. This is the secret of a priestly life that will be pleasing to Me, will build up My Church, and will glorify My Father.

My Immaculate Mother is present to you in each of these moments. It is she who obtains for you the grace to come to Me. When you stay with Me, she is there, even as she remained with Saint John in adoration of the mysteries of My Body and Blood. When you rise to go into the vineyard, she prepares the way for you and obtains the graces necessary for your labours. When you return to Me, she is still with you, and she offers her Magnificat as you offer the humble thanksgiving of your hearts to My Father.

Friday, February 6, 2009

I want you to live in silence and adoration.

Wednesday, February 11, 2009

Spend less time at the computer and more time in My presence. I wait for you here. I long to see you before Me. I want to give you all the signs of My friendship that My Heart has destined for you and for no other, but for this you must come to Me. Follow the promptings of My grace.

Thursday, February 12, 2009

There is no need for you to grow anxious or fearful. I will continue speaking to you so long as you come before Me with a quiet and trusting heart. I still have much to teach you. I want to form you in purity, in charity, in mercy towards your brother priests, and in the ceaseless adoration that I desire from you.

Wait upon Me. Come to Me. Open your heart to Me and I will open My Heart to you.

---

[1] Luke 24:49; Acts 1:4, 2:3, 10:19; Matt 10:20; John 7:39, 14:16–18, 15:26–27, 16:12–15; Ps 103(104):30; Ps 142(143):10; Isa 32:14–18.

[2] Matt 4:1; Luke 4:1, 11:13; Acts 8:26–40; Rom 8:14; Gal 5:18.

[3] John 15:1–8.

This is one of My most poignant sufferings: that I should encounter hearts that are closed to Me, even among My beloved priests, the friends whom I have chosen for myself. How can I have friendship with one who closes his heart to Me, who flees My presence, who cannot bear to be silent, still, and alone with Me and for Me?

Even for you this remains a struggle. There are so many lesser things that pull you away, that eat up your time, and that put stumbling blocks in the path of your coming to be with Me. Learn to recognize these obstacles for what they are. Some of them are your own doing; others are the work of the Evil One; still others come from the ordinary cares of life in a world that has forgotten how to be still in My presence. Do not let yourself be stopped by any of these things. Learn to come to Me quickly, generously, and gladly. I wait for you in the Sacrament of My love, and you will not be disappointed in coming to Me. This is really all I ask of souls, and especially of My priests—that they come to Me. And I will do the rest.

Friday, February 13, 2009

Of the sins cast into the fire of My Heart, nothing remains. They are completely annihilated—reduced, not to ashes, but utterly destroyed and forgotten. Love makes Me do this. When a soul laden with sin, even with sins against My divine Person—blasphemy, sacrilege, and revilement—comes to Me with a repentant and broken heart, My love envelopes that soul and purifies her in My Blood.[1]

I am the Saviour. I abhor sin and its ravages in My creatures. Sin given to Me ceases to exist; it is forever lost in the infinite ocean of My mercy, but sin clung to and held close to oneself becomes a poison, a cancer that spreads, destroying the spiritual organism that I designed for holiness and for eternal beatitude.

I want My priests to give Me their sins. I want all their sins because I have already paid the price for them. Why should My priests go about burdened with shame and handicapped by the weight of wickedness that they carry with them? Every sin given to Me disappears, and in exchange for every sin given to Me I will give a grace in return.[2] This is the exchange I propose to souls; this is the exchange I offer My poor priests. You have seen how I do this. You can attest to the beauty of this exchange in your own life and in the life of Father N. It is enough to sur-

---

[1] Matt 26:28; Mark 3:28–29; 1 John 1:7–10, 2:1–2; Acts 3:19; Eph 1:7; Heb 8:12, 10:17; Ps 31(32):1; Ps 102(103):8–12; Isa 1:18, 38:17, 43:25, 44:22; Mic 7:19.
[2] Rom 5:20.

render your sins to Me: in return I bestow an abundance of graces, precious graces that sanctify the soul and cause virtues to spring up where formerly there was nothing but a wasteland inhabited by the shadows of vice.

I want My priests to be the first to experience the immensity of My mercy. I want them to be the first to experience this exchange of sin for grace, of darkness for light, of sickness for health, and of sadness for joy. Let them come to Me in the Sacrament of My mercy, and then let them seek Me out daily, even hourly, in the Sacrament of My love, the Most Holy Eucharist. There I wait for them, there they will find everything their hearts desire.

I am Jesus. Mine it is to save, to heal, to vivify, and to make lovely in the sight of My Father the souls that consent to the operations of My mercy and to the secret action of the Holy Spirit. When you speak to My priests, remind them of the power and efficacy of a single act of confidence in My merciful love. Confidence opens the door to all the treasures of My kingdom. To one who has confidence in My merciful love, I can refuse nothing.

When I want to draw souls into union with Myself, I speak to them as I am speaking to you. The effect of My words is the union of the soul with Me in a silence that is all love and desire. I want to be desired. I want that souls should long for union with Me. My word will produce this longing in you, and I will fulfil it.

Make the writings of My little Josefa[1] known to the priests I will show you. They will find in them a remedy, a comfort, and a source of confidence in My merciful love. They are not for all; not all are humble enough to hear the message of My Heart, but the broken and the wounded, those devastated by sin will understand them and will rejoice in the message of My love.

Friday, March 13, 2009

So few souls remember to thank Me after receiving My Body and Blood. This is true even of My priests—My priests, My friends, My chosen ones from whom I expect more, from whom I desire more. Hearts have grown cold and indifferent towards Me in this the Sacrament of My

---

[1] Sister Maria Josefa Menéndez (February 4, 1890–December 29, 1923) was a Catholic nun and mystic, born in Madrid but entering, at 29, the Society of the Sacred Heart of Jesus in Poitiers. Her religious life as a coadjutrix sister was spent in menial tasks such as cleaning and sewing, and few were aware of the visions and revelations she received from Jesus, which were posthumously published under the title *The Way of Divine Love*.

love. For many, receiving Me has become a routine action devoid of faith and with no manifestation of adoration and of love. How has My Church come to this?

I will raise up holy priests to rekindle a burning love for the Most Holy Eucharist in the hearts of My faithful. I am calling many priests to adore My Eucharistic Face and to approach My open Heart in the Sacrament of My love. These are the priests whom I will use to minister first to their own brothers in Holy Orders and then, through them, to vast multitudes of souls who have never understood the mysteries of My Body and Blood offered to the Father and given up for the life of the world.

It is in these few precious moments after Holy Communion that My Heart seeks to hold conversation with My friends, but so many turn away from Me to busy themselves about many things.[1] Of you, My friend, I ask something more. Remain with Me for these few moments. Listen for the sound of My voice in your heart. Know that My desire is to speak to you and to listen to all that you have to tell Me. It is in these moments that I am most disposed to grant the requests made of Me in faith.

Saturday, March 14, 2009

Let Me instruct you and teach you what you are to say, both when you pray and when you preach.[2] This I do by sending upon you the grace of the Holy Spirit in a way that is always new, always fresh, and always adapted to your needs at a given moment. Yes, the Holy Spirit is your other Advocate, your other Friend,[3] and I would have you live not only in His company, but held fast in His intimate embrace. Thus will you be united to Me, and through Me to My Father.

Love the Holy Spirit and call upon Him with humility and confidence. He will never fail you. He is, as My Church calls Him, the "Father of the Poor."[4] He takes delight in descending upon those who are poor in spirit and He makes His tabernacle in their hearts. Seek His presence there and begin to live in constant dependence on His divine guidance. This is how My Apostles lived, and this was the life of My Virgin Mother.

---

[1] Luke 10:40–42; Matt 22:4–5; Sir 11:10, 38:24–25; Ps 126(127):1–2.

[2] Rom 8:26; Eph 6:18; Phil 1:19; Jude 1:20; Matt 10:19–20; Mark 13:11; Luke 4:18, 12:11–12; Acts 2:4, 4:31; 1 Cor 2:4, 2:12–14; 1 Pet 1:12; 2 Sam 23:2; Sir 39:6.

[3] John 14:16, 16:17.

[4] *Pater pauperum*, a title applied to the Holy Spirit in the Golden Sequence *Veni, Sancte Spiritus* appointed for Pentecost (and, in the *usus antiquior* of the Roman Rite, daily during its octave).

Call upon Him in the prayer that is familiar to you and address Him as the "Soul of your soul." Cardinal Mercier[1] was inspired to call this the secret of holiness. One who lives in an intimate union with the divine Paraclete will necessarily be united to My Immaculate Mother. She is present wheresoever the Holy Spirit is active; and where she is, the Holy Spirit enters in.

Saint John knew this and, in sharing his home with My Immaculate Mother, it became for him like the Upper Room on the morning of Pentecost. My Mother obtains for souls devoted to her and consecrated to her the grace of a perpetual interior Pentecost. At every moment the Holy Spirit is sent forth from the Father and the Son to gather souls into unity by uniting them with Me and among themselves.

Sunday, March 15, 2009

Show yourself grateful, sincere, and interested in others and in the things that concern them, first of all in their families. Reveal to all whom I send to you My Heart and My Face.

Monday, March 16, 2009

My love for you is unique and unfailing. Trust in My merciful love at all times and in all circumstances. Your weaknesses are not an impediment to My merciful love; on the contrary, they endear you to Me and draw

---

[1] Désiré-Joseph Cardinal Mercier (November 21, 1851–January 23, 1926) was Archbishop of Malines, Belgium from 1906 until his death. Besides the heroic leadership he demonstrated during World War I, Cardinal Mercier hosted the famous Catholic-Anglican dialogue known as the Malines Conversations, and obtained the establishment of the liturgical feast of the Blessed Virgin Mary, Mediatrix of All Graces, with its proper Mass and Office. His spiritual mentor was Blessed Dom Columba Marmion. Here, in his own words, is the daily practice he recommended: "I am going to reveal to you the secret of sanctity and happiness. Every day for five minutes control your imagination and close your eyes to the things of sense and your ears to all the noises of the world, in order to enter into yourself. Then, in the sanctity of your baptized soul (which is the temple of the Holy Spirit), speak to that Divine Spirit, saying to Him: 'O Holy Spirit, Soul of my soul, I adore Thee! Enlighten me, guide me, strengthen me, console me. Tell me what I should do; give me Thy orders. I promise to submit myself to all that Thou desirest of me and to accept all that Thou permittest to happen to me. Just make me know Thy Will.' If you do this, your life will flow along happily, serenely, and full of consolation, even in the midst of trials. Grace will be proportioned to the trial, giving you strength to carry it, and you will arrive at the Gate of Paradise laden with merit. This submission to the Holy Spirit is the secret of sanctity." Mercier was also a noted Thomist scholar, and the founder of the Higher Institute of Philosophy at Louvain University as well as of the *Revue Néoscholastique.*

down special graces upon you. So long as you trust in My abiding friendship for you, you will experience the signs of My merciful love in greater and greater abundance. I want to fill you with graces not for yourself alone, but for all My priests and, most of all, for those who have closed their hearts to Me, rejected My intimate friendship, and withdrawn into the comfortable life they have organized for themselves—but that sort of life apart from Me is the beginning of damnation, the beginning of that hell that is not something I inflict on souls but, rather, the state in which they put themselves by withdrawing little by little from Me until, in the end, the separation is complete and there is no return.

You were well on your way to this terrible separation from Me, but My Immaculate Mother intervened, Pope John Paul II interceded, and My merciful love triumphed in your heart. What I have done in you, I yearn to do in countless others. Pray then for your brother priests. Bring them into the light of My Eucharistic Face. Offer them to My Eucharistic Heart. I will receive your intercession on their behalf and, through the mediation of My Immaculate Mother, grant abundant graces of conversion, healing, and holiness to My priests through this work that I have asked you to do.

It is I who inspired My servant Pope Benedict XVI to proclaim this Year for Priests.[1] This is a sign and a confirmation that I am giving you. Hold fast to My words and be faithful to all that I ask of you. You will see a great outpouring of the Holy Spirit over the priests of My Church. Many lives will be changed. The Face of My priesthood will be renewed and all will wonder at its new-found splendour and purity.

Saturday, March 21, 2009
Transitus of Our Holy Father Saint Benedict

The purpose of any words that I speak to you is to unite you to Me in the silence of love. That is why friends and lovers speak one to the other: to express what they hold in their hearts. Once these things have been expressed, it is enough for them to remain united one to the other in the silence that is the more perfect expression of their love.

So many souls are afraid of the silence into which I would lead them if only they would let Me. Fear causes them to hide behind a barrage of

---

[1] On March 16, 2009, Pope Benedict XVI announced that a "Year for Priests" would be observed by the Church in celebration of the 150th anniversary of the *dies natalis* of St. John Mary Vianney. It would begin on the feast of the Most Sacred Heart of Jesus that year (June 19) and end on the same solemnity in 2010 (June 11).

words and concepts, when My desire is to unite them directly to Myself by means of faith, hope, and especially love. Love is the bond of My union with you and with every soul whom I have chosen to live in the gift of My divine friendship.

There are times when words are useful and necessary to your human weakness and to the need you have to be reassured of My love for you, but in the end, silence is the purest expression of My love for you and of your love for Me.

Little by little I will lead you into the silence of unitive love. I will not stop speaking to you altogether because you have need of My words and also because they will be useful to other souls, but I will teach you to imitate John, My beloved disciple, by resting your head—so full of thoughts and cares and fears and words—upon My Most Sacred Heart. There you will learn to find peace and perfect happiness in listening only to the steady eternal rhythm of My Heart, which beats with love for you and for all priests. It is not the length of these moments that matters but, rather, the intensity of divine love that fills them.

Monday, March 23, 2009

I will increase your love for Me. This is what I will do in you, because you ask it of Me, and in the souls of any others who ask it of Me, especially in the souls of My priests.

For you to love Me as I would have you love Me, you have need of My gift of love. Without Me, you can do nothing.[1] Those who have loved Me well, My saints in heaven, glorify Me eternally for having placed in their hearts the burning love with which they loved Me on earth.[2] Love Me, then, as I give you to love Me, and in that love you will find the one thing necessary.[3]

Wednesday, March 25, 2009
The Annunciation

I am your Mother, the Mother given you by my Son Jesus, from the Cross, in the solemn hour of His sacrifice. And you are my son, dear to my Sorrowful and Immaculate Heart, precious to me, and ever under the mantle of my protection. Let me live with you as I lived with John, the second son of my Heart and the model for all my priest sons down

---

[1] John 15:5.
[2] Rom 5:5; Ezek 11:19.
[3] Luke 10:42.

through the ages. Speak to me simply and with complete trust in the compassion of my maternal Heart and in the power given to my maternal intercession.

There is nothing that you cannot bring to me, nothing that you cannot present to me, nothing that you cannot offer me, even your very sins. Anything given to me by my sons, I press to my Heart; all that is impure, every vestige of sin is consumed in the flame of love that burns in my Immaculate Heart, in the fire of love that is the Holy Spirit in me, the very Fire of the Divinity. Give to me, then, all that you would offer to my Son and to His Father. It will be purified as gold in the furnace because I will press it to my Heart. Nothing impure can endure the flame of love that burns in my Heart. Only love remains.

Give me your weaknesses, your past sins, your daily faults, and I will present to my Son only the love with which, in spite of all your weaknesses, you desire to love Him, and with Him, love the Father.

I am your Mother. I am the Mother from whom you need hide nothing. Even those things that you think are hidden appear clearly to me in the pure light of the Godhead. When I see a priest son of mine disfigured or polluted by sin, I am moved, not to judge him but to show him mercy and to employ all the means at my disposal for his full recovery from the ravages of sin. So many of those who struggle against inveterate habits of sin and pernicious vices would find themselves quickly set free from them if they would only approach me with filial confidence and allow me to do for them what my maternal and merciful Heart moves me to do.

There are no limits to my intercessory power because the Father has so ordained it.[1] One can never go wrong in turning to me. No matter how complex the problem, no matter how sordid the sin, I am the handmaid of the divine mercy, the refuge of sinners, and the Mother of all who struggle against the forces of darkness. Come to me, then. I can even say those comforting words first spoken by my beloved Son: "Come to me, and I will give you rest."[2]

It is not enough to have some practices in my honour in the course of the day: I desire more, and you are called to more. You are called to reproduce the life of Saint John with me in the cenacle and at Ephesus.[3]

---

[1] John 2:1–11.

[2] Matt 11:28.

[3] Although some Church Fathers speak of Jerusalem as the home of the Blessed Virgin Mary after the resurrection of Christ, another longstanding tradition has her living near Ephesus with St. John, which harmonizes better with Our Lord's entrustment of her to the beloved disciple (John 19:26–27) and which is corroborated by Bd. Anne

If only you knew the bonds of love for Jesus, and of obedience to the Father, and of joy in the Holy Spirit that united John's soul to mine! We were the nucleus of a family of souls that has grown wondrously through the ages—the family of all those who, like John, lived with me, learned from me, and allowed me so to love them that love for my Jesus blazed in their hearts like a great fire, the fire that my Son came to cast upon the earth.[1]

I am happy to have spoken to you on this feast of the Annunciation that filled me with divine joy so many years ago in Nazareth. That divine joy remains. No one will ever make it decrease. In eternity it multiplies itself to infinity; it is an ocean of joy having no boundaries, and its depth cannot be measured. This is the joy that I would share with you and with all my priest sons today.

April 14, 2009
Tuesday of Pascha

Our Lord directed me to the two epistles given for the Mass of the Day on Easter.[2]

> *Has not Christ been sacrificed for us, our paschal victim? Let us keep the feast, then, not with the leaven of yesterday, that was all vice and mischief, but with unleavened bread, with purity and honesty of intent.*
> 1 CORINTHIANS 5:8

I call you to newness of life in purity of heart and in faithful adoration. Purity of heart is the effect of persevering adoration, and its fruit. One cannot abide before My Eucharistic Face day after day without being changed from one degree of purity—that is, of brightness—to another.[3] Those who adore My Eucharistic Face will be like mirrors in the Church, reflecting My holiness, My majesty, and My boundless pity for all to see.

This is how I would accomplish the transformation of My priests: I

Catherine Emmerich's vision, at the beginning of the nineteenth century in Germany, of the home of the Virgin Mary on Mt. Koressos, in the vicinity of Ephesus. Her detailed description allowed a team of explorers in 1881 to locate the site, which, under the Turkish name Meryem Ana Evi, has become a popular shrine whose visitors have included Popes Paul VI, John Paul II, and Benedict XVI.

[1] Luke 12:49; Deut 4:36.

[2] In the revised lectionary, the two options given for the second reading are Col 3:1–4 and 1 Cor 5:6b–8, which are commented on here in reverse order.

[3] 2 Cor 3:18; Heb 1:3; 1 Cor 15:41; Wis 7:24–30; Bar 5:3.

would have them remain in My presence until the reflection of My holiness in them and on their faces demonstrates to all that I am faithful to My promises and that the adoration of My Eucharistic Face is, for all My priests, a privileged means of transformation into Me.

I call you to newness of life, and the principle of that newness is your fidelity to adoration. You promised, in My presence and before the bishop I have given you, to live in persevering adoration. This is your call. This is the way I have opened before you for your healing and purification. This way is not for you alone. It is also for those whom I will send you, and for all My priests.

My priests rarely take the time to be with Me, to gaze upon My Face, to remain in My company. This coming Year for Priests will be fruitful for My Church in proportion to the response of My priests to the graces held out to them; most precious among these graces is My invitation to contemplate and adore My Eucharistic Face. The work of transformation into Me is My work. My priests have only to expose themselves to My Eucharistic Face. Little by little, the radiance of My Face will cause the indelible character of My priesthood in them to emerge from the sin that has obscured it and defaced it. It will begin to shine, and this will draw souls to Me though My priests.

The holiness of a priest is My life in him. The duties of the sacred ministry are sanctifying, but they are not enough. There must be in every priest a willingness, a desire to grow in My friendship, to abide in My presence, to surrender to My transforming love in silence and in repose before My Face.

> *Risen, then, with Christ, you must lift your thoughts above, where Christ now sits at the right hand of God. You must be heavenly-minded, not earthly-minded; you have undergone death and your life is hidden away now with Christ in God. Christ is your life, and when He is made manifest, you too will be made manifest with Him.*
> COLOSSIANS 3:1–4

This is the rule of life that I give you for this Paschaltide and, indeed, for the rest of your life. Live with Me, hidden in Me as I am hidden in the glory of My Father and hidden beneath the appearance of bread in the Sacrament of My love. Seek My Face, and I will seek yours, causing My brightness to penetrate your soul and transform you from within.

Those who turn away from Me in the Sacrament of My love choose the darkness over My light, and they will be deformed by the darkness that penetrates their souls and causes sin to rule them.[1]

---

[1] Inter alia, Matt 6:23; Luke 11:34; John 3:19; Job 24:13–17; Wis 18:4.

I have shown you the way to priestly holiness that I desire all My priests to follow. Would that My priests would take the time to abide before My Eucharistic Face and to surrender to the love of My Eucharistic Heart! This is how I will go about renewing the priesthood in My Church. This Year for Priests is the moment I have chosen to begin a universal action in the souls of My priests. I will separate the wheat from the chaff.[1] Some will be lost,[2] and already My Heart and the Heart of My Mother grieves over them, but many will enter into a new way of life marked by adoration and by the shining purity that is its fruit.

Wednesday, April 15, 2009

The path I have traced before you is the path of adoration. Walk this path in the light of My Eucharistic Face and you will see that it leads straight into My open Heart. This is the very path that I would set before all My priests. I want them to walk in the light of My Face,[3] forsaking all darkness, and desiring nothing so much as to rest within My sacred side.

My pierced Heart is the wellspring of purity, of healing, and of holiness for all My priests. How much I want them to draw near to My open Heart in the Sacrament of My love! It is enough for them to come to Me, even if they are weary and without words or affectionate thoughts. By the simple act of coming to Me, they demonstrate their love for Me and their desire for My healing and purifying action in their souls.

You must learn to remain in My presence, to abide there for as long as you can, for this is the very essence of the life to which I have called you here. When you forsake Me for other things, you are compromising the immense grace I have given you in bringing you here to be the priest adorer of My Eucharistic Face. The healing and purification of many priestly souls depends on your fidelity to this call to adoration and reparation. I have charged you with a grave responsibility for the healing of your brother priests and for the return of many of them to My open Heart. Their healing and sanctification depends on the love you have for them and on the expression of that love by fidelity to adoration. I have elected to associate you to Myself and to My most holy Mother in this work. You are not alone. There are many other souls whom I have

---

[1] Matt 3:12, Matt 13:49, 25:32; Luke 3:17; Jer 23:28.

[2] Inter alia, Matt 22:12–13, 25:24–30; Luke 13:2–5; 1 Cor 1:18, 2:15–16; 2 Cor 4:3–4; Phil 3:16–19; 1 Tim 1:19; 2 Peter 2; Rev 20:12–15.

[3] Ps 88:16 (89:15).

called to this life of adoration and reparation for My beloved priests. But you have your part to play in this design of My merciful love and no one can fulfil this part except you. You see, then, that I count on you. But do not be afraid. I will give you the grace to be faithful to all that I have asked of you. It is not you who will do great things for My priests, but rather Me living in you as in a *humanité de surcroît*,[1] another humanity marked by My priesthood, another humanity in which I can offer Myself to the Father and pour Myself out for souls.

This is the vocation of every priest: to allow Me to live out My mission of eternal Priest and Victim in them. This is how, from the beginning, I determined to save souls and to give glory to My Father. And this is why, on the very night before I suffered, I prayed that My apostles should be one with Me, even as I am one with My Father. The prayer you have been saying after Holy Communion is inspired by My own prayer for all My priests:

> O my beloved Jesus,
> unite me to Thyself,
> my body to Thy Body,
> my blood to Thy Blood,
> my soul to Thy Soul,
> my heart to Thy Heart,
> all that I am to all that Thou art,
> so as to make me with Thyself, O Jesus,
> one priest and one victim
> offered to the glory of Thy Father,
> out of love for Thy spouse, the Church...

And yes, I want you to add:

> for the sanctification of Thy priests,
> the conversion of sinners,
> the intentions of Pope Benedict XVI,
> and in sorrowful reparation for my innumerable sins

---

[1] A superadded humanity. This phrase is from the prayer "Ô mon Dieu, Trinité que j'adore" by Bd. Elizabeth of the Trinity: "O Feu consumant, Esprit d'amour, 'survenez, en moi,' afin qu'il se fasse en mon âme comme une incarnation du Verbe: que je Lui sois une humanité de surcroît en laquelle Il renouvelle tout son Mystère" (O Consuming Fire, Spirit of Love, 'come upon me' and create in my soul a kind of incarnation of the Word, that I may be for Him a superadded humanity in which he can renew His whole mystery).

against Thee in Thy priesthood
and in the Sacrament of Thy love.
Amen.

Every time a priest sins, he sins directly against Me and against the Most Holy Eucharist toward which his whole being is ordered. When a priest approaches My altar laden with sins that have not been confessed or for which he has not repented, My angels look on in horror, My Mother grieves, and I am again wounded in My hands and My feet, and in My Heart. I am again struck on My mouth and treated with a terrible ignominy. This is why I call My priests to purity of heart and to frequent confession. This is why I ask you to confess your sins weekly and to let the adoration of My Eucharistic Face purify your heart and make you less unworthy of offering My Holy Sacrifice. The sins of My priests are a grievous affront to My own priesthood and immaculate victimhood.

Every priest of Mine is to live *for* the altar and *from* the altar. Be conscious of this, and you will learn to hate sin and turn from it in disgust. Learn this and you will desire nothing so much as purity of heart and holiness of life.

When a priest sins, he sins against My Eucharistic Body and against My Mystical Body, so intimate is the relationship between his very being and the Sacrament of My Body and Blood offered to the Father, and given up for the life of My Spouse, the Church.

I asked Our Lord about reading during adoration.

It is all right to read a little in My Eucharistic presence, especially from the Scriptures, provided that your heart remains fixed on Me, and your eyes are illumined by the light of My Face.

Tuesday, May 12, 2009

Your weakness is My gift to you. Instead of offering Me your achievements, offer Me your poverty, your weakness, your very failure to achieve great things, and I, in turn, will accept your offering and, uniting it to My own all-sufficient Passion, will make it fruitful for My priests and for all My Church.[1] So long as you come to Me humbled by your weakness and animated by a holy desire for Me alone, I will overlook the other faults that affect you and in My mercy I will erase them

---

[1] 1 Cor 2:3; 2 Cor 8:9, 11:30, 12:5–10, 13:4; Heb 4:15, 5:1–2; Col 1:24; Gal 4:12–14; Matt 5:3; Luke 6:20.

and give you, in their place, graces and mercies that I have chosen and designated for you and for no other, and this from all eternity.

My plan for you is not the one you have created and entertained in your mind. My plan for you is the one that is unfolding day after day in all the humiliations and apparent failure to achieve great things that make up this phase of your life. Accept your weaknesses, and then offer them to Me; offer them to Me through My Mother. Place them in her hands and entrust them to her most pure Heart. Every weakness entrusted to My Mother becomes an occasion of grace and an outpouring of My merciful love into the soul that suffers it.

Trust not in what you do for Me but, rather, in what I will do for you, for I am all love, and I am all-powerful, and you have won the love of My Heart, and I shall never take from you what is Mine to give. How have you won the love of My Heart?, you ask. By learning to say sincerely and with confidence, "O Jesus, King of Love, I put My trust in Thy merciful goodness."[1] That little invocation expresses all that a soul needs to say to win My Heart's tenderness and favour.

Wednesday, June 17, 2009

Wait now for the promises I have made to you to be fulfilled, for the time of their fulfilment is now at hand. Receive from My most loving hands all that I will send you and let yourself be drawn by means of all these things into the secret sanctuary of My pierced Heart. There I will unite you to Myself as Priest and Victim, just as you ask Me to do each day at Mass. I will communicate to you a participation in My own priestly prayer to the Father, and this prayer shall be quickened in your soul by a new outpouring of the Holy Spirit.

Refuse nothing of what I have prepared for you. Enter humbly and gratefully into this plan of Mine. Your correspondence with My designs is the means by which I will sanctify you and use you for the sanctification of My priests.

Above all, be faithful to your times of adoration. I wait for you to come to Me in the Sacrament of My love. It is during these times of adoration that I will continue to communicate to you the secrets of My Heart, just as I communicated them to My beloved apostle John as he rested upon My breast at the Last Supper and gazed upon My pierced side on Calvary.

Live in the company of My most pure Mother and go to her as any son goes to his mother, full of confidence in her love for him. Never

[1] See p. 11, note 1.

doubt that she loves you most tenderly and that she is, at every moment, ready to comfort you, to help you, to lift you when you fall, and to instruct you in the plan of life that I have determined will be yours in this place.

Thank Me for the *dona disciplinae*[1] I have given you, for by them you will make great strides in a short time. These gifts of discipline enable you to follow the little way of a humble and loving fidelity from moment to moment, doing at the appointed time what is to be done, and trusting in My grace for all the rest. Do what you can do, what I have asked you to do, and all the rest will be given you besides in abundance, and with enough left over to come to the help of priests in need.[2] Now kneel and adore Me in the silence of love that unites you to My Heart.

Thursday, June 18, 2009
After First Vespers of the Most Sacred Heart of Jesus

I will renew My priests in holiness.[3] I will restore their honour in the sight of the nations, for they are Mine and all that pertains to their honour pertains to My glory. I will purify those who have fallen into the filth of habitual sin. I will heal those who are broken in spirit, and even those whose bodies are weary and limited by infirmity. They will discover that I am their Physician just as truly as I am their Friend.[4] I will leave nothing undone so that My priests may be renewed in the fire of My love.

A chastened priesthood will shine with chastity in the face of a world darkened by every fleshly vice and sinful excess. A meek and humble priesthood will astonish a world obsessed with power, and influence, and exploitation of the poor. An obedient priesthood will stand in contradiction to a world that, following its master, says, "I will not serve."[5]

I am about to renew in the hearts of all My priests the gift I made to John, My beloved disciple, from the altar of the Cross; I am about to give My Mother to each priest in a new and personal way. Those who

---

[1] "Gifts of discipline." The phrase refers to the humble, little practices of self-denial by which one can respond to grace in daily life: one might call them "little opportunities for renunciation."

[2] Luke 6:38, 12:31; 2 Cor 9:8; Ps 22(23):5; Ps 77(78):25.

[3] Ps 131(132):9 and 16; 2 Chron 6:41.

[4] On the physician: see, e.g., Ps 146(147):3, and, in Matthew alone, 4:23, 8:16, 9:12, 9:35, 12:15, 12:22, 14:14, 15:30, 19:2, 21:14; on the friend, see Matt 11:19; Luke 12:4; John 3:29, 11:11, 15:13–15.

[5] Jer 2:20; Isa 14:11–19; John 14:30–31; Eph 2:1–3.

will accept this most precious gift of Mine, and take My Mother into the inmost secret of their life, will experience a marvellous apostolic fruitfulness. Where My Mother is, there too is the Holy Spirit manifested in an abundance of charisms and signs given for the sake of My Body and My Bride, the Church.

Let My priests listen attentively to the teachings of the Pope [Benedict XVI], for I have inspired him to reach out to them and to call them out of the shadows into the radiant light of an authentic priestly holiness.

For this have I set My servant Jean-Marie Vianney before My priests.[1] They have everything to learn from his humility, his poverty, his purity, and his prayer. I want all My priests to imitate his zeal for souls, his compassion in welcoming sinners, and his clear and simple teaching of the truths of the faith.

As for you, beloved friend and priest of My Sacred Heart, remain faithful to the adoration I have asked of you, and trust Me to accomplish all that I have promised, for I am faithful in My friendship and I have pledged you My love in this life and in the next. Glorify My love by trusting Me in all things, great and small. Above all, seek Me and abide in My presence; your adoration is precious in My sight, and through it I will touch the hearts of many priests to draw them to Myself, just as I have drawn you to Myself and pressed you to My pierced side. Surrender to My love for you and let Me fulfil for you all the desires of My Heart.

My Father desires that My Sacred Heart should be made known again to all My priests, and through them and their experience, to the entire Church and to the world. My priests will discover the infinite treasures of My Heart by seeking Me in the Sacrament of My love and by abiding in My presence. Nothing can replace these times of closeness to Me in the Sacrament of My love. It is during these times that I sanctify My priests and configure them to Myself in view of the Holy Sacrifice they offer, and in view of their sacred ministry. Those priests who forsake all else to remain alone in My presence will be, of all priests, the most effective and fruitful workers in My vineyard.

---

[1] The French parish priest or *curé* Jean-Baptiste-Marie Vianney (May 8, 1786– August 4, 1859) was proposed as a model for parochial clergy when beatified in 1905 by Pope St. Pius X, and declared patron saint of parish priests four years after his canonization in 1924 by Pope Pius XI. In honor of the 150th anniversary of the death of the Curé d'Ars, Pope Benedict XVI declared a Year of the Priest, running from the Feast of the Sacred Heart, June 19, 2009, to the same feast one year later, on June 11, 2010. The homilies of St. John Vianney are exemplary for their clarity of teaching, memorable analogies, concrete moral applications, and spirit of fervor, particularly in connection with his intense Eucharistic piety.

Monday, June 22, 2009

I will direct your prayer and fulfil the prayer I direct. This will be the effect of the Holy Spirit whom I will send upon you in a new way to be the soul of your soul, and the light and life of your spirit. Yield to every movement of My Holy Spirit and you will go forward in serenity and security, preserved from the deceits of the enemy and from the illusions of self-love.

I will teach you to adore Me as I desire to be adored by all My priests, and I send you to My priests to communicate to them what I will have taught you. Thus will My plan be fulfilled of raising up in My Church during this Year for Priests a cenacle of priest adorers conformed to the designs of My Heart.

Tuesday, June 23, 2009
After First Vespers of Saint John the Baptist

When you pray for any soul, begin by uniting yourself wholly to My perfect will for that soul and by entering into all the designs of My Heart on that soul. Desire only what I desire. Will what I will. Let your prayer be a way of harnessing yourself to Me so that we might work together for souls and for My Father's glory. This is what I meant when I called My dear friends to take My yoke upon them. I wanted them to learn to labour with Me.[1]

By the prayer of adoration for My priests, you are working with Me for them. You are working with Me to lift them when they fall, to bind up their wounds, to deliver them from bondage to evil, to open them to My gifts, and to obtain for them a greater openness to the sanctifying action of the Holy Spirit.

Your union with Me in prayer lessens the resistance of many priests to entering resolutely upon the path of holiness that I am opening before them. When you represent My priests before My Eucharistic Face, you are obtaining graces for them, but also the grace to accept those graces that I long to bestow upon them. So much of what I long to give to My priests is refused because they are unable to move beyond their fears and their self-absorption.

I would work marvels in every place on earth through the ministry of My priests if they would accept the graces that I hold in reserve for them. I would first purify and sanctify them, and then, by means of

---

[1] Matt 11:28–30, 12:30, 27:32; Mark 15:21; Luke 11:23, 23:26–27; John 4:38, 6:27; 3 John 1:8; 1 Cor 3:8–9.

their sacred ministry, purify and sanctify a great multitude of souls, so as to make of them an offering of praise and thanksgiving to the glory of My Father.

Why do My priests refuse the gifts that I would lavish upon them? Many are self-sufficient, relying on their natural abilities and talents, and thinking that these natural gifts are sufficient for the success of their ministry. But their idea of success is not Mine. And the means that they would take are not Mine. And I have no need of their natural abilities and talents.[1] I can do more with one poor priest who, like the Curé of Ars, is humble and utterly united to Me by ceaseless prayer, than I can with a priest who astounds the world with his knowledge and presents himself brilliantly in the sight of men.[2]

When I find a priest who is open to My gifts, I lavish these gifts upon him. Nothing is lacking to the priest who comes before Me in his poverty, and even in his sins, provided that he give Me his poverty and entrust Me with his sins, and expose all his weaknesses to the transforming light of My Eucharistic Face.

This is what I ask you to do, not only for yourself, but for all My priests. I am about to renew My priesthood in the whole Church. I will purify the sons of Levi in fulfilment of the ancient prophecy, not those of a physical priestly lineage, but those who have taken the place of the former priesthood, and who are one with Me in the everlasting priesthood of the Order of Melchisedek.[3] I will change the face of the priesthood to make it resplendent with the light reflected from My Eucharistic Face.

Tuesday, July 7, 2009

My Heart is open to your prayers and I receive them with favour because it is I who inspire you to speak to Me in this way. This is the secret of prayer pleasing to My Heart: it rises out of a grace that I have already planted in the soul, even before you come into My presence, even before you open your mouth, or take up your pen, or begin to formulate words. These are the prayers that I answer most readily; these are the prayers that I answer unfailingly, because they are the fruit of the work of the Holy Spirit in the soul, teaching the soul to pray in perfect harmony with the desires and designs of My own Sacred Heart.

---

[1] Inter alia, Deut 7:7; Ps 146(147):10–11; Isa 31:3, 40:13–17; Sir 42:18–22; Rom 11:34–36.

[2] Isa 66:2.

[3] Mal 3:3; Gen 14:17–20; Ps 109(110):4; Heb 5–7; Luke 22:19; Acts 2:42, 2:46.

Yield to the prayer of the Holy Spirit by Whom you will pray as you ought, by Whose grace your prayers rise like incense in My sight.[1] This was the secret of the saints when they sought Me in prayer: little by little their own ways of praying gave way to a divine way of praying, to the ineffable sighs and groanings of My Holy Spirit within them.[2] Some of My saints were able, in fact, to translate this Spirit-given prayer into words; and so the Church has been enriched with a treasury of prayers inspired by the Holy Spirit, prayers that glorify My Father, prayers that touch My Heart and move Me to compassion.[3]

Pray in this way. Surrender to the Holy Spirit, and allow the Holy Spirit to cause prayer to well up within you like a fountain of living water.[4] This is the prayer that flowers into adoration in spirit and in truth.[5] This is the prayer that the Church has enshrined and, by the grace of the Holy Spirit, expresses in a new and living way in the celebration of the Sacred Liturgy. I want to bestow this gift of prayer on you. I want to send upon you My Holy Spirit to create in your heart a prayer that is, in every way, conformed to the prayer of My own Heart to the Father and to My will for your life and for your eternity. Humble yourself then in My presence and receive this gift of prayer, not as something human, not as an ability that comes from your nature, but as a divine gift and a manifestation of the Holy Spirit in your nature, even in your brokenness marked by sin and, in the past, darkened by collusion with evil.

Now I call you, I bring you into the pure light of a new life in My Eucharistic presence and, in order to fill this life with My gifts, I impart a grace of prayer by which you will learn to open yourself to all that I desire to give you. Be grateful, then, and open yourself to the Holy Spirit. Call upon the Holy Spirit, the Lord and Giver of Life, through My Mother's Immaculate Heart, and you will experience the surpassing joy of His presence.

---

[1] Ps 140(141):2; Rev 5:8, 8:3–4.

[2] Rom 8:26; Luke 10:21; John 11:38; Ex 2:23–25; Ps 6:7 (6:6); Ps 37:9–10 (38:8–9); Ezek 9:4.

[3] As we read below, these would include, in a preeminent way, the prayers of the sacred liturgy. Hence Christian tradition ascribes elements of the Roman Rite of Mass to St. Damasus, St. Leo I, and St. Gregory I, and Byzantine anaphoras to St. John Chrysostom, St. Basil the Great, and St. James. Certain saints enriched the liturgy in their own times with the addition of sublime poetry: St. Romanus the Melodist in the East, St. Thomas Aquinas in the West.

[4] John 4:10–14, John 7:37–38; Esther 11:10; Ps 35:10 (36:9); Prov 18:4; Song 4:15; Isa 58:11; Zech 13:1; Sir 21:16; Rev 21:6.

[5] John 4:23–24.

Then I told Our Lord that I feared being deluded or deceived or led astray by my imagination in receiving words such as these. This is what He answered:

See all that I have done for you to bring you closer to Myself, to make you live in My presence and in the light of My Eucharistic Face. See the changes I have wrought in you, and know from these things the truth of our conversations, for My desire is, and remains, to speak to your heart, even as a man speaks to his friend.[1]

When doubts come, dismiss them. Know that I speak to you in a language drawn from your own experience and from the resources of your own imagination and mind. The message nonetheless is Mine. It is I who am communicating with you in this way to hold you fast in My divine friendship, and to draw you into the sanctuary of My Heart, there to worship and glorify with Me the Father Who is the Source of all heaven's gifts. There too, in My Heart, are you filled with My Holy Spirit and lifted into a union with My priestly prayer that no human effort can merit or produce. All of this, you see, is My gift to you, a gift offered to you out of My gracious and merciful love.

Do not yield to fear, to doubt, and to a purely human scrutiny of something which is of Me, and which I freely communicate to you out of love. Above all else, be grateful, and allow My peace to descend into your heart and fill you with a holy joy.

Wednesday, July 8, 2009

My Heart grieves over so many priests who have no desire to approach Me in the Sacrament of My love. Their hearts have grown cold, but My Heart burns with love for them still. How I suffer from their coldness, their indifference, their lack of desire for Me and for the friendship I offer them. I make Myself a beggar before them. I plead with them to accept My friendship and to give Me each day but an hour of their time. So much of their time is wasted pursuing things of no value, things of no consequence, and I, all the while, wait for them to come to Me.

Will they hear My call during this Year for Priests? Will they turn from the perishable things that fascinate them and hold them enslaved, and turn to Me who will make them truly happy, and Who will give them what no creature can?

My priests are in need of a great revolution, a revolution of love. I have seen the lives of so many priests; I know their sufferings. Nothing is hid-

---

[1] Ex 33:11; 2 John 1:12.

den from Me. I will raise up a company of faithful friends of My Heart, priest adorers of My Eucharistic Face. I will gather them together as once I gathered the Twelve in the Upper Room, and will speak to them heart to heart, as a man speaks to the friends he has chosen for himself. I will heal those who are wounded. I will refresh those who are weary. I will sanctify them all, but only if they heed My appeal and, following the sound of My voice, seek Me out and learn to abide in My presence. This is how I will renew My priesthood during this year of grace.

I do not ask that My priests live all the day in church, as did My faithful servant John Vianney, but I do ask of every priest one hour in My presence, one hour in the light of My Eucharistic Face, one hour close to My Heart. Let them come to Me, and I will do for them more than they can ask or imagine.[1]

I am calling My priests into My company. I am pressing them to come into the cenacle and, there, to be radiant in the light of My Face. I would have them listen to the secrets of My Heart, to those secrets that I have reserved for this generation and for the joy of My Spouse the Church in this year of grace.

As for you, be the consoler of My Eucharistic Heart. Abide in My presence. Speak to Me as the Holy Spirit moves you to speak. Listen to Me and receive the words that I address to you, words that communicate something of the fire of love that blazes in My Heart for you and for every priest of Mine.

Console Me, console Me, for My own have rejected Me. Console Me, for I am forsaken by those whom I chose for Myself, expecting that they would respond to My love with love, and to My tenderness with a like tenderness. You, at least, give Me all the tenderness of your heart, and know that My Heart is open to you to receive you and to be the sanctuary of your priesthood here and in the world to come.

Thursday, July 9, 2009

My Heart overflows with merciful love for My priests. There is not one of them for whom I would not suffer the most bitter betrayals and humiliations of My Passion over again, so great is My desire to see every priest of Mine made whole, washed clean in My precious Blood and sanctified in the fire of the Holy Spirit. All that I suffered once—especially the sufferings of My priestly Heart—remains available until the end of time to the priests of My Church, the chosen friends of My Heart. My suffering remains for them a wellspring of healing, and from

---

[1] Eph 3:20–21; Prov 9:4.

My wounds there flows for My priests a balm of purity and of love. If only My priests would approach Me and apply to themselves the merits and power of My most bitter Passion and of My most precious Blood!

There were moments in My Passion—the darkest moments of all—when My Heart was crushed as in a winepress, beneath a weight of sorrow that no words can describe: when I was suffering particularly for My priests. I saw them passing before Me, a seemingly endless procession until the end of time. I saw each one's sins, each one's betrayals, sacrileges, and cold-heartedness. I saw too those who lived and walked in the light; these were My consolation, and in each of them I saw the influence of My most pure Mother. She formed them for Me, and this she will continue to do until the last priest is ordained and the sacraments I gave My Church pass into the blaze of glory that they signify in time. I looked into the eyes of each of My priests. In some I saw a burning love and a desire to please Me in all things. In others I saw a mercenary spirit, an inability to move past the necessary organization of My Church into the mysteries for which she came forth from My wounded side and received the Holy Spirit at the third hour on Pentecost. In still others I saw a terrible indifference, a loss of their first love, a betrayal of all that My priesthood represents. It is these who added immeasurable sorrow to the sufferings I endured.[1]

In this Year for Priests, I ask for priestly souls to console Me and to make up for what is lacking still in a part of My priesthood. For the coldness of so many, I ask for an undivided and tender love. For the indifference of so many, I ask for a holy zeal. For the irreverence of so many, I ask for a renewed awareness of My divine majesty and of the holiness that befits My sanctuaries.

The time is measured and it will pass quickly. Let My priests return to the wound in My side. Let them follow the beacon that shines from My Eucharistic Face to drawn them into My presence. I wait for them. With a great desire I desire their company and the consolation that only they can offer My pierced Heart.

---

[1] Cf. the intention and prayer for the eighth day of the Divine Mercy novena: "Today bring to Me the souls who have become lukewarm, and immerse them in the abyss of My mercy. These souls wound My Heart most painfully. My soul suffered the most dreadful loathing in the Garden of Olives because of lukewarm souls. They were the reason I cried out: 'Father, take this cup away from Me, if it be Your will.' For them, the last hope of salvation is to run to My mercy. / Most compassionate Jesus, You are compassion itself. I bring lukewarm souls into the abode of Your most compassionate Heart. In this fire of Your pure love, let these tepid souls who, like corpses, filled You with such deep loathing, be once again set aflame" (text from the Marians of the Immaculate Conception, http://www.thedivinemercy.org/, accessed August 19, 2016).

Friday, July 10, 2009

Go forward in simplicity, free of fear and trusting in My merciful providence to prepare all things for a future full of hope. Leave the preparation of the future entirely in My hands. Your part is to remain faithful to the adoration I have asked of you. By corresponding to your vocation to be the priest adorer of My Eucharistic Face and the consoling friend of My Heart, you are already participating actively in the preparation of My work here in all its dimensions.

Listen to the inspirations of the Holy Spirit. When it is time to act or to move on any particular question, this will be made clear to you. Until you have that certainty, be content to persevere in this hidden life of adoration. The work is Mine and I will fulfil that which I have promised you. I will send you sons and brothers. I have already chosen and called them, and when they present themselves to you, you will recognize them as the men I have prepared to share with you in this work for the glorification of My Eucharistic Face and the sanctification and healing of My priests.

Reparation is at the heart of this work: adoring Me for the priests who do not adore Me; seeking Me for those who flee from before My Face; trusting Me for those who place all their trust in themselves and in the ways of the world. Above all, love Me. Love Me for the sake of those priests of Mine whose hearts have grown cold.

Priests must offer themselves as victims for their brother priests. This is how I intend to purify, and heal, and sanctify, and restore the beauty of holiness to My priesthood[1]: by associating victim priests to My own Sacrifice renewed on the altar, and by taking the offering of their sufferings into My own, so as to make them co-redeemers with Myself, co-redeemers of those priests who must be brought back from the distant regions of sin where Satan has held them captive for too long.[2]

Saturday, July 11, 2009

The desire of My Heart is that My priests should adore Me, setting aside time each day to abide before My Eucharistic Face. There I will fill them with all the graces necessary to their sacred ministry. There I will give them the virtues without which they will be incapable of showing My Face and My Heart to souls.

I would compel My priests to come in from the highways and byways where they have wandered, and where the Evil One lies in wait to

---

[1] 1 Chron 16:29; 2 Chron 20:21; Ps 28(29):2; Ps 95(96):9. In the KJV, each of these verses uses the expression "beauty of holiness."

[2] Col 1:24; Matt 4:16; Luke 10:30–34, 15:13–14; Isa 9:2; Ezek 34:25–31.

ambush them.[1] I would have them come in to Me, for I wait for them with a Heart full of divine friendship for each one. There will be no reproaches and no condemnation, but only forgiveness, and a great joy among the angels of heaven[2] that My priests are, at last, taking their place in adoration before My altars.

Make known to My priests this pressing desire of My Heart. The time is short. I will renew the face of My priesthood by filling it with the reflection of My own Eucharistic Face. Thus will My priesthood be transformed. The Church and the world wait for holy priests. And I wait to sanctify them in the Sacrament of My love.

Sunday, July 12, 2009

You think that your inability to pray without distractions is an obstacle to My grace. Were that so, I would not have been able to sanctify a great number of those whom My Church honours as saints. Distractions, when they are not entertained wilfully, are no obstacle to My work in a soul. My grace passes through them to touch the centre of the soul wherein all is still and in readiness for My healing and sanctifying touch.

Come to Me with a lively desire to surrender to Me: that is sufficient. Come to Me for My sake, to offer Me your companionship as an expression of grateful love. I need nothing from you[3]; My Heart's desire is to respond to all your needs with an abundance of spiritual gifts. My Heart's desire is to draw you into the closest union with Myself.

Bring Me your desires, your good will, a profound regret for all your sins, and, above all, a boundless confidence in My merciful love. Come to Me to receive what I desire to give you. When you receive from Me with simplicity and with a grateful heart, you glorify My mercy.

I am not a taskmaster in prayer. I do not ask of you anything burdensome or difficult to achieve. I ask you to offer Me the companionship of a loving friend and the affection of your heart. I ask you to remain in My presence, content to be before My Eucharistic Face, close to My Eucharistic Heart. A prayer made with sleepiness and distraction is no less pleasing to Me than one made in consolations and alertness. Your subjective dispositions do not impede the action of My grace in your soul. Learn, then, to trust in Me to do the things that you cannot do of yourself, and allow Me to work in you secretly, in a manner perceptible to the gaze of My Father, and by the operation of My Holy Spirit.

---

[1] Matt 22:9; Luke 14:23; Jer 6:25; Ezek 21:21; Hos 6:9–7:1; 1 Macc 5:4.

[2] Luke 15:10.

[3] Ps 15(16):2: "I have said to the Lord, Thou art my God, for Thou hast no need of my goods"; Ps 39:7 (40:6); Ps 49(50):8–14; Mic 6:6–7; Isa 40:15–17; Acts 17:25.

Thursday, December 3, 2009

Your union with Me, My beloved, will take place through My Immaculate Mother and by the gentle but continuous operations of the Holy Spirit in your soul. Together, the Holy Spirit and My Immaculate Mother put themselves at the service of souls who seek union with Me. Is not this a wonderful thing? God the Holy Spirit, the source of all holiness in creatures and the substantial Love by which My Father and I are eternally one, puts Himself wholly at the service of a finite and sinful creature to bring about a union with Me that is the perfect expression in a human soul of the union of My human soul and of My divinity with My Father.

> In that day you will know that I am in My Father, and you in Me, and I in you.
>   JOHN 14:20

And in this work of uniting a soul to Me, no one can take the place of My most pure and loving Mother. She is the Mediatrix of all graces, and just as no one can come to the Father except through Me, so too can no one come to Me except through her in whose virginal womb I took flesh.[1]

If only My Mother's role and the greatness of her work, even now from her place in heaven, were better known! Then there would be a great springtime of holiness in My Church and, first of all, among My priests, for I have entrusted each one of them to her as to the most attentive and compassionate of mothers. All the resources of her Immaculate Heart, full of grace, are at the service of her motherhood of the souls of My priests.

Priests have the right and the privilege of calling upon My Mother in every need, trial, failure, and sin, confident of receiving from her help and solace, mercy and healing, comfort and peace. Too few of My priests have entered into the relationship of filial love and of spousal intimacy with My most holy Mother that I desire for them, and from which their holiness will flow as from a pure spring. In a word, this relationship with My most pure Mother is the secret of priestly holiness. My priests have only to seek Mary, My Mother, and all the rest will be given them in abundance. The greatest saints knew this, but today many priestly hearts have grown dark and cold, and their relationship with My Mother, which is to be a reproduction of My own relationship with

---

[1] The classic exposition of this truth is St. Louis Marie de Montfort's *True Devotion to Mary.*

her, is almost non-existent. The renewal of holiness in My priests will come about as I have promised only when they become little and child-like, and consecrate themselves entirely to My Mother's Immaculate Heart. Their hearts need her Heart. That is My message today. That is what I so desire My priests to learn and to put into practice. Those who do this will quickly advance in holiness and their virtue will shine for the joy of the Church and for the glory of My Father in heaven.

Today you must speak to N. of silence and humility, of gentleness, meekness, and restraint. At the same time, comfort and encourage him. Assure him of your fatherly love and encourage him to go to My Mother and to abandon himself entirely into her keeping.

Did I not ask you never to speak critically of any priest? Hold fast to that resolution and I will bless you and all the priests with whom you concern yourself.

Tuesday, December 8, 2009
Immaculate Conception of the Blessed Virgin Mary

My own Heart overflows with love for you and I rejoice greatly to see you here in prayer before Me. Trust My providence. All things will unfold as I have promised and you will not be disappointed in your hope. I am almighty, all-merciful, and all-attentive to your every prayer and sigh. So few believe in My personal love for each soul.

December 13, 2009
Gaudete Sunday

Whenever you want to intercede with Me for another, it is enough for you to make your prayer as it comes to you through the inspiration of the Holy Spirit, knowing that I will hear you and that My Heart is, at every moment, open to your supplications. I am more attentive in lis-tening to your prayers than you could ever be in making them. Trust in Me. Believe in My tender and faithful love for you. I am your Friend, and I have chosen you to be the friend of My Eucharistic Heart. Why then would I not listen to your prayers and, in My infinite wisdom and merciful love, respond to them as I see fit?

Trust that My response to your prayers is always the best of all possi-ble responses, and never fail to thank Me, even as you make your peti-tions, for no prayer of yours goes unanswered.

✠

Saturday, January 2, 2010

I have not asked you to found a monastery, but rather to adore Me, to love Me, to seek My Eucharistic Face and draw near to My Eucharistic Heart. I have asked you to trust Me and to place in Me alone all your hope and all your dreams for happiness and peace. Seek Me, trust Me, and all the rest will be given you besides. I will build the monastery stone by stone, and I will fashion the men I have chosen for it.[1] You have only to remain humble and little and faithful. Without Me, you can do nothing, but to Me, nothing is impossible.[2]

Be faithful, then, to *Me,* not to a project or to an ideal. I am your all. Live for Me alone. Seek Me. Seek My Face. Take comfort close to My broken Heart. See how I love you, even to the piercing of My Heart by the soldier's lance, even to the last drops of blood and water. There is nothing I will not do for you, and this because I love you and because you are Mine. Only allow Me to act freely, choosing the means, and the day, and the hour.

Here in the Sacrament of My love, you have everything. Here you have all of Heaven. Here you have the Creator of earth and of all that it holds, and of every human being who has ever seen the light of day. I am all yours. Be all Mine. Ask Me to unite you more and more to Myself, until you are completely hidden in the secret of My Face.

When I prayed, "Attune me to Thy Heart," He said:

To be attuned to My Heart is to be attuned to My will, for My will is all love: love in its origin, love in its realization, love in its reward.

I have several communities of fervent Benedictines in My Church, and they glorify Me according to the gifts imparted to them, but I have nowhere a house of priest adorers to keep Me company in the Sacrament of My love, and to offer themselves for their brother priests. This is what I ask of you. This is what I will do through you. You have only to be faithful, even in the measure of your weakness. Your weakness is no obstacle for Me; it is, rather, a channel through which I will give you My grace in great abundance.

The Benedictine framework and the commitment to the choral liturgy will protect and sustain the life of adoration and the work for priests—the interior work of self-offering in all things—and the exte-

---

[1] 1 Pet 2:4–6.
[2] Job 42:2; Ps 118(119):91; Wis 7:27, 11:23; John 15:5; Matt 17:20, 19:26; Mark 9:23, 10:27, 14:36; Luke 1:37.

rior works of hospitality, spiritual counsel, and availability to priests in their times of need and of inner darkness. At the heart of the vocation I have given you is the assent to My divine friendship, the "Yes" to My merciful love uttered on behalf of all priests through your presence in adoration before My Eucharistic Face.

This is how I will purify and heal and sanctify My priests: by drawing them into the radiance of My Eucharistic Face and the warmth of My Eucharistic Heart. They forget that I am present in the Sacrament of My love to offer them all the good things that come from friendship: companionship, conversation, joy, comfort, hospitality, strength, and, above all, love. I am hidden in this Sacrament and My Face is veiled by the sacramental species; My Heart, too, is hidden, but I am present, True God and True Man, alive, seeing all, knowing all, burning with desire that all should come to My tabernacles, but first of all, the priests whom I have chosen to be My intimate friends, the friends of My Heart.

A priest who, in adoration, assents to My friendship, will want for nothing and will make great strides along the path of holiness. Virtue is not difficult for one who abides in My friendship. The friendship of Jesus for His priests: let this be the subject of your conversations with priests and of your preaching to them.

Speak of what you know, of what you have experienced, for already I have given you countless signs of My friendship. I have shown you that I am your beloved Friend and that I have chosen you to abide in the friendship of My Heart as did Saint John, My beloved disciple. A priest who abides in the friendship of My Heart will accomplish great and wonderful works for souls. This is the secret of a fruitful priesthood.

Ask My Mother to keep you faithful to My divine friendship. Ask Saint John to teach you the way of friendship with Me, and of joy in the love of My Heart.

Priests who come to adore My Eucharistic Face will discover quickly My Heart, and in My Heart they will discover the friendship for which I created them and to which I have called them. The single greatest deficiency among My priests is that they are—so many of them—ignorant of the tenderness and strength and fidelity of My friendship for them. How will this deficiency be remedied? By adoration before My Eucharistic Face. This is why I have called you to this specific work and vocation. It will begin humbly and in an almost hidden way, but I will bless you and those whom I will send you, and the radiance of My Eucharistic Face will reach an ever greater number of priests, until My priesthood shines in them with all the splendour of My own holiness.

Thursday, January 7, 2010
Saint Raymond of Peñafort

I am delighted and consoled by your presence close to Me. This is what I asked of you, and you responded to the pleas of My Heart. Above all things, remain faithful to your times of adoration. Invisibly and imperceptibly I am at work in your soul and in the souls of the priests whom you represent before My Eucharistic Face. Your adoring presence before Me permits Me to reach them, and to touch even those whose hearts are hardened against Me. This is your primary ministry to My priests. So long as you remain faithful to this vocation of adoration, reparation, and representation of your brother priests in the sight of My Eucharistic Face, I will bless you and pour out upon you the treasures of mercy reserved for you in My Sacred Heart.

To be sure, there are many ways of reaching out to My priests, and of ministering to them, but of all of these, Eucharistic adoration is the most efficacious and the most fruitful. Already My priests are experiencing the effect of your presence to Me in the Sacrament of My love. Remain faithful to this, and I will save and sanctify a great number of priests. In heaven they will be for you an eternal source of joy and of thanksgiving.

Friday, January 8, 2010

This is the prayer I want you to say in all circumstances of life:

> My Jesus, only as Thou willest,
> when Thou willest,
> and in the way Thou willest.
> To Thee be all glory and thanksgiving,
> Who rulest all things mightily and sweetly,
> and Who fillest the earth with Thy manifold mercies.
> Amen.

Pray in this way, and so you will allow Me to deploy My grace and manifest My munificence in all places and in all the circumstances of your life. I desire to heap blessings upon you. I ask only that you give Me the freedom to act upon you, and around you, and through you, as I will.

If more souls would give Me this freedom to act as I will, My Church would begin to know the springtime of holiness that is My burning desire for her. These souls, by their entire submission to all the dispositions of My providence, will be the ones to usher in My kingdom of peace and holiness on earth.

Look at My most pure Mother; this was her way and this was her life—nothing but My will and the will of My Father, in complete submission to the Holy Spirit. Imitate her, and so will you too bring My presence into a world that waits for Me.

Saturday, January 9, 2010

Make Me the object of all your desires and you will never be disappointed. Seek Me and you will find Me. Ask for the grace of My presence in the inner sanctuary of your soul, and there hold conversation with Me, for I am in you, and you are in Me. I am your life, and apart from Me, all that this earthly life offers you is bitter and unable to satisfy your heart. I have created you and called you to live in My friendship and to long for Me on earth until that longing is satisfied in heaven.

In the meantime, for as long as your earthly exile lasts, you have Me in the Sacrament of My love. There you have My Heart; there you can contemplate My Face; there you can hear My voice; there you can enjoy My friendship and live in My presence. I was no more really present to My Apostles than I am to you at this moment in the Sacrament of My love.[1] Do you believe this?

I replied, "Yes, Lord, I believe. Help my unbelief."[2]

I will strengthen your faith in My real presence and make it so strong that the rest of your life will rest upon it as upon a solid rock.[3] I am making you the priest adorer of My Eucharistic Face that I have so long desired. Allow Me to form you, to shape you, to purify and to illumine you in preparation for the work that I have given you to do among My priests. For this to happen, you have only to abide in My presence. The work of adoration is also, and first of all, My work in you. When you are before My Eucharistic Face and so close to My Heart, I am acting in you

---

[1] The category of substance does not admit of degrees: a given substance is either fully what it is (e.g., a man, a horse, a dog) or not that thing at all; it cannot be half-man, half-horse, half-dog. This is the basis of the pro-life position: either the embryo is human or not human, and if human, it has the same dignity and deserves the same honor as any human person, regardless of what the accidents—the size, shape, color, weight—may be. Similarly, because the *substance* of Jesus Christ is present in the Blessed Sacrament, and substance does not admit of degrees, the essential reality of Our Lord is there, neither more nor less real than it was for His apostles. Although His accidents do not appear to us and we see, hear, taste, and touch those of bread, the very same *Person*, in His divinity and humanity, is present in our midst, under the sacramental veil.

[2] Mark 9:24.

[3] Matt 7:24–25; Luke 6:48–49; 1 Cor 3:11; Eph 2:20; 2 Tim 2:19.

and acting upon you. Your whole being is subject to My divine influence when you present yourself before Me to adore Me.

This is why I so insist on adoration for all My priests. It is the crucible of their priestly perfection. It is the furnace of love in which I purify them like gold in the fire.[1] It is the nuptial chamber in which I draw them to My Heart, and speak to them face-to-face, as a bridegroom to his bride, and as a man to his friend.[2] The nuptial bond of the priest with Me pertains to the relationship between My divinity and the priest's soul. My humanity offers the priest a divine friendship,[3] but that friendship leads to the union of the soul with My divinity and to a fruitfulness that surpasses every action and work of the priest acting of his own initiative.

Consent to My friendship and I will espouse your soul.[4] Thus will you be Mine in a way that exceeds every purely human notion of union, even the union between two souls in the purest charity. I created your soul for these espousals with My divinity, and your soul will have failed to attain that for which I created it, and that for which I destine you, unless you allow Me to love you and to purify you and to unite Me to yourself, not only as Friend to friend, but also as the One and Thrice Holy God to His beloved creature. I am one with My Father and with the Holy Spirit, and when I love a soul and espouse a soul to Myself, that soul is also united and espoused to the Father and to the Holy Spirit. Here, 'espoused' is but a human word. These mystical espousals have about them nothing carnal or material. I speak of the union of the soul with her God, the realization of that for which she was created, and the fulfilment of her truest longings.

Espousal means the most intimate union in love; it is in this sense that the soul is espoused by the Persons of the Adorable Trinity. The Father nonetheless unites Himself to the soul as a Father; the Son unites Himself to the soul as Bridegroom and as the Father's only-begotten Son; the Holy Spirit unites Himself to the soul as the fruition and completion of love.

All of this you can read in the Fourth Gospel. For Saint John, in resting his head upon My Heart, was given an understanding of all these mysteries. He is the patron and friend of all who seek perfect union with Me, and through Me with the Father, in the Holy Spirit. For this reason

---

[1] Prov 17:3; Sir 2:5; Wis 3:5–7; Job 23:10; Zech 13:9; Mal 3:2–4; 1 Pet 1:7; Rev 3:18.

[2] Ex 33:11; Song 2:4, 7:10; Deut 33:12 (Vul.).

[3] Because it is always the person who acts, not the nature as such, this statement can be understood to be saying: "In my humanity (or according to my human nature), I, the Son of God, offer the priest a divine friendship…"

[4] Hos 2:19–20; Ezek 16:8; 2 Cor 11:2; Rev 19:7–9.

I have given him to you to be your protector and to intercede for you in these final years of your life on earth. I desire that you should be for Me another Saint John, and that many priests should be led to the imitation of Saint John in his friendship with Me and in his sublime union with My divinity.

Read now[1] and understand.

I expressed the fear of being deluded or of falling prey to my own imagination. Our Lord replied:

Why should I not hold conversation with you who are the friend of My Heart? I speak in this way to many souls but not all recognize My voice, and very few welcome My conversation and receive My friendship as the freely given gift it is. It is My delight to hold conversation with those whom I love. Understand this: I hold conversation with you because I love you with an infinitely merciful and tender love and because I set My Heart upon you long ago to make you entirely My own.

When the enemy who hates Me and who hates all whom I love saw that My love was preparing you for union with Myself, he set about corrupting you by every means at his disposal. Many things happened that put you at risk and threatened the fulfilment of My plan for you. My Mother, however, knowing of My special love for you, and loving all whom I love, interceded for you and pleaded your cause until, at last, My infinite mercy prevailed over the iniquity of the Evil One and his plans for your destruction in hell.

All of this has been going on, visibly and invisibly, for so many years, but now I have led you into the harbour of peace and of holiness that I have prepared for you. This life of adoration is your harbour of salvation, just as it will be a harbour of salvation for many priests who risk being shipwrecked in the stormy waters of lives stirred up by sin and darkened by the shadows of evil. Thank Me that I have brought you here, and now begin to love Me more, desiring Me and choosing My love over all else. You are Mine.

Sunday, January 10, 2010

Only love heals, only love liberates, only love redeems. By bringing love into the depths of My Passion and by putting all the bitterness and hatred of sin expressed in My sufferings in contact with My love, I redeemed the world, atoned for sin, and restored to My Father the glory

[1] The Gospel of John.—*Author*.

that is due Him from the creatures whom He created to bless Him and fill the world with the sound of His praises.

The redemption is the work of love. I loved in the face of hatred. I loved in the face of death. I loved even in the netherworld, where the just of the ages awaited My coming among them. It is by love that I vanquished hell, by love that I triumphed over death, by love that I undid what Satan, in his envy, had plotted against the creatures whom I so love and whom My Father destined for the praise of His glory.[1]

Love is not a feeling; it is an act of the will, a movement of the heart, a glance of hope directed to My Father—for where there is love, there is confidence, and where there is confidence, the victory of love is assured.

Monday, January 18, 2010

Work a little each day on transcribing the notebooks and then present the text to Bishop N. He will indicate what the next step ought to be. I desire that My words and those of My Mother should reach a great number of priestly souls to bring them comfort and courage and light. I have spoken to you not only to comfort you and give you the assurance of My merciful love and friendship, but also so that, through My words to you, other priests may come to know of My burning love for them and of My desire to welcome them into the embrace of My divine friendship. Offer the Mass of the Holy Spirit today for this intention. My words to you will continue because I desire to instruct you, to uphold you, and to unite you to Myself through them.

Be not anxious when listening for the sound of My voice in your heart. You will recognize My words, and this will happen without anxiety or stress on your part. Be at peace. You will receive the words that I want you to hear and those that I give you for the comfort and upbuilding of your brother priests and of the sons that I am giving you. One of the signs that these words originate in My tender love for you, and not in your own thoughts, is that, when you re-read them and meditate them, you will experience the peace and joy of My presence.

When you have to choose between preparing a talk or homily and spending time in My Eucharistic company, choose the latter. I will give you all that you will need to say, and your eloquence will be greater and more compelling than if you had focused on preparing your words for the occasion.[2]

[1] Eph 1:12–14.

[2] Ps 88:35 (89:34); Jer 19:2, 23:16, 26:2; Ezek 3:10, 11:25; Sir 39:8–9; Matt 10:19; Luke 4:22; John 3:34, 15:26–27, 16:13, 17:8; Acts 5:20; 1 Pet 4:11.

Allow Me to give to you abundantly. Allow Me to speak through you, to act through you, to heal through you, and to bless through you. Trust Me to provide you with all that you need to do the things I ask of you. Fidelity to adoration is the key that will unlock for you all the treasures and infinite riches of My Heart.

Tuesday, January 19, 2010

My Heart's desire is that you should prefer nothing to your time before My Eucharistic Face,[1] for this is the very essence of the call I have given you. Remain close to My Heart. I will not fail you nor will I forsake you in your time of need. I am attentive to you in all the details of your life and I am, at every moment, disposed to hear your prayers with kindness and with an immense self-giving love.

Allow Me to guide you and to direct your steps. Come to Me with your questions, your perplexities, and your needs. Nothing is too small for Me, and nothing too great. I am here for you. I wait for you to share with Me all that preoccupies you, and all the questions that arise in your heart.[2] Worrying and daydreaming are useless. What I ask of you is dialogue with Me in the Sacrament of My love, and a boundless confidence in My loving friendship.

Your role is to remain hidden and to keep watch before My Eucharistic Face, praying at all times, and receiving those who come to you as you would receive Me, for, in them, it is I Myself who visit you and wait for you to tend to My needs.[3] I am sending you N. so that there will be another adorer to keep watch before My Face.

Whenever you perceive a conflict in your obligations and duties, come to Me and I will resolve it for you. Learn to depend on Me in all things. Let your first recourse be to Me, for I wait for you at every moment in the Sacrament of My love. I am never disturbed or importuned by your requests and your visits. I yearn for the company of My priests and every visit from My priests brings joy and consolation to My Eucharistic Heart. My sacred humanity is divinely sensitive to every mark of friendship and trust on the part of My priests.

---

[1] This echoes *The Holy Rule* of St. Benedict, who says in ch. 4: "nihil amori Christi praeponere" ("let nothing be preferred to the love of Christ"), which is repeated more forcefully in ch. 72: "Christo omnino nihil praeponant" ("let them prefer nothing whatsoever to Christ").

[2] Mark 2:8, 9:9; Luke 5:22, 24:38.

[3] Matt 10:40–42, 18:5, 25:31–46; Mark 9:37; Luke 9:48; John 13:20; Rom 15:7; Gal 4:12–14. *The Holy Rule* of St. Benedict states in ch. 53: "Let all guests that come be received like Christ . . . let Christ be worshipped in them, for indeed he is received in their persons."

You are beginning to understand that I love you with a merciful love that is tender, faithful, particular, and eternal. I will give you the grace to correspond to My love for you with the love that I Myself will place in your heart. Thus will you burn with love for Me, and be capable of loving all whom I love, as I love them.

Believe in My love for you, and enter by faith into My pierced side. There you will know the height and depth and breadth of My infinite love, and there, united to Me by Love, that is, by the Holy Spirit, you will worship the Father in spirit and in truth.[1] My Heart is the sanctuary wherein true adorers adore My Father as He desires to be adored by His children.

See how I have surrounded you with loving friends to help you remain faithful to the path of love that I have opened before you! No one of My friends corresponds to My will in isolation from others. I am forming a community of friends—of those souls nearest and dearest to My Sacred Heart—who will support each other in corresponding to My love and in fulfilling My will as I show it to them. You are one of these friends, as is N., and there are many others besides. Remain faithful to My love for you, and never doubt of My Heart's friendship for you, My beloved priest, for I want you to be for Me another John.

My Heart's desire is clear. I have asked you to sacrifice yourself in adoration and reparation and intercession for My beloved priests. Do this and I will attend to all the rest. Do first what I have asked you to do. Follow My plans as I reveal them to you. The time is short and this work for the sanctification of My priests is urgent. I desire that it go forward as soon as possible, and I will make possible even those things that, to men, seem impossible.[2] I will give you light sufficient for each step.[3] Thus will you grow in confidence and in faith.

Allow Me to build this monastery so dear to My Heart. Allow Me to build this sanctuary of adorers wherein the radiance of My Eucharistic Face will heal My priests and restore them to purity. I will do this, even as I have promised it.[4]

As for you, remain humble and obedient to Me. Allow Me to lead and to direct you in all things. Come to Me with every question, doubt, and fear, and I will answer you out of the tenderness and wisdom of My

---

[1] Eph 2:4–6, 3:17–19; 1 John 3:16, 4:8; John 4:23–24.

[2] Job 42:2; Ps 118(119):91; Wis 7:27, 11:23; John 15:5; Matt 17:20, 19:26; Mark 9:23, 10:27, 14:36; Luke 1:37.

[3] Ps 42(43):3; Ps 104(105):39; Ps 118(119):105; Matt 6:8, 7:11; John 11:9–10, 12:35–36.

[4] 1 Thess 5:24; Gen 21:1; Josh 21:45; 2 Sam 7:21; Rom 4:20–21; Heb 10:23.

Heart. This work will be done according to My design, for I have organized all things in My wisdom, and it remains only for My plan to unfold. You are but an instrument in My pierced hands. Allow Me to use you as I see fit. Above all, be faithful to the adoration I have asked of you. It is by adoration that My monastery will be built, and it is by adoration that I will cleanse and heal and sanctify My priests, the priests whom My Heart loves with an everlasting love.

There is nothing that you cannot discuss with Me, nothing that you cannot bring to Me in the Sacrament of My love. Friendship grows through conversation. Therefore, I have called you and chosen you to dialogue with Me and to open all that is in you to the radiance of My Eucharistic Face.

Friday, January 22, 2010

I want you to consult Me in all things, even in those that seem most insignificant. I am with you at every moment in every area of your life. My eyes are upon you and My Heart is open, never again to be closed.[1] Listen to Me when you seek My counsel, and I will speak to your heart, or reveal to you in some other way what is best for the glory of My Father and for the salvation of your soul and of the souls of the many whom I give you to influence, to encourage, and to console.

Sunday, January 24, 2010

When I asked Our Lord about my physical weaknesses, swollen hands, and shortness of breath:

Accept these things and offer them to the Father in union with My Passion for the sanctification of priests and the healing of those whom you have offended or wounded by your sins.

My beloved Jesus, attach me to Thyself, even as Saint John, Thy beloved disciple, was attached to Thee.

> *Abide in Me, and I in you. As the branch cannot bear fruit of itself, unless it abide in the vine, so neither can you unless you abide in Me. I am the vine; you the branches: he that abideth in Me, and I in him, the same beareth much fruit, for without Me you can do nothing.*
> JOHN 15:4–5

---

[1] 2 Chron 7:15–16; 1 Kings 9:3.

Abide in Me, suffer in Me, love in Me, and I will use all that you do and suffer to repair the evil you have done and to bring healing and peace to those whom you have injured. Trust Me with your past and with its heavy burden of sin; give Me all that you have: the present moment. Offer the present to Me, and I will attend to repairing your past and to preparing your future. Your future is to be united with Me eternally in heaven by means of the same love with which you will have loved Me during these remaining years on earth.

Tuesday, January 26, 2010

Do you not see how much I have been calling you to trust in Me? Trust is the key that opens all the treasures of My merciful and infinitely loving Heart. I am touched by a single act of trust in My merciful love more than by a multitude of good works. The soul who trusts in Me allows Me to work freely in her life. The soul who trusts Me, by that very fact, removes the obstacles of pride and self-determination that impede My freedom of action. There is nothing I will not do for the soul who abandons herself to Me in a simple act of trust.

> Do Thou in me and through me, O my beloved Jesus,
> all that Thou desirest to find in me and do through me,
> so that, in spite of my miseries, my weaknesses, and even my sins,
> my priesthood may be a radiance of Thine,
> and my face reflect the merciful love that ever shines
> on Thy Holy Face
> for souls who trust in Thee and abandon themselves
> to Thy divine action.

Wednesday, January 27, 2010

Will you allow Me to suffer in you, to complete in your flesh and in your heart that portion of My Passion reserved for you by My Father from all eternity?[1] I will send upon you the Holy Spirit, the Comforter, so that you may be able to suffer joyfully and in the peace of a complete submission to all the designs of My Heart upon your life.

I need your sufferings and I ask for them for the renewal of My priesthood in the Church and for the spiritual regeneration of priests weakened by sin and held in bondage to evil. By your submission to My Father's will and by your humble participation in My Passion, many priests will be healed and purified, and restored to holiness. Will you

---

[1] Col 1:24; Rom 8:17; Matt 25:34; John 6:32, 15:2, 17:14–15, 18:11; Gal 6:12–17.

give Me your "yes"? Will you consent to this work of Mine in you and through you? Trust.

My Jesus, how can I refuse Thee anything? All my trust is in Thee. In Thee is all my hope. I am all Thine, and Thy friendship is my assurance of happiness and of Thy unfailing grace. I give Thee my heartfelt "yes." I am all Thine, beloved Jesus: a priest in Thine own priesthood and a victim with Thee in Thy pure, holy, and spotless oblation to the Father. Amen.

Look to My Eucharistic Face and I will strengthen you in all your sufferings. You will suffer not as one defeated by the forces of evil, but as one already united to Me in the triumph of My resurrection.[1] I will suffer in you, giving to everything you endure out of love for Me and for My beloved priests a value far exceeding what can be measured in human terms.

My Heart will beat in yours and yours in Mine. This is the union to which I am leading you. This is the ultimate meaning of your passage on earth. I am preparing you now for an eternal union with Me in the glory of heaven. There you will find the home that I have prepared for you in My love for you even from before the beginning of time.[2]

Your sufferings will be made of weakness and weariness and dependence on others. I will send you physical sufferings, but I will also strengthen your heart and unite you more and more to Myself in a joy transcending all suffering and in a strength transcending every weakness. You will be with Me on the altar of the Cross, and your life will become to the eyes of all a continuation and prolongation of My sacrifice on Calvary. Thus will you be that father in Jesus Crucified that I have chosen you to be: a father to the souls of many priests, a father with a heart pierced like My own Heart, and with an ever-flowing fountain of love for the healing of souls and the sanctification of My priests, My beloved priests. Do you accept this?

Yes, Lord Jesus, I accept all that Thou proposest. All my trust is in Thee. All my confidence is in Thy Heart's friendship for me.

While reposing the Blessed Sacrament:

---

[1] John 16:33; Luke 24:26, 46; Acts 5:41–42; Rom 6:3–11, 8:17–21; 2 Cor 2:14, 4:8–18; Col 2:12–15; Phil 3:8–11; 2 Tim 2:12; 1 Pet 4:13, 5:1.

[2] Isa 64:4; Matt 25:34; John 14:2–3, 17:24; 1 Cor 2:9; Eph 1:3–5; 2 Tim 1:8–9; Rev 13:8.

I will always give you strength to adore Me, to come before My Eucharistic Face, and to sing My praises.

Thursday, January 28, 2010

Beloved Jesus, Thou knowest in detail every one of N.'s questions. I wait upon Thy answers, and I ask Thee to open my ears, my eyes, and my heart to perceive all of Thy answers, directives, and counsels.

There should be three houses for priests, in reference to the three tabernacles that Saint Peter wanted to build on Mount Tabor because it was "good for them to be there."[1]

The land itself will provide exercise, refreshment, and rest.

Build the church according to what I will show you.[2] It will be a temple of adoration to the glory of My Eucharistic Face, a sanctuary of My Heart, a dwelling-place for the Holy Spirit, under the gaze of My Father.

Once the money comes you will find the land, and it will be possible to begin, for the time is short and My Heart yearns for the completion of this temple of adoration and house of refreshment for the souls of My priests. Once you begin, complete what you have begun, for the time is short, and I will renew My priests, as I have promised, in the light of My Eucharistic Face, close to My Eucharistic Heart. They will come and My blessing shall be upon this work for it is Mine, and I conceived it for you and for all My priests in the depths of My Heart.

Build and establish this work of Mine so that My designs may be carried out in security and in peace, with no anxiety for the cares of this world, for it is passing, but the holiness of My priests will endure forever, and they will shine like stars in the firmament of My kingdom.[3]

Be at peace. Trust in My infinitely tender love for you and in the abiding friendship of My Heart, for you are Mine and I am yours, and I will not forsake you, nor will you be disappointed in your hopes.

Lord Jesus, I ask Thee only this: that the souls of those who are in any way connected with this work of Thine, or who will collaborate in its realization, may be delivered from all evil, preserved in holiness and peace, enjoy abundant blessings, and be drawn into the radiance of Thy Eucharistic Face and the fire of love that blazes in Thy Heart.

---

[1] Matt 17:4; Mark 9:4; Luke 9:33.
[2] Ex 25:40; Wis 9:8; Heb 8:5.
[3] Dan 12:3; Wis 3:7; Matt 13:43.

This—and more still—will I do for them, for your happiness is My delight. I have always loved you and I will continue to love you, to protect you, and to draw you to Myself, until you are one with Me forever in heaven. Be at peace. Have no fear. My love for you is assured, and My mercy has blotted out those sins that still cast a shadow over your memories of the past.

I forgive you and I heal you as I will forgive and heal those who were caught up with you in the web of evil by which the Enemy sought to destroy you and pull you after him into the abyss of darkness and torment that is the lot of those who refuse My Heart's merciful love. My Heart condemns no one to hell; My Heart grieves over every soul that withdraws from My willingness to pardon and to receive it into the embrace of My forgiving love. Believe in My mercy, trust in My mercy, and through your belief and trust in the mercy of My Heart, many souls will be spared the pains of hell.

There are priests who doubt of My love for them, who refuse to believe in the friendship of My Heart for each of them. I will change their hearts in the light of My Eucharistic Face and they will begin to trust in My love for them, and My mercy will wash over their souls and renew in them the joy of their youth.[1] I have said this and I will do it, for I am faithful.[2]

Saturday, January 30, 2010
Anniversary of the Death
of Blessed Columba Marmion, O.S.B.

I have brought so many of My saints and blessed, so many of My friends here in heaven with Me, into your life to help you, to guide you, to intercede for you. You are not always aware of their presence nor of their intense activity on your behalf. I give tasks to My saints. I share with them the ministrations of My merciful love to souls. I invite them to enter into the lives of My servants and friends on earth, and to educate and guide those whom I love and have called to eternal glory.

The life of My saints in heaven is one of cooperation with Me in My twofold mediation as eternal High Priest. Through Me, and with Me, and in Me,[3] they glorify and praise My Father; and through Me, and

---

[1] Ps 42(43):4; Ps 102(103):5; Isa 40:31.

[2] 1 Thes 5:24; Heb 10:23; 1 John 1:9; Isa 40:5, 49:7, 58:14; Ps 36(37):5.

[3] An echo of the doxology at Mass: "Per ipsum, et cum ipso, et in ipso, est tibi Deo Patri omnipotenti, in unitate Spiritus Sancti, omnis honor et gloria per omnia sæcula sæculorum."

with Me, and in Me, they dispense graces to souls and intervene with a perfect love in the lives of their sisters and brothers who walk as pilgrims on the earth.

I have charged so many of My saints to walk with you, to attend to your needs, to obtain for you the graces of repentance and illumination and union with Me that My merciful Heart so desires to give you. Some of these saints, though not all of them, are known to you. They have adopted you, some as a brother, others as a spiritual son. Their interest in all that you do and say and suffer is continuous, and they are attentive to you at every moment.

Call upon My saints. Ask for their help. Walk in their company. Invoke those whom I have made known to you. Welcome those whom I will make known to you. One day you will be united with them, in Me, in the glory of heaven where My Face will fill your soul with an ineffable joy, the same joy that is the delight of all My saints,[1] and the reward of those who have sought My Face on earth.

Invoke those whom I have already brought into your life and remain open, for there are others whom I will present to you, and to whom I will entrust you in the years to come.

Saturday, February 6, 2010

Be at peace. There is no need to force yourself to write or to be distressed if I seem silent. I am here before you. You are enveloped in My Eucharistic love and in the radiance of My Eucharistic Face. What more could you want? Here you have already all that you will have in heaven—except that here you have the merit of believing without seeing.[2]

Love Me, believe in Me, hope in Me, and adore Me, trusting that I will accomplish in you, in My own way, all that My Heart desires to see in you. I will re-create you, by the power of My grace and by the inward action of the Holy Spirit, into the man I want you to be, into the priest who will correspond in all things to My will and the desires of My Sacred Heart. There is no need to be anxious, no need to fear My silence. Rather, I ask you to enter into My Eucharistic silence and allow Me to act upon your soul through it.

---

[1] The final title under which the Litany of the Sacred Heart addresses Our Lord is "Cor Iesu, deliciae Sanctorum omnium."

[2] John 20:29; 1 Pet 1:3–9; Heb 11:7–13; Luke 1:45; Pope Leo XIII, Encyclical Letter *Divinum Illud Munus* (May 9, 1897), §9.

February 7, 2010
Sexagesima Sunday

I have called you to friendship with Myself. I will not fail you. I am drawing you into an intimate union with Me in My sufferings and in My Eucharistic life. Just as I am the perpetual Victim and interceding Priest in the Sacrament of My love, so do I intend to make you like Myself a perpetual victim and interceding priest for the sake of all My priests. Suffer and pray always.[1] I will sustain you with My love, and the anointing of the Holy Spirit will rest upon you in such abundance that it will no longer be you who suffer and pray but I Myself who will suffer and pray in you. This is My plan for you. Tell Me that you accept it.

My beloved Jesus, I accept Thy plan and all the designs of Thy Heart on my life—only sustain me by Thy love even as Thou art sustaining N. in his life as a victim of love and of prayer.

Monday, February 8, 2010

You will suffer as I suffered, that is to say, with an ineffable love. The love that will consume you and sustain you and refresh you in your sufferings is the burning Flame of Love, the Holy Spirit. My sacrifice upon the wood of the Cross was a holocaust of love consumed in the Holy Spirit. This is what I want for you, that you too should become a holocaust of love united to Me on the altar of the Cross and consumed in the fire of the Holy Spirit. Suffering is the fuel of love's holocaust.

Lord Jesus, if that is the case, then I accept whatever sufferings Thou wilt send me, that through them I may be united to Thee in the holocaust of love that is Thy Cross.

This is what I meant when I told you at —— that you would be a father in Jesus Crucified. You will enter into the fatherhood of the Cross that is the mysterious fecundity of suffering with Me for the life of the world[2] and, especially, for My beloved priests. The fatherhood of Love Crucified was prefigured in Abraham when, in obedience to My Father, he prepared to sacrifice his beloved Isaac. Abraham's fatherhood was broken open and, in some way, already filled the earth with descendants, when he consented to the suffering asked of him by My Father.[3] You,

---

[1] Luke 18:1, 24:53; Acts 10:2; Rom 1:10; 1 Cor 1:4; 2 Cor 4:8–11; Eph 5:20; Phil 1:4, 4:4; Col 1:3; 1 Thes 1:2, 5:16–18; 2 Thes 1:11, 2:12; Heb 13:15; Ps 33:2 (34:1).

[2] John 6:52.

[3] Gen 22:1–19.

too, will enter into a fatherhood wider and deeper and more far-reaching than anything you can imagine, by accepting the sufferings that I will send you, the sufferings by which I will unite Myself to you.

As Thou willest, O my Jesus,
when Thou willest,
and in the way Thou willest,
for Thou art God who rulest all things mightily and sweetly,
and who fillest the earth with the abundance of Thy mercies.
Amen.[1]

Tuesday, February 9, 2010

Nothing surrendered to My Heart is ever lost. If you would place the persons and the things you love in the safest place of all, surrender them to My Sacred Heart.

O my beloved Jesus,
I surrender to Thy Sacred Heart
all that I love.

February 14, 2010
Quinquagesima Sunday

Your sleepiness in no way impedes My action in your soul. If My action depended on your state of attention, I would be limited indeed. My action in your soul is deeper than your outward states of attention or sleepiness, deeper too than your thoughts and imaginings. You have only to come before Me intending to adore Me and to offer yourself to My Heart, and I will do all the rest.

Monday, March 1, 2010

Suffer and adore.

Suffering and adoration are two expressions of the love that I desire to see burning in your heart. Suffer in love for Me, and adore Me out of love. It is love that gives suffering its value in My eyes and in the eyes of My Father, and it is love that makes adoration worthy of Me and pleasing to My Heart. This is your vocation: to suffer and to adore, always in love. The love that reaches Me through suffering is a source of graces for the whole Church. The adoration offered Me out of love consoles My

---

[1] For a slightly different version of this prayer, see above, under January 8, 2010.

Eucharistic Heart and wins an immense outpouring of graces for the sanctification of My beloved priests.

Suffering, for you, is the humble acceptance of every limitation, fatigue, humiliation, disappointment, and sorrow. It is the joyful acceptance of infirmity and weakness. It is adhesion to all the manifestations of My will, especially those that you are incapable of understanding in the present moment. Suffering offered in love is precious in My sight.[1] Accept the sufferings that I allow and that I will for you; thus will you participate in My Passion through patience and accomplish the mission that I have entrusted to you.

Adoration is the second aspect of your vocation. In adoration, and from it, as from an ever-flowing fountain, you will receive the love that makes suffering precious and makes you like Me in the hour of My Sacrifice on the altar of the Cross. The more you adore Me, the better equipped you will be to accept suffering and to live it in union with My Passion, for the renewal of My priesthood in the Church and for the redemption of the souls of priests held in bondage to the forces of evil.

Listen to N.'s desire for more adoration, for I am speaking to you through him. Your fears are groundless. You will see that much more will be accomplished by using more freely and more generously the charism of adoration that I have already given you.

Adore Me more generously; make the offering of your time out of love, trusting in My power to bring about the impossible, and you will see wondrous things.[2] Adore Me more generously and I will bless you more abundantly. Show Me your willingness to be the adorers that I have been asking you to be for so long a time already, and I will show you that I am faithful and that I will accomplish all that I have promised, even down to the last detail.[3]

It is your failure to adore Me generously and freely that impedes My work and delays the manifestation of My glorious providence among you. Give Me the first place and I will attend to all the rest. Such is My promise to you, and I am faithful to My promises.

When I asked for a sign of confirmation:

Are My words not enough for you? Why do you doubt of My promises? It is not for Me to give you signs to prove the truth of My words to you;

---

[1] Ps 115:6 (116:15).

[2] Matt 17:19, 19:26; Mark 10:27; Luke 1:37, 18:27; Ps 71(72):18; Ps 85(86):10.

[3] Isa 46:9–10, 55:10–11.

it is your place to go forward in obedience and in faith, relying on My words and trusting in the infinite love of My Heart.

I have called N. to this life of adoration. He has the grace to live it generously and fervently. Do not obstruct the unfolding of My plans for him. Tomorrow allow him to increase his hours of adoration, and you, as an act of faith and trust in Me, do the same. You will not be disappointed. You can always begin preparing your meals in advance. N. will help to make the time for more adoration. You have only to ask much of him. He is capable of responding generously because I have enkindled a fire of Eucharistic love in his heart and nothing will be able to extinguish it.

Respond generously to My desires and I will provide generously for all your needs. That is enough for now.

Tuesday, March 2, 2010

I am about to carry out the plan for the renewal of My priesthood that for so long I have held within My Heart. These days of shame and of darkness that have come upon My priests in so many countries are about to be changed into days of glory and of light. I am about to sanctify My priests by a new outpouring of the Holy Spirit upon them. They will be sanctified as were My Apostles on the morning of Pentecost. Their hearts will be set ablaze with the divine fire of charity and their zeal will know no bounds.

They will assemble around My Immaculate Mother,[1] who will instruct them and, by her all-powerful intercession, obtain for them all the charisms necessary to prepare the world—this sleeping world—for My return in glory. I tell you this not to alarm you or to frighten anyone, but to give you cause for an immense hope and for pure spiritual joy.

The renewal of My priests will be the beginning of the renewal of My Church, but it must begin as it did at Pentecost, with an outpouring of the Holy Spirit on the men whom I have chosen to be My other selves in the world, to make present My Sacrifice and to apply My Blood to the souls of poor sinners in need of forgiveness and healing. They will preach My word in the power of Saint Peter on that Pentecost long ago,[2] and at the sound of their voices, hearts will be opened and miracles of grace will abound.

I ask you to undertake this work of adoration because it is the necessary preparation for all that will follow. Pope Benedict XVI, My faithful

---

[1] Acts 1:14, 2:1.
[2] Acts 2:14–39.

and trusted servant, will see the fruits of his Year for Priests, and his heart will rejoice at the rising light of a new priestly holiness on the dark horizon. Your part is to represent the priests of the world before My Eucharistic Face, and to allow the radiance of My divine Countenance to purify you, to heal you, and to transform you into My image for the joy of the whole Church. What I propose to do in you is what I desire to do in every priest of Mine.

Once priests begin to see the changes wrought in the lives of their brother priests by exposure to My Eucharistic Face, they will be obliged to admit that therein lies the secret of a priesthood renewed and restored to its rightful place of honour and dignity even in the eyes of the world. The world will continue to hate and persecute My priests,[1] but no one will be able to deny that they are men transformed by an experience that transcends all that is purely human. My priests must bear witness to Me by their purity, by their charity, by their zeal, and by their shining holiness.

I will that My priests shine in the darkness of this present age so as to draw many souls out of the shadows of sin into the radiance of My Face reflected on their faces. This is why I call all My priests to become adorers of My Eucharistic Face. Let them come to Me and open their eyes to the radiance that shines from the Sacrament of My love; it is the light of My Face, and they are to reflect it by lives that are holy and pure.

When I asked Our Lord about more vocations:

Trust Me with the timing of all things. One plant must be deeply rooted before another one can be planted beside it.

I am alive in the Sacrament of My love and, at every moment, divinely active, doing from My place upon the altar all that I did during My sojourn on earth. From the Sacrament of My love I heal the sick, I give sight to the blind, I cause the lame to walk, the deaf to hear, and the mute to speak. I am the healer of souls and of bodies. Those who approach Me in faith will not be sent away empty-handed.[2] Those who come to Me trusting in My Eucharistic love will experience its healing power.

Bring Me all those priests of Mine who are in need of healing in body, in mind, and in soul, and I will heal them according to My perfect will for each one. I long to restore My priests to purity of life and to wholeness. You, then, represent them all before Me, so that through your sur-

---

[1] John 15:18–25; Matt 23:34; Mark 10:30, 14:55; Luke 11:49, 21:12; 1 Thess 2:14–16; Jer 26:8.
[2] Luke 1:53; Ps 106(107):9.

render to My Eucharistic love, I may touch and heal at least some of them. Every day that you adore My Eucharistic Face and draw near to My Heart for the sake of My beloved priests, I promise to deliver and heal and sanctify some of them. This is why I ask you to be generous and faithful in the vocation that I have given you. Your fidelity means deliverance from sin, healing, and holiness for a great multitude of priests. Trust these promises of Mine. I will fulfil them for I am faithful, and even the world will be obliged to see that I love My priests and that I am sanctifying them.

The attack on My priesthood that appears to be spreading and growing is, in fact, in its final stages. It is a satanic and diabolical onslaught against My Bride the Church, an attempt to destroy her by attacking the most wounded of her ministers in their carnal weaknesses; but I will undo the destruction they have wrought and I will cause My priests and My Spouse the Church to recover a glorious holiness that will confound My enemies and be the beginning of a new era of saints, of martyrs, and of prophets.

This springtime of holiness in My priests and in My Church was obtained by the intercession of My sweet Mother's Sorrowful and Immaculate Heart. She intercedes ceaselessly for her priest sons, and her intercession has obtained a victory over the powers of darkness that will confound unbelievers and bring joy to all My saints.

Wednesday, March 3, 2010

You do not yet understand the value and the meaning of what you are doing when you abide in adoration before My Eucharistic Face. You are participating in a divine work, in a work of grace. You are before Me as an empty vessel to be filled with the power and sweetness of the Holy Spirit, that souls might drink of My love and, drinking, see that My love is sweeter than any earthly delight.

You are before Me as the intercessor in whose soul the Holy Spirit is sighing with ineffable groanings,[1] and [you are] obtaining from My Father, through Me, all that the Father desires to give My priests in this world and in the next.

You are the reparator opening yourself to receive the love that so many others ignore, refuse, or treat with indifference, coldness, and disdain. By offering yourself to Me in an adoration of reparation, you console My Eucharistic Heart, which burns with love and so desires to fill souls with My tender mercy.

[1] Rom 8:26.

When you are before Me, you are the privileged friend of My Heart, keeping Me company in My loneliness and allowing Me to share with you My sorrows, My grieving over sin, and My designs for a priesthood made pure and radiant with holiness.

When you are before Me, you are with Me a victim of love, handed over and bound to remain at your place before the altar with no desires or plans other than to love, to adore, to make reparation, and to represent all priests in a prayer that is simple, confident, and life-changing.

When you are in adoration before My Eucharistic Face, you are not idle; you are working in a way far more efficacious than any human undertaking can be.[1] This is your work and it is My work in you. This is a work that many will criticize and not understand. You are here in a divinely active collaboration with Me, who from the Sacrament of My love continue My priestly mediation before the Father on behalf of poor sinners.

Never doubt of the value of your hours of adoration. It is this that I have asked you to do, and I will draw from your presence in the sanctuary a great good and a superabundance of graces for My priests. Now, by giving Me the better part of the day, you are beginning to realize that for which I called you here, and that for which I set you aside long ago.

Friday, March 5, 2010

O my beloved Jesus, show me how Thou wouldst have me spend this hour in Thy presence.

I leave you free. You need not do anything. You need not say anything. All I desire is that you should be present, focused on My presence, and allowing Me to act in your soul.

Monday, March 8, 2010

You pleased Me by praying the Chaplet of Reparation[2] and by offering My precious Blood to My Father for the purification and sanctification of My priests. I received that prayer and brought it before My Father; abundant graces fell upon the priests of My Church in response to that simple prayer. I am pleased by every effort, no matter how humble or

---

[1] See Robert Hugh Benson, "In the Convent Chapel," contained in the collection *The Light Invisible* (1903).

[2] For the Chaplet of Reparation or Offering of the Precious Blood for Priests, see Appendix I, p. 269.

simple. In fact, I prefer the prayers of the humble and simple heart,[1] prayer made without pretence, in faith, in hope, and in charity. I will hear the prayers of those who recite this chaplet and My priests will experience its fruits in their lives.

Learn from My saints. Study them. Receive their teachings. Draw inspiration from their friendship with Me. But do not try to imitate them.[2] Each of My friends arrives at union with Me by the path traced for him by the Holy Spirit. Even when two paths may appear similar, know that they are not identical. All of these paths converge in union with Me, in the light of My Face, and all of them lead to the open door of My Sacred Heart.

Yours is the way of adoration. I have called you to abide before My Eucharistic Face and to make it possible for others to follow that same vocation. Even when many souls are called to the same way of life, each soul has its secret of love, a way of experiencing My friendship most intimately, that can be shared with no one else.

My love is a personal love. I love each soul that I have created as if that soul were the only soul in the universe, and I adapt My infinite love to the particular sensibilities and needs of that soul with all the wisdom and tenderness of My divine Heart.[3]

Trust in the path that I have opened before you and be faithful to it. N. is the first of a family of sons who will grow and flourish in the radiance of My Eucharistic Face.

Allow My love to direct all things. Remain little and humble. Prefer to stay in the background, allowing Me to direct and determine the course of events and the growth of this work of Mine. The more faithful you are to adoring Me in the Sacrament of My love, the more will I be faithful to you in manifesting the wonders of My providence.

Your fatigue and your distractions in adoration are no impediment to My action in the depths of your soul. I have assured you of this before. Come before Me and remain before Me even when you feel that your adoration is no more than a struggle and a failure to remain attentive in love and focused on My Eucharistic Face.

---

[1] Ps 39:18 (40:17); Ps 101:18 (102:17); Isa 66:2; Judith 9:16; Sir 3:19–21.

[2] As is clear from the surrounding context, "imitate" here means "copy," rather than "emulate." For, as St. Paul says, "Be imitators of me, as I am of Christ" (1 Cor 11:1; cf. 1 Cor 4:16, Heb 6:12), thus teaching us that we must strive to emulate the saints, while not attempting to mimic them or assume that the path on which the Lord led them is the very same as the one on which He intends to lead us.

[3] Gal 2:20; Song 7:10; Rom 14:7; John 4:2–42, 10:3–4; Ex 33:17; Isa 40:26–31, 43:1–2.

Here, your feelings are of no importance. What matters in My sight is your humility and your willingness to endure distractions, fatigue, and even sleepiness while adoring Me from the heart of your heart. Know that even when you feel that your adoration has been a waste of time, in My plan it is something fruitful and it is very pleasing to Me. I do not see things as you see them nor do I measure their value as you measure it.[1]

Friday, March 12, 2010

Listen to Me and write, for My time has come. I am about to bring to fulfilment My plan for you and for those whom I have sent you. My Eucharistic Face will shine over this new hour of building and of work for My glory and for the sanctification of My priests.

Your place is before Me, adoring Me and consoling My Heart, My Heart that so grieves over the sins and betrayals of My beloved priests. It is not too late for My priests in league with the darkness to turn to Me and begin to live in the light of My Countenance. My Heart waits for them. The wound in My side is an open door and I am ready to welcome them into the closest bonds of a friendship restored and made even more intimate by the work of My mercy in their souls.

So many of My priests are strangers to Me. They stand at the altar to represent Me before My Father and before My Body, the Church, and in their hearts there is no love for Me. They have grown cold towards Me, and they have given their love to passing things and to affections that violate their sacred promise to live for Me alone and to keep themselves pure as bridegrooms of My Church and as the closest friends of My Heart. I am betrayed by My own! There are so many priests who have placed themselves outside of the company of My friends and consolers, and they have made themselves My torturers, and are numbered among those who afflict Me most grievously.

I will receive them back. I wait for their return. I love all My priests with an indefectible love. Nothing they have done can keep My Heart from loving them, and in loving them I will do all things for them, and wash them in My Blood, and heal them, and restore them to the company of those who love Me, and console Me, and are safe within the sanctuary of My wounded side.

Did you think that I had forsaken you? Our conversations will continue. Believe in Me and know that, at every moment, My Heart yearns to share with you its secrets of love, of sorrow, and of mercy.

---

[1] Isa 55:8–9.

Saturday, March 13, 2010

You console My Eucharistic Heart by giving Me signs of your friendship; of all these, the one that most consoles Me is your presence before My Eucharistic Face. There are many ways of expressing friendship and of responding to the love of one's friend, but the one that is most satisfying to the heart is the simple act of companionship, of presence, of being together. Experience has taught you this in human relationships, but you have yet to apply it to your relationship with Me as generously as I desire. Come to Me, remain with Me. Seek Me out in the Sacrament of My love and, by remaining with Me, adore Me with tenderness and give Me your heart's friendship and affection.

What I ask of you, My beloved, and what I am asking of all My priests, is not difficult, nor is it impossible for the weak, the sick, and those who are homebound. If you cannot come before My Eucharistic Face, you can be transported there spiritually by an act of desire coming from the depths of the soul. Ask Me to transport you before those tabernacles of the world where I am most forgotten, neglected, and even despised. I will transport your souls into My presence and receive from your adoration and from your love the consolation that I await from My friends.

You have the privilege and the joy of living with Me under the same roof. Do you understand what this means? Do you see how like the life of My Immaculate Mother and of Saint Joseph your life is? Do you not want to avail yourself in every way and at every moment of My presence here? Cultivate this adoring adhesion to My sacramental presence. Let everything in this house and in your own life acquire an habitual and spontaneous referral to Me. Show Me that you are grateful for My sacramental presence by coming to Me often, by including Me in every aspect of daily life, and by consulting Me concerning all things. Do not treat Me as a guest in the house who remains aloof and distant in a formal parlour, one with whom you dare not share life as it really is. Rather, integrate My Eucharistic presence into every detail of your life.

My Eucharistic Face radiates from the tabernacle and from the monstrance into every nook and cranny of this house. This is My desire for the houses of My beloved priests as well. I want to sanctify their rectories and transform their homes into sanctuaries of adoration and of love. Encourage those priests who are considering arranging an oratory with My Eucharistic presence in their homes. I will bless them. I will draw them more intimately into the grace of My divine friendship. I will change their habits and purify the very atmosphere in which they live and work. As a result, they will grow in holiness and souls will benefit from their new-found intimacy with My Eucharistic Heart.

It is not enough to reserve My true Body in the tabernacle. In how many religious houses am I sacramentally present and yet left alone with little attention paid to My abiding real presence? Make reparation for this neglect, coldness, and lack of gratitude towards the Sacrament of My love in so-called religious houses. These houses where I am neglected and treated coldly are on the verge of a great collapse. They will not stand. I can no longer bear the mistreatment to which I am subjected in such places. They have become places of business and like the worldly residences of the comfortable—and I, I am forsaken under their very roofs.

Religious houses where I am loved and honoured and adored will flourish. The radiance of My Eucharistic Face will be their light, and the fire of love burning in My Eucharistic Heart will be their warmth. Souls will be drawn to them and, from among these, I will call many to be My friends, My consolers, and even My spouses.

The renewal of religious life will follow upon the Eucharistic renewal of My priesthood. Holy priests will foster vocations to a holy form of consecrated life, one in which I am at the heart of all things, giving life to all,[1] and drawing all to My wounded side and to the wellspring of living waters.[2]

Yes, much of what I am saying to you needs to reach other souls. Go about this prudently and in obedience to your Father, the Bishop. He will read and understand that this little light should not be hidden under a bushel basket. It should be protected and carefully passed from hand to hand so that more souls may rejoice in My warmth and in the light of My Face.

Do what you can do and I will help you, and what I will will be accomplished. Only be patient and faithful, and believe in My love for you.

Monday, March 15, 2010

My love for you is unchanging. It is faithful and it is as strong as it is tender. I will never forsake you and you must never doubt that I have chosen you to be a privileged friend of My Heart, and this in spite of the sins by which you so grieved Me and wounded My little ones.[3] All is forgiven; the past has been consumed in the fire of My merciful love. Now,

---

[1] Deut 32:39; 1 Sam 2:6–7; Neh 9:6; Isa 38:16; Job 5:18; John 3:16, 5:21, 6:33, 6:52; Acts 17:25–28; 2 Pet 1:3; 1 John 5:11.

[2] John 4:10–14, 7:38; Rev 21:6; Num 20:6 (Vul.); Song 4:15; Jer 17:13–14; Zech 14:8.

[3] For the Lord Jesus all souls are His "little ones." When "one of the least of His brethren" is offended, His Sacred Heart feels it as an offense done to Himself.—*Author.*

you have only to rejoice in the love with which I have turned your life into an act of adoration and of obedience to My designs. Trust in the love of My Heart for you. Go forward with confidence and with peace, for I am with you and you are Mine and My love will never fail you.

Tuesday, March 16, 2010

I accept the renewal of your offering. It is good that you should renew the offering of yourself to Me; it is a necessity of love. The beloved offers herself again and again to her lover, and so must you offer yourself again and again to the love of My Heart, so as to live in a constant state of offering and of openness to My love for you.

Yes, I call you to a life of reparation. Very few souls understand that a creature can console her God, and that God should desire the consolation of a mere creature, even of one created in His image and likeness. As God, I am love and the source of all love, and the life of the Most Holy Trinity is a circulation of living love that is perfect, complete, and utterly sufficient unto itself. But this same love was poured out in My creation and, in creating man, I gave Myself a being capable of receiving My infinite love and of responding to it with a love like unto My own. Man cannot contain infinite love, but he can be contained by it and lifted up into its current of life, sharing in the life of the Most Holy Trinity by means of union with Me, and by the gift of the Holy Spirit. Thus does My Father see in every soul united to Me by grace the one object of His eternal love and the reflection of My Face.

From among these brothers of Mine, sons of the eternal Father, sealed with the gift of the Holy Spirit, I choose some in whom I desire to reproduce My victimal priesthood. These I choose to drink of My chalice and to ascend with Me the altar of the Cross by offering My sacrifice day after day in the sacramental form that I left to My Church on the night before I suffered. These priests of Mine are also the friends whom I choose to enter into the sorrows of My Heart and to console Me through the ages.

When My love is spurned, when the gift of My Body and Blood is not discerned,[1] when it is not received worthily and adored by loving and grateful hearts, I suffer a divine affliction. That is to say, I am wounded in love, wounded in My Heart. I look to My beloved priests to console Me and to make up for the coldness, the cruel indifference, the ingratitude, and the irreverence that I suffer, hidden in the Sacrament of My love.

---

[1] 1 Cor 11:29.

There is a consolation that only My priests sojourning on earth, in the valley of the shadow of death,[1] can offer Me. Only those who live for the altar and from the altar can give Me the consoling and adoring love that delivers Me from the sorrow that constrains My Sacred Heart. This is a mystery, a mystery of love, that I, who am all-glorious and the source of heaven's glory and bliss, should nonetheless suffer the effects of man's refusal to respond to My Eucharistic love with love.

I ask My priests to offer themselves as victims of adoration and reparation to My offended and outraged Eucharistic love. Soon My Church will be singing the Reproaches of the Good Friday liturgy that express so well My Heart's sorrows and My grievances against My people. Who will come forward to offer Me a kiss, not of betrayal, but of faithful love and of consolation?[2] This is the privilege, first of all, of My beloved priests. I have chosen you to live this mysterious vocation of adoration and reparation. It is not difficult to carry out what I have asked of you. Give Me your presence. Offer Me your companionship. Abide in the radiance of My Eucharistic Face. Offer yourself to My Eucharistic Heart to be loved, and transformed, and used as an instrument of love and of healing for My priests, your brothers.

Saturday, March 20, 2010

My words to you are a daily gift of My Sacred Heart to your heart that remains so much in need of these assurances of My love for you. I will not stop speaking to you, but you must continue to dispose yourself to hear My voice by remaining confident and adoring in the radiance of My Eucharistic Face. I still have much to reveal to you, just as you have need of discussing with Me the struggles and sorrows, the joys and graces of each day. Treat Me, then, as your dearest friend, as your loving and faithful companion even in this valley of tears, for I am with you always in the Sacrament of My love. There I am waiting for you, and there you will find Me. There too you will discover that My Heart burns with love for you and that nothing can separate you from the love of My Sacred Heart.[3]

Trust in My Heart's love for you and offer yourself as a victim to My merciful love. By doing this you will open yourself to My love for you

---

[1] Ps 22(23):4.

[2] Inter alia, Gen 45:15, 50:1; Ex 4:27, 18:7; 1 Sam 20:41; 2 Sam 20:9; Prov 7:13, 27:6; Song 1:1; Matt 26:48–50; Mark 14:44–45; Luke 7:38, 22:47–48; Acts 20:37–38; Rom 16:16; 1 Cor 16:20; 2 Cor 13:12; 1 Thess 5:26; 1 Pet 5:14.

[3] Rom 8:35–39.

and receive in abundance the gifts and graces that, in My mercy, I have held in reserve for you for so long a time. Now you are ready to receive the graces and gifts that I long to give you. You have only to come before Me and surrender to My Eucharistic love. This is the love that radiates from My real presence, drawing souls to My Eucharistic Face and to My pierced Heart. Surrender to that love and to all that I desire to do in you and through you.

My beloved Jesus, I surrender to Thy Heart's love for me and I offer myself to Thee as a victim of adoration and reparation for all whom I have hurt or offended, that they may be healed and restored to Thy friendship within Thy Church, and for all Thy priests, especially for those who are still wallowing in sins and blind to the sweet light of Thy Countenance.

My Jesus, I give myself as a victim of love to Thee who gave Thyself as a victim of love for me. I desire to have no will apart from Thy will, the perfect expression of Thy Heart's love for me and for all Thy priests. I offer myself to Thee also for all the intentions of Pope Benedict XVI. I ask Thee to strengthen him and to console him, and I consecrate him to Thy Mother's Immaculate Heart.

I will purify and renew My Church in Ireland, but first I require of all My priests there a conversion of life and a return to sincere, heartfelt prayer daily in the presence of My Sacrament of love. There they will meet Me; there I will speak to them. There I will heal their wounds, detach them from sin, and console them. There I will sanctify them and strengthen them for their mission as priests and victims in a society that has turned away from My Cross.

I want My priests to go in pilgrimage to Knock. There My Mother waits for them. There abundant graces will be given them. There they will recover the joy of their youth and the purity and innocence that makes My Church shine in a world threatened by the darkness from below.

Let My priests in Ireland go to the feet of My Immaculate Mother at Knock. Let them seek the company of Saint Joseph and of Saint John. And let them wash themselves in My precious Blood, for I am the Victim Lamb, the perpetual Victim, the Priest who offers and the offering of propitiation. My precious Blood must wash the priests of Ireland from the first to the last, beginning with My bishops. Only then will a new day dawn for the Church in Ireland that I have long loved and still love with an everlasting love.

Monday, March 22, 2010
Feast of the Transitus of Saint Benedict (transferred)

When you come into My presence to adore Me, and prefer Me to the other things that solicit your attention and make claims upon your time, I am consoled and glorified. The proof of friendship is the choice of one's friend over all else. I want you to prefer Me, to give Me time that could be given to other persons and things. In so doing, you will show Me your love and offer Me the consolation of a true friendship.

I would ask this preferential love of all My priests. Friendship, if it is to thrive, must be practiced. This is as true of friendship with Me as it is of human friendships. I wait for the companionship of My priests. With them I hold My priesthood in common—and My victimhood. This is what makes the friendship of My priests so precious to My Sacred Heart. With them, too, I share the purest joy of living in the presence of My Immaculate Mother and of experiencing her maternal care in all the circumstances of priestly life. Given that friendship is based on treasured things held in common, My friendship with My priests is unlike that with other souls. The more My priests come to Me and linger in My presence, the more can I share with them the secrets and the treasures reserved for them in My Sacred Heart.

Priests, yes, even My priests, are sometimes fearful of finding themselves silent and alone in My presence. When they come to adore Me and to offer Me the consolation of their company, I do not require that they speak to Me; it is enough that they remain in the radiance of My Eucharistic Face, allowing their hearts to reach out to My Eucharistic Heart. Those who have experienced this movement of the heart to My Eucharistic Heart will know of what I speak. Words are not always necessary. The engagement of the heart, on the other hand, is indispensable.

Weariness and fatigue are no obstacle to a fruitful time of adoration. They are incidental; what matters is the desire to seek My Eucharistic Face and to abide in My company.

For one who loves, the time in My presence passes quickly, storing up immense treasures of merit for souls. The merits of your adoration I consider as belonging to the neediest and most broken of My priests. Is that not the meaning of the prayer by which you begin your adoration?

You will not see in this life the good done to the souls of My beloved priests by your fidelity to adoration, but in heaven it will be revealed to you, and this revelation will cause you an immense increase of delight in My presence.

Adoration is the first duty proper to this specific form of Benedictine life. Be faithful to it and you will flourish. This I promise you today. Be the adorer of My Eucharistic Face and draw other souls, those whom I will send you, into its radiance.

April 11, 2010
Divine Mercy Sunday

Today My divine mercy flows like a river, rushing into the souls of those of My priests who will receive it. By placing yourself before My Eucharistic Face, you opened your soul to the abundant streams of divine mercy that ever gush from My wounded side. Receive My mercy for the sake of all My priests and for the sake of those who refuse it now, that they may receive it at the hour of their death.

Nothing grieves My Heart more than the death of a priest outside of My grace. I pursue My priests—even the most sinful and hardened among them—even into the moment of death, that last opportunity to consent to My forgiving mercy, and still there are some who refuse My mercy, thus condemning Me to suffer again the grief that invaded My Heart when Judas refused to turn to Me and trust in My mercy.

I love all My priests. Even those who are sunken deep into sin and vice remain the privileged friends of My Heart, friends who have forsaken Me, their only hope, friends who have betrayed Me, friends who have broken My divine Heart with a sorrow surpassing all human sorrows. I love them all and My Heart will be their refuge and their hospice; they have only to turn to Me, trusting in My mercy and believing in My Heart's love for them.

Every day priests die, and some of these are saved only at the last moment by a merciful intervention of My Immaculate Mother, or by the sacrifices and prayers of some little soul known to Me alone and to My Mother.

Pray for priests who are dying. Pray for those who will meet a sudden death. Death for a priest of Mine is meant to be a crossing over into the sanctuary of heaven where, marked with the indelible character of My own priesthood, he will participate forever in My glorification of the Father and in My love for the Church, My Bride. Those priests who are on the point of dying in a state of sin can be saved, even *in extremis*, provided that they cast themselves, repentant and sorrowful, into the purifying mercy of My Heart.

Live each day as if you are to die. Enter each night in peace with Me and with all men.[1] Relinquish and renounce every attachment to sin

---

[1] Mark 9:50; Luke 2:29; 1 Thess 5:13; 2 Pet 3:14; Eph 4:26; Ps 4; Sir 10:6, 28:7.

and to enmity, and every collusion with evil. Prepare to die as a victim of love offered upon the altar of My Sacred Heart. Thus will you make of your death a final priestly act of oblation.

Wednesday, April 14, 2010

Yes, I am here for you, just as I am here, in the Sacrament of My divine friendship, waiting for all My priests. I yearn for their company. I want them to offer Me the gift of their time. I want them to rest in My presence and to discover what My Eucharistic Heart so desires to give them.

Where are My priests? Why am I left alone in thousands of tabernacles all over the world? Why do so many of My priests rush by Me, never stopping to linger in the healing and strengthening radiance of My Eucharistic Face? Why are so many of My priests indifferent to the friendship I hold in reserve for them in the Sacrament that I instituted in order to be close to them and have them close to Me?

My priests are the chosen companions and friends of My Heart. Just as I experience joy when they come before My Eucharistic Face, so too do I experience sorrow when they pass Me by or forsake Me in the Sacrament of My love. If only My priests would return to Me in the Sacrament of the Altar, if only they would give Me their hearts by beginning to offer Me the sacrifice of their time, what miracles of grace would I not work in them, and for them, and through them? My priesthood will be purified, healed, and sanctified when, one by one, My priests return to Me and discover the joy and refreshment of abiding before My Eucharistic Face, close to My Heart, the wellspring of divine friendship.

Thursday, April 15, 2010

I who am here before you, I am the Word. No book, however beautifully written, can speak to your heart as I do, for I am eternal Wisdom, infinite Love, and uncreated Beauty in dialogue with your soul. My words are not like the words of men, My words surpass even the words of My saints, though I often speak through them and continue to touch souls through their writings. My words are like arrows of fire shot into the heart and wounding it so as to inflame it and heal it with divine love.[1]

Make yourself vulnerable to My words. Allow Me to speak to you in such a way as to wound you with the piercing of divine love. When you come before Me and wait upon Me in silence, you are, in effect, allowing Me, when I choose and in the way I choose, to wound you with

---

[1] Song 4:9; Ps 37:3 (38:2); Ps 76:18 (77:17); Isa 49:2.

an interior word and to set you on fire with a communication of divine love. Expect Me, then, to speak to you, to console you, and to enlighten you, but also to wound you.[1] Unless I wound you in this way, you will be incapable of withstanding the attacks of the enemy and of bearing witness to Me in the midst of darkness and tribulation.

In the spiritual battle that is coming, only those wounded by Me will emerge victorious. This is why I call all My priests to seek and to accept the healing wounds of My love. Those who keep watch before My Eucharistic Face will be among the first to be so wounded. I have called you to adoration because I desire to wound you not once, but again and again, until your whole being is wounded, and so purified and set ablaze with the fire of My love. Would that your soul were wounded as many times as I was wounded in My body for love of you in the combat of My most bitter Passion! Allow Me, then, to pierce you through and through until, wounded by divine love, you are wholly sanctified and made fit for My purposes and designs.

This I desire not only for you, but for all My priests. I would wound each one again and again with My burning love so as to purify the whole priestly order in My beloved Church, and present it to the eyes of the world as a victim priesthood made holy in the holocaust of divine love.

Until My bishops and My priests allow Me to wound them with the fiery arrows of My divine love, their own wounds—wounds of sin—will continue to fester and to spread a filthy infection of corruption and of impurity in the Church. Let each one beg Me to wound him, for in wounding My beloved priests, I will heal them, and in healing them, I will sanctify them, and in sanctifying them, I will offer glory to My Father and fill the world with the radiance of My own Face and the love of My own Heart.

This, in truth, is who you are: a sinner held fast in the embrace of My divine friendship. When I withdraw this grace of conversation with Me for a time, it is so that you will not mistake it for the product of your own imaginings, and also so that you will not grow accustomed to My words and so, little by little, fail to take them to heart and to treasure them. I speak to you so that you might share My words when the occasion arises to do so. Share My words humbly, with no thought for yourself. Remain hidden in Me: I will hide you from the observations of men in the secret of My Face, I will prepare for you a secret place deep within

[1] Prov 20:30, 27:6; Job 5:18; Jer 30:12–17, 33:6–8; Zech 13:6; Heb 12:6; Rev 3:19; Luke 10:34.

the sanctuary of My pierced side.[1] There you can go to remain hidden and silent, sharing My words freely and without the fear of being noticed or praised.

Ask Me to hide you in My wounds. There is a place for you in each of My five wounds; each of them represents a refuge against the temptations that threaten you, and the traps set by the devil, who would ensnare you and rejoice to see you fall.

The wound in My right hand is your refuge from sins of disobedience and self-will. Take refuge there when you are tempted to take the path that is easy and broad.

The wound in My left hand is your refuge from sins of selfishness, from directing all things to yourself, and grasping the attention of others by seeking to take to yourself what your right hand has given Me.

The wound in My right foot is your refuge from sins of inconstancy. Take refuge there when you are tempted to be inconsistent, and when you waver in your resolutions to love Me above all things, and to place Me first in your affections and in your desires.

The wound in My left foot is your refuge against sins of sloth and of spiritual lethargy. Take refuge there when you are tempted to give up the struggle and to consent to despair and discouragement.

Finally, the wound in My side is your refuge from every false love and every fleshly deceit promising sweetness, but giving bitterness and death instead.[2] Take refuge in My pierced side when you are tempted to look for love in any creature. I have created you for My love, and My love alone can satisfy the desires of your heart. Enter, then, the wound in My side and, penetrating even into My Heart, drink deeply of the springs of love that will refresh and delight your soul and wash you in preparation for the wedding of your soul with Me, for I am the Bridegroom of your soul, your Saviour from all that would defile you, and your God who is love and mercy now and unto the ages of ages.

Sunday, May 2, 2010

Speak of My Immaculate Mother, of her humility, her obedience, her silence, her purity, and her single-hearted love for Me. Speak of her delight in praising and thanking My Father for the superabundance of graces lavished upon her. Speak, too, of her oblation with Me on Calvary and of her mystical participation in My priesthood.

---

[1] Col 3:3; Ps 26(27):5 (Vul.); Isa 45:3, 49:2; 1 Pet 3:4; Rev 2:17.
[2] Inter alia, Mark 4:19; Rom 1:26–32, 6:16–23, 7:5, 8:1–13; Gal 5:13–24, 6:8; Eph 2:3; 1 Pet 1:11; 2 Pet 2:17–22; 1 John 2:15–17; Jude.

My Mother is the shining model of every monk and nun and oblate. She is the mould in which monks are shaped and formed according to My Father's plan for each one. In order to grow up into holiness, one must enter the Virgin's heart and hide oneself, as it were, in her virginal womb. Thus is one born again into the life of perfection that I desire to see in every member of My Mystical Body. My most holy Mother is indispensable to life in Me, with Me, and through Me. One who seeks union with Me will find that union more surely, more safely, and more sweetly by going first to My Mother and by consecrating himself unreservedly and forever to her Immaculate Heart.[1]

Friday, May 7, 2010

My Heart is both loving and generous. I am generous to My friends, to those who trust in My love for them, and to those who approach Me, confident in My goodness and expecting to receive good things from the treasury of My Sacred Heart.

Such is My love for you. I love you with a tender and faithful love, with a merciful and redeeming love. There is nothing that I will not do for you, for you are Mine, and I have set My Heart upon you, making you My friend and My priest forever.

So many souls make little or no progress in the holiness that I desire for them because they do not trust in My grace. They attempt to change themselves by making use of purely human means, and forget that I am all-powerful, all-merciful, and ready at every moment to heal and sanctify those who entrust themselves, with their weaknesses and sins, to My most loving Heart. I do not ask for perfection from those whom I have chosen to be My friends; I ask only that they give Me their imperfection and the burden of their sins, and allow Me to do for them what, of themselves, they are incapable of doing.

Did I not say to My Apostles on the night before I suffered, "Without Me, you can do nothing"?[2] Why is this word of Mine so often forgotten? It is a word of immense power for the healing and liberation of souls because, understood rightly, it obliges them to run to Me in every necessity of body, mind, or spirit, and to allow Me to be their Saviour, their Physician, and their God.

You did not displease Me over these past few days. You needed to rest in many ways, and I provided you with an opportunity to take the rest

---

[1] For a full exposition of the truths stated here, see St. Louis Marie de Montfort's *True Devotion to Mary*.
[2] John 15:5.

and refreshment that you need. I am not as demanding of you as you are of yourself. I ask only that you cling to Me and prefer nothing to My love,[1] and that you bear patiently the infirmities of body, of mind, and of spirit that I have allowed to weaken you and humble you in My sight.

When you offer Me your physical limitations and infirmities for the sanctification and healing of My priests, I immediately put that offering to use, and My priests experience the effect of your offering because it is an act of love, and love knows none of the limits imposed by time and space, or even by death itself.[2]

Never think that I have withdrawn from you the gift of our conversations. I am ready at every moment to welcome you in My presence, to receive whatever you desire to give Me or say to Me, and to speak to you heart to heart and face-to-face, as a man speaks to his friend.[3] I have told you this before, but you easily forget My words and My promises to you. Call upon the Holy Spirit to keep My words and My promises alive in your heart, and to call them to mind in your hours of need.

Sunday, May 16, 2010

When I have something to say to you, nothing can interfere with the word that I would give you, apart from your own lack of preparation or refusal to hear My interior voice. This is the voice that is interior to you, but that comes from Me. It is the expression of My Heart's desire for you, and of the things that I would share with you, heart to heart, as a man speaks to his friend.[4] Remain open, then, to the sound of My voice, and let nothing deceive you into thinking that I have forsaken you or that our conversations have come to an end. I have so much to say to you that the rest of your earthly life will not suffice to hear it all, but you will hear nonetheless all that I want you to hear, and all the rest will become clear for you in paradise.

Yes, I have united your heart to the heart of My servant Benedict XVI, and this from the very beginning of his pontificate. Listen well to all his teachings. Receive them and make them known, for he is My messenger and My victim-priest in the midst of a world that closes its ears to My word and that still derides the mystery of the Cross. Soon I will give the world a sign that will convert many hearts. Many others will remain

---

[1] Deut 4:4, 10:20, 13:4, 30:20; Josh 22:5, 23:8; Ps 72(73):28; cf. *The Holy Rule* of St. Benedict, chs. 4 and 72.

[2] Song 8:6; 1 Cor 13:7–8.

[3] Ex 33:11; 2 John 1:12.

[4] Ibid.

closed and, in their refusal to listen and to be healed of the ravages of sin, they will be like hearts turned to stone, and incapable of responding to My redeeming love.[1]

This is My sorrow: that so many, even within My Church and in the ranks of the clergy, My chosen ones and My friends, have hardened their hearts against Me and, to My immense grief, will die in their sins.[2]

As for you, study well the words of My servant Benedict XVI, and use them in your preaching to priests and in your ministry to those who intercede and offer themselves for My priests. You will see how closely I have united you to the Holy Father. Give your life for his life. Offer yourself for his intentions. Support him by listening well and by carrying out all that he desires for the Church and for priests. The soul of the Holy Father is, in many ways, not unlike your own. You both have received a penetrating intelligence of the Sacred Liturgy—My mysteries celebrated for the life of the Church and for the salvation of the world—and you both have been led by the Holy Spirit into a deeper and more intimate union with My Immaculate Mother. For both of you, My Holy Face is a light shining in the darkness and the beauty that has captivated your souls and filled them with a holy desire for union with Me. And upon My Face, both of you are learning to read the secrets of My Heart. The Holy Father senses that there are souls united to him, souls who intercede for him, souls who offer their sufferings for him. I have, in fact, surrounded him with a legion of such souls, for without their effective self-oblation and constant prayer, he would falter beneath the weight of his office and experience a suffering too heavy for him to bear.

Tell N. that all her suffering and trials are precious in My sight, and that having weighed them in the balance of Crucified Love, I found them to be of greater value than the finest gold. With this offering of hers, I will work marvels of merciful love in the souls of many priests. She is not to fear the future and what it holds, for I am ever with her, and all that concerns her is My own affair. I will protect her and provide for her, and in My loving care she and N. shall want for nothing.

Write also to N. and tell him that the love of My Heart for him is a blazing furnace and that I have accepted his holocaust of suffering and of prayer. He is My victim-priest: I offer myself to the Father in him and through him, and he becomes through Me an oblation worthy of the divine majesty and a fragrant incense consumed upon the altar of a burning love.

---

[1] Ex 8:15; 1 Sam 6:6; 2 Kgs 17:14; Prov 28:14; Dan 5:17–21; Wis 17:20–21; Rom 2:1–6; 1 Pet 2:7–8.

[2] John 8:12–30.

Continue offering Me your infirmities and sufferings. They, too, are precious in My sight, and nothing of what you give Me is lost. On the contrary, I unite your offering to My own Sacrifice, and so it becomes part of the priestly intercession that ceaselessly rises from My pierced Heart to the Father.

My Mother takes delight in this little monastery where you love her and honour her. The more you show her the grateful and tender affection that is due her from all her sons, the more will she show herself a Mother,[1] full of loving kindness and ever ready to intervene and to act on your behalf. Love My Mother and all the rest will be given you besides.[2] Love her with a boundless love, for so do I love her, and My will is that My love for her should be continued in the hearts of all My priests until the end of time.

I speak to souls not only by means of interior words, but also by the suggestions that come from the Holy Spirit, and by events and circumstances ordered by My most loving providence so as to allow souls to rise above the earthly considerations that hold them in bondage to the things of earth,[3] and to be more closely united to Me, who desire the love of their whole heart, and their whole mind, and their whole strength.[4]

Nothing escapes the purview of My providence, and I order all things sweetly and mightily for the good of souls and the glory of My Father.[5] You have only to accept all that I will and all that I permit, with a trusting heart, with a heart that recognizes in all things the work of divine love and the overtures of My infinite mercy.

Tuesday, May 25, 2010

You are right to put your trust in My merciful goodness, for I am faithful to My friends and all that I promise them I can give them. I ask only that you not tire of waiting upon Me. Your human way of calculating things and of measuring time does not correspond to My own simple perception of all times and ages in an eternal now. Your prayers now will not be without effect in ages to come, and the prayer of many who prayed to Me in ages past is availing to you now. My arm is not shortened nor is My

---

[1] Cf. verse 4 of the hymn *Ave Maris Stella*: "Monstra te esse matrem" ("Show thyself a mother").

[2] Matt 6:33; Luke 12:31.

[3] Phil 3:18–20; Col 3:1–7.

[4] Matt 22:37; Mark 12:29–33; Luke 10:27.

[5] Wis 8:1; Rom 8:28.

Heart closed to your requests.[1] Continue to honour and adore My precious Blood, have recourse to My five glorious wounds and, above all else, trust in My Sacred Heart's love for you. Nothing touches Me as much as a soul who trusts Me and counts on Me alone.

Thursday, May 27, 2010

There is no need for you to become fearful and anxious. All will come to pass as I promised, but according to My perfect plan and at the time I have chosen, the best possible time for you and for all concerned. Continue to trust Me and tell Me often that all your trust is in the merciful goodness of My Heart. I will not fail you nor will I leave you open to the destructive influences that are seeking to undermine this work that is Mine. I chose you, the most broken and sin-sick of all My priests, in order to fill your poverty with My gifts and to display My power in your weakness.[2] Your soul was marked by deep wounds, the wounds inflicted by impurity and by sin at so tender an age. You could have continued down the path of evil prepared for you by Satan and his instruments, but My Mother intervened to save you, and she obtained from Me that you should carry out this work of adoration, reparation, and service to My beloved priests.

The work will begin slowly and it will encounter every manner of opposition, criticism, and resistance, but the merciful love of My Heart will prevail, and the light of My Eucharistic Face will shine in places long claimed by the powers of darkness. Continue to trust Me, and have recourse to My Mother, to Saint Joseph, and to Saint John, for I have given them to you to watch over you, to protect you, and to obtain for you an abundance of treasures from My Eucharistic Heart.

Friday, May 28, 2010

I receive your petitions and your prayers and take them into My Sacred Heart, the burning furnace of charity[3] and the wellspring of every grace and blessing.[4] Every prayer received into My Heart is wondrously ful-

---

[1] Isa 50:2, 59:1.

[2] Ps 34(35):10; Ps 71(72):13; Ps 80:11 (81:10); Joel 3:10; Wis 9:5–6; Rom 5:6; 1 Cor 1:25–27, 4:10; 2 Cor 11:29–30, 12:5–10, 13:3–4; 1 Tim 1:15.

[3] *Fornax ardens caritatis*: from the Litany of the Most Sacred Heart of Jesus.

[4] An echo of the *Supplices te rogamus* of the Roman Canon: "Humbly we beseech Thee, Almighty God . . . that those of us who shall receive the most sacred Body and Blood of Thy Son by partaking thereof from this altar may be filled with every grace and heavenly blessing."

filled, for My Heart cannot remain indifferent to prayers offered in confidence, humility, and faith.

Saturday, May 29, 2010

My Heart speaks to you so that you may speak My words to the hearts of many others, those whom I will send to you and those to whom I send you to preach. So long as you remain faithful to keeping watch before My Eucharistic Face, I will give you My words and see to it that they remain in the treasury of your soul, to be drawn out and offered to other souls on the day and the hour foreseen by My providence.[1]

Your most effective preparation for the preaching that I ask of you is your time in My presence. There I surround you and immerse you in My love. Any word spoken out of this immersion in My love will be supremely effective. Thus will I, through you, touch souls, and heal them, enlighten them, and set them ablaze with love for My love.

Be faithful to your times of adoration. Seek My Eucharistic Face, for I never cease from seeking your face. This is the mystery of My divine friendship: that I, the infinite and all-holy God, should seek the face of a sinful creature, love the sight of it, and take delight in seeing it turned toward Me. Amen. This is My Heart's desire: to see the faces of all My priests turned toward My Eucharistic Face, and lifted up in adoration to receive the reflection of My Face and the imprint of every sentiment and movement of My Sacred Heart.

Tuesday, June 1, 2010

I offered myself to the Father from the altar of My Mother's Sorrowful and Immaculate Heart. She accepted, consenting to bear the full weight of My sacrifice, to be the very place from which My holocaust of love blazed up. She, in turn, offered herself with Me to the Father from the altar of My Sacred Heart. There she immolated herself, becoming one victim with Me for the redemption of the world. Her offering was set ablaze in My holocaust by the descent of the Holy Spirit. Thus, from our two hearts become two altars, there rose the sweet fragrance of one single offering: My oblation upon the altar of her heart, and her oblation upon the altar of Mine. This, in effect, is what is meant when, using another language, you speak of My Mother as Co-Redemptrix. Our two hearts formed but a single holocaust of love in the Holy Spirit.

---

[1] Matt 12:35, 13:52; Luke 6:45; Job 23:12; Prov 2:1–5; Isa 45:3; Tob 4:7–10.

Thursday, August 26, 2010

There are so many tabernacles on earth where I am, for all intents and purposes, like one buried, hidden, forgotten, and out of sight. My divine radiance is diminished because there are so few adorers to act as the receptors of My radiant Eucharistic love and to extend My radiance through space and into the universe of souls.

Where there is faith in My real presence, there will be adoration; and where there is adoration, there will also be an efficacious radiance of My presence, drawing souls to My Eucharistic Heart and surrounding them, even at a distance, with the healing influence of My Eucharistic Face.

In those places where I am exposed upon the altar to receive the adoration, the reparation, and the companionship of My friends—and, first of all, of My priests—My radiance is powerful and strong. Faith, adoration, and love act as receptors; thus is My power drawn out and made effective, invisibly but really, in space and in time. It was the same with My sacred humanity during My life on earth: the faith and love of My friends drew out the virtue of My divinity, and an invisible radiance acted in souls and upon them, bringing healing, holiness, and many graces of conversion.

When I am adored in a place, My hidden action upon souls is wonderfully increased. The place where I am adored becomes a radiant centre from which love, life, and light are diffused in a world in the grip of hatred, darkness, and death.

Chapels of adoration are not mere refuges for the devout. They are the radiant, pulsating centres of an intense divine activity that goes beyond the walls of the place where I am adored to penetrate homes, and schools, and hospitals; to reach even those dark and cold places wherein souls are enslaved to Satan; to penetrate hearts, heal the infirm, and call home those who have wandered far from Me.

For these reasons, the work of perpetual adoration, or even of prolonged daily adoration, is intensely apostolic and supernaturally efficacious. Would that My bishops understood this! They would not hesitate to implement the request that came to them from Rome already three years ago.[1] But, alas, they put their trust in human schemes, in plans devised by the worldly-wise, and in programs drawn up along short-sighted human principles. And so they go, and they will continue to go from failure to failure, and from disillusionment to disillusionment.

---

[1] See Pope Benedict XVI, Post-Synodal Apostolic Exhortation *Sacramentum Caritatis* (February 22, 2007), §67; Congregation for the Clergy, *Letter for the Sanctification of the Clergy* (December 8, 2007). The latter document contains the injunction: "We are asking,

I have not set bishops over My flock to govern, to teach, and to sanctify out of their personal abilities and by making use of the wisdom of this passing world. I have set them as lights upon a lampstand to shine in every dark place,[1] and I have equipped them with supernatural gifts and divine power to accomplish that for which I chose them and set them over My Church. Woe to those bishops who trust in purely human solutions to the problems that beset My Church! They will be grievously disappointed, and many souls will fall away because they have neglected to take up the supernatural weapons I have prepared for them in this time of spiritual combat.[2]

My presence in the Blessed Sacrament preached, and confessed, and surrounded by adoration, love, and heartfelt reparation is the single greatest remedy for the evils that afflict My Church and for the sorrows that weigh so heavily upon My priests. My ways are not your ways,[3] nor do I act according to the principles of worldly success. I act in the silent, humble, hidden reality of My Eucharistic presence. Adore Me, and the radiance of My Eucharistic Face will begin to change the face of the earth,[4] even as it heals My priests, calls sinners home to My Heart, and enlivens the hearts of those grown weary and sad (like the disciples on the road to Emmaus[5]) with a spark of divine vitality and with the fire of My Eucharistic love.

I speak to you in this way not only for you, beloved friend of My Heart, but also for those who will receive these words, ponder them, and draw out of them the inspiration to love Me more generously, more fruitfully, and more joyfully. I speak to you for the sake of My priests. You will be astonished at the reception given to these words of Mine. Many souls of priests will be quickened and consoled by them. Many priests will be moved to spend time in the radiance of My Eucharistic

therefore, all diocesan Ordinaries who apprehend in a particular way the specificity and irreplaceability of the ordained ministry in the life of the Church, together with the urgency of a common action in support of the ministerial priesthood, to take an active role and promote—in the different portions of the People of God entrusted to them—true and proper cenacles in which clerics, religious and lay people, united among themselves in the spirit of true communion, may devote themselves to prayer, in the form of continuous Eucharistic adoration in a spirit of genuine and authentic reparation and purification."

[1] Matt 5:14–16; Mark 4:21; Luke 11:33–36; Rev 2:5, 4:5; 2 Pet 1:19; Ps 131(132):17.
[2] Eph 6:13–17; Rom 13:12–14; 2 Cor 6:4–10, 10:3–5; 1 Thess 5:8; Ps 149:6; Song 3:8; Luke 11:21–22, 22:36–38; Heb 4:12; Jer 50:25; Sir 46:1–3; Wis 5:18–22.
[3] Isa 55:8–9; Ezek 18:25–32.
[4] Ps 103(104):30.
[5] Luke 24:13–33.

Face, and to abide close to My pierced Heart. This is My desire for them. I want to draw all My priests into the radiance of My Face, and then into the sanctuary of My open Heart.

⊕

Saturday, February 19, 2011
After First Vespers of Septuagesima Sunday

It is not by privileges, special graces, or mystical experiences that souls are perfected in love; it is by a total adhesion to My will, and by a real death to all that is not My will. This life of yours will pass quickly. In the end, you will take comfort in one thing only: in the "Yes" that you will have said to My love for you, and in your adhesion to My will as it will have unfolded minute by minute, hour by hour, and day by day in your life.

Tell Me, then, that what I will, you will. Tell Me that all that is outside of My will for you is so much rubbish.[1] Ask Me to cleanse your life of the accumulated rubbish of so many years. Ask Me to make you clean of heart and poor in spirit.[2] Seek nothing apart from what My Heart desires you to have. Ask only for what My Heart desires to give you. Therein lies your peace. Therein lies your joy. Therein lies salvation and glory.

Your plans, your desires, and your anxieties are but puffs of smoke blown away by the wind. Only what I will endures. Only what I will gives you happiness. Seek then what I will, and trust Me to give you what you seek. Souls who chase after rainbows pass by the treasures that I have laid beneath their feet, leaving them behind to pursue a future that is not, and that will not come to be. This is an exhausting exercise for you and for so many souls like you, who, enchanted by an ideal, fail to see My work, and the splendour of My will for them, revealed in the present.

Live, then, in the present moment. Choose to be faithful to Me in the little things that I give you and ask of you from minute to minute, from hour to hour, and from day to day.[3] It is foolish to pin your hopes and to spend your energy on an imaginary good, when the real good that I offer you is here and now.

It is not forbidden you to dream dreams or to imagine a future that

---

[1] Phil 3:8; Deut 7:25–26.
[2] Matt 5:8, 5:3; Ps 50:12 (51:10); Prov 20:9.
[3] Luke 12:42–44, 16:10, 19:17; Matt 24:45–46, 25:20–23, Sir 19:1.

you think will make you happy—I give you your imagination and I am not offended when you use it. The imagined good becomes an evil, however, when it saps you of your energy; when it drains you of the vitality that I would have you offer Me in sacrifice by being faithful to the reality that is here and now; and when you use your imagination to flee from obedience and submission to Me in the circumstances and in the places where I have placed you at this time.

Plan for the future by living in the present. Open your heart to My voice each day, and cling to the smallest manifestations of My will. Renounce all that springs from your own desires and imaginings, and say "Yes" to all that springs from My most loving and merciful Heart. Therein lies your peace, your joy, and your salvation.

I speak to you every day. I am at work in you and all around you. You are My priest and I will use you to speak words of comfort, of light, and of life to My people. You are My priest, and in you I stand before My Father, pleading for sinners and glorifying His infinite mercy. Be just that: My mediating priest, and allow Me to use you as I see fit. By virtue of your priesthood—My priesthood engraved indelibly in your soul—you are in Me and I am in you, at every moment bringing God to men and men to God. At the altar this priestly mediation attains the highest degree, that of My death upon the Cross, that of My own priestly sacrifice on Calvary.

Is this not enough for you and for every priest of Mine? Woe to the priest who looks for works apart from this one work: the great work of love that is the Cross, and the Cross renewed at the altar in the Holy Sacrifice of the Mass.

Today it was I who inspired you to answer N., saying that you would have adoration from 5 to 7. I would like you to do this. It will be a time of special grace for you and of consolation for My Eucharistic Heart. Listen to the inspiration that I give you through your guardian angel, and you will prosper in all that you do.

March 13, 2011
First Sunday of Lent

Preach the love of My Father who is in heaven. Make His love known to all who will hear you preach during these holy days of Lent. How little known is My Father's love, how little known is the immense pity of His Heart for sinners. If souls but knew of My Father's love, they would run to throw themselves at His feet and He, being all love, would lift them up to be held fast in His embrace. Of those who profess to know My Father, too many fear Him and keep themselves at a distance from Him, while He, being all Father, yearns with a divine longing to have His children close to His Heart.

Preach My Father. Make known the tender pity of His Heart for all His children. Teach souls that His Majesty, though it is infinite and causes even the purest of angels to tremble in His sight, submits to the paternal movement of His Heart whenever there is a question of attaching a soul to Himself.[1] Speak of My Father's meekness and of the gentleness of His strength. Only those who do not know My Father fear Him and fail to entrust themselves to Him.

Abandon yourself to My Father, place yourself in His keeping, and teach other souls to do the same. The world so needs to hear the Gospel of My Father. It was to make Him known to men that I became man, and My joy is to see men won over to My Father because they have heard Me and believed in Me. He who sees Me sees the Father; the Father and I are one.[2]

Tuesday, March 15, 2011

Listen to Me, My friend, My brother, My adorer, and My priest. One who has not known the joys and the security in love of divine sonship cannot receive the grace of supernatural fatherhood. One learns to be a father by being a son and, even in the perfection of spiritual fatherhood, one remains a little child, a son beloved of My Father, full of confidence in His providence and ready, at every moment, to embrace His Will as it unfolds.

So many of My priests are retarded in the exercise of their spiritual paternity because they are wounded in their identity as sons. I am about to heal many of My beloved priests who bear, deep within their souls, the wounds of a sonship that did not unfold as I would have wanted it to unfold because of the sins of fathers, and this over many generations.

I desire to fill My Church with spiritual fathers by healing a great number of wounded sons among My priests. I desire the reconciliation of sons with their fathers, and of fathers with their sons.[3] Through this reconciliation the wounds inflicted on the souls of My priests will be healed, freeing them to enter fully into My love for the Father, into My obedience to the Father, into My glorification of the Father.

Those who will be healed in this way will become fathers of souls, participating in the tenderness and strength of the eternal Father and

---

[1] Hos 11:8–9; Jer 31:18–20; Isa 49:14–16; Benedict XVI, Encyclical Letter *Deus Caritas Est* (December 25, 2005), §10.

[2] John 14:9, 10:30.

[3] Mal 4:6; Luke 1:17; Sir 48:10.

sharing in the fatherhood that the Apostles recognized in Me whilst I lived on earth among them in the flesh. I revealed the Fatherhood of God to My Apostles and graced them with a new birth into My own divine Sonship. Thus were they rendered capable of a supernatural fatherhood that even today generates life in My Church.[1]

O My priests, I call you to Myself in the Sacrament of My love. There I will heal you of those childhood wounds that have impaired your response to My Father for too long. I will free you to enter into the grace and mystery of My own Sonship, and you will discover, each one for yourself, what it means to be "a son in the Son." This is My desire. This is My plan for you. Let Me heal your souls. Let Me restore you to the security and joy of divine sonship. Let Me call you to fatherhood in My Church and to a strong and tender care for souls.

Monday, March 21, 2011
Transitus of Our Holy Father Saint Benedict

Allow Me to guide you into the way of total filial dependence upon My Father in all things and for all things. This will be the expression of My filial life in you. I would have you look to the Father in every need, trust the Father in every adversity, depend upon the Father in every weakness. Thus will you glorify My Father, and thus will I glorify Him in you.[2]

My Father's goodness and love remain hidden from so many souls. They have not understood that I came into the world to reveal My Father who is all love, and to draw souls to Him in filial confidence and in the joy of abandonment to His goodness. Love our Father. Trust our Father. Depend upon our Father in every weakness.

This revelation of God as a Father who cherishes His children, and so loves them that He sent Me, His only-begotten Son, into the world to suffer and to die, lies at the very heart of My Gospel.[3] Love My Father and open your heart to the immensity of His love for you. Thus will you become for Him, in Me, a beloved son in whom He takes delight.[4]

Friday, April 29, 2011

My Heart is moved to pity for those whom you recommend to My merciful love. There is no limit to My merciful kindness. Souls that doubt

---

[1] Cor 4:15, 3:5–9; Phil 2:22; Philemon 1:10; 1 Thess 2:11; Eph 3:14–15.
[2] John 14:13–14.
[3] John 3:16; 1 John 4:9.
[4] Matt 3:17, 17:5; Mark 1:11, 9:7; Luke 3:22, 9:35; 2 Pet 1:17.

My mercy or fear Me as a severe judge is feared grieve My most loving Heart. What I want from souls is their confidence in Me and their trust in My merciful goodness. Accept My merciful love, accept it for those who refuse to accept it, for those who turn away from Me to go in search of false comforts and deceptive teachers.[1]

Too many priests have lost confidence in My mercy, and for this reason they are unable to inspire confidence in My mercy in the souls entrusted to them. One cannot speak convincingly of My divine mercy without having first experienced it.

I wait for My priests in the Sacrament of My love. Let them all approach Me to experience My mercy. Then will I make them channels and heralds of My mercy in a world that needs the divine mercy more than anything else.

Sunday, July 10, 2011
After First Vespers of Our Holy Father Saint Benedict

Long ago in My love for you and in My infinite wisdom, I established your soul in a special relationship with My servant Saint Benedict. I gave you to him as a son, and I gave him to you as a father. He has followed you faithfully, even during those times when you strayed from his teachings and turned away from his paternal care for you.

Now, you are a father sharing in Saint Benedict's fatherhood of souls. I want to unite you even more closely to him so that his virtues may flourish in you, and so that you will be able to communicate to your sons a portion of the spirit you have received from him.[2] I will give you a penetrating insight into the wisdom of the Holy Rule, not for you to draw glory from it, but so that you might change your life and go forward day by day in a deeper conformity to the spiritual heritage that I have bestowed upon you through Saint Benedict.

Saint Benedict had the grace of a profound union with Me in the adorable mysteries of My Body and Blood. He lived from the altar and for the altar. His adoration in My presence was filled with a profound reverence for My divine majesty and, for Saint Benedict, adoration was the school of humility, of victimhood, and of sacrifice.

Without adding anything fanciful to the sober traits of his existence, you must understand that his entire life was profoundly Eucharistic. He could not conceive of a day without partaking of the daily bread of the

---

[1] Matt 23:8; 1 Tim 1:6–7; 2 Tim 4:3–4; Gal 2:4; Heb 5:12; 2 Pet 2:1–3; 1 John 4:1; Rev 2:2.

[2] Num 11:25; 2 Kgs 2:9–15.

pure in heart that is My Body given for you. In the Sacrament of My divine charity he saw the pattern of the monastic way of life: a life dead to sin and hidden away from the world,[1] a life in union with My priesthood and with My Sacrifice, the very Sacrifice that I renew upon the altars of My Church through the ministry of My priests.

Catherine-Mectilde de Bar[2] was given an insight into the Eucharistic quality of Benedictine life, and she transmitted it in her writings so that others, and now you and the sons I have given you, might live from what she understood and so desired to share.

The monk is a victim immolated with Me for the glory of My Father and for the reconciliation and healing of sinners. You are a victim immolated for the praise of My Father's glory[3] and in reparation for the affronts to that glory perpetrated by priests, priests whom I chose and love even now. Offer yourself for them, for all of them. Take their place before Me. Let the light of My Eucharistic Face so penetrate your soul that I may use you to give light to priests who live in the outer darkness and in the company of the damned.

This is the darkness from which I saved you, and the intercession of Saint Benedict and a multitude of other saints obtained for you the grace of living in My light, in spite of the Evil One's attempts to win you for the darkness and drag you into the horrors of hell. By means of your adoration, thank Me, and respond to the merciful love of My Heart for you with all the love of your heart. Thus will I make your heart pure and capable of seeing Me one day face-to-face in light.[4]

Remain close to Me and I will unite you to My own adoration of the Father.

Remain close to Me and I will unite you to My priestly intercession for souls.

Remain close to Me and I will give you the peace that the world cannot give.[5]

---

[1] Rom 6:2–4, 6:10–11; Col 3:3.

[2] Catherine-Mectilde de Bar (December 31, 1614–April 6, 1698), a spiritual guide and writer of the stature of St. Gertrude the Great and St. Teresa of Avila, laid the foundations in 1653 of a branch of the Benedictine family dedicated to perpetual adoration of the Most Blessed Sacrament, in a spirit of reparation and ceaseless praise. Her profound spirituality, centered on the Holy Mass, the Divine Office, and Eucharistic devotion, anticipates by several centuries the teaching of Joseph Ratzinger/Benedict XVI. Mother Mectilde's fervent and illuminating writings deserve to be much better known.

[3] Eph 1:12–14.

[4] Matt 5:8; 1 Cor 13:12–13; Col 1:11–14.

[5] John 14:27, 16:33, 20:19–22; Rom 1:7, 5:1, 8:6, 14:17, 15:13; Eph 2:14–17; Phil 4:7; Col 1:20, 3:15; 2 Tim 3:1–5.

Remain close to Me, that I may hide Myself in you and hide you in My Sacred Heart.

Adore Me in My silence and I will make you silent.

Adore Me in My solitude and I will separate you from all save from Myself.

Monday, July 11, 2011
After Second Vespers of Our Holy Father Saint Benedict

Adore Me in My humility and I will make you humble.

Adore Me in My obedience and I will make you obedient.

Adore Me in My prayer to the Father and I will begin to pray My Father in you.

Adore Me in My merciful love for sinners and I will save sinners through you.

Adore Me in My weakness and in My poverty, and I will make you strong in My grace and rich in heavenly blessings.[1]

Adore Me, and I will live in you.

Adore Me, and at the hour of your death I will take you to myself and show you the beauty of My Face unveiled in glory.

Sunday, August 7, 2011

My Heart burns with love for you and for the brothers I have given you. Yes, they are also your sons, for I have entrusted them to your fatherly care, and I ask you to love them with a paternal tenderness. Do not be weak in loving them nor afraid to challenge them to conversion of life and to growth in holiness. I give to you and to them all the graces necessary to go forward and to bear fruit that will last for the sake of My beloved priests and for the holiness of My Bride the Church, even in the face of her enemies.

The role you play in the unfolding of My plan may seem insignificant and even worthless, and yet I tell you that nothing of what is said and done in this little monastery is without value in My eyes, for I have accepted your offering and that of those who will unite themselves to

---

[1] An echo of the Roman Canon: "Supplices te rogamus ... ut quotquot, ex hac altaris participatione sacrosanctum Filii tui Corpus et Sanguinem sumpserimus, omni benedictione caelesti et gratia repleamur" (Humbly we beseech Thee ... that as many of us as shall receive the most sacred Body and Blood of Thy Son by partaking thereof from this altar may be filled with every heavenly blessing and grace). Cf. 1 Cor 1:5; 2 Cor 8:9; Eph 1:7–8, 2:4–7, 3:8; Phil 4:19; Col 1:27; Jas 2:5; Rev 2:9, 3:18; Matt 8:20; Luke 9:58; Isa 52:13–53:12.

you for the regeneration of a priesthood marked by the beauty of holiness,[1] and by a true configuration to Me in the mystery of My self-offering to the Father.

N., too, is counted among you. He is, in every way, as much a part of this little monastery as are those of you who are here before Me now. His sufferings weigh heavily in the balance on the side of love, of reparation, of thanksgiving to the praise of My glory. I receive his self-offering together with yours, and it pleases Me that you pronounce his name at the altar while offering My Holy Sacrifice.

All of these things are part of My perfect plan for the purification and renewal of the priests of My Church. There will be an immense tide of grace invading the hearts of all My priests, and flowing in a mighty torrent from My Eucharistic Heart, especially in those places where My real presence is confessed and where I am adored and loved in the Sacrament of My love.

Be faithful, then, to the mission I have given you. To be faithful, you need only trust in Me and rely on the infinite resources of My grace.

Tuesday, August 9, 2011

My thoughts are not your thoughts nor are My ways your ways.[2] Yet a little while and you will see what I have prepared for you and your heart will rejoice.[3] Then you will see that all shall be well and you will go forward in peace, full of confidence in My providential love for you. There is no need to be frightened or to rush into situations that have only the appearance of solutions. Wait for Me to act.[4] Show Me that you trust in Me, and at the hour willed by My love for you, you will see My plan unfold.

Pray much to My Mother, the Queen of Ireland and the Lady of Knock, that you may be ready to enter into My plan when the time comes.

Monday, August 22, 2011

Nothing in your life is more important than the time you spend in adoration before My Eucharistic Face. Your energy and your capacity to do

---

[1] 1 Chron 16:29; 2 Chron 20:21; Ps 28(29):2; Ps 95(96):9. In the KJV, each of these verses uses the expression "beauty of holiness."

[2] Isa 55:8–9.

[3] John 14:2–3 and 16:16–22; 1 Cor 2:9.

[4] Ps 26(27):14; Ps 36(37):9; Prov 20:22; Isa 8:17, 30:18, 49:23, 64:4; Lam 3:24–26; Mic 7:7; Hab 2:3; Rom 8:25; Sir 2:3, 2:7, 36:16.

other things efficiently and in due order will grow in proportion to the time you consecrate to Me alone.

I yearn for the gift of your love in response to My love, and for your presence to My sacramental presence. How long must I beg you for your time, your love, and your companionship? I am here for you; be here for Me. Allow Me to fill you even as you empty yourself before Me. I am all yours; be all Mine. Prefer nothing whatsoever to My Eucharistic love.[1] Come before Me giving thanks.[2]

Tuesday, August 23, 2011

Adore Me always and in all places by a simple movement of your heart. Consider that wherever you are, I see you and know your heart's desire.[3] Desire to adore Me always, and know that I accept that desire of yours with great delight.

Come to Me as frequently as you can. Use every opportunity to come before Me in the Sacrament of My love. There is no need to calculate the length of time you give Me in the course of a day. If your heart is always in a state of adoration, you will find your way to My tabernacle frequently and you will abide in My presence willingly and gratefully.

Allow Me to lead you and instruct you in the life of adoration to which I have called you. The Holy Spirit will be your infallible guide and the teacher of your adoration.

Saturday, August 27, 2011

You have experienced how I answer you whenever you come to Me with your questions and difficulties. I am, at every moment, available to you and attentive to your prayers. Speak to Me freely of all the things that preoccupy you and weigh down upon your heart. Ask Me whatever questions you feel are necessary and seek My gentle guidance in all things.

If I delay in answering you, it is so that you will trust Me to reveal the answer you seek in the persons who surround you or communicate with you, in events, in circumstances, and in those barely perceptible signs of My providence by which I communicate My love to little souls.

Never refrain from conversation with Me. Every conversation includes both questions and answers. Speak to Me confidently and with-

---

[1] Cf. *The Holy Rule* of St. Benedict, chs. 4 and 72.

[2] Ps 94(95):2; Ps 99(100):4; Luke 17:16; Col 1:12, 3:17; Tob 2:14, 11:7.

[3] St. Benedict says this in *The Holy Rule* in chs. 4, 7, and 19.

out fear of being misunderstood or judged. I know your inmost thoughts, and the questions you bring to Me in the Sacrament of My love are clearly known to Me. Nonetheless, I desire to hold conversation with you because I have chosen you to be My friend and to abide in love, close to My Heart.

Thursday, September 1, 2011

If you remain close to Me, abiding in the light of My Eucharistic Face, and close to My Eucharistic Heart, I will not allow you to be deceived in the words you hear from Me, nor will I allow you to lead others astray. You have only to prefer My company to every other companionship, the love of My Heart to the love of every other heart, and the sound of My voice in the silence of your soul to every other voice.

I have called you to be for Me another John, and this vocation of yours remains My plan for you. You have only to abide close to Me, to seek Me before all else, and to put nothing whatsoever before My love for you and the love I have placed in your heart to love Me in return.[1]

Love Me in this way not only for yourself, but for all your brother priests whose hearts have grown indifferent and cold. Love Me for them. Take their place before My Eucharistic Face. Persevere in loving Me and in adoring Me for those poor priests of Mine who no longer love Me and who never adore Me. They are many, and the sorrow of My Heart over such priests is a sorrow that no human language can describe, for it is a divine sorrow; it is the grieving of a divine Heart. It is the pain of an infinite love rejected again and again by finite creatures who have become blind in a terrible darkness of the spirit.

Love Me, then, and console My Heart by adoring Me for them. When I see you before Me, I will see them, and in seeing them, I will be moved to show them pity, and many of those who are far from Me will return to My tabernacles[2]; and many of those who have spurned My divine friendship will, in the end, surrender to the embrace of My mercy. Do your part, and I will fulfil all that I have promised.

Monday, September 5, 2011

There is no need to force your prayer, as if it were something of your own doing. It is enough to remain with Me, content to be in My presence as I am content to be in yours.

---

[1] Cf. *The Holy Rule* of St. Benedict, chs. 4 and 72.
[2] Inter alia, Neh 1:9; Isa 19:22, 44:22; Jer 3:12–14, 24:7; Hos 2:7, 6:1.

Adore Me and trust Me to restore your energy, your health, and your joy in My service. Those who adore Me know that My presence renews the soul and the body. Experience this—as you already did today—and teach others to find in My presence the rest for which they long, the peace that the world cannot give, the joy that renews the heart, and the strength to follow Me in My sufferings, even along the way of the Cross.

To adore Me is to demonstrate that all your hope is in Me. To adore Me is to show Me that you count not on yourself nor on others, but on Me alone.[1] To adore Me is to give Me the freedom to act within you and upon you, in such a way as to unite you wholly to Myself, as you have asked Me to do: My Heart to your heart, My Soul to your soul, My Body to your body, My Blood to your blood.

The work of adoration is little understood, even by those who claim to be My adorers. There is no need to fill up the time of adoration with thoughts and words, as if it all depended on your doing something. It is sufficient to speak to Me as the Holy Spirit gives you to speak, to listen to Me with the ear of your heart,[2] and to abide in the light of My Face for those who languish in the darkness of sin and in the refusal of My love, My truth, and My life.

There is no work more precious than this work. In My presence, you are ministering to souls in every time and place. In My presence, I am using you to accomplish all that My Heart desires to communicate to souls, and, first of all, to My priests. I have not called you to build or to organize, nor have I called you to speak much, nor have I called you to appear much in the sight of men. I have called you to a life as hidden as is My life in the Sacrament of My love.

Consent to be hidden. Let Me hide you as you hide Me in the tabernacle. My Heart is your tabernacle, and you are My host.

This I ask you to share with the brothers, for until now you have kept the light I have given you under a bushel basket; you have not allowed the flame of this vocation to give light to all in the house.[3] It is time for you to speak clearly, trusting in My faithfulness and in My power to heal old wounds, to change hearts, and to draw souls to Myself in love.

I am using you to help the Sisters and to engender in them the life I will for them. You are the friend of the Bridegroom, My friend, and I am the Bridegroom, the Lamb to whom they will vow their lives.[4] You will

---

[1] Jer 17:5; Ps 39:5 (40:4); Ps 59:13 (60:11); Ps 145:2 (146:3); 2 Chron 14:11; Judith 9:7; Prov 3:5; Isa 31:1.

[2] Cf. St. Benedict, *The Holy Rule,* Prologue.

[3] Matt 5:15–16; Mark 4:21; Luke 11:33–36.

[4] John 3:29–30; Matt 9:15, 25:1–13; Mark 2:19–20; Luke 5:34–35; Rev 19:7, 21:9.

disappear and they will remain. You will speak to them on My behalf, and then I will hide you in the secret of My Face. I will give you words, and then I will give you silence in My presence.

Tuesday, September 6, 2011

You are still too fearful in your prayer, too attached to yourself, to your own ideas and words. Perfect love casts our fear.[1] Be little and poor in My presence, and abandon yourself to My transforming love, to the love that radiates from My Eucharistic presence.

Wednesday, September 7, 2011

When you intercede for another, do so with a boundless confidence in My love for that soul. At the same time, relinquish every desire to see the outcome of your intercession as you would imagine or desire it to be. Allow Me to receive your prayer and to respond to it in ways corresponding to My infinite wisdom, to My love, and to My perfect will for the person you bring before My Eucharistic Face.

Do not come to Me with solutions; come to Me only with your problems, and allow Me to provide the solutions. I have no need of your solutions, but when you bring Me problems, sufferings, questions, and needs, I am glorified by your confidence in My merciful love.[2]

Bring Me your questions, your problems, and your fears, and I will attend to them; for Me darkness itself is not dark and night shines as the day.[3] There is no situation and no suffering so heavy that I cannot make it light to bear, and even, if such be My will, remove it altogether from those who are crushed beneath its weight.[4]

Pray to Me with confidence and with abandonment, and not with a secret desire to force My hand and to obtain from Me only what you have in view.

Ask and you shall receive.[5] Only ask with a trusting faith, believing that whatever I will give is best for you and most glorious for Me and for My Father. Seek and you shall find. Yes, seek, but allow Me to guide you

---

[1] 1 John 4:18.

[2] John 14:13–14, 17:10; 2 Thess 1:10–12; 2 Macc 3:30.

[3] Ps 138(139):12.

[4] Num 11:14–17; Ps 54:23 (55:22); Ps 80:7 (81:6); Isa 9:4; Matt 11:30; 1 Cor 10:13; 2 Cor 4:16–17; 1 John 5:3–5.

[5] Matt 7:7, 21:22; Luke 11:9; John 16:24; 1 John 3:21–22; Ps 12:6 (13:5); Ps 36(37):3–5; Prov 3:5–8.

to the object of your seeking. Seek My Face, and all the rest will be given you besides.[1]

There are souls so attached to what they think I should give them in answer to their prayers, that when I give them what is best for them, and most glorious for Me and for My Father, they fail to see it. This is because they do not intercede or ask in the Holy Spirit. Instead, they pray out of the obscurity, blindness, and narrowness of their own perceptions, limiting what I can do for them, and using their prayer as an attempt to control My loving omnipotence.

When you ask, do so with a complete abandonment to My wisdom, My love, and My perfect will. Pray in this way, and you will begin to see wonders surpassing all that you can imagine.

How unfortunate are those who come to Me proposing their own solutions, when all they need to do is to bring Me their problems, their needs, and their requests. When you intercede for one who is ailing, it is enough for you to say to Me: "Lord, the one whom Thou lovest is sick."[2] Leave all the rest to My most loving Heart. If you ask for a cure or healing, do so with such confidence in My love that your faith is ready to embrace My response to your prayer in whatever form it takes.

If I am teaching you how to intercede before My Eucharistic Face, and how to present souls to My Eucharistic Heart, it is because I want you to intercede much, to ask boldly, and to obtain great things from My omnipotent love. If you are praying well, that is, praying as I teach you how to pray, then act boldly and confidently,[3] for I am with you and I will not forsake you, and My blessing will rest upon all that you do with a pure heart for My glory and the glory of My Father.

Thursday, September 15, 2011
The Seven Sorrows of the Blessed Virgin Mary

Yes, my beloved little son, the eighth sorrow of my maternal and Immaculate Heart is that my Son is so offended in the Sacrament of His love. This sorrow of mine will endure until the end of time, when the real presence of my Son in the Most Holy Sacrament will give way to the sight of His divine majesty. Then will faith give way to vision, and hope

---

[1] Matt 7:7–11; Luke 11:9–13; Acts 17:26–28; Deut 4:29; Jer 29:13–14; Wis 6:12–16; Sir 32:14.

[2] John 11:3.

[3] Ps 26(27):14; Ps 30:25 (31:24); Deut 31:6; 1 Chron 19:13, 22:13, 28:20; 2 Chron 32:7; 1 Macc 2:64; 1 Cor 16:13.

to possession. Then will love be secure and everlasting for all who will have died in the embrace of His divine friendship.

Until then, know that my maternal Heart suffers and grieves over the irreverence, the coldness, and the ingratitude of so many souls towards the Sacrament of my Son's undying love. It is in this Sacrament that He loves His own, loving them to the end[1]—to the end of every created possibility and to the end of this passing world. His Eucharistic love surpasses all the laws of perishable nature: there is no greater miracle on the face of the earth than the real presence of my Son in the Sacrament of the Altar. Even so, He is forsaken, neglected, and handed over to sinners to be betrayed, again and again—and this by His chosen ones, His beloved priests, the men whom He chose to be the consolation and joy of His Heart. This is my own Heart's eighth sorrow: the betrayal and neglect of my Son in the Most Holy Eucharist.

How is He betrayed? His priests, my own sons, betray Him when they fail to make Him known, when by not teaching the mystery of His real presence they leave souls in the darkness of ignorance, without fire or light.[2] They betray my Son when, by their example, they discourage reverence, and adoration, and a loving attention to His presence. They betray Him when they offer the Holy Sacrifice of the Mass unworthily, and when they hand Him over to sinners who have no intention of giving Him their hearts and seeking His mercy and His pardon for their sins. They betray Him when they leave Him alone in locked churches and when they make it difficult or impossible for souls to approach His tabernacles and rest in the radiance of His Eucharistic Face. They betray Him when they allow His churches to become places of noise and worldly chatter, and when they do nothing to recall souls to the living mystery of His love, that is, His presence in the tabernacle.[3]

Shall I tell you more of this eighth sorrow of my Heart? It is when you are lacking in generosity, when you fail to respond to love with love, when you are not generous in being present to Him who is present in the Most Holy Eucharist for love of you. I speak here not only to you, but to all my priest sons and to all consecrated souls who live with my Son under the same roof, and yet treat Him coldly, or casually, or with a distant formality.

---

[1] John 13:1; Luke 22:15.

[2] Matt 6:23; Luke 1:78–79, 11:34–36; John 12:35, 12:46; Acts 26:16–18; 2 Cor 4:6; Eph 4:18, 5:8–11; 2 Tim 4:1–5; Tit 2:15; 1 Pet 1:14–16; 1 John 1:6; Wis 14:22.

[3] Isa 56:7; Jer 11:15, 23:11; Ezek 23:39, 44:7; Matt 21:12–13; Mark 11:15–17; Luke 19:45–46.

This, too, is the eighth sorrow of my Heart: that the Holy Sacrifice of the Mass is celebrated quickly, with little reverence, with no thanksgiving, and with all the attention given, not to my Son, the Lamb, but, rather, to the human presence of His minister, who, by calling attention to himself, takes from God what belongs rightly to God alone: the loving attention of every heart during the Holy Mysteries.[1]

What more shall I tell you? Do you not grieve with me over this eighth sorrow of my Heart, made up of many sorrows repeated again, and again, and again? Grieve with me today, and console my maternal and Immaculate Heart by adoring my Son, the blessed fruit of my womb, and by giving Him all that you are in an immolation of love.

Friday, September 16, 2011

You, adore Me, and all the rest will be given to you besides.[2] Seek My Face and abide close to My Heart. This is your life's work: not to write much, nor to be published, nor to speak much in the sight of men, nor to appear much among the rich and powerful, but to choose silence, to embrace all that is lowly, to enter into My hiddenness, and into My Eucharistic humility.

There, it will remain for you to love Me: to love Me for those who do not love Me, especially My poor priests blinded by the attractions of the world and the deceits of the Evil One; and to adore Me, in reparation for those who have set up false gods; and to hope in Me alone, in reparation for those who trust in their own strength.

Yours it is to praise Me for those who never praise Me, and to thank Me for those who never thank Me. Yours it is to keep a vigil of faith before the Sacrament of My love, until the veils fall, and I call you to see Me face-to-face eternally.

Live now in this world as one completely dead to it.[3] Remain untouched by its interests and unspotted by its corruption.[4] Hide yourself in Me until the tempest passes by,[5] for in Me alone is your peace,[6] and to be near Me is your only happiness in this vale of tears and strife.[7]

---

[1] 1 Chron 16:24–29; Ps 122(123):2; Eccles 5:1; Mal 1:6–7; 2 Macc 9:12; Matt 22:21; Mark 12:17; Luke 20:25; Rom 12:1–3; 1 Thess 1:9–10; Heb 5:1, 12:28–29; Jas 4:5–10.

[2] Matt 6:33.

[3] Rom 6; Col 3:3; John 17:14; 2 Cor 10:3; Gal 2:20, 5:24, 6:14.

[4] 1 John 2:15–17; Eph 1:4; Col 1:22; 2 Cor 7:2–3; Jas 1:27; 2 Pet 1:3–4, 3:14.

[5] Ps 30:21 (31:20); Ps 56:2 (57:1); Isa 26:20.

[6] Ps 4:9–10 (4:8–9); Ps 84:9 (85:8); Isa 57:19; Bar 3:13; Ezek 37:26–28; Luke 2:29, 19:42; John 16:33.

[7] Ps 64:5 (65:4); Ps 72(73):28; Deut 30:20; Phil 1:21–23.

Trust in Me and continue to adore Me. Remain in My company and I will work things beyond your imagining. Follow the indications of My providence as you perceive them, and trust more in Me and in My love for you than in yourself.

Tuesday, September 20, 2011

Observe Me in the Sacrament of My love. The Sacred Host that you see is silent, still, humble, poor, and hidden. Imitate Me in the Sacrament of My love. Become silent, still, humble, poor, and hidden. Hide yourself in Me as I am hidden in the tabernacle, and as I am hidden beneath the appearance of the Sacred Host.

Outside of Me there is nothing for you, and with Me, in My presence, is all that your heart desires.[1] Do not look outside of Me for anything to fulfil your heart's desires. Instead, hide yourself in Me, as I hide myself for love of you in the Most Holy Sacrament of the Altar.

How I love hidden souls! In them I see a reflection of My Mother's hiddenness, and of the hiddenness of Saint Joseph, My foster father on earth.

Hiddenness is the virtue of those who adore Me hidden in the Sacrament of My love. I am a hidden God,[2] but I reveal myself face-to-face to those who hide themselves in Me.

Withdraw more and more from the sight of men. Seek to go unnoticed. Hide yourself in Me and with Me in the bosom of My Father. Rest in Me, and be content to abide where you are not seen, or known, or praised. Do the work that I entrust to you, and then be content to disappear, once you have led souls to the contemplation of My Eucharistic Face and to the love of My Eucharistic Heart.

The grace of hiddenness and silence is not given to all, but it is the grace by which I mark souls destined to a Eucharistic life, to a life of adoration in which they grow in resemblance to Me, hidden in the Sacrament of My love. This does not happen all at once, but it will happen to all who give their consent to the work of My love in their souls, and who are faithful to the adoration of My hidden Face, My Eucharistic Face. This hiddenness cannot be imposed from without, nor can it be taught as one would teach a skill. It is My gift, and the realization of My likeness in the souls I have called to a life of Eucharistic adoration.

---

[1] Deut 4:39; 1 Sam 2:2; Isa 45:18–22; Mark 12:32; Acts 4:12; Bar 3:36 (3:35); Ps 33:11 (34:10).

[2] Isa 45:15; Ex 20:21; Deut 5:22; 1 Kgs 8:12; Ps 17:10–12 (Ps 18:9–11); Ps 96(97):2; Sir 45:5.

See how hidden I am in the Gospels. Even when I reveal myself, I remain hidden. Only the Father knows Me, and those to whom the Father gives the knowledge of My hiddenness.[1]

Thursday, September 22, 2011

I am a hidden God,[2] and those whom I call to adore Me must hide themselves in Me, becoming hidden from the eyes of the world, and hidden even from themselves,[3] having a pure gaze fixed upon Me alone, even as My pure filial gaze is fixed upon My Father in heaven. Learn what it means to be hidden: it is to be free of preoccupations with yourself, with the opinions of others, and with what the world may say of you or of Me.[4] It is to live for Me alone, even as I live for the Father.

Hide yourself in Me as I am hidden in the glory of My Father. Hide yourself in Me as I am hidden in the bright cloud of the Holy Spirit.[5] Hide yourself in Me as I am hidden in the sacred species. Hide yourself in My Heart as I am hidden in the tabernacles of the world, unseen, unknown, and forgotten by men.

I call you to this hidden life because I am the hidden God and because My Eucharistic life in your midst is a hidden life. Those who would be My adorers must consent to live in My tabernacle, hidden with Me and, at the same time, loving as I love: loving the Father as I love Him, loving souls as I love them, suffering coldness, rejection, misunderstanding and abandonment with Me and for Me.

Understand these things and you will have begun to understand the Eucharistic life to which I call you more and more. Apart from those souls whom I call to this life of adoration, such a hiddenness will appear foolish and inhuman, but it will act as a leaven upon the whole mass of dough until it rises and becomes a perfect loaf fit for My oblation.[6] It is a spark of light being kept burning for a world plunged into darkness. It is a drop of divine sweetness in a sea of bitterness and misery.[7] It is a presence of love in a world from which love is absent.

---

[1] Matt 11:27; Luke 10:22–23; John 6:44–46, 17:1–8.

[2] Isa 45:15; Ex 20:21; Deut 5:22; 1 Kgs 8:12; Ps 17:10–12 (Ps 18:9–11); Ps 96(97):2; Sir 45:5.

[3] 1 Cor 2:2, 4:3–4; Col 3:3.

[4] Ex 23:2; Ps 111(112):6–7; Prov 14:7; Eccles 9:17, 10:12–14; Sir 9:15; Mark 4:19; John 14:31; Rom 14:1; Gal 6:14–17; 1 John 4:5.

[5] Matt 17:5; Luke 9:34–35; Acts 1:9; Ex 16:10, 24:15–18, 33:9–10; Job 37:15; Ezek 1:28, 10:4; Sir 24:4.

[6] Matt 13:33; Luke 13:21.

[7] Cf. the intention for the third day of the Divine Mercy novena: "Today bring to Me all devout and faithful souls and immerse them in the ocean of My mercy. These souls

Love My hiddenness and hide yourself in Me. Withdraw from all that solicits your attention, your energy, and your time into the secret of My Eucharistic Face. There I will show you how best to do the things I ask you to do. There I will give you a peace that no one will perturb or take from you.[1] There I will use you for the sanctification of My priests and for the consolation of My Church.

Do you want this?

Yes, Lord Jesus, because Thou askest this of me. I consent to it with all my heart and I want all that Thou willest for me.

Do you accept to be separated from those whom you love, from those who know you and from those who love you, in order to lose all, save Me and My love?

Yes, Lord Jesus, I consent to lose all save Thee, for in possessing Thee, I will lose nothing, and in loving Thee I will be loved by Thee, and in that love find perfect happiness and the grace to love others as Thou hast loved me.

Do you accept to disappear from the eyes of the world and to live hidden in Me as I am hidden in My tabernacles?

Yes, Lord Jesus, I accept the hidden Eucharistic life to which Thou callest me, and I desire nothing else.

Know, then, that today I accept your "Yes" to My plans for you. Because you have given your consent to Me, I give My consent to you. Live henceforth as My adorer hidden in Me, hidden with Me. Seek no other way of life. Your life is henceforth hidden with Me in the Sacrament of My love and in the glory of the Father.[2] I promise you joy in the secret of My Face and an unending sweetness that is the taste of the Hidden Manna, a sweetness not of this world, but of the next, a sweetness that I give as a foretaste of heaven to those who drink the bitter chalice of My Eucharistic solitudes on earth.[3/4]

---

brought Me consolation on the Way of the Cross. They were that drop of consolation in the midst of an ocean of bitterness."

[1] John 14:27, 16:22; Isa 26:3, 32:17, 54:10; Ezek 37:26.

[2] Col 3:3–4; Rom 5:2; Mark 16:19; 1 Tim 3:16.

[3] There are as many solitudes as there are forsaken tabernacles on earth.—*Author.*

[4] Rev 2:17; Ex 16:31; Deut 8:3; Neh 9:20; Ps 77(78):24; John 6:31–33, 57–59; Ps 30:20 (31:19); Wis 16:20; Matt 20:22–23, 26:39, 27:34; Mark 10:38–39, 14:36, 15:23; Luke 22:42; John 18:11; Ps 59:5 (60:3); Isa 5:2, 63:2–3; Jer 23:9.

This is the perfection of the life to which I have called you. The time is short. Enter into the life I have prepared for you. Let go of all else. Our life is one: your life in Me, and My life in you, in a mystery of hiddenness that glorifies My Father and builds up My Church.

September 23, 2011
Ember Friday
Saint Pio of Pietrelcina

My way is one of gentleness, of mercy, and of compassion. I offer My Cross to souls, but I never impose it, and when a soul begins to say "Yes" to the sweet and terrible exigencies of My love, I fit My Cross to her shoulders, and then help her to carry it step by step, increasing its weight only as that soul grows in love and in the fortitude that comes from the Holy Spirit.

Conversions that are sudden and excessive are not My habitual way of leading souls in the way of holiness. I prefer to see souls advance by little steps along a way of spiritual childhood,[1] trusting in Me to bring them to Calvary and to the fullness of joy in My presence and in the presence of My Father.[2]

This way is no less demanding than the high road along which, by reasons known to Me alone, I lead certain other souls. The little way, marked by little steps, is, nonetheless, the way I prefer, because it perfects souls quickly in the image of My own littleness, My poverty, and My abandonment to the Father's will.[3]

Teach this little way to souls and many will benefit from your teaching. But first of all, practice it yourself by obeying My inspirations in little things, and by doing all things out of love for Me, who desire to perfect you in one thing only: love. This little way suits best those whom I call to be My adorers and the consolers of My Eucharistic Heart. It leads a soul in the path of My Eucharistic virtues, those that you see when you gaze upon My Eucharistic Face: hiddenness, littleness, stillness, silence, poverty, peace, constancy, and a radiant love that rejoices the hearts of those who come into the circle of its influence.

This is what I desire for My priests, not a holiness that is excessive in

---

[1] Ps 130(131); Wis 12:2; Prov 13:11; Matt 18:3–4; Mark 10:15–16; Luke 18:17.

[2] Ps 15(16):11; Ps 20:7 (21:6); John 15:11, 17:13.

[3] Phil 2:5–8. As St. Thomas Aquinas says in the Prologue to the *Compendium theologiae*: "To restore man, who had been laid low by sin, to the heights of divine glory, the Word of the eternal Father, though containing all things within His immensity, willed to become small. This He did, not by putting aside His greatness, but by taking to Himself our littleness."

its demands and harsh in its exigencies, but one that is entirely childlike, peaceful, and humble. This is the imitation of My Eucharistic life, and it is this that I want for you and from you.

Here I speak to you, My beloved priest and the friend of My Heart. Enter into the imitation of what you see when you contemplate My Eucharistic Face: silence, hiddenness, peace, stillness, poverty, and a love that is radiant, but without great flashes that would blind the soul. You, begin to practice all these things and I will perfect them in you until you become as I am in the Sacrament of My love, a radiant Host hidden in the tabernacle to save souls and to glorify My Father here on earth until the end of time.

The words I give you are for your instruction, for your consolation, and for the conversion of your heart in love, but they are not for you alone. Others will read them and they too will be moved to repentance. They will be comforted, and begin to seek My Face and draw near to My Heart in the Sacrament of My love.

September 25, 2011
Fifteenth Sunday after Pentecost

The answer for you lies in the writings of My servant Mectilde, to whom I have entrusted your future in a special way. Until now the time was not right nor were you ready to receive her teaching and enter into the hidden life of adoration and reparation to which I have always destined you. Now you will be able to go forward, enlightened and strengthened by a great company of heavenly friends, who see the unfolding of My plan for you and who marvel at My mercy, My wisdom, and My loving providence.

Have no fear, and let all your questions cease, for now I will show you clearly the life to which I am calling you and those whom I will send to you. It is not the life you planned for yourself, nor is it the fruit of your reflections or the realization of your dreams. It is, rather, the fruit of My tender love for you, the manifestation of My unfailing providence, and the realization of My perfect will for your life.

You will adore Me with a great love and, in adoring Me with a great love, you will make reparation for your own sins and for the sins of all your brother priests, who, like you, fell for a moment, and still fall in the darkness of sin, far from My Eucharistic Face and far from the fire of love that ever burns for them in My Eucharistic Heart. This is your vocation and it is, in essence, simple and pure. It is to remain in love and in adoration before My Face, making reparation to Me in the Sacrament of My love.

I could have called you to any number of other works and to the realization of other projects for My glory and the good of souls, but this is the work that My Heart prefers for you above all others. This is the hidden life of adoration in love and of reparation that I ask of you. This is the life to which I call you. This is the life, which I am about to make possible for you in a way corresponding to My power, to My providence, and to My tender love for you and for My priests.

There is no need to fear or to be anxious over the details, for I have placed all of this in the hand of My most pure Mother, and she is about to show you the delicacy and attention of her maternal Heart. It was she who asked this work of Me and who obtained it for you. It is her doing, and she will provide for you out of the infinite resources that are hers by the will of My Father and by the operation of the Holy Ghost, her divine Spouse. All who see this work will recognize her hand in it, and they will be compelled to acknowledge that My Mother has acted out of her love for Me and out of her love for you and for all her priest sons.

You will adore and make reparation, and this in the school of My spouse and handmaid Mectilde de Bar, and, like her, you will give rise to a school of adoration and reparation in My Church, one for which My Heart has longed and for which I have waited until now. There is no need to concern yourself with the working out of details that, in any case, are beyond what you can accomplish.

I ask only that you immerse yourself in the writings of Mother Mectilde. I will fill them with a special penetrating sweetness, and they will delight and pierce your soul. And then I will ask you to adore Me faithfully and to make My real sacramental presence the centre of your life, your one treasure here below, the pearl for which you must sell all else,[1] and the foretaste of the glory I have already prepared for you in heaven.

Until now, you have not been ready to enter into the vocation that is yours. But now, the hour of its fulfilment is close at hand. Enter into the cenacle where I wait for you, and abide there in adoration, resting upon My Heart and gazing upon My Eucharistic Face. This will be your reparation, and, through it, great numbers of priests will find their way back to My tabernacles, and they too will begin to persevere in prayer with My Mother,[2] adoring My Eucharistic Face, and tasting of the merciful sweetness of My Heart's love for them.

Accept these things as I speak them to you, and give Me your "Yes," your consent to all that My Heart holds in store for you. Say with My

---

[1] Matt 13:44–46, 19:21; Luke 12:21; Col 2:3; Deut 33:18–19; Sir 6:14–16.
[2] Acts 1:14; Matt 2:11; John 2:1, 19:27.

Immaculate Mother, "Be it done unto Me according to Thy word,"[1] and it shall be done just so.

Be it done unto me according to Thy word. Lord Jesus, I accept Thy plan. I give my free and full consent to Thy will. I am willing to forsake all else and leave all else behind. I am Thy servant and, by Thy infinite mercy, the friend of Thy Heart. Amen.

Monday, September 26, 2011
Saints Cosmas and Damian, Physicians and Martyrs

The Mectildian charism[2] will become for Benedictine life what the Teresian charism was for the reform of Carmel. Until now, the work of My handmaid and victim-spouse Mectilde has remained incomplete, for it calls for a sacerdotal complement in monasteries of men devoted exclusively to adoration and reparation to Me, who live and wait for the return of all My priests to the Sacrament of My love.

Behold, the hour has come for the fulfilment of this desire of My Heart, and for the realization of that part of what I gave to Mother Mectilde that, until now, has remained hidden like a grain of wheat buried in the earth.[3] You are the tender shoot breaking through a rocky soil, and beginning to stretch upward toward the light of My Eucharistic Face. This little shoot is My Mother's work and it will be the object of all her solicitude and maternal attention.

Plunge yourself into the writings of My servant Mectilde. I will speak to you through them and I will show you that the charism given to her is about to flower again for the joy of My Church and for the good of a great number of souls, especially those of My priests.

Begin with what you have at hand, and the rest will be provided for you. The essential thing is to receive with an open heart and to ponder in My presence the mission that I gave to Mother Mectilde, and that I am about to renew in your soul for the good of many.

I have prepared you for this work and called you to carry it out. Go forward humbly, but confidently and boldly. Say only what needs to be said, but live the fullness of this vocation with a manly generosity and vigour. I will give you health and strength, even in your weakness, and you will be able to bring to fruition this mission that, long ago, I reserved

---

[1] Luke 1:38.
[2] See p. 176, note 2.
[3] John 12:24; 1 Cor 15:37–38.

for you. You are not alone in being called to this life; others will come, for I have prepared them and placed within their hearts the same vision and the same desire, but you will be their father, and you will be their shepherd, leading them to the green pastures that I will show you.

Banish every doubt and hesitation. There is no time for uncertainty and fear. The hour has come. Go forward, trusting in My love for you and in the nearness of My Immaculate Mother, who will attend to every detail of this work for the glory of My Father and for the joy of My Bride, the Church.

Understand that the Mectildian charism is, at once, priestly and victimal. As such, it contains within itself the seeds of a great revival of holiness among My priests, and the renewal in My Church of the work of reparation for priests and by priests at the very core of their existence: My Most Holy Sacrament of the Altar. Until priests return to My tabernacles in adoration, weeping for their own sins and for the sins of the people, loving Me and offering Me their broken hearts, the entire Church will continue to languish.

Do you see now why this work has been kept hidden in My providence until now? Be Mectildian and Benedictine: that is, be adorers and victims, offered at every hour to Me in the Sacrament of My love.

Wednesday, September 28, 2011

My Heart's desire is to see you settled safely in a permanent home where, free from the uncertainties and struggles of a situation that, even in this life, is provisional, you may at last devote yourself, unfettered and free from fears, to the One Thing to which I have called you. There are powers of darkness working against the fulfilment of My plan, but I will prevail, and I will establish you in the place I have prepared for you—and this will be a triumph of My merciful love in the hearts of many.

The time is very close for your departure; indeed, this very day you will better understand what you must do. Go forward manfully,[1] trusting in Me and unaffected by the shadows that appear to be threatening My work.

I give you Saint Vincent[2] to prepare the way. I give you Saint Thérèse to move the hearts and wills of those who, by their word, will open the

---

[1] Ps 26(27):14; Ps 30:25 (31:24); Deut 31:6; 1 Chron 19:13, 22:13, 28:20; 2 Chron 32:7; 1 Macc 2:64; 1 Cor 16:13.

[2] Saint Vincent de Paul, who helped Mother Mectilde de Bar when she and her daughters were homeless after fleeing the war in Lorraine.

way before you. I give you Mother Mectilde and Abbot Marmion to instruct you in the life of hiddenness and of praise to which I call you for the sake of My priests and of My Church. I give you My angels to keep a guard about you and to preserve you from the plots and intrigues of the unseen Enemy of your soul and of the souls of all priests. I give you Mother Yvonne-Aimée as a close friend and intimate companion. She will remind you of her little invocation[1] and spur you on to act with a manly courage in all My interests.

And I give you My own most pure Mother, the Immaculate Queen of Ireland, who appeared at Knock, and who weeps and intercedes for her children in Ireland, but most of all for her priest sons, who have lost their way in a land of mists and of spiritual dangers at every turn. She is the Mother of the Lamb and of the Shepherd. She will guide all those priest sons of hers who turn to her in humble prayer—especially in the prayer of the Rosary, so pleasing to her Heart—and she will guide My priests into the green pastures I have prepared for them, where they shall rest in safety and drink deeply of the waters of peace.[2]

Now have I pulled back the veil on what I intend to do for you. Be courageous, and let not the small setbacks that are inevitable in any work undertaken for My glory discourage you or cause you to call everything into question. I am with you. Do not fear.

Saturday, October 1, 2011
Saint Thérèse of the Child Jesus and of the Holy Face

St. Thérèse spoke to me thus:

This calling that you have received, my little brother, it is love: it is love in the heart of the Church[3]; it is the love that adores, the love that makes reparation, the love that keeps company with Love in the Sacrament of love.

Do not become discouraged. Be manful. Be confident, and go forward. The Lord is with you as a mighty warrior who takes up your cause,[4] and I, for my part, shall accompany you from here even to the

---

[1] "O Jesus, King of Love, I put my trust in Thy merciful goodness." See p. 11, note 1.

[2] Ps 22(23); Song 2:16, 6:3; Joel 2:21–23.

[3] Cf. St. Thérèse of Lisieux, *Story of a Soul*, 3rd ed., trans. John Clarke, O.C.D. (Washington, DC: ICS Publications, 1996), 194: "O Jesus, my Love . . . my *vocation*, at last I have found it . . . MY VOCATION IS LOVE! Yes, I have found my place in the Church and it is You, O my God, who have given me this place; in the heart of the Church, my Mother, I shall be *Love*. Thus I shall be everything, and thus my dream will be realized."

[4] Ex 15:3; Isa 42:13; Jer 20:11; Deut 4:34; Sir 46:5–6.

house that the Lord has reserved for you and that I myself am making ready for you and for your sons, so that, in this land of Ireland, where still today I am much loved, this work of love, and of reparation to Love in the heart of the Church, will come to flower.

I know you, and I have been following you for a long time, for many years. We will continue our friendship now, but it shall be clearer and more evident. We are going to work together for the souls of priests, and, together, we will give priests the taste of Love, so that they might burn with love and spread the fire of love around them and in all the Church.[1]

Yes, it is great, this work of love for priests, but your part shall be to adore for those who do not adore, and to represent your brothers, especially the weaker among them, and those who have fallen from their priestly dignity, before the Eucharistic and so merciful and compassionate Face of Jesus, who waits for the return of all those whom He has chosen to share in the glory of His priesthood.

Be faithful, and be courageous. You have nothing to fear. Go forward and believe in Love, for you are greatly loved and nothing will be able to wrest you from Love, which possesses you and has marked you with His seal.[2]

Wednesday, October 5, 2011
Saint Faustina and Blessed Bartolo Longo

Go forward with confidence in Me and with trust in My Heart's undying love for you. You are precious in My sight, because I have set My Heart upon you and I have rescued you from the snares that were set for the ruin of your life in this world and in the next. I have kept you from falling into the deep pit that was dug for you by the enemies of your soul, by those who hate Me, and abhor My priesthood, My Church, and My Blood. This was obtained for you by My Mother and by the multitude of saints in heaven who have followed you through your life, and have interceded for you with Me and with My Father, with a most tender and solicitous friendship.

You are not alone in this great undertaking. Remain little and hide yourself in My tabernacle, that is, in My open side. There I will purify you in the fire of My love, and prepare you for the work for which I have destined you.

---

[1] Luke 12:35, 12:49, 24:32; John 5:35; Isa 62:1; Jer 20:9; Sir 48:1.
[2] Song 8:6; Ps 134(135):4; Rom 8:35–39.

Thursday, October 6, 2011
Saint Bruno

No soul need ever be afraid of meeting My gaze, for in My eyes there is naught but mercy and love.

Those who turn away from My gaze, those who fear the encounter with Me face-to-face, are those who fall away from My love.

I call you to a life of adoration so that you might contemplate My Face and read thereon all the love of My Sacred Heart for poor sinners, and especially for My priests. Whenever a soul seeks My gaze, My Heart is moved to show that soul an immense pity, to lift her out of the sin into which she has fallen, to bind up her wounds,[1] and restore her to the joys of friendship with My Heart.

When a priest begins to avoid looking at My Face, he has begun to alienate himself from the merciful love of My Heart. Thus will he begin, little by little, to lose confidence in My mercy, to consent to sin, and to descend into the darkness of a life from which I have been exiled.

Look upon Me for those who turn away from Me. Seek My Face for those who avoid My divine gaze. Accept My friendship for those who refuse it. Remain with Me for those who flee from My presence. This is the reparation I ask of you. Offer yourself to Me as did the little Thérèse[2]; thus will you allow Me to love you freely, and through you, My merciful love will triumph even in the souls of hardened sinners.

The "Yes" of even one soul to My merciful love is of immense benefit to a multitude of souls who fear to say it, or who are hardened in the refusal of My love.

Sunday, October 9, 2011

Yes, you need to be manly and resolute in carrying out My will, the will that I have shown you and that My servant N. has confirmed for you in My Name. The enemy will try to defeat you by insinuating imaginary fears and by playing upon your insecurities and your past sins. Send him away in the power of My Name,[3] and step into the breach for the sake of My priests, for I am with you. Take your place there in Ireland; I will place you at the heart of the Church to adore Me and to make the reparation inspired by love.

The very place of this work of Mine is already prepared for you. Go,

---

[1] Ps 146(147):3; Isa 61:1; Jer 33:6; Ezek 34:16; Hos 6:1.

[2] Cf. St. Thérèse of Lisieux, "Act of Oblation to Merciful Love," in *Story of a Soul*, 276–77.

[3] Mark 16:17; Luke 10:17; Phil 2:9–11.

and take possession of the land that I am giving you,[1] for I will make it a place of blessing and of healing for many souls. Priests will be drawn there to experience the radiance of My Eucharistic Face, and in that radiance, their hearts will be converted to Me, and set aflame with zeal and with love.

This is no time to hesitate, for the hour has come. Go in faith and in total reliance upon Me, and fear nothing. I will defend this work as the apple of My eye and I will surround it with a wall and a rampart of angelic protection.[2] You will see that the work is Mine; you are but My instrument, chosen by My Mother, so that My grace and My mercy may be glorified in one already marked by the powers of darkness for a terrible end. But they have been defeated, and their plan has been foiled. My love will triumph in your heart and in your life, and your priesthood will have been for many souls a means of encountering Me in the Sacrament of My love, and a force for the healing of My most broken and wounded priests.

For this to happen you have only to give your consent, and you have given it, and it is accepted in the court of heaven, and now My plan of mercy and of love will be carried out.

Abide in My presence. Seek My Eucharistic Face. This is what I ask of you above and before all else. I give you My Heart, My Eucharistic Heart, as the pledge of My fidelity and as your sure refuge in every temptation and trial. My sacred side is open to receive you. Abide in Me, and My love will triumph in you and around you for the glory of My Father.

Saturday, October 15, 2011
Saint Teresa of Jesus

I spoke to you in the words of Psalm 90 to give you an assurance of My protection and of My care for you at every moment, but especially now in these days that will lead you into the fulfilment of My plan. Trust in My protection. Go forward without fear. I will illumine the hearts of those with whom you will have to deal, and the doors will open before you, because this is My work and its hour has come.

My Mother is your foundress and your abbess[3]; the saints are her collaborators; the angels are her messengers and the protectors of those

---

[1] Deut 9:23, 11:31; Josh 1:11, 18:3.

[2] Deut 32:10; Ps 16:8 (17:7); Zech 2:8; Ex 14:19, 23:20; Ps 33:8 (34:7); Ps 90(91):11; Isa 63:9; Dan 6:22.

[3] In the Mectildian tradition, the Virgin Mary is always considered the abbess of the community and is acknowledged and venerated as such.

whom she loves. This is a divine work, and the realization of a desire of My Sacred Heart. I chose you for it because your life has made you humble in My sight, and your weakness has fitted you to be My instrument.[1] There is nothing in your past that I will not redeem and use for My glory and the good of souls. You will repair souls and build up My priests because I have repaired you and rebuilt your priesthood. I love you and you are Mine. Go forward with complete confidence in My protection and in My care.

Monday, October 17, 2011

Your prayer of intercession for *N.* is pleasing to Me because it is an act of love. No act of love goes unrewarded, not in this life, nor in the next. Love calls to love.[2] Prayer is the expression of love[3]; it engages with divine love and so, divine love—the love of My Heart for the Father and the Father's love for Me and the flame of unifying Love that is the Holy Spirit—descends into the soul of the one who prays. Thus does your soul possess heaven within itself, for heaven is the abode of Trinitarian love.[4]

It is My desire to see you pray always in this way. Allow yourself to be moved by love towards love, and so love will descend to you and take up its dwelling within you. Where love is present, all things are possible, for where love is, there am I, together with My Father and the Holy Spirit. You are indwelt by love. Believe this, and go forward in confidence and in peace.

Saturday, October 29, 2011

Fear not. The temptations you have suffered have not separated you from the love in which I hold you fast, close to My Heart. Be on your guard, nonetheless, for the enemy of all that is true, and pure, and

---

[1] 1 Cor 1:26–31, 9:22; Joel 3:10.

[2] Cf. Ps 41:8 (42:7).

[3] Cf. St. Thérèse of Lisieux: "For me, prayer is a surge of the heart" (quoted in the *Catechism of the Catholic Church,* at n. 2559).

[4] 1 Cor 3:16; cf. Bd. Elizabeth of the Trinity, *Letter* 122, to Madame de Sourdon: "We possess our Heaven within us, since He who satisfies the hunger of the glorified in the light of vision gives Himself to us in faith and mystery, it is the same One! It seems to me that I have found my Heaven on earth, since Heaven is God, and God is [in] my soul" (*The Complete Works,* vol. 2, trans. Anne Englund Nash [Washington, DC: ICS Publications, 1995], 51); *Letter* 172, to Germaine de Gemeaux: "The entire Trinity rests within us, this whole mystery that will be our vision in Heaven: let this be your cloister" (ibid., 116).

lovely, circles about you, seeking a point of entry into the castle of your soul. Seal every entrance and window with the sign of My Cross and with the power of My Blood, and you will remain secure under My protection.

Be at peace. Pray for N. as you pray for all priests, but without dwelling on him in a particular way. He, too, is called to a great holiness and to the grace of friendship with Me, but the temptations of the world, and of the flesh, and of the devil, have prevailed thus far, and he is, for the moment, deaf to My loving entreaties. Pray for him peacefully, and do not let your own heart be troubled.[1] I will care for him as I have cared for you, with all the mercy of My Heart.

Those who know Me have a boundless confidence in My mercy, and trust Me to resolve even the most difficult situations with a love that is at once tender and mighty. Pray to Me with confidence then, for I am the King of Love, and I want to be recognized as such. I rule in souls, not by coercion, but by My most sweet love.[2] I rule as a Child King, with gentleness and with an affection that is wholly divine. I am not a tyrant, nor will I force My rule upon anyone. I am the Child King who comes in the guise of a beggar, seeking the hospitality of one heart after another.[3] To those who welcome My rule, I impart warmth and light, food and drink, a glorious raiment, and a share in My kingdom forever.[4]

Make Me known as the King of Love, as the little poor One who waits to be admitted into your company, and welcomed into the midst of you, there to rule, not by might, but humbly and with an infinite compassion. If souls knew My kingship for what it is, they would submit to Me in an instant, and I, in response, would fill them with happiness in My presence. Love Me, then, and allow Me to love you with My Royal Heart. It is a great thing to be loved by the Heart of a King, and I am the King of all that is, that was, and that will be. My Heart is yours. Give Me your heart in return. Thus will our friendship be sealed in heaven and on earth.

Thursday, November 3, 2011

When all seems confused and inconsistent, then you must turn to Me with an even greater confidence, for I remain all wisdom, all love, all mercy, and nothing escapes My providence. Have no fear, for I remain

---

[1] John 14:1, 14:27.
[2] Matt 11:29–30; Rom 8:5; Gal 2:4, 5:1; Ex 6:6; Jer 30:8.
[3] Matt 25:37–43, as well as the story of St. Martin of Tours and the beggar at the gate.
[4] John 6:55; Rev 2, vv. 7, 10, 17; Rev 3, vv. 5, 12, 21; Isa 61:10.

constant even when you are inconstant.[1] I am strong when you are but weakness. I am holiness itself when everything in you seeks compromise with sin. I am wholeness and peace when you are broken and disordered.

Come to Me, then, and receive from Me all that you, in your poverty, do not have. I will give to you freely and you will rejoice in My beneficence.[2] Know that I am with you, and that My plan for you is constant, not changing. Trust in Me as it unfolds, even in the midst of uncertainties and setbacks, for I am faithful to all My promises and I have set My Heart upon you and upon this work, which is all Mine.

When you doubt, or when you are assailed by temptations and fears, come to Me, and rest a while in My presence. I will restore your confidence in My plan and I will give peace to your troubled heart. Too many souls, when they are in the throes of temptation or beset by doubts and fears, avoid coming into My presence, when it is there and only there that they will find peace of heart and trust in My merciful goodness.

Sunday, November 6, 2011

When you come to pray, it is not so much the words that matter; it is your loving attention to My presence that consoles My Heart. Give Me your attention, and I will work the wonders of My merciful love in your soul. Hold yourself facing Me. Abide in My presence gently, without forcing yourself to produce thoughts, feelings, or sensations. None of these things is necessary to a prayer that pleases Me and gives Me the freedom to act in a soul. All that is necessary is faith, and with faith, hope, and with hope, the love that binds the soul to Me and makes union with Me a reality.

I speak to you because you need the assurance of My friendship and the guidance that only I can give you in this way. You may not recall all that I say to you, but My words are not without a lasting effect, even if you forget them, or no longer read them. No word of Mine is vain. Every word that I utter is fruitful in the soul that offers no resistance to it.[3]

You have not resisted My words—quite the opposite: you have received them according to your ability, and so I am making them bear fruit in your soul, and in your preaching, and in your life as it unfolds.

There is no priest to whom I would not speak in this way or in

---

[1] Matt 14:29–31.

[2] Matt 10:8; Rom 10:12; Jas 1:5; Rev 21:6; Ps 83:12 (84:11); Ps 111(112):9; Hos 14:5 (14:4).

[3] Isa 55:11; Matt 13:23; Mark 4:20; Luke 8:15; Jas 1:18.

another way adapted to his hearing, provided that he believe in My divine friendship, and in My own choice, in love, of the men whom I have called to share in My priesthood.

Have I not told you before that the priesthood is, above all else and before anything else, a relationship of intimate friendship with Me?[1] The priests who do not understand this have no notion of what their priesthood means to Me and to My Father in heaven. This is one of the great sorrows of My Sacred Heart: that priests do not approach Me as a friend, that they fail to seek My company, to abide in the radiance of My Face, and to rest close to My Heart.

Seminarians are taught many things, some useful, and others less so, but are they taught to love Me, to give Me their hearts, to remain in My presence, to seek My Face, and to listen to My voice? If they are not taught these things, they will have learned nothing useful, and all their efforts will remain shallow and sterile. Why are the seminaries of My Church not schools of love, and furnaces of divine charity wherein the dross is burned away and the pure gold of holiness is produced, a gold capable of reflecting the glory of My divinity and the splendour of My truth in a world plunged into darkness?

Woe to those who allow men to pass through their institutions without teaching them the one thing necessary![2] Will I be obliged to say on the last day to those whom I have chosen, "You have not yet come to know Me, and though I know you through and through, I find in you coldness and resistance to My grace"?[3]

Pray, then, not only for My priests, your brothers, but also for the men whom I have called to be My priests, that they may learn to *love Me* before investing their talents and their energies in a multitude of other things that are perishable and have no value except in the hands and in the mind of one wholly converted to the love of My Heart.

Every seminarian and every priest needs to consecrate himself to the maternal and Immaculate Heart of My Mother. Apart from My Mother they risk growing tepid, and then cold. Apart from her they will succumb to habits of sin and find themselves too weak to rise when they fall. Apart from her their lives will be devoid of joy, of tenderness, of sweetness, and of the warmth that her Immaculate Heart diffuses in the souls of those consecrated to her.

Love My Mother, and make her loved. In this there can be no exaggeration; have no fear of loving My Mother excessively. Your love for My

---

[1] John 15:14–15; Mark 6:31–32; Song 5:16; Isa 41:8.
[2] Luke 10:42.
[3] Matt 7:21–23, 25:11–12, 26:69–75; Luke 6:46–49, 13:24–27; Acts 7:51.

Mother will never approach Mine in tenderness, in filial piety, in attention to all the desires of her Heart.[1] I loved My Mother and made her loved during My life on earth; first of all, I made My apostles love her, and by loving her they grew in love of Me. After My Ascension they assembled around her as around a hearth of fire and of light.[2] Thus were they prepared to receive the outpouring of the Holy Ghost at Pentecost.

A priest according to My own Heart will love My Mother with all his heart. A priest according to My own Heart will attend to all that My Mother desires; he will listen to her and follow her counsels. The remedy for so many of the evils that have disgraced My priesthood and brought shame upon My Church lies in the consecration of priests and seminarians to the Immaculate Heart of My Mother. I saw all My priests until the end of time from the height of the Cross, and it was to each one that I said, "Behold thy Mother."[3]

Saturday, November 12, 2011

My love for you is constant and unchanging. It does not fluctuate according to moods or seasons. My love for you glows and burns like a steady flame that is tall and bright. Never doubt of My prevailing love for you, the love that will triumph in you and around you, provided that you come to Me with confidence and offer Me all your infirmities, your weaknesses, and even your sins.

Nothing so grieves My divine Heart as the doubt of My merciful love. Sin in all its forms and manifestations offends Me and grieves My most loving Heart, but one who doubts of My merciful love grieves Me in a way that you cannot imagine. It is because I am love, and all love; it is because My mercy is the expression of My love towards sinners, that My Heart suffers when these same sinners close themselves to Me by doubting that I am all love and ready to forgive all.

Never let sin become a pretext for staying away from Me. Instead, let sin be a catalyst pushing you into My presence. There, in My presence, as in a furnace, sin is consumed in the fire of merciful love,[4] souls are made clean, healed, and restored to My friendship. I reject no one who comes to Me with confidence in My merciful love. My arms are open to receive repentant sinners into the embrace of My merciful love; even more, My side was wounded, so as to give sinners a way into My inmost Heart:

---

[1] Luke 2:51; John 2:3–5.
[2] Acts 1:14.
[3] John 19:27.
[4] Deut 4:24; Zech 13:9; Heb 12:29.

their hospital, their refuge, their place of healing, refreshment, and holiness, that is, separation from all that is incompatible with My love.

When you are weak, come to Me. When you are burdened, come to Me. When you are fearful, come to Me. When you are assailed by doubts, come to Me. When you are lonely, come to Me. Let nothing separate you from My Heart, which is ever open to receive you. It is the Evil One who seeks to turn souls away from My Heart. It is the Evil One who sows the seeds of doubt, of fear, of sadness in souls, so as to turn them away from Me and drive them into the cold pit of darkness and despair that he himself inhabits.

My Mother, on the other hand, raises souls when they fall; she instils in them a confidence in My loving mercy, a readiness to believe in My merciful love, a desire to come into My presence and to expose to Me, the divine physician, the wounds suffered in spiritual combat. My Mother is the Mother of Holy Hope.[1] She is the Mother of Holy Confidence. One who entrusts himself to My Mother will never fall into the pit of despair. Even when sorely tempted, there will remain in that soul enough confidence to turn to Me, and to make an act of abandonment to My merciful love that will touch My Heart and release from it a torrent of forgiveness, healing, and mercy.

You did not expect to receive these words from Me today, but I speak them to you to strengthen your confidence in My merciful love and to comfort souls caught in the throes of temptations against My mercy and against the unchanging love of My Most Sacred Heart.

Wednesday, November 16, 2011
Twenty-Fifth Anniversary of My Ordination to the Priesthood
Feast of Saint Gertrude

I have indeed saved you from many dangers when your priesthood and your very life were threatened with shipwreck and with complete destruction. I saved you for Myself because I love you and because I had set My Heart upon you, choosing you for Myself from the womb.[2] My choice remains, for I am changeless, and My decrees of love cannot be undone, not even by the fickleness of sinful men. You are Mine, and I am yours, and this, forever.[3]

Believe, then, in My love for you. Go forward with courage and act with faith, trusting in the love that is Mine. There are no obstacles over

---

[1] Sir 24:24.
[2] Ps 21:11 (22:10); Ps 70(71):6; Isa 44:2, 44:24, 49:1, 49:5; Jer 1:5; Sir 49:7; Gal 1:15.
[3] Ps 118(119):94; Song 2:16, 6:3; Isa 43:1; Ezek 18:4.

which My love cannot triumph. My love is a victorious love, even when all appears sunken in defeat and bound in the fetters of death. I am the God who brings new life out of what is old, decayed, and buried. I am the God who renews all those things upon which My gaze rests. I am the God for whom nothing is impossible and whom all things obey.[1] Trust, then, in My love for you, and go forward.

I have prepared the way before you, and I will remove the obstacles that will arise as easily as a child removes a leaf from the ground before him while he plays. Adore Me and keep Me company, for this is what I ask of you, and I will do all the rest. The more you abandon your power-lessness to Me, in confidence and in the humble prayer of adoration, the more you will see that I order all things mightily and sweetly[2] and that My plan will prevail.

The house that I am giving you will be built up by hours of adoration and by the faithful recitation of My praises by day and by night. One who praises Me, however humbly and simply, trusts Me, and for the one who trusts Me, there is nothing that I will not do. What matters in My sight and what charms My ears is not the outward pomp and solemnity given to My praise of the Father in the midst of My Church, and in the hearts of those whom I have called to this work. It is the humble fidelity to this work by day and by night, the continuity of a solemn commit-ment to be with Me, who am present in the Sacrament of My love, and to enter into the mystery of My glorious priesthood in heaven. It is this that opens heaven over the face of the earth; it is this that fills the heart of My Church with the splendour of heaven. Seek to be faithful. How-ever simple, however poor your worship is, when you are united to Me in the Sacrament of the Altar on earth, that worship becomes My own in the courts of heaven.

Even when you find yourself alone, My own prayer enters yours, and your prayer enters Mine. In this is My Father glorified.[3] Pray always. Do not lose heart.[4] To pray is to believe in My love for you. To pray is to allow Me to work the wonders of My love in your soul. To pray is to open the Church to a renewing and purifying wind that cleanses all things and fills the earth with a divine fragrance that originates in heaven.

There are things that I will not tell you now; it is enough for you to persevere in prayer if you would see them come to pass.

---

[1] Job 42:2; Judith 16:14; Esther 13:9; Ps 118(119):91; Wis 7:27, 11:23; John 15:5; Matt 17:20, 19:26; Mark 9:23, 10:27, 14:36; Luke 1:37; Rom 9:19.

[2] Wis 8:1.

[3] John 14:13, 15:8.

[4] Luke 18:1–8; Rom 12:12; Col 4:2.

So few of My priests believe in Me with all their hearts. They live as if I were not real for them, and their hearts sink deeper and deeper into a deathlike sleep of indifference and lukewarmness. It is by faith that they will change themselves, because it is by faith that I will begin to act in them.[1] What is prayer, if not a demonstration of faith in Me? Let them pray, then. Teach them to pray. Help them to pray. Only then will My priests begin to find hope. Only then will they become the witnesses of My joy in a world shrouded in sorrow and blinded by too many tears.

I have more to say to you but, for the moment, this is enough. Take My words and read them until they impress themselves in your memory. You will need them on the day of temptation and in the hour of trial, for that hour will come. But I shall triumph over all, and you will emerge as the priest of My Heart, whom I have chosen and hidden from the world in My open side.

Saturday, November 19, 2011

When you come to Me in this way, you allow Me to work in your soul. My desires for you are being fulfilled in proportion to your submission to My love in the Sacrament of My divine friendship, in the mystery of My real presence. When you adore Me, you submit to all that I desire, and you give Me the freedom to work the wonders of My healing grace within you. When you adore Me, know that I am working in you, silently but efficaciously uniting you to Myself, purifying your sinful heart, and enlightening your soul with the radiance of My divinity.

This is what I would do for all My priests, but there are very few who come to Me, seeking My Face in the Sacrament of My love, and resting close to My most loving Heart. Why do they stay away from Me, when I have performed this miracle of love that is My real presence in the Most Holy Sacrament of the Altar in order to be close to them? Why do they stay away, grieving My Heart by their coldness, their indifference, and their ingratitude, when I am ready to receive them at any hour of the day or night in the very tabernacles where their own hands have placed Me?

Why are they obstinate and hard-hearted, wallowing in worldly pleasures and suffering the terrible boredom of those who look to this world and its deceits for the joy that only I can give? Why have so few of My beloved priests turned to Me in the present darkness and in the crisis that afflicts My Church in nearly every place? They are like the sick who refuse to see the physician. They are like the lonely who refuse to open the door to the friend who desires only to visit and comfort them. They are like the hungry who turn away from the food set before them. They

---

[1] Heb 11; Matt 17:19, 21:21; Mark 11:22; Acts 3:16; Eph 3:12.

are like the thirsty who will not drink of the stream that flows, fresh and clean, at their very feet.

These priests of Mine grieve My Heart, and yet I will pursue them with My merciful love until they surrender to My Heart and allow Me to be their Friend, the joy of their hearts, the light of their eyes, their physician in sickness, their food, their drink, their shelter and—in a word—their all.

I have nothing but benefits and mercies to offer My priests, but they turn away from Me close-fisted and unwilling to receive like little children the gifts that I wait to lavish upon them. Where have they learned to treat Me in such a way? Why do they resist all My efforts to warm their hearts, to illumine their minds, and to fill their empty lives with My abiding presence? I wait for My priests to turn, and to return, to Me in the Sacrament of My love. I wait for them to claim Me, and no other, as their first and finest Friend. I wait for them to pour out their hearts in My presence, to tell Me of their sufferings, their failures, their joys, and their sins. I will not refuse any priest who comes to My Eucharistic Heart seeking grace in time of need, light in darkness, and a companion in loneliness.

Oh, let them return to My tabernacles where I wait for them, and let them open My churches so that the souls entrusted to them may also seek Me out in the Sacrament of My love, and be filled with My blessings in their time of need. I will withhold no grace from the priest who seeks My Face in the Sacrament of My love. Not a single one will I send away disappointed or empty-handed, for I am the Lord of heaven and earth, and I await them in the tabernacles where they themselves have placed Me. In so many places I am the divine Solitary, when I would be to each of them, and for all My faithful, the divine Friend, ever ready to receive those who seek My Face.

Monday, November 21, 2011
Presentation of the Blessed Virgin Mary

I will show you how to touch many hearts by giving you a message that comes from My Heart, burning with love for My priests in the Sacrament for which they were ordained, for every priest is ordained for the care and service of My Body.[1] The priest is essentially Eucharistic. The priesthood is ordered to the renewal of My Sacrifice upon the altars of My Church, from the rising of the sun to its setting.[2] I would populate

---

[1] See St. Thomas Aquinas, *Summa theologiae*, III, q. 82, a. 3.
[2] Mal 1:11; Ps 112(113):3.

the earth with My priests so that in every place My Body may be made present and My Church, My Bride, may grow in holiness and in beauty for all to see.

The vision has been shown to you; you have written it down. Now is the time to make it known. Hearts will be moved, and through the kindness of a multitude of little ones I will provide what is needed for My work to go forward. You have not been active enough in sharing—through writing, and by spreading what you have written—the work that I have entrusted to you.

I do not call you to an activism that would exhaust you and draw you away from prayer but, rather, to a courageous engagement in the project that I have shown you, and that I yearn to fulfil, not as something for you alone, or even for your lifetime, but as a gift to My Church and My beloved priests. Write, spread the word, and then trust Me to open hearts. The support for the work will come, but it will come mostly from the little and the poor to whom I have given hearts of compassion for My priests who suffer.

The realization of My work is happening even now, in this very moment, because you are here before My Face, and because I see you, and My Heart is moved to pity for all the priests whom you represent. I have called you to hiddenness; nonetheless, out of that hiddenness, and without leaving it to court the favour of the rich and the powerful, I want you to write, and by writing, doors will open and you will marvel at how perfectly My wisdom and My love have ordered all things. This is not the time to give in to discouragement and to draw back in doubt. It is the moment to go forward, making use of the gifts that I have given you, and of those of your sons.

Speak when you are called upon to speak, but prefer silence in My presence to speaking in the sight of men. Appear when you are called upon to appear, but prefer hiddenness in the secret of My Eucharistic Face.

The time is short, and this work of Mine must go forward because the spiritual needs of My priests are immense. I want to save My priests from the snares and entrapments laid in their path by the Evil One who seeks their destruction, and through their destruction, that of My Bride, the Church. My priests stand in the front lines; when they fall, My Bride, the Church, is left with no defence, and he who has hated Me from the beginning will advance to cause her downfall.[1] I will thwart his plans for the destruction of My priesthood and of My Church by raising

---

[1] John 8:44; 1 John 3:8; Mark 4:15; Luke 4:13, 8:12, 22:3–4, 22:31; 2 Cor 12:7; 2 Thess 2:9–12; 1 Pet 5:8; Rev 12:1–9; Job 40:20–41:25 (Vul.); Zech 3:1–2.

up a cohort of adorers, priests who will adore for priests, sons of My Virgin Mother, who, like John, My beloved disciple, will stand firm in the face of persecution and remain the consolers of My Eucharistic Heart that, more and more, is abandoned and forsaken in the tabernacles where I dwell.

The Evil One plots My betrayal, a betrayal by My chosen ones, by the priests whom I love even in their filth, their sin, and their cold-heartedness. Your role is to represent them before My Face. In doing this, you will cause many to return to Me, to repent of their connivance with the lies of the Evil One, and to return to an obedience that is loving and sustained by prayer and by the presence of My most holy Mother.

These are the things that I have to say to you tonight. For now, it is enough. Be at peace. You are in My Heart, and I love you.

Tuesday, December 20, 2011

The practice of adoration is not difficult. It is a gentle abiding in My presence, a resting in the radiance of My Eucharistic Face, a closeness to My Eucharistic Heart. Words, though sometimes helpful, are not necessary, nor are thoughts. What I seek from one who would adore Me in spirit and in truth is a heart aflame with love, a heart content to abide in My presence, silent and still, engaged only in the act of loving Me and of receiving My love. Though this is not difficult, it is, all the same, My own gift to the soul who asks for it. Ask, then, for the gift of adoration.

Adoration is an austere prayer because it rests upon faith alone. Out of faith there rises the pure flame of hope, and out of the flame of hope, I enkindle in the soul a great conflagration of charity—that is, a communication to the soul of the fire that blazes in My Eucharistic Heart. The fire of divine love does not destroy what I created: a soul fashioned in My image and likeness. It purifies that soul and burns away only what is incompatible with My infinite holiness, and with the purity of My Essence. The soul, however, is not annihilated. The soul remains, even in the midst of the purifying flames of divine love, fully capable of believing, of hoping, and of loving Me.

Adoration is a furnace and a forge. The soul called to a life of adoration must expect to suffer the intensity of the fiery furnace, and the reshaping of all that is misshapen in her in the forge of My divine will. For this to happen, it is enough that the soul offer herself to My love, and remain humble, peaceful, and quiet as I purify and transform her in My presence. If only souls knew the power to purify and to transform that emanates from My tabernacles!

If only My priests knew this, they would hasten into My presence and remain there, waiting for Me to do in them what, of themselves, they cannot do. It is the simple prayer of adoration that renders a priest fit for the sacred ministry by giving him a pure heart and by correcting all that is incompatible with My divine holiness and with My priestly love in his life. This way of holiness through adoration is a secret revealed to My saints in ages past, and it is a gift that I am offering to My priests in these times of impurity, persecution, and darkness.

To overcome impurity, I will give them a shining purity that will blaze before the eyes of the world as a testimony to divine love. To overcome persecution, I will give them a manly strength and a resoluteness of purpose that will confound those who plot their downfall. To overcome darkness, I will give them a clear light by which to order their steps and see what choices are pleasing to My Heart.

Time spent in My presence is not time wasted. It is the ground and support of every word spoken by My priests in the exercise of their ministry; it is the secret of a priestly action that is supernaturally fruitful, bearing fruit that will last.

If this is true of the priests whom I have chosen to labour in the vineyard of My Church, how much more must it be true of those whom I have chosen and set apart to live cloistered in the cenacle with My most holy Mother and with Saint John, My beloved disciple. John was most at home in My Eucharistic presence and in the company of My Mother. John understood better and more than the other Apostles the mysteries that I instituted in the cenacle on the night before I suffered. John was the first of a long line of Eucharistic priests called to love Me and abide in My Eucharistic presence, close to My Heart, and in the radiance of My Face. This is the particular grace that Saint John would share with those who, responding to My call, will find their way to the cenacle of adoration that I am bringing to birth as a living organism within My Church, enlivened by the Holy Spirit and formed in the Heart of My Immaculate Mother.

Be faithful, then, to this work to which I have called you. You have only to cooperate with Me, for I am leading and guiding you. Act boldly, trusting in My power to confirm and ratify all that you do for love of Me with a pure heart and a humble spirit.[1]

---

[1] Cf. the prayer in the Offertory of the *usus antiquior* of the Roman Rite: "In spiritu humilitatis et in animo contrito suscipiamur a te, Domine…" (May we be received by Thee, O Lord, in a spirit of humility and in a contrite heart).

Tuesday, December 27, 2011

All that you have asked Me to give you, I will give, and more besides, for I have chosen you to be for Me another John, a friend for My Heart, a consoler in My loneliness, an advocate on behalf of poor sinners, especially on behalf of fallen priests and those who have lost hope in My infinite mercy. Be a companion for Me in the Sacrament of My love, the Sacrament of My divine companionship for every human wayfarer in this valley of tears.

I remain unknown. I am left alone. Even those who claim to profess the mystery of My real presence in the Sacrament of the Altar forsake Me. I am treated with a terrible indifference, with coldness, and with a lack of respect that causes the angels to weep because they cannot offer Me reparation for the coldness and indifference of human hearts.[1] Only men can make reparation for men.[2] What is lacking is the loving response of a human heart to My Eucharistic Heart, pierced, alive, and beating in the Sacrament of the Altar. Only a human heart can make reparation for a human heart. For this reason the angels are sorrowful.

The adoration and the praise they offer Me is angelic. It is the expression of the perfections I have placed in their angelic nature. Without ever dying, they immolate themselves before Me in the tabernacles where I dwell on earth by lowering themselves in the most humble adoration and by placing all their angelic perfections—their beauty, their strength, their intelligence—beneath My feet.[3] The angels are like living flames who burn in My Eucharistic presence, without ever being con-

---

[1] Since angels do not have bodies, and since the good angels are completely caught up in the bliss of heaven, "weeping" here is a metaphor for some kind of spiritual lamentation that is difficult for humans, and fallen humans no less, to understand.

[2] Cf. Heb 2:9–17, 5:1, 10:5; St. Thomas Aquinas, *Summa theologiae*, III, q. 1, aa. 2–4; q. 22, a. 2; q. 46, aa. 1, 3.

[3] Ps 102(103):20; Ezek 1; Isa 6:1–7; Tob 12:15–20; Matt 4:11, 13:41, 16:27, 25:31, 26:53; Mark 1:13, 8:38, 13:27; Luke 2:13–14; John 1:51; 2 Thess 1:7; 1 Tim 3:16; Heb 1:3–14, 12:22–24; 1 Pet 1:12, 3:22; Rev 4:6–11; 5:11–14, 7:11–12, 8:2–4, 19:9–10, 22:8–9. Cf. *The Prayers of Saint Gertrude and Saint Mechtilde of the Order of St. Benedict* (London: Burns and Oates, 1917): "O ineffable God, we are now drawing near to those tremendous mysteries which neither cherubim nor seraphim nor all the virtues of heaven suffice to comprehend, for Thou alone knowest with what energy of love Thou dost daily offer Thyself to God the Father upon the altar as a victim of praise and propitiation. And therefore all choirs and orders of angels adore this Thy most sacred and impenetrable secret with lowliest prostration, and behold with awe their King and their Lord, Who once came down from heaven in unutterable love to redeem man, now again mysteriously present upon the altar, hidden beneath the mean and lowly species of bread and wine for the salvation of men. . . . Hail, most glorious Body and most precious Blood of

sumed.[1] Yet for all of this, My angels cannot replace a single human heart in My presence. What I look for from men, what I wait for, above all, from My priests, My angels cannot give Me.

And so I turned to Saint John to comfort Me; to love Me when the love of others grew cold; to hope in Me when the trust of others was shaken; to remain faithful to Me when the faith of others was put to the test.[2] John was, among the Apostles, My loving friend, My adorer, the one who understood the mystery of reparation to My Heart.

John made reparation for Peter's denial of Me, not by standing in judgment over Peter, whom he honoured and loved as a father, but by weeping with Peter, and by offering himself in reparation for Peter's fall.

Again, it was John who offered Me faithful love in exchange for Judas's faithless betrayal. He made reparation to My Heart that suffered so grievously when Judas walked out of the cenacle into the night.[3] In that moment, John gave Me all the love of his heart, begging Me to accept it in reparation for Judas's cold and calculated plot against Me.

Be another Saint John for My Heart. Offer Me reparation by offering Me *yourself*: in the place of those who flee from before My Eucharistic Face; in the place of those who cannot bear to remain in My presence, close to My Heart; in the place of those priests of Mine who have time for all else, except for Me.

Give Me your companionship, give Me your confidence, give Me your grateful affection. Let nothing keep you from carrying out this design of Mine. One who makes reparation for My priests will discover on the last day that his own sins, though they be many, will be covered over by a single act of reparation, for reparation is the exercise of love, and love covers a multitude of sins.[4]

Love Me, and you will fulfil all that I am asking of you. Love Me, and I will fulfil all that you ask of Me. I desire a company of Johannine souls, priest adorers and reparators, and upon them I will pour out rivers of grace for the renewal of My priesthood and the joy of My Spouse, the Church.

☩

my Lord Jesus Christ, here truly present beneath these sacramental species; I adore Thee with all that devotion and awe wherewith the nine choirs of angels worship and adore Thee."

[1] Heb 1:7; Rev 4:5, 10:1; Ex 3:2; Acts 7:30; 2 Thess 1:7; Ps 28(29):7; Judg 6:21, 13:20; Isa 6:2–7; Song 8:6.

[2] John 13:21–27, 19:26, 20:1–9.

[3] John 13:30; Ps 40:10 (41:9); Ps 87:19 (88:18).

[4] Luke 7:47; Ps 31(32):1; Rom 4:7; Isa 1:18, 43:25, 44:22; 1 Pet 1:1, 4:8; Sir 3:30; Tob 12:9.

Sunday, January 7, 2012

Rise earlier. Give Me the first hours of the day. Come to Me before seeking anything or anyone else. I will strengthen you to use well the hours of each day begun in this way.

I have called you to be My adorer; all else is secondary. I wait for you in the Sacrament of My love and I am often disappointed because you allow other things to absorb your time and consume your energy. Give Me as much time as you can, and I will give you time and energy to do all that you must do. You will see that by coming to Me first, everything else will appear to you in its just proportions. You will do one thing after another, and all that you do will be marked by serenity and by an inward adoration toward My abiding presence in the tabernacle. Is not this what you learned from reading the Epiphany instruction of My servant, Mother Mectilde?[1]

I call you to a life of perpetual adoration. Perpetual adoration is a loving attention to My presence. It is a seeking after My Face and a drawing close to My Heart that never ceases and that suffuses every moment of life. This perpetual adoration nonetheless begins with and returns to times of real adoration spent before My Eucharistic Face, during which all other things are left aside.

Come, then, to the place apart that I have prepared for you.[2] I wait for you there. Come to My tabernacle and abide in My presence. I will fill you with joy, with serenity, and with wisdom for the demands of the day. Begin always by adoring Me. Do not allow your heart to grow cold towards My Eucharistic presence. I have called you to this life for one thing only: to adore Me for the sake of My beloved priests, your brothers, especially for the sake of those who never come into My sacramental presence to find, close to My Heart, refreshment, light, peace, and, above all else, the love for which I created them and of which I have made them My servants.

I forgive your weaknesses in this matter, but I invite you to pick yourself up and to return to the generosity of a love that brooks no delay and is defeated by no obstacle. What I am telling you is simple, but it is the

---

[1] Reference is made to the great conference Mother Mectilde, at the age of eighty, delivered to her daughters on Epiphany in 1694. This conference gives sublime expression to her spiritual doctrine, centered on the Holy Eucharist as the summation and re-presentation of all the mysteries of the life of Christ, the connection between adoration, sacrifice, and heavenly glory, and the simple way of faith that eschews extraordinary manifestations.

[2] Matt 14:13, 25:34; Mark 6:31–32; Luke 9:10; John 14:2–3.

secret of a strong vitality and of a wisdom that sees all things rightly and judges them prudently.

The principal difficulty in your life and in the lives of so many priests of Mine is the neglect of adoration. In your life I want it to hold the first place. You are, before anything else, the adorer of My Eucharistic Face and the consoler of My Sacred Heart. This is your mission, and it alone is the justification for everything else you undertake. I am pleased with the adoration you offer Me, but I wait for a greater generosity from you. Seek Me first in the Sacrament of My love, and I promise that I will give you all else besides, and that you shall want for nothing.[1]

Adoration is the exchange of love, and the exchange of love is the source of all fruitfulness. If the fruits are meagre, it is because you have been sparing in the exchange of love with My Eucharistic Heart. Do not begin by saying, "I must make three hours of adoration a day." Begin, rather, by adoring Me as much as you can. The rest will follow effortlessly.

There is a special grace that I have attached to the Office of Matins for those who, by vocation, are called to it. Recite it quietly and peacefully in My presence, and I will visit your soul with the sweetness of My divine love and with the fragrance of My presence within you. I am consoled when souls rise while it is still dark, and make their way to My tabernacle to chant My praises and to unite themselves to My own adoration of the Father. The psalms will unite you to My Heart, and you will emerge from the Night Office refreshed and strengthened in love.

Wednesday, January 10, 2012

Intercession for other souls is a work of love. It consists in placing oneself with Me before the Father, with a boundless trust in the merits of My Passion and in the wounds that I present to the Father on behalf of all who approach Him with confidence, through Me.

I live in the Sacrament of My love as I live in heaven, in a ceaseless state of intercession for all who believe in Me and come to Me with the weight of life's burdens and sorrows. There is nothing that I will not do for the soul who approaches Me with confidence.

For this reason did I wish to remain present in the Sacrament of My love until the end of time: so that souls might know where to find Me, and approach Me easily, certain of being heard, and trusting in the mercy of My Heart for a world marked by suffering and ravaged by sin. There is no form of intercessory prayer more efficacious than that of the

[1] Matt 6:33; Luke 12:31.

soul who approaches My Eucharistic presence, certain of finding Me and certain of being heard. I am not distant from souls in need. I have made Myself close to them, as close as the nearest tabernacle. Would that My people understood this! My churches would be filled to overflowing at every hour of the day and night. I would never be left alone in the Sacrament of My love.

The exercise of faith increases faith. The exercise of confidence causes confidence to grow. One who approaches My tabernacle in faith is giving evidence of a complete reliance on My merciful love. The Most Holy Sacrament of the Altar is My Heart, open to receive those who will respond to My timeless invitation: "Come unto Me, all you that labour, and are burdened, and I will refresh you. Take My yoke upon you, and learn of Me, because I am meek and humble of heart, and you shall find rest to your souls. For My yoke is sweet, and My burden light."[1]

One who approaches Me frequently in the Most Holy Sacrament of the Altar will discover that he is yoked to Me by an unbreakable bond of love. He will discover, by personal experience, that I share in all his sorrows, that I bring him relief in afflictions, that I carry his burdens with him, and that he is never, not even for a moment, forsaken or left to himself alone.

What I am teaching you is more than the simple visit to Me in the Sacrament of My love; it is a way of approaching Me marked by absolute confidence in My intercession with the Father. It is an act of faith in My merciful love, and a way of disposing oneself to receive the waters of life that stream abundantly from My open side.

Do souls believe in My real presence in the tabernacles of My churches? Have they altogether forgotten who I am and where I am to be found? Has the faith of My priests in the Sacrament of My love grown so tepid and so weak that the souls entrusted to them have lost the simple instinct of the believing heart—that is, to seek Me out in the Most Holy Eucharist, and to abide in My presence, loving Me, and allowing Me to love freely those who come to Me, to heal their wounds, and to draw them into the sanctuary of My open side?

The emptiness of My churches is an affront to My love, to the love that compelled Me to give Myself by the hands of My priests, under the forms of bread and wine, so that no one might perish from hunger or thirst on the road to eternity.

I am all love in the Sacrament of My love. My Heart is open to receive all, even those who have in their souls no more than the faintest spark of

---

[1] Matt 11:28–30.

faith in My real presence. Let them come to Me, and that little spark will become a shining flame, giving joy and hope to all who perceive its light.

The emptiness of My churches apart from the hours of the liturgical offices is an indictment, first of all, of My priests, and then, of My faithful. My Eucharistic presence meets with coldness, with indifference, and with a chilling ingratitude, even on the part of My priests and of consecrated souls. They fail to recognize in the mystery of the Most Holy Eucharist the pearl of great price, the treasure once hidden in the field but now offered freely to all who would partake of its inexhaustible riches.[1]

I am left alone in a world where so many lament their loneliness. If only souls would come to Me and would tarry in My presence, they would discover a love that fills the heart so completely that it dispels every loneliness and becomes wondrously fruitful in the lives of those who accept it.

Your life, your vocation, your mission now is to abide in My sacramental presence. It is to console My Eucharistic Heart and to expose your soul to the radiance of My Eucharistic Face for the sake of so many of your brother priests who stumble about in a darkness that no earthly light can dispel.[2]

Friday, January 27, 2012

O my beloved Lord Jesus, truly present here, I adore Thee with all the love of my heart. It is for this and for no other thing that Thou has brought me here: to adore Thee, to abide in Thy company, to seek Thy Face, and to rest upon Thy Heart. Keep me faithful to the calling Thou hast given me, and let nothing distract me from Thee, who art the One Thing Necessary, and apart from Whom there is nothing in heaven or on earth to which I will give my heart.[3] To be near Thee is my happiness. Hold me in Thy presence, and let me never depart from the radiance of Thy Eucharistic Face. Amen.

Jesus, Jesus, Jesus, let nothing take me out of the radiance of Thy Eucharistic Face; rather, let all things work together to compel me to seek Thy Face and to adore Thee.

Adoration! Adoration! Adoration! This is what I am asking of you, because adoration is the exercise of love, and love fulfils all else.[4] Give to

---

[1] Matt 13:44–46.

[2] Isa 59:10; Job 5:14; Sir 37:15–16.

[3] Luke 10:41–42; Ps 72(73):25.

[4] Josh 22:5; Song 8:7; Rom 13:8–10; 1 Cor 13, 16:14; Gal 5:14; Eph 3:17–19; Col 3:14; 1 Tim 1:5; 1 John 4:16; Jas 2:8; Rev 2:4.

no other work the importance that I am asking you to give to the work of adoration. Take it upon yourself until others come with whom you will be able to share it. Were it not for this work of adoration, I would have had no reason to allow the birth of this little family over which I have placed you as a father and a servant. Let others do the work to which I have called them, but as for you, do the one work to which I have called you before and above all else.

It is because I am left alone in the Sacrament of My love that such darkness has fallen over the souls of My priests. It is this that grieves My Sacred Heart more than anything else, and this because the Most Holy Sacrament of the Altar is the supreme expression of My personal love for every priest, and there are so few who understand this and respond to My love with love.

The work of reparation is a substitution freely undertaken out of love, for those who remain far from the radiance of My Eucharistic Face and from the warmth of My Sacred Heart. The loneliness that I suffer in so many tabernacles is caused by the indifference of My priests. Their lives are ruled, not by My love for them, and their love for Me, but by a thousand other created things unworthy of the character that I inscribed in mystic fire upon their souls when they were ordained for the service of My Body.

O My priests, priests of My Heart, priests upon whom rests the gaze of My Eucharistic Face, return to Me! Return to Me and be forgiven.[1] Return to Me and be healed. Return to Me and be refreshed.[2] Return to Me and I will so unite you to Myself that you and I will appear before My Father as one Priest and one Victim offered to Him for the praise of His glory and out of love for our one spouse, the Church.[3]

Until now, the precious grace of Eucharistic adoration has remained unknown to far too many of My priests. This accounts for the weaknesses, the scandals, the shame, and the falling away of so many. The world has grown cold, and it will become even more cold as the darkness of the Enemy enfolds it and turns to ice the hearts that I consecrated to be for Me hearts of love.[4]

This is why I am pleading with you to adore Me in the Sacrament of My love and, by your adoration, to bring many priests into the light of

[1] Isa 44:22; Jer 4:1; Joel 2:12; Mal 3:7.
[2] 2 Chron 7:14; Job 5:18; Isa 57:18–19; Jer 17:14, 33:6–9; Hos 14:4; Matt 9:21–22; Luke 5:17, 8:43–48.
[3] Eph 1:9–14, 5:25–29.
[4] Matt 24:12.

My Eucharistic Face. This return to adoration will save My priests from the devastation that the Enemy is plotting against them. When a priest flies to My Heart and rests his head upon My breast, he is safe from all harm, and the plots of the Enemy against his soul are thwarted and brought to nought.

Who among My priests will survive the tribulation that is coming? Only those who will have listened to My plea for priest adorers, for priest reparators, for priests who will allow Me to befriend them, and who will give Me their time, their minds, and their hearts in the essential work of adoration. I call this work essential because the right order of things has been subverted and because a great disorder and confusion has overtaken the hearts and minds of My beloved priests. Adoration will be for them and for you the restoration of the only right order: the order of divine love poured into the hearts of men by the Holy Spirit Who is Love.[1]

So important is this work that I have entrusted it, and you with it, to the compassionate and glorious Heart of My own Mother. This work is her work, in the whole Church and in the hearts of those priests who have made themselves hers by an act of consecration. To this work of Mine and this work of My Mother I have associated my saints in glory, and the angels who worship before My Face and surround My tabernacles with a celestial adoration on earth. There is nothing that can reverse My plan now. The hour has come for priests to hear My appeal and to return, penitent and joyful, to the foot of My altars.[2] It is there that I wait for each one, full of mercy and ready to receive them into My Heart.

Saturday, January 28, 2012

O strengthen my loving attention to Thee, Thou who art lovingly attentive to me in this the Sacrament of Thy love.

What matters is that you have come into My presence, seeking My Face and offering Me all the love of your heart. This is enough. With this little act of adoration and love, I will do great things. I do not ask for things beyond your strength. I am not a harsh and demanding taskmaster; I am the most loving and grateful of friends. No moment spent in My sacramental presence goes unrewarded, for I love those who love Me.[3] I show My Face to those who seek Me, and I give My Heart to those who yearn

---

[1] Rom 5:5.
[2] John 5:25; Ps 42(43):4.
[3] Prov 8:17.

for My friendship. It is a ploy of Satan to make souls believe that I am a harsh and demanding God, that I am never satisfied with the humble offerings of My children, and that I withdraw My presence from those who seek Me, spurning their attempts to find Me, and frustrating all their desires to know Me and to know My love for them. Lies, all lies to prevent souls from approaching Me. I am, of all friends, the most gentle and the most grateful.

Come to Me, for I wait for you in the Sacrament of My love. It was no mere development of ritual practice when My Church began to reserve My Most Holy Body in the tabernacles prepared for Me. It was a glorious and long-awaited inspiration of the Holy Ghost, for the Sacrament of My Body and Blood is more than the perpetuation in time of My eternal sacrifice. It is more than the nourishment by which I enter souls to unite them to Me and to one another in a single Body. It is also the pledge and the expression of My divine friendship and the sign of My Heart's desire and resolve to remain present until the end of the ages,[1] for the sake of all who seek My friendship and would know the love of My Heart for them. There are those who argue that such was not My intention on the night before I suffered, when I gave My apostles to eat and drink of My Body and Blood, yet in all truth it *was* the intention of My Heart and My Heart's desire, for I looked far into ages to come and saw that the greatest hunger of the human heart would be for My divine friendship, and for My companionship and presence in this earthly exile.[2]

There is nothing I will not do to make Myself close to the souls who seek My presence and yearn for My friendship. Loneliness is a consequence of sin, for all sin alienates men from their true selves, from their Creator and their God, and from one another. Loneliness is, I repeat, the consequence of sin, by which the perfection of My plan for human happiness is fractured and rendered unintelligible. Sin causes man to

---

[1] Matt 28:20.

[2] Our Lord is referring to twentieth-century liturgists who argued against the practice of Eucharistic adoration on the basis of its seeming lack of accord with the symbolism of food and drink. The Magisterium of the Church has always firmly resisted such prandial reductionism and has consistently reaffirmed the spiritual fruitfulness of the now long-standing practice of adoring Christ's Body, truly present in the Blessed Sacrament. In fact, our Lord is already nourishing us spiritually by the very power of His real presence and by our loving adoration of Him. See Pope Benedict XVI, Post-Synodal Apostolic Exhortation *Sacramentum Caritatis* (February 22, 2007), §66; Alcuin Reid, ed., *From Eucharistic Adoration to Evangelization* (London/New York: Burns & Oates, 2012), esp. pp. 17–40 and 151–66.

see himself distorted as in a broken mirror.[1] Come, then, to the Sacrament of My love, and gaze into the perfect and immaculate mirror of souls, by which I reveal to souls all that I would have them be in the sight of My Father and in the Body that is My Church.[2] I have no desire apart from your eternal happiness. For this did I create you, calling you, at the very instant of your conception, into the fullness of life with Me, in the bosom of My Father, and in the love of the Holy Ghost.

I will that all knowledge of Me lead to love of Me. Theology is useful only insofar as it leads to communion with Me in humble prayer and in adoration. Theology is at the service of love. Separated from love, it is a monstrous science that separates even from Me.

Sunday, January 29, 2012

Lord Jesus, Thou askest not the impossible of me, for even when Thou askest what, to my eyes, appears impossible, Thou art already making it possible by Thy grace. To Thee, and to those who love Thee, nothing is impossible.[3] I can do all things in Thee who strengthenest me to do them.[4]

Monday, January 30, 2012

A prayer for those who would offer one hour of adoration and reparation at home, at work, in hospital, in prison, or while travelling:

Lord Jesus Christ, although I cannot, during this hour,
approach Thee physically in the Sacrament of Thy love,
I would approach Thee by desire and by faith.
Transport me, I beseech Thee, by the lifting up of my mind and heart,
to that tabernacle in the world where Thou art, at this hour,
most forsaken, utterly forgotten, and without human company.

Let the radiance of Thy Eucharistic Face so penetrate my soul
that by offering Thee adoration and reparation,
even as I am busy doing ordinary things in an ordinary way,
I may obtain from Thy Sacred Heart
the return of at least one priest to the Tabernacle
where Thou waitest for him today. Amen.

---

[1] Ps 10:6.

[2] Wis 7:24–30; Jas 1:23–25; 1 Cor 13:9–12.

[3] Job 42:2; Ps 118(119):91; Wis 7:27, 11:23; John 15:5; Matt 17:20, 19:26; Mark 9:23, 10:27, 14:36; Luke 1:37.

[4] Phil 4:13; Rom 8:37; cf. *The Holy Rule* of St. Benedict, ch. 68.

That[1] was no distraction that you had in adoring Me this morning; it was My desire, and it was I who inspired you to undertake this work for love of Me in the Sacrament of My love for you, and for the sanctification of My priests. Live the message I have given you, and then make it known, for by means of it I will touch the hearts of many of My priests and bring them back to Myself. I wait for each one in the Sacrament of My love.

I yearn to gather My priests about My tabernacles, and to draw each one of them to My Heart. I will allow each one to rest upon My breast, to listen to My divine heartbeats, and to learn of My everlasting love for him, the love by which I created him, and chose him, and united him forever to Myself as priest to Priest, and as victim to Victim.

I am about to send My Holy Spirit as a blazing fire of purity over all the priests of My Church. Those who submit to this purifying and sanctifying action will flourish in My Church for the joy of My Heart and for the glory of My Father. Those who resist this purifying and sanctifying action will grieve Him, will bring great sorrow to My Heart, will provoke the justice of My Father, and will dry up like branches cut off from the vine and ready to be cast into another fire.[2] He who refuses the flames of divine love will suffer the flames of divine justice. This is hard for you to hear, but I say it out of love, filled with an immense pity for every one of My priests, for I love each one to the point of what men of the world call madness; but it is not madness, it is the very nature of the divine love that blazes in My Sacred Heart.

Begin, then, the work of the Confraternity of Priest Adorers. It will be integral to the mission of your little monastery. And you, live the message. Live it daily. Live it generously. Adore me with a holy zeal, and know that I will not be outdone in zeal.[3] As you are zealous for Me, so will I be zealous for you. Work for Me and for My interests, that is to say, adore Me, adore Me, persevere in coming before My Eucharistic Face and in abiding close to My Eucharistic Heart, and I will work in you to purify you, to sanctify you, to fill you with joy in this life and with glory forever in the next.

---

[1] The reference is to the Confraternity of Priest Adorers, to which more explicit reference is made just below, as well as in the entry for June 2, 2012.—*Author.*

[2] Mal 4:1; Judith 16:20–21; Matt 3:7–12, 13:40–43; Luke 3:16–17; John 15:1–6; Heb 6:4–9; 2 Pet 3:10.

[3] Ps 68:10 (69:9); John 2:7; Rom 12:11; 1 Pet 3:13; Rev 3:19; cf. St. Benedict, *The Holy Rule,* ch. 72.

Tuesday, January 31, 2012

Eucharistic adoration becomes for My priests the means by which they begin to say sincerely and with an immense joy in their hearts, "To be near God is my happiness, and my happiness lies in Thee alone."[1] I want My priests to be happy, not with the happiness that the world gives (for it fades quickly, leaving a bitterness on the palate of the soul), but with the happiness that is the fruit of My presence sought, adored, and glorified in the Sacrament of My love. My priests will be happy insofar as they are Eucharistic priests.

The happiness of a priest is directly proportionate to his experience of My friendship, My nearness to him in the Sacrament of My love, and My readiness to receive him there, to press him against My Heart, and to refresh his soul. The priest who allows days and weeks to pass without tarrying before My Eucharistic Face will soon find his soul drained of the supernatural happiness that is the fruit of adoration.

Far too many priests become melancholy and bitter because they keep Me at a distance from their hearts, even when I am sacramentally present and available to them in a tabernacle which may be no more than a few steps away. Priests think that ministry is the whole of their vocation, forgetting that I call them, first of all, *to be with Me*, to abide in My presence, and to become My intimate friends, the closest friends of My Sacred Heart.

For many, the business of religion has driven out the joy that is an infallible sign of My presence in one's life. I Myself am no longer central to the priestly ministry of too many of My chosen ones: they exhaust themselves in a constant flow of activities and conversations, never taking time to be silent in My presence, and to listen to what My Heart longs to speak to their hearts. This is true not only of diocesan priests; it is, alas, true of far too many of those whom I have called to live for Me alone in the silence of the cloister. Even there, the spirit of activism has penetrated, drawing men from one enterprise to another, causing them to build castles in the sand, playthings that will be swept away again and again by the vehemence of My love, until they learn to find happiness in Me alone.[2]

---

[1] Ps 72(73):28; Ps 15(16):2. The latter verse can also be rendered "Thou hast no need of my goods" or "I have no good apart from Thee."

[2] Priests and religious who are tempted to follow a false philosophy of activism, pragmatism, and utilitarianism, or who waste their time on entertainments and distractions, will suffer God's loving judgments. He will make bitter their false delights, destroy their enterprises, and weaken the efficacy of their work in order to wake them up to their calling of intimate friendship with Him as the source of happiness and the condition for all fruitfulness.

These are things that must be said. I say them first to you, that you may change your own life, and become for the sake of all your brother priests the priest adorer and reparator that I have chosen you to be.

Make these words known. They will touch many hearts and I will make them fruitful in the souls of those who will read them with simplicity and with faith. There is nothing new in the words that I speak to you; their newness is in the way I am expressing My Heart's desires and My abiding love for My priests, to you and through you, for the sake of many. Be simple, then; pass on what I say to you during these times of adoration, and trust Me to give growth to the seed thus scattered abroad.[1]

Wednesday, February 1, 2012

When you come to adoration, hold yourself before My Eucharistic Face like a mirror before the sun. Thus will you capture the radiance of My Countenance and the fire that blazes in My Heart; thus will you become both light and fire for souls plunged into darkness and hearts grown cold.

How many precious souls perish because the priests I have sent to them are not men of light and of the fire of divine love! There are priests of mine who act as though they were ministers of Satan, bringing darkness with them, and causing souls to shudder for the lack of supernatural warmth. But this can change, if only My priests would return to Me and allow Me to make them all fire and all light in this world of yours, growing so dark and so cold. This world of yours is My world, for I created it, and I would fill with life and light all that I create. It is men who extinguish My light in the world and snuff out the fire of love that I came to cast upon the earth.[2]

O priests of Mine, when will you be converted and turn to Me, seeking My Face in the Sacrament of My love? When will you flee the coldness of the world to live close to the fire that can never be extinguished because it is the fire of love that burns in My Heart? I am not asking for anything difficult or hard to attain; I ask only that you seek Me out in the nearest tabernacle, where I am waiting for you. And when you have found Me there, abide with Me. Place your soul before Me as a mirror before the sun, and I will do great things in you and through you, for My love is a consuming fire of purity and the salvation of a world grown cold.

---

[1] 1 Cor 3:6–7; 2 Cor 9:7–15; Col 2:19; Jas 5:7–8; Mark 4:26–29.
[2] John 3:19–20; Luke 12:49.

When my priests return to My tabernacles, seeking My Face and yearning to rest upon My Heart, you will begin to see wondrous things in My Church—in My Church that has grown accustomed to living in mediocrity and lukewarmness. This is not My doing, for I am, in truth, a consuming fire.[1] It is, rather, the slow but relentless work of the Evil One who would see all that I created plunged into darkness and frozen in evil.

I am light and I am fire, and those who come to Me in the Sacrament of My love will become light and fire in Me. Do you not see this happening? Is this not your own experience? Love Me, then, and let love compel you to run to Me in the Sacrament of My love for you. More good can be done in a single hour of adoration than in a hundred days of uninterrupted preaching and apostolic labours, for when you are with Me, I am working for you. Time spent in My presence is not time lost. It is the multiplication of time and the magnification of your limited strength into an energy that comes from Me, an energy by which I will do great things through you.

All that does not proceed from Me is lost.[2] All that does not proceed from Me will be swept away on the day of temptation. All that does not come from Me is of no value in the kingdom of heaven. Seek, then, not to do much, but to love Me above all other things. One who loves Me will seek My Face, and find My Heart, and be set ablaze with the love that radiates from My sacramental presence.

I long to see priest adorers return from all sides to My Eucharistic presence. I long to see priest adorers discover that there is no better place on earth than the place reserved for them before My tabernacle. I long for priest adorers who will die to themselves and forsake all things for love of Me,[3] Who for love of them have made Myself so fragile, so little, and so hidden in the Sacrament of the Altar.

Friday, February 3, 2012

Behold, I stand at the door and knock.[4]

Fear is the great obstacle in interior prayer. Prayer, and Eucharistic adoration in particular, is a dangerous transaction because it threatens the state of mediocrity into which one has settled. In adoration I act

---

[1] Ex 24:17; Deut 4:24, 9:3; Ps 49(50):3; Isa 29:6, 30:27–30, 33:14; Heb 12:29.

[2] Inter alia, Eccles 2; Isa 49:4; Rom 14:23; Rev 18:13.

[3] Matt 10:37–39, 19:27–29; Mark 10:28–30; Luke 9:23–24, 14:33, 18:28–30; John 3:30, 12:24; Gal 2:20, 5:24, 6:14; Phil 3:8; 1 Pet 2:24.

[4] Rev 3:20.

upon the soul directly: the soul is exposed to Me in her poverty, her nakedness, and all her sins.

Adoration gives Me the space in which to work in a soul. It is the great corrective for those who, by their personality and character, are in constant movement and ever restless. Be still and know that I am God.[1] Open to Me the door of your heart and I will enter therein.[2] I will show you My Face and reveal to you the thoughts of My Heart. I will converse with you face-to-face, as a man converses with his dearest friend. There are those who go through life keeping Me at a distance because they fear what I might do should they allow Me to come close to them.

These souls do not yet know Me, for if they knew Me, they would know that I am love, and that all that I do is love. Eucharistic adoration is the remedy for the fear that keeps souls at a distance from Me. Why? Because it obliges one to stop, to quiet oneself with one's impulses, thoughts, desires, and projects, to abide close to Me, and to learn from Me that I am meek and humble of heart.[3] In adoration, one who labours for Me will find rest and refreshment for his soul.

A little reading during adoration is not a bad thing; it can dispose the soul to listening to Me directly when I speak to the heart.

Monday, February 6, 2012

As for you, love Me, count yourself for nothing, and believe always that you are held safely in My paternal love for you. There are things over which you will have no control. Humble yourself before Me, adhere to all My designs, and trust in My perfect love for you. I am not a cruel tyrant. I am the most loving of fathers, the Father from whom every fatherhood on earth derives its name.[4]

Thursday, February 9, 2012

Do one thing after another, calmly and quietly. I am with you to assist you in this work, and if you are attentive to My inspirations and obedient to the sound of My voice speaking to you inwardly, you will discover that everything is unfolding according to My plan of wisdom and love for you.

---

[1] Ps 45:11 (46:10).
[2] Rev 3:20; Song 5:2; Ps 23(24):7–10.
[3] Ps 45:9–12 (46:8–11); Matt 11:29.
[4] Eph 3:14–15.

Wednesday, February 22, 2012

All that is happening now is in My hands, and My love has ordered all things, even down to the smallest details, so as to make My care for you shine before the eyes of men. Thus will I confound the naysayers who doubt that I am at work in what you are doing by My inspiration. Go forward fearlessly and joyfully, trusting Me absolutely to provide for you, to protect you, to feed and clothe you,[1] and to instruct you in the mysterious designs of My Heart over you and over those whom I am sending to you.

Some of those who are most in need of what I am doing will resist and criticize it.[2] Do not let their resistances and criticisms slow the pace of your progress. The work is Mine and I desire to see it flourish, even if, at times, it seems that there is no hope and that all My promises have been vain delusions and empty fabrications of your own making. Such is not the case. It is I who have inspired this work in you, and I will bring it to completion. It is a work of My Sacred Heart. To doubt of what I am doing here is to doubt of My love for you. My love for you will never fail. Be humble, and trust in My love for you. Be bold, and act bravely.[3] I am with you, and so long as you are faithful to the adoration that I ask of you, all will unfold according to My plan, and I will stand by your decisions, and affirm the fatherhood that is My gift to you. Stay close to Me and know that I am in you, and with you, and at every moment attentive to your prayers.

I have gathered into this cenacle, as into the hospital of My Sacred Heart, the broken-hearted, the empty, the fearful, and the lonely. This I will continue to do, for My Heart is the refuge and rest of all who trust in My love.

Tuesday, March 6, 2012

Come to Me in adoration, and I will make straight your path before you.[4] I will remove the obstacles that loom in the distance, and I will provide for every need as it arises. Listen to Me and write My words, for I am speaking to you as I have done in the past and as I shall continue to do, for you are the friend of My Heart, and I have chosen you for this work which is Mine.

My Mother continues to protect you. She is your advocate and your

---

[1] Matt 6:25–34; Luke 12:22–32.

[2] John 16:1–4; Matt 15:7–9, 23:13; Luke 5:30–32, 12:54–56; Acts 7:51–53.

[3] Deut 31:6–7, 31:23; Josh 1:18, 10:25; 1 Kgs 2:1; Ps 26(27):14; Dan 10:19; Haggai 2:5 (2:4); 1 Macc 2:64; 1 Cor 16:13.

[4] Prov. 3:6, 4:27 (Vul.).

defence. She holds you close to her maternal Heart, and she will adopt in a similar way all whom I shall send you. Each one will be a son of Mary modelled after Saint John, to whom I entrusted My Mother from the Cross, that she might form him and teach him the secrets of My Heart, held within hers as in a tabernacle.[1]

From her did John receive the Word of Life, which became in his Gospel a light illumining the whole world and a fire of Eucharistic love giving warmth to souls grown cold.[2] Expose yourself often to My words in the Gospel of Saint John. Allow them to fall into your soul and to act upon it. You will discover that the Gospel of Saint John, drawn from the Immaculate Heart of My Mother, contains within itself a power to draw souls out of darkness into light, and out of the shadow of death into the radiance of My brightness.

So few souls understand that My Gospels are spirit and life.[3] One cannot hear My Gospel—the Gospel of My beloved disciple, in particular—without being drawn to My Heart, whence came the Sacrament of My love, by which I nourish My Church and make Myself present to her all days, even until the end of this passing world.[4]

There is nothing that I will not do for those who approach Me in the Sacrament of My love. Look at Me! Here I am vulnerable, exposed, hidden, and yet entirely delivered over to you. The Eucharist is the invention of My love, and nothing surpasses it in all My works. The Eucharist is more than creation itself[5]; it is the crown of My work of redemption in this world, and the foretaste of the glory that I have prepared for those who love Me, in the next.[6]

If souls understood what treasures of love are freely given to those who approach Me in the Sacrament of My love, My churches would be filled day and night, and unable to contain the multitudes drawn to them. But the Evil One has schemed and plotted to cover the mystery of

---

[1] John 19:25–27; Luke 1:41–43, 2:19, 2:51, 11:27–28.

[2] Phil 2:16; 1 John 1:1; John 1:9, 3:19–21, 8:12, 9:5, 11:9–10, 12:46; 2 Cor 4:4; Wis 17:19 (17:20).

[3] John 6:63.

[4] Matt 28:20; Eph 5:29; Col 2:19; Rev 12:14.

[5] As St. Thomas teaches, Christ as God is the extrinsic good to which the entire universe is ordered (see *Super I ad Cor.*, cap. 12, lec. 3), and the whole Christ is present in the Eucharist.

[6] For liturgical texts that convey the same truths, see the Office of the Feast of Corpus Christi composed by St. Thomas Aquinas. Consider the Magnificat antiphon for Vespers: "O sacrum convivium, in quo Christus sumitur: recolitur memoria passionis eius: mens impletur gratia: et futurae gloriae nobis pignus datur. Alleluia" (O sacred banquet, in which Christ is received, the memory of His Passion is renewed, the mind is filled with grace, and a pledge of future glory is given to us. Alleluia).

My presence with a dark veil of neglect, of irreverence, of forgetfulness, and of unbelief. He has obscured the mystery of My real presence, and so My faithful, beginning with My priests, have walked away from Me, one after the other, even as they did when first I spoke plainly of Myself as the living Bread come down from heaven to give life to the world.[1]

Satan hates those who, resisting his lies, have remained close to Me, adoring Me in the Sacrament of My love, and consoling My Heart that is so afflicted by the ingratitude of men and their lack of faith in the mystery of love that is My real Eucharistic presence. Because of these things that so grieve My Heart, I have called you to a life of adoration and reparation. Through your adoration and reparation, countless priests will return to My altars and to the Sacrament of My love, where I wait for them, never tiring of waiting for them, and ready to receive them into the embrace of My Eucharistic love.

Saturday, March 10, 2012

O my beloved Jesus, I am happy to be in Thy presence. Thy psalmist said it: "To be near God is my happiness."[2] There are no words to describe what it is to have Thee—God from God, Light from Light, Very God from Very God—so close.

Thou art hidden, but I see Thee.
Thou art silent, but I hear Thee.[3]
Thou art immobile, but Thou reachest out to draw me in
and hold me against Thy Heart.
One who possesses Thee in the Sacrament of Thy love,
possesses everything.
Because Thou art here, I lack nothing.
Because Thou art here, I have nothing to fear.[4]
Because Thou art here, I cannot be lonely.
Because Thou art here, heaven itself is here, and myriads of angels
adoring Thee and offering Thee their songs of praise.
Because Thou art here, I need not search for Thee anywhere else.[5]
Because Thou art here, my faith possesses Thee, my hope is anchored
to Thee, my love embraces Thee and will not let Thee go.[6]

---

[1] See John 6, esp. vv. 41–66.
[2] Ps 72 (73):28.
[3] Zeph 3:17 (Vul.); Rev 8:1.
[4] John 6:20; Isa 12:2, 44:6–8; Jer 1:8.
[5] John 20:11–18.
[6] Eph. 3:17; Heb 6:19; Song 3:4.

You, then, be silent, because I am silent; be hidden, because I am hidden; be humble, because I am humble.[1] Efface yourself, because here I have effaced Myself in order to remain with you, in order to give you the radiance of My Face in a way that illuminates your soul without blinding you.

I withhold nothing from those who love Me and seek Me in this the Sacrament of My silent, living presence. Those who come to Me, and abide in My presence but once, if they allow Me to touch their souls, will return to Me again and again. They will find in Me all that is necessary for happiness in this world, even when suffering abounds and when a darkness seems to have fallen over all things. In the Sacrament of My love, I am the pearl of great price and the treasure hidden in the field.[2] I am the lasting happiness of the man who sells all that he possesses in order to possess Me.

I am here for you, beloved friend and priest of My Heart. I am here for you, and nothing will keep Me from giving to you according to My Heart's desire. Come to Me and receive what I wait to give you. You will never be disappointed nor will you go away empty.

Give to me, Lord Jesus, according to Thy Heart's desire. I am an empty vessel waiting for Thee to fill me. I would remain before Thee, silent and empty, and prepared to be filled with whatever it shall please Thee to pour into me. Fill me according to Thy desire, not only for myself, but for others, for the souls whom Thou wilt send to me, that I may give them something pure, something divine to drink.

Tuesday, March 13, 2012

No moment spent in My presence is without value. Every moment given Me is precious in My sight and becomes fruitful for the whole Church. It is not a question of quantity, of spending long hours in My presence when the duties of one's state in life require something else. What I ask instead is the moment of pure adoration and of love offered to Me from a simple, childlike heart. Just as a mother takes as much delight in a single wildflower offered by her child as in a great

---

[1] On silence, cf. Zeph 1:7, 3:17 (Vul.); Zech 2:13; Job 6:24; Wis 18:14; Matt 26:63; Mark 14:61; Rev 8:1. On hiddenness, cf. Isa 45:15; Ps 30:21 (31:20); Hab 3:4; John 8:59, 12:36; 1 Cor 2:7; Col 2:3; 1 Pet 3:4; Rev 2:17. On humility, cf. Judith 9:16; Sir 10:17–21; Matt 11:29, 18:4.

[2] Matt 13:44–46.

bouquet of flowers, so too do I take delight in the moment offered Me out of love.

Begin, then, by offering Me what you can. You will see that I will move you to add moment to moment, until you are giving Me all the time of adoration and of love that I desire from you. Too many souls are discouraged when they attempt to pray. They think, wrongly, that unless they can undertake much, they should undertake nothing. And so they abandon prayer and leave Me alone, leave Me waiting for their little moment of presence, a consolation to My Heart.

Give Me the little moment of adoration and of love and I will multiply it, making it possible for you to give Me hours of adoration and of love, as they become available in your life, and as I ask them of you. Too many souls try to do too much, and end up doing nothing. It is better to begin by doing what is very little, and by entrusting that little offering to Me, confident that I will receive it and turn it to My glory and to the glory of My Father.

Thursday, March 15, 2012

It is the little and the poor who come to Me in the Sacrament of My love and who console My Heart by their presence to Me. It has always been so. The proud and the worldly have no time for Me, because I am hidden, because I am poor, because I am silent, in the Sacrament of My love.[1] But those who are themselves humble and poor are drawn to the humility and the poverty of My Eucharistic presence. I welcome them. I take comfort in their presence, and I recognize them as those blessed of My Father to whom belongs already the Kingdom of Heaven.[2]

Sunday, March 18, 2012

Thou hast called me to this hidden life of adoration and reparation because Thou desirest to have, close to Thy tabernacles on earth, men who will imitate Thy hidden sacramental life in the adorable mystery of Thy real presence.

Unite me, then, I beseech Thee, to Thy Eucharistic humility, to Thy silence, Thy hiddenness, and Thy ceaseless prayer to the Father. Unite me to the uninterrupted oblation of Thyself to the Father in the Sacrament of Thy love. There is no moment in which Thou art not offering Thyself, no moment in which Thy immolation on the Cross is not re-presented to the

---

[1] 1 Cor 1:18–31.
[2] Matt 25:34.

Father from the silence of Thy tabernacles. Let nothing, then, separate me from Thyself,[1] the Lamb of God by Whose Blood the world is redeemed, souls are washed clean of sin, and the Father's Heart is moved to pity for the most hardened sinners and for the very least of His creatures. Amen.

Friday, April 20, 2012

O my beloved Jesus, I adore Thy Eucharistic Face, the radiance of which is my unfailing light in the shadows of this earthly exile. So long as Thou art with me, I will fear no evil. Thou art here, close to me, and I am here, close to Thee, to believe in Thee, to hope in Thee, to love Thee, and to adore Thee. Apart from Thee I desire nothing on earth, and without Thee, what is heaven?[2] Here in Thy Eucharistic presence is heaven on earth. Here is the joy eternal of all the angels and blessed. Here is the fulfilment of the longing in hope that burns like a fire in the souls of purgatory.[3] Here is the heart of the Church on earth and the glory of the Church in heaven. Here is the stupendous miracle of Thy love for us: Thy abiding presence as the Lamb who was slain, and the triumph of Thy Cross and Resurrection.

Why, then, art Thou left alone in this Most Holy Sacrament? Why art Thou forsaken in Thy tabernacles? Why are Thy churches empty or so rarely visited? Reveal Thyself again in the Sacrament of Thy love! Make known Thy presence here to those who doubt, to the ignorant, the indifferent, and the cold-hearted. Draw all—baptized and unbaptized—into the radiance of Thy Eucharistic Face, and let not a single soul escape the embrace of Thy Eucharistic friendship. Thus wilt Thou satisfy Thine own thirst for the faith and love of our souls, and thus wilt Thou satisfy Thine own Heart's longing for the love of the hearts which Thou hast created for Thyself and no other. Amen.

Monday, April 23, 2012

The gift you asked of Me, the gift of adoration, has already been given to you. You have only to make use of it. You will see it multiply in souls around you. Thus will this place become the house of adoration that My Heart has so long desired. Trust in these My words to you, and make use of the gift I have given you.

---

[1] Cf. the second prayer of the priest before receiving Holy Communion in the *usus antiquior* of the Roman Rite: "Fac me tuis semper inhaerere mandatis, et a te numquam separari permittas" (make me always cleave to Thy commandments, and suffer me never to be separated from Thee).

[2] Ps 15(16):2; Ps 72(73):25; Prov 3:15.

[3] See St. Catherine of Genoa, *Purgation and Purgatory*, trans. Serge Hughes (New York: Paulist Press, 1979).

Sunday, April 29, 2012

Do you not see the love with which I have prepared all things for you in bringing you to this place? Yes, I shall make it a place of healing and of hope for many, beginning with those who are here at this moment. I shall cause My Eucharistic love to radiate into every heart from My Face, which, though hidden, shines more brightly than the sun in this Sacrament of My abiding presence among you.

Let My adorers take their place before Me. Their faith, their hope, and their surrender to My merciful love will cause a great tide of healing love to pour forth from My sacred side and radiate from My Face. Thus will My adorers, without leaving My sanctuary, become also My apostles: messengers and instruments of My merciful love and of My burning desire to gather in the lost, to bind up the bruised, to tend the wounded, and to heal the broken-hearted.

I am speaking to you now as I have already spoken to you in the past, and as I will continue to speak to you for your own sake and for the sake of those who will read My words. My love for you has not diminished, nor have the dispositions of My Heart towards you changed. I love you tenderly, faithfully, mercifully; and I will draw you into the embrace of My friendship, and hold you close against My sacred side until, at length, you come to abide in My Most Sacred Heart, the sanctuary of My elect, and the refuge of poor sinners.

Trust My love for you, and go forward, acting boldly and bravely, for I am with you, and this work is altogether Mine. It is a work of My merciful love for priests, for the men I have chosen out of millions of others to be the cherished friends of My Heart and intimate sharers in My Passion of love.[1]

Allow Me to love you, by coming before Me and by remaining in My presence. This is what I ask of you before all else. Seek Me first, and you will discover that I will provide you with time to come before Me.[2] Listen closely to My inspirations and to the suggestions that I make through your guardian angel, through My Immaculate Mother, and through our friends, the saints whom I have charged to support you, to guide you, and to walk with you in this life.

All of these are co-workers with the Holy Ghost, acting in union with the uncreated Love that is the bond of My union with the Father and with all My elect, the saints in heaven and on earth. Nothing done by

---

[1] Song 5:10; Ps 104(105):26; Hag 2:24 (2:23); Matt 22:14; John 13:18, 15:16; Acts 1:2, 10:41; Heb 5:1.
[2] Matt 6:33; Luke 12:31.

My saints in heaven is accomplished apart from the Holy Spirit, and all that My saints do, by way of signs and miracles, manifests the creative power of the Holy Spirit at work in the Church, not only through the sacraments I instituted and gave her, but also through the intercession of the angels and saints in glory.

Love me, then, and trust in My love for you. Ask the Holy Spirit to inflame you with the same fire of love that burns in My Sacred Heart and in the hearts of all My saints. It is in the prayer of adoration that this love grows strong, becoming a fire that gives light and warmth to all who approach it, burning in the hearts of My loved ones.

May 17, 2012
Ascension Thursday

Listen to me. It is in silence that I speak to souls. Those who flee silence will never hear My voice. Encourage silence and practice it yourself with a renewed dedication, for it is in silence that the Holy Spirit descends, and it is in silence that He works in souls, bringing them to holiness of life, and to the perfection that I desire for each one.

Enter into the Cenacle with My Mother and My apostles. Invoke them and live these days in their company. The spirit of the Cenacle is one of charity, silence, effective separation from the world, and perseverance in prayer. This is what I ask of you. A week or more of silence will bring nothing but benefits to mind, and soul, and body.

I love silence—look at My sacramental life[1]—and I love those who follow Me into the silence of My Eucharistic presence. The Eucharist is the most silent of sacraments. Once the words of consecration are spoken, I am present, and My presence is wrapped in a profound silence. I am silent in the Sacrament of My love because there I am humble. There I lower Myself to live hidden, and often forgotten, in a silence that only the lowly of heart can understand.

May 27, 2012
Pentecost Sunday

Come, Holy Ghost!
Come, living Fire!
Come, Anointing from above!
Come, living Water!
Come, Breath of God!

---

[1] That is, the Sacred Host.—*Author.*

Mark me with an incision of fire for the work to which I have been called. Sign my soul deeply and indelibly for the adoration of the Eucharistic Face of the Son and for the consolation of His Eucharistic Heart. So burn the mark of this vocation into me that I will suffer from every betrayal of it, and from every infidelity to it. So seal me for this vocation that I will find Thee only in fulfilling it and in its perfection in the lasting adoration of heaven, where Thou livest and reignest with the Father and the Son.

Let the adoration of the Lamb begin for me here on earth today, and let it increase and deepen in my life until it becomes ceaseless: a spring of joy flowing from an inexhaustible source, Thine own indwelling presence in my soul, to quench the thirst of the Bridegroom Christ,[1] and to make fruitful His priesthood in the Church. Amen.

Saturday, June 2, 2012

You have begun this month of June well by offering yourself as a victim to the merciful love of My Heart. I will take you into the radiance of My Eucharistic Face, and I will consume you in the fire of My Eucharistic Heart. Spend yourself in loving Me, seek My Eucharistic Face, abide close to My Eucharistic Heart, and I will do all the rest. You will lack nothing. I am your provider, your lover, your friend. I am your food, your drink, your clothing, and your shelter. I am your counsellor in uncertainty, your comforter in tribulation, your companion in exile.

Refer all things to Me. Let nothing distract you from your essential work: to abide in My presence, loving Me for those who do not love Me; trusting Me for those who do not trust Me; thanking Me for those who do not thank Me; and offering yourself to Me for those who withhold themselves from Me—above all, for My poor priests, your brothers in this valley of tears. Be faithful to this essential work, and I will make it prosper. Priests will return to the love of My Heart and begin to dwell in the light of My Eucharistic Face. Thus will the whole Church begin to be renewed in the shining holiness that is My Heart's desire and My will for her.

Do not neglect the Confraternity of Priest Adorers; establish it as soon as possible. Through it My Heart will be consoled by My priests. The radiance of My Face will shine from their faces, and many of those who have lived far from Me in darkness will return to live and to walk in the light of My Face. It is time for you to present this to your bishop. Then, go forward, trusting in Me to move the hearts of many priests to adhere to this initiative of My Heart and of the maternal Heart of My Immaculate Mother.

---

[1] Isa 12:3; John 4:13–14, 19:28; Rev 7:17.

Thursday, June 7, 2012

It is by adoring Me that this little monastery will be brought to life and will become the centre of love, and of mercy, and of grace for priests that I want it to be. Here, by adoring Me, you are building this monastery—or rather, by adoring Me, you are allowing Me to build it and to provide for all that the fulfilment of My plan requires.

Saturday, June 9, 2012

You are always in My presence, and when your heart is directed towards My Heart, there is no distance between us. My sacramental presence, though unique, substantial, and real, is not the only form of My presence.[1] It is not possible for you to remain at every moment of the day close to Me in the Sacrament of My love and before My altar, but it is possible for you to adore Me at every moment in the inner sanctuary of your soul, where I am also present, together with My Father and with the Holy Spirit.

Adhere to My will at every moment, and you will be adoring Me at every moment. I understand the complexities and circumstances of your life. Be with Me by desiring to be with Me. The desire never to leave My sacramental presence is, in effect, as precious in My sight as if you were physically before Me, adoring Me, listening to Me, speaking to Me. Learn from My servant Mother Mectilde how to adore Me perpetually without forsaking the things that require your attention. I am present intimately, and in the secret sanctuary of the soul, to all who desire to be with Me, to all who seek My Face, and who desire to rest upon My Heart.

Give Me your inability to carry out all that you propose to do, and I will receive your incapacity, and change it, by My love, into an offering more pleasing than the successful accomplishment of what you propose to do. Trust Me with your weaknesses. Give Me your inability to do even what I have inspired you to do. Your poverty, your infirmity, even your inconstancy is no obstacle to My work in your soul—provided that you abandon all to Me with complete confidence in My merciful love. Do what you can reasonably do, and what you cannot do, give to Me as well. I am as much pleased with the offering of the one as I am with the offering of the other. Let these words comfort you. Know that I am not a taskmaster, but a friend, and the most loving and welcoming of friends.

---

[1] Cf. Pope Paul VI, Encyclical Letter *Mysterium Fidei* (September 3, 1965), §§20–21.

What friend would greet the one he loves with a reproach rather than with a tender welcome?

Yes, I have called you to a life of adoration and of reparation, but I call you also to humility, to the little way of spiritual childhood, and to a boundless trust in My mercy. Adore Me, then, in the Sacrament of My love, as much as you can, and when you are unable to do this, adore Me in the meeting place with Me that is your infirmity, your weakness, and the needs of the present moment.

Adore Me ceaselessly in the sanctuary of your soul, and know that your adoration there glorifies Me in the Sacrament of My love and in the glory of heaven, where, one day, I will unite you to Myself forever.

Friday, June 22, 2012

Listen to Me, for I am speaking to you now as I have spoken to you in the past. You were not deceived, and any inaccuracies in what you wrote came from your imagination, not from the Evil One, and these inaccuracies are few. It was I who was speaking to you to console you, to strengthen you in your love for Me, and to draw you into the silence that is the particular grace of those whom I unite to Myself in love.

Be at peace, then, and have no fear for the future. I am speaking to you now as I have in the past, from the depths of My Heart's love for you. Believe in My love for you, and I will protect you from the errors of your own imagination and from the deceits of the Evil One. I want our dialogues to continue, for I have chosen you to be the intimate friend of My Heart, and friendship thrives on conversation and on the intimate exchange of one heart with another.

This is the friendship that I desire to have with every one of My priests, but because so few accept it, I have chosen you to be the friend of My Sacred Heart, to be for Me another John. In this way, you will make reparation for your brother priests, and console My Heart, which is wounded by their coldness, ingratitude, irreverence, and indifference.

There are those who will not believe that I have spoken to you, or that I am speaking to you still. Do not allow this to trouble you. What I say to you will be recognized as coming from Me by the fruits it produces in your life.[1]

Do not dwell on apprehensions and fears of going astray. Trust in Me, and in the guidance of the Holy Ghost, who dwells within you, and rests upon you.[2] So long as you hear in My words to you nothing that varies

---

[1] Matt 7:16–20.
[2] John 16:13; 2 Tim 1:14; 1 Thes 4:8; 1 Pet 4:14; 1 John 2:27.

from the teaching of My Church, you can go forward in peace. You will know when the Evil One is trying to counterfeit My words to you by the unrest that they will cause. And you will also know when certain elements in our conversations come from your own imaginings, fears, or desires. Be at peace. Listen to Me, and abide in My love for you.

Thursday, June 28, 2012

Let Me do My work in your soul and in this place that I have chosen for you and for many other souls. I will make it a place of restoration, of healing, and of peace. I will renew souls in the radiance of My Eucharistic Face, and I will draw them into the silent sanctuary of My Heart. There they will know the love of My Father and the sweet fire of the Holy Ghost. Here, too, souls will come to experience the maternal care of My Mother's Immaculate Heart.

Thursday, July 5, 2012

Adoration is the soul of what I am doing here. Should adoration cease, the physical body of the monastery will begin to disintegrate, the community will fail, and nothing will remain of it but an empty shell.

Adoration continues the priestly action that is Mine in the Mass, and engages you in it. Adore, then, and all shall be well. This is My promise to you.

This will be the monastery built by adoration. I will do great things here and manifest the merciful love of My Heart to all who approach Me in the Sacrament of My love.

Friday, July 6, 2012

Had I given to other men the grace of adoration that I have given you, you would be tempted to allow them to do in your place what My Heart requires and expects from you alone. You must be the first adorer of this house. You will adore Me in response to My Heart's desire, and, then, from you, others will catch the spark of adoration, and so a great fire of love, of adoration, and of reparation will blaze up before My Eucharistic Face. Thus will My plan and My desire be fulfilled here.

Others will come later who have the grace of adoration, but at this time, adoration is your essential work, and I want it first from you. The day will come when adorers of My Eucharistic Face will fill My house and succeed each other in keeping a vigil of adoration, reparation, and love, close by My Eucharistic Heart. In that day will My Heart's designs on this place be fulfilled for the greater joy of the Church and for the consolation of My Sacred Heart that is grievously wounded by the indifference, coldness, and irreverence of so many of My priests.

You will make reparation for them, and so become the father of a family of souls who will understand that reparation is the response of love to My sorrowful love; sorrowful because it is refused by those whom I would cherish above all other men, My own priests; sorrowful because the very men whom I am pleased to call My friends turn from My Heart's friendship, and look elsewhere for the satisfaction of their own need for love, for companionship, and for understanding.

You will make reparation for them, and thus, little by little, My priests—even those far off from Me—will find their way back to My altars, and will discover that I wait for them in the closed tabernacles where their own hands will have placed Me.

Sunday, July 15, 2012

What matters is not what you are thinking or saying,[1] for I am pleased and comforted and glorified by your simply being with Me. Be present in My presence. This is what I ask of you. So many others among My priests leave Me alone in the Sacrament of My love. They grow cold, indifferent, and hard-hearted. An hour spent in My presence would be enough to reinflame their hearts, to move them to gratitude and love, and to open their souls to the grace of My friendship. I ask only that My priests return to My altars, and that they seek Me in the tabernacles where I am truly present and waiting for them. So much sin can be avoided and so many sins repaired by a simple act of loving presence to My Eucharistic Heart!

I am here for My priests. I will draw them to My Heart. I will reveal to them the priceless grace of My divine friendship. And, from the Sacrament of My love, I shall renew the face of the priesthood in My Church. The shortage of priests in some places is caused, not by Me, but by the laxity that has come to prevail and, above all, by the great diminishment of prayer in the hearts and on the lips of My priests.

Wheresoever My priests return to prayer, there will I cause a vast harvest of priestly vocations to spring up.[2] I will multiply My priests just as I multiplied loaves and fishes to feed the multitude in the desert.[3] When

---

[1] The context shows that Our Lord is referring to one who is at Eucharistic adoration.

[2] Jesus connects the prayer of the disciples to the raising up of vocations in Matt 9:37–38 and Luke 10:2.

[3] The miracle of the feeding of the five thousand with five loaves and two fishes is recounted in all four Gospels: Matt 14:13–21; Mark 6:31–44; Luke 9:10–17; John 6:5–15.

priests forsake prayer, they forsake Me, and so I withdraw My blessing from their labours, and leave them to themselves, for without prayer—without Me—they can do nothing.[1]

Thursday, July 26, 2012

Come to Me whenever you can and as often as you can. There is not a moment when I am not waiting for you, not a moment when My Heart is not open to receive you. Do you not believe in My friendship for you? Have you forgotten that I chose you to be My companion and the consoler of My Heart, in reparation for those of My priests who reject My companionship, and who, by their coldness, grieve My Eucharistic Heart?

I came to you today as a gift in the form of M. Yvonne-Aimée's little King of Love. I came here as the King of Love to bring peace and healing to each one of you, and to all who will visit here or enter this house. I came to show My Heart to you and to your sons. I came to heal the long-festering wounds of childhood, and to establish souls in security and in confidence in My Heart's merciful goodness.

Receive Me as the King of Love. Consecrate yourselves to Me. Honour My image, and I will produce in you and in this house marvels of healing, of holiness, and of compassion. I enter here as a little child, as the Child King. Receive Me, welcome Me, and I will receive and welcome each one of you.

This is your vocation. Do not lose sight of it. Come to Me more often, and remain quietly in My presence. There is no need for you to say or do anything. You have only to expose your soul to the penetrating radiance of My Eucharistic Face, believing and trusting that I will act in you to do in you what no human being can do in himself. Yield to My divine action. Give Me permission to act in you and upon you. Resolve to abandon yourself to My love, and then be at peace, for in this one resolution is the secret of all holiness.

Honour My love by allowing Me to love you. There is no more effective way to grow in holiness and to acquire the virtues that will make you My instrument and the priest that I would have you be.

M. Yvonne-Aimée, your faithful friend in heaven, obtained this gift and this grace for you, to show you that she is present to you, and attentive to your needs. You are not alone. My saints in heaven follow you closely, to encourage and to comfort, to guide and to console, to instruct

---

[1] Jer 17:13–14; John 15:5.

and to correct. Live with My saints, the servants of My kingly munificence and the collaborators in all the works of My merciful love.

I came to you today as the little grandchild of Joachim and Anna. Tell Me that you are happy to have Me in this house, and invite Me to rule over your heart and in your life.

Monday, November 12, 2012
At the Priory of ——

While praying before the Most Holy Sacrament at night:

A great work of love is being done here, one that proceeds directly from My Eucharistic Heart, to glorify My Father and to redeem the world—for the work of redemption is continued in the Sacrament of My Body and Blood until the end of time.[1] I have chosen you to share in this Eucharistic work of Mine by calling you to this very life of adoration and reparation that you see here.

I am here in the Most Blessed Sacrament for you and for the whole world. Take your place here before Me, and abide before My Face, close to My Heart that is all love.

It is no little thing for a poor human creature of Mine to prefer My Eucharistic love to an hour of sleep in the night. Only in heaven will you know the worth of an hour so spent. Come to Me, then. Visit Me, and remain with Me by night, and I will work for you, and with you, and through you by day. By nocturnal adoration you will obtain from My Heart things which cannot be obtained from Me in any other way, especially the liberation of souls from the influence and oppression of the powers of darkness. More souls are saved and liberated by adoration made during the night than by any other form of prayer: this is the prayer that unites you most closely to My own nights passed entirely in prayer during My life on earth.[2]

Come to Me, then, by night, and you shall experience My power and My presence at your side during the day. Ask of Me whatsoever you will by coming to Me at night, and you will experience My merciful help at break of day. I love with a love of predilection those whom I call to be

---

[1] Cf. the Secret for the Ninth Sunday after Pentecost: "Concede nobis, quæsumus, Domine, hæc digne frequentare mysteria: quia, quoties hujus hostiæ commemoratio celebratur, opus nostræ redemptionis exercetur" (Grant to us, we beseech Thee, O Lord, that we may worthily frequent these mysteries: for as often as the memorial of this Victim is celebrated, the work of our redemption is wrought).

[2] Luke 6:12; Matt 26:36.

with Me during the hours of the night. The prayer of adoration at night has the power and efficacy of that prayer made with fasting that I recommended to My apostles as the means of expelling demons from the souls whom they torture and oppress.[1] For this reason, the demons fear and hate adoration made at night, while the angels rejoice over it, and place themselves at the service of the soul who desires to do it.

⊕

March 28, 2013
Maundy Thursday

The first thing I asked of My priests, My newly-ordained apostles—and of these, the three closest to My Heart—was to watch and pray with Me.[2] I did not send them out immediately, nor did I entrust them with any priestly task apart from keeping watch with Me in prayer, lest they fall in the hour of trial. I wanted them close to Me to console Me, to comfort Me in My agony by their union with My prayer of obedience and abandonment to the Father. This was their first priestly action, their first mandate as priests of the New Covenant: not to preach, not to teach, not to heal, not even to baptize, but to watch and pray with Me.

I wanted them to understand by this that unless a priest keeps watch and perseveres in prayer, all else will be in vain. He will dispense the substance of My mysteries, but without the sweetness of a heavenly unction, without the fire and light of a personal experience of My divine friendship. This is why I beg My priests to become adorers, to begin to watch and pray, close to Me in the Sacrament of My love.

If you could have heard the urgency and sorrow of My plea to Peter, James, and John! I did not merely ask them to watch and pray, I begged them to do so. I needed their prayer at that hour, just as I need the prayer of all My priests in this final hour that is coming and that is already upon My Church.[3]

Only the prayer of My priests, made in union with the prayer of My Heart to the Father, will be able to preserve and console My Church in the darkness that lies ahead. I beg for the prayer of My priests, for a

---

[1] Matt 17:20; Mark 9:28.

[2] Matt 26:41; Mark 14:38.

[3] Our Lord needs us not in the sense that He is weak or incapable of achieving certain ends, but because in His goodness He wills to need us and make use of us. See Pope Pius XII, Encyclical Letter *Mystici Corporis Christi* (June 29, 1943), §44.

prayer of adoration, of reparation, and of supplication. I ask them for a prayer that is sincere and persevering, for a prayer that will become in their hearts a ceaseless murmur rising to the Father as a spiritual offering.

When will My priests begin to pray as I have asked them for so long—lo, all these centuries—to pray? I want priests who will watch and pray with Me. I need such priests. Without their prayer, My mystic agony will be prolonged and be without consolation from the friends whom I have chosen to abide with Me in the trials that will soon beset My Church, My poor, frail Bride.

The crisis in My priesthood will continue and will even grow worse unless My priests, the chosen friends of My Heart, forsake this passing world's vanities and empty pursuits to become adorers in spirit and in truth.

I pleaded with My apostles to watch and pray, and they slept.[1] Still do I plead with My priests to watch and pray, and still they sleep, even at this hour when My Church invites them to stay with Me, to linger close to My real presence, and not to forsake Me in the darkness and terror of this night. Where are My priests? I wait for them. I call to them. I desire that they leave all else to offer Me their companionship, their presence, their wordless love, and their tears.

Those who are responding to My plea, and to the first mandate given to My Apostles, are still too few. Offer yourself so that others may find their way to My altars and learn that there is no sweetness, no comfort, and no presence like the sweetness, the comfort, and the presence that I offer them in the Most Holy Sacrament, which they themselves consecrate for My Church.

The words that I have given you are given not for you alone, but for the priests whom I will send to you. Share with them this desire of My Heart for priests who will keep watch close to My altars and abide in My presence, even if this means forsaking things that are, in themselves, innocent, and good, and gratifying. The hour is late. Soon there will be no time left to offer Me the prayer and companionship that I have always sought and still seek from My priests. I say this not to cause panic or fright, but because priests must begin to realize that what I asked of My Apostles in Gethsemane perdures. It is My request, here and now, and it is no less urgent today than it was in that awful night in Gethsemane.

---

[1] Matt 26:36–46; Mark 14:32–42.

Let them begin to carry out the first request I made to My priests, the first mandate I gave them: to watch and to pray. Only then will they live to see the splendour of My glory on the day of My return.

Why, beloved Jesus, were there so many false starts in my life? So many attempts to reach Thee that turned to bitterness, or delusion, or failure?

These were all an attempt to escape from the pain and inner confusion that had been inflicted upon you as a child. I allowed all of these things to befall you; I allowed you to make mistakes and to knock at the wrong doors because, by this, I was preparing you to accept My plan for you. I humbled you so as to make of you an instrument for My use.

May 20, 2013
Pentecost Monday

Why, beloved Jesus, hast Thou brought Mother Mectilde and so many other holy women into my life? Hast Thou really put me in the school of Mother Mectilde? Am I not in Thine eyes a son of Saint Benedict?

From the beginning I chose you to be My adorer, like Saint John, and adoration does not come easily to men. Just as I placed Saint John in the school of My Mother to learn what it is to adore, so have I placed you in the school of Mother Mectilde to learn to adore Me as I would have you adore Me. Mother Mectilde's institute is the school of My Mother; by enrolling in the school of Mother Mectilde, you have entered the school of My own Virgin Mother, like Saint John.

Saturday, June 15, 2013

There is no suffering that I cannot heal, and if I allow certain souls to suffer for a longer period of time, giving them no sign of My healing power, it is because out of their suffering I intend to bring a great good. You must believe this and help others to believe it, for out of this truth there will come confidence and hope, even in the darkest hours.

I do not measure time as men measure it, nor do I judge the intensity of suffering as men do. I know what I am doing, even when I hide My plans from men in order to test their faith in Me, and cause that faith to grow strong and indomitable.

There are, alas, many souls who, in their hour of suffering, stop believing. They lose their faith in Me, and descend into hopelessness, and even despair. To rise from their suffering, they have only to make the smallest act of faith; it will dispel the darkness and lift them out of their despair. A little act of faith is immensely powerful; it is a spark of fire and of light in the vast cold darkness of sin and disbelief.

Faith will not always remove suffering, but it will make it bearable, and will suffuse it with a supernatural hope. Others can make this act of faith for the ones who are suffering until, helped by their prayers, they have enough strength to make it for themselves.

You are doing this when you come before Me in the Sacrament of My love. Is this not an act of faith? Does not your adoration express utter confidence in My plan and complete adherence to My will? You can make your adoration for those who cannot make it for themselves. You can believe for those who have (or think they have) no faith, for those who are without hope, and for those in whose hearts love has grown cold.

Do this for the one you have presented to Me in his sufferings. Do this, and leave all the rest to Me, following My counsels as I make them known to you, and trusting in Me to act. There is no more effective way to bring comfort to those who suffer, to obtain healing for those who are ill and deliverance for those whom the powers of darkness oppress and persecute.

I am always here for you, and there is no time at which you cannot come to Me with the things that weigh upon you. Come to Me and I will refresh you. I will show you the way in which you are to go forward. I will speak to you heart to heart, as a man speaks to his closest friend.[1] Do not stay away from Me. On the contrary, come to Me frequently, as often as you can. Abide with Me. Wait upon Me. Listen to Me. And you will experience the wonders of My loving mercy in you and around you, for I am the King of Love, and this place is Mine. I have claimed it all for My own Heart and for the glorification of My Eucharistic Face by a family of faithful adorers and by souls of reparation, souls of a great love, a love drawn from My Eucharistic Heart as heat is drawn from a furnace that burns without ever going out.

I am here for you. Come, and be here for Me. Take your place before Me and wait for Me to act. I will speak to you again as I have spoken to you in the past, and your soul will thrive and flourish in the radiance of My Face and because of the power of My words, all of which are words of love and emanations of the love of My Heart.

---

[1] Ex 33:11; 2 John 1:12.

IN SINU JESU

Saturday, September 7, 2013

In re-reading the life of Father Antoine Crozier,[1] I was given to understand:

It is normal that a priest be stigmatised; what is not normal, in fact, is that he not be. The real union with the Crucified each day at the altar should leave the traces of His holy wounds in his hands, in his feet, and in his heart. In offering the Holy Sacrifice of the Mass, the priest is totally assimilated to Jesus crucified. This the Father sees; this the angels see; it is only men who do not see it.

The depth of the impression of the wounds of Jesus in the heart and in the soul of the priest is proportionate to his degree of abandonment to the embrace of Jesus, who desires only to unite him to Himself. In some, the interior impression is so strong that it manifests itself even in the flesh of the priest; in others, the identification with the Crucified remains all interior and hidden; in still others, it is barely sketched in the soul of the priest, because he rebels against the idea of letting himself be crucified with Christ, and wants to keep his life for himself.

To ascend to the altar to offer there the Holy Sacrifice is already to offer oneself to the piercing of the nails and of the lance, and to the crown of thorns. To offer the Holy Sacrifice of the Mass is already to risk the secret interior stigmatisation that the Father sees, who sees in secret, and the angels who are admitted to contemplate the immolation of the Lamb renewed in the body and in the soul of a man.

To offer oneself to the interior stigmatisation is entirely in the logic of priestly ordination. In some men, God permits it to be manifested visibly, with outpourings of blood. In others, the same mystery is lived in secret, without any outward manifestation. It remains that every priest is chosen to bear the marks of the Passion of Christ, and to be the living icon of His immolation each day upon the altar.

Then I asked, "Who is explaining all this to me?"

[1] Antoine Crozier (February 8, 1850–April 10, 1916) was ordained a priest for the archidiocese of Lyon in 1877. After he became chaplain of a Carmel, and encouraged by its prioress, he published *Comment il faut aimer le bon Dieu* [How We Must Love the Good God], which became very popular. His meeting with a Carmelite visionary, Antonine Gachon (1861–1945), led to his founding in 1888 of a union dedicated to the cult of the Sacred Heart. This union, and Fr. Crozier's personal friendship, later played a major role in the life of Bd. Charles de Foucauld. On January 10, 1901, Fr. Crozier received the stigmata during Mass, but asked Jesus to make the wounds invisible, a prayer that was granted. Fr. Crozier nevertheless continued to suffer the pain of the wounds until his death.

It is I, Antoine Crozier, priest of Lyon, who am explaining this to you; it is the entire meaning of my life and of yours, insofar as you are priest and victim. Do not refuse what the Lord is asking of you. Offer yourself to Him each day, so that He may impress in the depth of your heart the marks that are the proof of His love—of that love that He wants to put in you so that you may be transformed into Him.

Friday, November 15, 2013

Leave aside the things that distract you from Me. I am the one thing necessary to you in this life.[1] Save your eyes, your ears, your mouth, your hands, and your heart, your whole being for Me, and I will unite you to Myself. Close your eyes to vanities, and your ears to flattery and deceit. Open your mouth to praise Me, to sing My glory, to speak of Me, and to speak good things to your neighbour. Keep yourself for Me, as I keep Myself for you in the Sacrament of My love.

Know that I wait for you. There is a consolation that only you can give Me. It is your friendship that My Heart desires, and this friendship of yours cannot be replaced by any other. You are Mine and I am yours.[2] Abide in Me and I will abide in you,[3] speaking through you, and touching souls through your words.

Allow Me to be the physician of souls and bodies through you. I want to live in you and pursue on earth all of those things that I did out of love and compassion when I walked among men in My flesh. You are My flesh now, and you are My presence in the world. It is through you that I make Myself visible to men. It is through you that I will speak to them, and comfort them, and heal them, and draw them to My Father in the Holy Spirit.

There is nothing that I will not do for souls through My priests. Let them be visible and present in the world that needs them and, without knowing it, seeks them and waits for a word from them: a word of life, a word of hope, a word of compassion, a word of forgiveness. Let My priests be visible, not in order to make themselves seen and admired by men, but in order to make *Me* seen, and known, and loved in them and through them.

The world is looking for fathers, and in My priests I have given souls the fathers whom they need. There are false fathers who would abuse souls and lead them along, and exercise seduction and power over them.

[1] Luke 10:42.
[2] Song 2:16.
[3] John 15:4.

These are not the fathers whom I am sending into the world. The fathers whom I send to souls are men in My own image and likeness: humble, meek, self-sacrificing, tender, and strong. I will give to these fathers, chosen and sent out by Me, a wisdom and a courage that the enemies of My Cross will not be able to confound.[1] Let My priests forsake all self-ishness and worldly aggrandisement, and so become fathers to souls in need of love, comfort, direction, guidance, and courage. It is through My priests—fathers in whom the tenderness and mercy of My own Father will be revealed to His children in this valley of tears—that the world will be healed of the sufferings inflicted upon it by the absence of true fathers. Let My priests be fathers! Let them beg Me for the grace of spiritual fatherhood, and I will give it to them in abundance.

Such a man was Saint Joseph. He was the living image of My Father, and he was chosen by My Father to be a father to Me in My sacred humanity. Let My priests go to Saint Joseph. He will obtain for them this priceless gift of spiritual fatherhood, and he will guide them in the delicate and difficult work of being true fathers to souls.

⊕

Thursday, January 16, 2014

What matters above all else is that you come to Me, that you abide close to Me, and that you have confidence in My merciful love for you. There is nothing that can separate you from My love: not your sins, nor your fears, nor your weaknesses, nor your vain imaginings.[2] I am here for you, to welcome you, to embrace you, and to hold you quietly, in peace, against My Heart. Let this be enough for you.

Do not worry over how, or when, or in what form I will speak to you. Abandon yourself to My love, and trust that I will never abandon you, nor let you fall victim to the deceits of the Enemy. Humility is the armour that frustrates and confounds the enemy. Remain humble and trusting in My presence, and the Enemy will have no way to poison your mind or your heart.

Take heart! Trust in My love for you. I will not abandon you. I will

---

[1] Luke 21:15.

[2] Cf. Rom 8:28–39. Mortal sin expels sanctifying grace from the soul, and in that way separates a man from God's friendship. This defective condition on the sinner's part, however, does not change God's will of love and His will to restore the sinner to friend-ship, according to His own plan. In that way, it may truly be said that while we can place obstacles in the way of our salvation, nothing can defeat God's love for us.

never forsake you, because you are Mine and I have set My Heart upon you. Do you think that I am fickle and unfaithful? I am unchanging and nothing can change My will,[1] for My will is the expression of My love, and My love is everlasting.[2] There is no detail of your life that is unknown to Me, and I see your life in the light of My providence. It is I who lead you, correct you, and keep you in the path that I have prepared for you. Be humble and trust in Me, and I will guard you. I will provide for you. I will show you the light that you need to take the next step in obedience, in trust, and in abandonment to My Heart.

Sunday, January 26, 2014

It is enough for you to be with Me. This is all I ask of you. I do not ask for elevated thoughts, or for emotional outpourings, or for nicely constructed phrases. I ask only that you stay with Me. I need your company even now, just as I needed the company of Peter, James, and John in Gethsemane. They slept on, it is true, but I knew they were there, and their mere presence was a consolation to My agonizing Heart.

You are afraid of distractions, of daydreams, and of foolish thoughts; these do not offend Me because they are no more than flies buzzing in the background.

I am absorbed by your presence before Me. Does it shock you that I should say such a thing? But I am absorbed by you: My eyes rest upon you; My Heart is all yours; I am listening intently to you; and all My attention is focused on you when you come seeking Me. Believe that I am totally absorbed by you, and soon you will be totally absorbed by Me. I speak here using human terms, using the language of friendship, of affection, of love. I am present here in all the sensitivity and tenderness of My humanity. I am here offering you My friendship, ready to spend as much time with you as you are ready to spend with Me.

I want you close to Me: as close as John was to Me when, at My last supper, he rested his head upon My breast. Prayer such as this cannot be calculated or measured in terms of minutes and hours. It is what it is— and this, for as long as you abide in My presence.

Even when the time of your adoration is ended, I remain with you. I am in you, all attentive to you, all loving, ready at every moment to enter into conversation with you, to strengthen you in temptation, to comfort you in your sorrows, to be a light for you in your darkness. It

---

[1] Inter alia, Num 23:19; Esth 13:9; Ps 109(110):4; Isa 46:9–10; Mal 3:6; Jas 1:17; 2 Cor 1:17–20.

[2] Jer 31:3; Isa 54:8.

requires but a little bit of faith to realise that one is never alone, to become aware of My presence, of My readiness to communicate Myself to you wordlessly by an infusion of My grace.

Use what I am telling you now to comfort others who struggle in their prayer, who think that prayer is difficult, and arduous, and wholly exceptional in the lives of ordinary people. For the man who seeks My Face and desires to rest upon My Heart, I make prayer something very simple: wordless, peace-giving, cleansing, and divinely fruitful.

May 29, 2014
Ascension Thursday

I am ascended to My Father, but I remain present to My Church. The same desire that caused Me to return to the Father with an inexpressible joy causes Me to remain present to My Church with an inexpressible love. When I said "I go to My Father," I did not mean "I abandon My Church," for the Church is My Spouse and with her I am one Body, and I am the Head of My Church.[1] My own Spirit animates the Church in all her members, so that I live in My Church, and My Church lives united to Me.[2] My presence to the Father is not an absence from My Church. I am present in the adorable mysteries of My Body and Blood, just as I am present, Body and Blood, in the glory of the Father, in the hidden sanctuary of heaven, where I serve as High Priest and offer Myself ceaselessly as a spotless Victim of propitiation.[3]

What I do in heaven, I do ceaselessly on earth.[4] Every tabernacle where I am present in the Sacrament of My Body and Blood is an image of the heavenly tabernacle into which I have ascended, and in which I offer Myself to the Father in a sacrifice that is unending. My life in so many earthly tabernacles is the very life that is Mine in the glorious tabernacle of heaven, in the Holy of Holies where I carry out My priestly service of the Father by offering Myself to Him as a glorious Victim, as the pure Victim, the holy Victim, the spotless Victim[5] by whom earth is reconciled to heaven, and heaven to earth; by whom the Father's perfect

---

[1] John 14:13; John 20:17; Matt 28:20; Eph 4:7–16; Eph 5:22–32; 1 Cor 10:16–17; 1 Cor 12:12; Col 1:24.

[2] 1 Cor 12:13; Rom 8:9; Acts 9:4.

[3] Heb 7:24–25, 8:1–2, 9:11–28.

[4] Note that there is here no question of repeating an offering, as with the priests of the old covenant, but rather of making ever present the once-for-all sacrifice of the Cross, which is the earthly echo of the eternal stance of the Son towards the Father.

[5] A reference to the Roman Canon: *hostiam puram, hostiam sanctam, hostiam immaculatam.*

plan is brought to completion; and by whom the kingdom of God is established forever.

Come to Me in the Sacrament of My love, and enter there into the mystery of My oblation. I am not inactive, nor am I present after the manner of a thing that has in itself no life, no movement, no breath. I am present in all the glory of My humanity and in all the power of My divinity; just as I am present in heaven, so am I present in the tabernacles of My Church on earth.[1] In heaven, My glory is the bliss of all My saints; on earth, that same glory is veiled in the Most Holy Sacrament to be the bliss of My saints here below. My sacramental joy is the unfailing joy of the saints on earth. If there is, at times, so little evidence of joy among My people on earth, it is because they ignore My real presence and fail to seek Me out where I am to be found: in the Sacrament where I wait for sinners, to love them, to forgive them, to heal them, to hold conversation with them, and to nourish them even with My very self.

Priests of Mine—priests who serve with Me in the sanctuaries of My Church on earth, even as the angels serve with Me in the sanctuary of heaven; priests who represent Me on earth, even as I present Myself before My Father in heaven: make known the mystery of My presence! Call the faithful to My tabernacles! Tell them that I await them there, that I am no absent God, and that, even in the mystery of My Ascension, I remain bodily present, although hidden beneath the sacramental veils, to all who seek My Eucharistic Face.

Why are My churches empty? Why am I forsaken in the Sacrament of My love? Why have men rendered vain the intentions of My Heart when, in the cenacle, I instituted the Sacrament of My abiding presence in My Church? Is My presence not to benefit those for whom I instituted so great a mystery of love? Am I to be rejected and forsaken in the Sacrament of My divine friendship for souls? Have My priests altogether forgotten that they are raised to configuration with Me in order to effect My sacramental presence, to offer Me to the Father in the perfect sacrifice of My death on the Cross, and to nourish the souls of the faithful with My own Body and Blood? Why are My priests so cold towards Me in the Sacrament of My love?

---

[1] As the Council of Trent (Session 13 and Session 22) and other magisterial documents teach, it is one and the same Lord Jesus Christ—the same reality, substance, and Person—who is present in the Blessed Sacrament and in heaven, but not in the same mode or manner of presence. In heaven, He is present in His own proper mode and species, while on earth He is present in a unique sacramental mode, under the species of bread and wine.

Why do My priests remain far from My altars? The priest is for the altar, and the altar is for the priest. It is the Evil One, the enemy of My Church on earth, who has driven a wedge between too many of My priests and the altars at which they are united to Me in a holy victim-hood, in a perfect oblation. Let nothing come between My priests and their altars, just as nothing came between Me and the wood of My Cross, the altar of My bloody sacrifice on Calvary.

Let the hearts of My priests be turned, at every moment, to the altar, where they are to offer themselves in sacrifice with Me to the Father, where I am present, and where I wait, silent and humble, for their companionship, for their adoration, and for their grateful love.

If the reality of heaven has become vague and far from the thoughts of so many in My Church, it is because they have forsaken the very mystery of heaven already present and given to them in the Most Holy Sacrament of the Altar. The Eucharist is heaven on earth; the Eucharist is My Church on earth already assumed into heaven. Heaven is wheresoever the words of consecration have been pronounced over the bread and wine in the holy oblation, for there I am present, even as I am present in the glory of My Ascension, adored by the angels, praised by all the saints, held in the divine gaze of My Father, and burning with the fire of the Holy Spirit.

Amen. Amen. Believe this and you will find heaven on earth, while waiting and hoping to see My Face in glory.

Friday, November 28, 2014

Trust Me when, for one reason or another, you take your distance from Me and no longer come to seek My Face in the Sacrament of My love, nor abide close to My Eucharistic Heart. If you do not come to Me, I will go out in search of you and bring you back to Myself, so that where I am, you also may be.[1] Your absence is to Me a greater suffering than My absence is to you, and this because I love you more, and because My divine Heart is infinitely sensitive to the actions and choices of those upon whom I have set My love.

Mine it is to arrange things in such a way that those whose place is, by vocation, before My Eucharistic Face, should be compelled to return to it, even if I am obliged to go out in search of them and bring them back to the foot of My tabernacle, where all along I have waited for their return patiently, silently, and sorrowfully. I am the keeper and the guarantor of the vocation I have given you. Events and circumstances, sick-

---

[1] John 12:26.

ness and distractions may interfere in your response to My call, but My call remains unchanged, and I will, in My own time, so arrange things that you will come back to Me, adoring Me with all your heart and responding to My Eucharistic love with a repentant and confident love of your own.

I do not judge you harshly, any more than the shepherd judges harshly the sheep that, in its stupidity, separated itself from the flock and lost its way. I see all the circumstances that come between Me and your desire to be with Me. I harbour no resentment in My Sacred Heart, nor do I hold a grudge against those who, because of human weakness, or ill health, or fatigue, find it difficult to honour their promise to abide in My presence often and even daily.

Life is not linear; it is made up of twists and turns, of detours and setbacks, of obstacles and of trials. It is the man who perseveres in coming to Me through all these things who comforts My wounded Heart by offering a worthy and costly love.

There is a kind of guilt that keeps souls far from Me—such guilt is the effect of a wounded pride, of a deep disappointment in one's flawed self. Never succumb to the guilt that whispers: "Stay away. It is no use. There is nothing left here for you. You are incapable of the vocation you thought you heard. Accept your failure to live it and admit that you were deceived." This is not My voice. It is rather the voice of the accuser who borrows all the voices of your past, still alive in your memory, and makes use of them to assault you with a barrage of lies that are calculated to bring you down and cause you to despair.

My voice is always one of comfort and of love, producing peace in the soul—even when My words are cutting, even when they pierce the heart like the surgeon's scalpel. Trust, then, in My words to you, and close the ear of your imagination and heart to all else. I am He who comforts you, not the one who would assault you, accuse you, condemn you, and cast you out. I am the one who welcomes you with joy. I am the father delighted to see the face of his son and to hear his voice.[1] I am the bridegroom who longs for the sweet company of his beloved bride. I am the friend who takes delight in the conversation of the friend whom he has chosen and to whom he has bound himself by a lasting pledge of friendship. Come to Me, then, without fear, for with Me you always find a divine welcome, a loving embrace, consoling conversation, and the courage to continue in the way of life that I have traced out for you.

---

[1] Luke 15:20–24.

Afternoon

Here you are safe. You are under My protection and under the protecting mantle of My most holy Mother. Let the storm rage without; as for you, remain hidden here in the secret of My Eucharistic Face. Nothing will touch you, for you are Mine, and I protect those who trust in My love for them and flee to Me in the time of trouble and disarray.

N., My faithful servant and friend, suffered much. He was wrongly accused, suspected, maligned, and condemned by those who should have gone to him in charity, protected him against his accusers, and comforted him in his sorrow. Thus did he share in My sufferings, and this without giving into despair. You have suffered and will continue to suffer some of what N. endured in meekness, silence, humility, and even joy, for he was united to Me in the Sacrament of My extreme humiliation, and so had to share in the ignominy of the Sacred Host when It falls into the hands of My enemies.

I shall protect you. I shall preserve you from the malice of the Evil One, who speaks through the mouths of the envious and who seeks always to sow division and fear. Trust in Me. Come to Me in the Sacrament of My love as to a secure place, a refuge, a fortress,[1] and I will hide you in My Face, and hold you in My Heart, and give you rest in My love.

Tuesday, December 2, 2014

There is no problem or difficulty that cannot be solved or resolved by faithful persevering recourse to My Mother's most holy Rosary. The Rosary is My Mother's gift to the poor and to the simple, to the little ones who alone are capable of hearing the Gospel in all its purity and of responding to it with a generous heart. It is to such as these—the child-like and the weak, the poor and the trusting—that the Rosary is given. It is to such as these that the Rosary belongs.

There are no sufferings that cannot be borne peacefully, so long as a soul is praying the Rosary. Through the Rosary, all the grace and power of My mysteries passes through My Mother's Immaculate Heart into the hearts of the little ones who invoke her, repeating the angel's "Ave" over and over again. There are illnesses that can be cured through the Rosary. There are clouds of darkness and confusion that only the Rosary can disperse, and this because it is My Mother's favourite prayer, a prayer that originated in the heights of heaven and was carried to earth by My Archangel, a prayer echoed and amplified in the Church

---

[1] Ps 17(18):1–2.

through the ages, a prayer loved by all My saints, a prayer of disarming power and of immense depth.

There are those who find the Rosary difficult. The difficulty lies not in the Rosary but in the complexity of those who struggle to enter into its simplicity. Invite souls to the prayer of the Rosary; through it I will heal the sick of mind and body, through it I will give peace where there is conflict, through it I will make great saints out of great sinners, through it I will sanctify My priests, give joy to My consecrated ones, and raise up new vocations in abundance.

Listen, then, to My Mother's plea in so many places.[1] Listen to her, take her plea to heart, pray her Rosary and, for you, as for her, My Father will do wondrous things.

Wednesday, December 3, 2014

When you come into My presence, pour out your heart before Me: all that you suffer, all that you question, all that you fear, give all to Me. This you do already when you pray the psalms. It was through the psalms that I poured out My own Heart to My Father, and in the prayers of David and the holy ones of Israel, My Father heard My voice and inclined to listen to the prayer of My Heart.

So does My Father now when My Bride, the Church, pours out her heart before Me in the Divine Office. I receive the prayer of My Church expressed in the age-old psalmody, already so familiar and so dear to My soul, and unite the prayer of the Church to My own ceaseless pleading before the Father in the heavenly sanctuary. It is this that confers upon the psalmody of My Church such impetratory power, such vehemence, such a resonance in the sanctuary of heaven.

When you chant the psalms, you are giving Me all that you hold in your heart and all that makes up your life. There is no human experience, no suffering—not even the evil that is sin—that cannot be tendered to Me by means of the psalmody of My Church.

For this reason, it is a tragic loss and an immense woe when the psalmody of My Church falls silent in a land or in a diocese. It is a silence of death, like that of the netherworld in which no one intones a song of praise, a lament of repentance, a hymn of thanksgiving, an ode of love.[2] My Church will be restored when the sound of her praises— the expression of My own praise of the Father in heaven—begins once

---

[1] Most notably, at Fátima in Portugal, where Our Lady, in each of her six apparitions from May 13, 1917 to October 13, 1917, urged the faithful to pray the Rosary daily.

[2] Ps 6:5; Ps 87(88):11–13; Ps 113:25 (115:17); Isa 38:18; Bar 2:17.

again to echo from place to place, filling the nations of the earth with the *sacrificium laudis*.[1]

I came from heaven to bring to earth the liturgy of the heavenly sanctuary—wherein I, the Word, am the Priest and Great Doxologiser of My Father—so that My Church might give voice on earth to the mystery of My life from all eternity facing the Father and glorifying Him, and offering myself to Him in a ceaseless oblation of love to His love.

Let no one doubt of the singular efficacy of the Divine Office. When the Office ceases in a given place, there the Church has become mute; she has lost her voice; she no longer has the means by which I want her to pour out her heart in My presence. When the Church no longer intercedes, praises, thanks My Father, and weeps over sin, an icy death-like silence begins to spread, not the silence of adoring love, but the silence of a tomb filled with corruption.[2]

The renewal of the Church among the nations is intrinsically related to the restoration of the public celebration of My praises: to the restoration of the Divine Office, however humbly and simply, in all those places where it has fallen into abeyance. My bishops have the duty of providing for the solemn public worship of the churches in their care. For this reason, My Church, united in Council, was right to teach and uphold that a [particular] church in which there is no form of contemplative monastic life remains underdeveloped, stunted in the growth that I will to give her.[3]

I promise to bless every nation and every church in which the solemn celebration of the prayer of My Bride, the Church, is restored to honour and fostered. Therein My people, especially My people caught in the throes of suffering and in the shadow of death, will find a voice to express all that they bear within their hearts, and therein they will find a wellspring of joy: the sound on earth of the liturgy I ceaselessly celebrate in the courts of heaven.

Do not doubt that I have given you these words: I have prepared you over a lifetime to receive them and to transmit them.

---

[1] "The sacrifice of praise," frequently mentioned in Scripture: Ps 49(50):14, 23; Ps 106(107):22; Ps 115:8 (116:17); Amos 4:5; Jonah 2:10; Heb 13:15; Tobit 8:19. Cf. Pope Paul VI, Apostolic Letter *Sacrificium Laudis* (August 15, 1966).

[2] Matt 23:27.

[3] Second Vatican Council, Decree on the Missionary Activity of the Church *Ad Gentes* (December 7, 1965), §18: "Cum enim vita contemplativa ad plenitudinem praesentiae Ecclesiae pertineat, oportet apud novellas Ecclesias ubique instauretur" (Since the contemplative life belongs to the fullness of the Church's presence, it is necessary that it be established everywhere among new churches).

Saturday, December 6, 2014

These are days of grace for the Church and for the world, because the mystery of My Mother's Immaculate Conception is a wellspring of pure light for all who dwell in the shadows of this earthly exile where the Church, My Church, My precious Bride, makes her way as a pilgrim amidst great sorrows, persecutions, and attacks from below.

All who fix their gaze on My Mother, the all-lovely, the Immaculate, will find themselves inwardly illumined and warmed. My Mother communicates something of the fullness of grace that is hers to all who call upon her name, and even to those who do no more than glance at her image with affection and with hope.

My Mother is present to My Church in this world. Her glorious Assumption has not set her at a distance from My Church; it has, on the contrary, made it possible for her to be wherever the suffering members of My Mystical Body are most in need of her ministrations and of her simple consoling presence. It is My Mother who makes even the darkest nights bright with the radiance of her beauty and, in so doing, she comforts souls who see nought but darkness all about them, and she leads them on securely and in a great inner peace.

Souls who look to My Mother as to their star shining in the night will never go astray and will never lose sight of the path that leads to Me and to the glory of My kingdom. There is no safer way of coming to Me than through My Mother and under the mantle of her protection. Those who think they can journey through this life without My Mother's companionship and intercession are blinded by a terrible pride and they sin against My dispositions made from the Cross: "Woman, behold thy son. Behold thy mother."[1] It is My positive will that *all* souls should learn of My Mother and live in her company. It is My positive will that souls should so abandon themselves into My Mother's keeping that they will be like little children held tightly against her Immaculate Heart.

Who will speak to souls of My Mother? Who will tell them that they need not fear the darkness of the night, so long as My Mother is near? Who will tell them that souls entrusted to My Mother are protected, and guided, and led along the path that I have laid out for each one? There is no better way of fulfilling one's mission in this life than by giving oneself over to My Mother in an act of irrevocable and total consecration.

Those who have made such an act know of what I speak. My Mother honours every consecration made to her Sorrowful and Immaculate Heart, and even if one should forget that one has uttered such a prayer,

---

[1] John 19:26–27.

My Mother does not forget it. She remains faithful to her own children, even when these are distracted by the world and turn away from her brightness shining like a star over the stormy seas of life.

My Mother waits for souls to remember her and to return to her maternal Heart, and when they return to her, she welcomes them with an immense tenderness and joy. Never does she pronounce a word of reproach to the child who returns to her, who keeps watch at her gate, who seeks to meet her loving gaze. My Mother is the Queen of Mercy. She is the refuge of sinners. She is the safe hiding place of those who live in fear of being attacked or harmed by the powers of darkness, or wounded in spiritual combat.

All of this must be announced to souls—but it must be lived first of all by My priests, for My priests are Mary's privileged sons, the children for whom her Heart has a predilection that I placed there when I gave her My beloved friend, My disciple Saint John, from the Cross. In that hour, I gave My Mother an abiding tenderness for all priests; it is an inexhaustible tenderness that she exercises in favour of all My priests, now and until the end of the age.

✠

Thursday, December 10, 2015

I want to draw a veil between your soul and the world. I want to reserve you for Myself alone, and hide you far from the gaze of demons and of men. I want to cover you with a veil and draw you into the sanctuary of My Heart, there to exercise with Me, through Me, and in Me, a hidden priesthood and a hidden victimhood.

This is the hiddenness into which I drew My most holy Mother, beginning with her Presentation in the temple and perfected in her glorious Assumption. This is the hiddenness into which I drew the friend of the Bridegroom, Saint John the Baptist,[1] and Saint John, the disciple beloved of My Heart. This is the hiddenness into which I still draw souls who consent to renounce appearances and enter into a state of apparent death, of silence, of uselessness, of nothingness in the eyes of the world.

This is the hiddenness of the Host, My true Body, now exposed before your eyes, and then hidden away in the tabernacle. Looking at the Host, the world sees nothing: no action, no usefulness, no message, no significance. Looking at the same Host with the eyes of faith, what do you see?

---

[1] John 3:29.

Do you not see, however faintly and obscurely, what the Father and the angelic hosts see: the Lamb slain from before the foundation of the world[1]; the very work of redemption unfolding; the glory of My Face filling the universe with the radiance of My divinity; the one Face that all the world desires to see?

Consent to be hidden, even as I am hidden, and you shall want for nothing. Consent to be hidden, and I shall give you all that I created you to receive from Me, all that My Father would give you because He loves you even as He loves Me: you in Me and I in you.[2]

⊕

Thursday, January 28, 2016

Your whole life has been a preparation for this present moment. All that you have experienced, all that you have suffered, all that you have learned, all that you have done or left undone, even all of your sins, constitute a preparation for this present moment. There is nothing in your life that I have not willed or permitted in order to bring you to this moment. As often as you go to the altar to offer the Holy Sacrifice of the Mass, you bring with you all that you are in that moment, and all that you have been and said and done until that moment.

Every moment of your life is a preparation for the Holy Sacrifice of the Mass, just as every moment of My life was a preparation for, and a slow ascent to, the Sacrifice of the Cross. Understand this and you will see that nothing in your life is foreign to My plan for you: everything you have done, every place you have ever been, every person with whom you have been or are connected, is part of My design for your life. All of your life moves towards the altar, just as all of My life moved towards the Cross. Even the things you have suffered are part of My preparation of your priesthood, part of the things by which I fit you to stand in My place as victim and priest.

When you bring to your Mass all that you have experienced—your whole life story—you allow Me to redeem those things that are most dark, bitter, and painful by taking them into the mystery of My sacrifice. Come to the altar with your sins, even with those of which you are most ashamed, and I shall show you that I have already taken them upon Myself and expiated them in My Blood. Come to the altar with every

[1] Rev 13:8.
[2] John 14:20.

troubled and broken relationship of your past, with every betrayal, every failure, and every sacrilege, and I shall cast all these things into the ocean of My mercy, never again to be recovered or named or used by the Accuser against you.

Live for the next Holy Mass you will offer, for the next Holy Mass that I will offer in you, My priest and victim—the priest and victim in whom and through whom I renew My sacrifice in an unbloody manner, and again give My Body and Blood to My Spouse, the Church.

Never doubt that every moment of your life is, and has been, and always will be a preparation for the next Holy Mass you will offer. You are My priest for this: to make the mystery of My sacrifice present again, and to stand in My place as the visible representative of My priesthood and My victimhood in the Church.

Later

No saint of Mine has come into your life except by My design and by My will to speak to you, comfort you, and instruct you through each one. Attend, then, to the saints whom I have charged with a mission in your life. They are more attentive to you than you can ever be to them, and this because they are perfected in charity and united to My Heart in the glory of paradise. There are saints whom I have sent into your life as My emissaries, like the *senpectae* sent by the merciful abbot to comfort the wavering brother lest he fall into too great a sorrow.[1]

Thursday, February 4, 2016

For this one thing did I call you out of the life you were living. For this one thing did I bring you first to —— and then here: that you should tarry in My presence and wait upon Me in love, even as I wait upon you in love in this the Sacrament of My love. In this moment, you are doing that for which I brought you here. Even if you were to do nothing else, this adoration would be enough, because it is *this* that I have asked of you. Do this one thing. Adore Me, and wait upon Me, and you will see in astonishment that I will do all the rest. There is but one obstacle to My plan here, and it is that you lose the grace for which I brought you here by becoming distracted and consumed by a multitude of other things. Be faithful to what is essential, your being with Me—and all the rest will be given you besides.[2]

---

[1] See *The Holy Rule* of St. Benedict, ch. 27.
[2] Matt 6:33; Luke 12:31.

I have asked nothing else of you but that you adore Me and linger in My presence: the rest I have promised you, and I will be faithful to My promises. Give yourself to Me and I will refuse you nothing. It is your love that I want, and love is the gift of yourself poured out in My presence. Even your healing, the healing for which you are praying through the intercession of Mother Mectilde, even this will be given you in My Eucharistic presence.

You have not yet understood that by coming to adore Me, you open yourself to miracles of grace and to a mighty deployment of My power in your infirmity. What I say to you, I would say to all My priests: come to Me.[1] Abide with Me.[2] Give Me your time, for time is the currency of friendship and the proof of your love for Me.

Come to Me, and I will make possible the very things that, in your shortsightedness, you deem impossible. To the man who values My friendship above all else, I will refuse nothing. To the man who has no time for Me, I can give nothing, for he is not with Me to receive My gifts, to listen to My words, to know Me as I would have him know Me.

Thursday, February 25, 2016

But Jesus answered them, saying: "The hour is come that the Son of man should be glorified. Amen, amen I say to you, unless the grain of wheat falling into the ground die, itself remaineth alone. But if it die, it bringeth forth much fruit. He that loveth his life shall lose it; and he that hateth his life in this world, keepeth it unto life eternal. If any man minister to me, let him follow me; and where I am, there also shall my minister be. If any man minister to me, him will my Father honour."
JOHN 12:23–26

There is a very real sense in which the prayer of adoration is a loss of one's life. It is a kind of falling into the ground to die. Remember this when you come to adore Me. Look at the Sacred Host and see Me, who am the grain of wheat fallen into the ground and risen to life, and become the food of a vast multitude of souls, and this until the end of time. The grain of wheat that I was has become the Host that I am.

When you adore Me, forgetting yourself and forsaking all things for Me, you imitate Me, for adoration is a kind of death. It is a passing out of everything that solicits the senses and a cleaving to Me alone in the bright darkness of faith. So it will be in the hour of your death.

---

[1] Matt 4:19, 11:28, 14:29, 22:4; John 1:39, 7:37, 21:12.
[2] John 15:4.

The more deeply you sink into adoration, the more deeply are you planted in the earth, there to die, and there to sprout, and finally to bring forth much fruit.

Sink into the ground of adoration. Consent to disappear, to forsake appearances, and to die. Enter into the silence of the Host. Become by grace what you contemplate in faith. Here, I am hidden, silent, and forsaken by all, save a very few whom I have chosen to enter into My hiddenness, My silence, and My solitude. If you would serve Me, follow Me into My Eucharistic state. Lose all that the world counts as something and become with Me something that the world counts as nothing.

"Where I am, there also shall my servant be."[1] You are here because I am here and was here before you. Adoration is the humblest and, at the same time, the most fruitful expression of service. To adore Me is to serve Me, and "if anyone serve Me, my Father will honour him."[2] When you adore Me, you serve Me, and in serving Me, you are united to Me who hide Myself, and give Myself, and reveal Myself in this Sacrament. This is the life of adoration: it is the mystery of the grain of wheat buried and hidden in the darkness of the earth. It is the promise of life in abundance and a foretaste of the face-to-face vision that awaits you in glory.

Thursday, March 3, 2016

Let not your heart be troubled. You believe in God, believe also in Me.
JOHN 14:1

A troubled heart is always an indication of one's lack of trust in Me. Trouble, interior disquiet, comes from wanting to control and manage the things that are better left to My Father's providence. At every moment, I provide you with occasions to trust Me and to abandon to Me the things that you would prefer to see other than they are. Whenever you come up against something that contradicts your plans or fails to meet your expectations, give that thing, that situation, that disappointment to Me. Entrust it to My Heart, and then relinquish all worry over it.

I am not distant from you nor am I removed from your life and all that makes up your days. Not a hair falls from your head without My Father permitting it. Make frequent acts of trust and abandonment. Let go of the things that you cling to most tightly. Come to Me with empty hands. Hold on to nothing, not even to your own plans and desires for good things. If the things that you want for yourself are good, know, beyond any doubt, that the things I want for you are infinitely better.

[1] John 12:26.
[2] Ibid.

When you find something difficult, or beyond your strength, ask Me to do it in you or even to leave it undone as I see fit. There are things that you would want to do that are alien to My plans, and there are things that I would have you do that you, of yourself, would never think of doing. It is your attachment to doing what you want that impedes the rapid fulfilment of My perfect designs for you and for this place.

I called you here to adore Me. You have found other things to fill your days and your nights, but none of these will advance My plans, nor will they contribute to the unfolding of what My Heart has conceived for this place. Give the first place to the adoration that I have asked of you, and still ask of you, and you will see wonders.

The doing must be Mine. Yours it is to trust Me, to wait upon Me, to abide close to My Heart like the beloved disciple. When you are to do something that springs from My plan for you, you will find that thing easy to do, for I will give you light and strength and perseverance in the doing of it.

Consecrate to Me the hours of prayer that I have asked of you. Follow your Rule, and all else will fall into place. When you are close to Me in the Sacrament of My love, you are working with Me, and I am working in you, and this in a way that is divinely efficacious and supernaturally fruitful. When the time to end your adoration comes, take leave of Me with the same freedom and joy with which you came into My presence. By following your Rule, you do not forsake Me; you cleave to Me and allow Me to speak, to act, to do in you things that would otherwise be impossible for you.

The things that weigh upon you most heavily, the things that cause you the most anxiety and distress, are the very things that I want you to abandon to Me. When a particular brother becomes for you a cause of worry and distress, give that brother to Me and represent him before My Eucharistic Face. You will see changes in him that only My grace can produce. When something becomes a cause of anguish, or makes you fearful, or robs your heart of peace, give that thing to Me immediately, and once you have given it to Me, think of it no more.

I order all things mightily and sweetly. Carry out your duties with freedom and simplicity. Do one thing after another. Give all things to Me upon beginning them, and offer all things to Me upon completing them. Work quietly in My presence, and then return to My presence here in the Most Holy Sacrament of the Altar to find rest for your soul and to console My Heart with your friendship.

March 24, 2016
Maundy Thursday

This is the night when I am closest to My priests who are suffering. This is the night of the suffering priesthood. I send out My angels in great numbers—vast shining multitudes of angels—to comfort My suffering priests; to heal some; to protect them all from the attacks of the Enemy; and even to bring some to Myself.

It is a special grace to die in the night of My agony; it is a participation in My redeeming Passion. Unite all that you suffer to My own sufferings and, in advance, unite your agony and death to My agony in the garden and to My death on the Cross.

My eyes search the earth for priests according to My own Heart[1]: priests who will suffer with Me, priests who will allow Me to pray, in them and through them, all that I prayed in Gethsemane and, then, from the Cross.

When I find a priest who suffers—and who suffers with Me—becoming a victim with Me in the Holy Sacrifice of the Mass and in every moment of his life, I embrace that priest with all the divine tenderness of My Heart, and I draw him to the wound in My side, there to drink deeply of the refreshing torrent that ever flows from My Heart.

It is in My suffering priests that I live My victimhood and bring many souls to salvation who, were it not for My Passion continued in My priests, would be lost to My love for them. I will to save souls through the sufferings of My victim priests. They are lambs for the slaughter, but I am their life, and their sufferings and death are precious in My sight.

Thursday, March 31, 2016

You came to Me wanting to discuss your sins, but your sins are of no interest to Me. Look not at your sins; look, rather, at My face and at the wound in My side. Look at the wounds in My hands and in My feet, and receive from them the streams of grace that will heal the wounds of sin, and purify them, and cause them to become signs of the triumph of My mercy in you.

I do not deny sin. I know it in all its ugliness and horror. I know sin from having borne the consequences of it in My flesh and from having allowed it to disfigure My face, making Me an object of scorn from which men turned away their gaze.[2]

---

[1] 1 Sam 13:14; Jer 3:15; Acts 13:22.
[2] Ps 30:12 (31:11); Ps 108(109):25; Isa 53:2–3.

My Immaculate Mother also knew sin in all its ugliness and horror. She saw all that sin wrought upon My Body, the very Body she bore in her virginal womb, and, in seeing the ravages of sin on My Body and on My Face, her Heart was pierced by a sword of sorrow in fulfilment of Simeon's prophecy.[1]

We know sin, and because we know it for what it is, we ask the friends of our Hearts to turn away from sin in its ugliness and horror and to look instead at the divine radiance that illumines My Face hidden in the Sacrament of My love and at the gentle countenance that so perfectly reflects this divine radiance, the countenance of My Mother.

Too few are the souls that fix their gaze upon us. A single glance at My Eucharistic Face, a single lifting of one's eyes to My Mother, is enough to cure a soul of the ills that darken and disfigure it. This is the grace of the Holy Rosary. It is a long, sustained exchange of looks. It is the encounter of our gaze with the gaze of souls who consider our Mysteries, and cry out to us with a prayer that is persevering and humble.

For this reason, the Rosary has become a medicinal prayer for souls devastated by the effects of sin. It is the application of a divine remedy to all that disfigures souls created in My image and likeness. Make use of this humble prayer in struggling with the sins that cause you such distress, and you will find in it the remedy and the defence that you need and that you seek.

Thursday, April 7, 2016

He who abides in Me, and I in him, he bears much fruit; for without Me, you can do nothing.
JOHN 15:5

If you would abide in Me, according to My word, you must begin by abiding *with* Me. The union to which I have called you, a fruitful union with Myself, will begin in the time you dedicate exclusively to Me and to My companionship.

Behold, I stand at the gate, and knock. If any man shall hear My voice, and open to Me the door, I will come in to him, and will sup with him, and he with Me.
APOCALYPSE 3:20

Those souls who never abide with Me remain closed to the graces of union with Myself that I so desire to give them. Time spent in My presence softens the heart and makes it permeable to the love that radiates

---

[1] Luke 2:35.

from My Eucharistic Heart. Time spent in My presence allows the eyes of the soul to adjust, in faith, to the brightness of My Eucharistic Face.

Love Me and show your love for Me by offering Me the gift of your time. Be like the candle that exists only to burn itself out in My presence. It is enough that you are there in My presence, offering Me the flame of your love and allowing yourself to be consumed in quiet adoration.

Speak to Me freely, or simply remain in silence. I do not ask for many words; I ask for your companionship, for your presence, and for the loving attention of your heart. Thus will you attain to the union with Me that I desire for you: a fruitful union by which you will abide in Me and I in you.

Give Me this, the sacrifice of your time in My presence, and I will give you all else, even those things that, at the moment, seem impossible. The monastery will be built not in agitation and in much worry but in quietness and in abandonment to My action and to the love that radiates from My Eucharistic Heart.

Mobilise your sons, as you are already doing, to watch before My Eucharistic Face in humble adoration and in submission to My action. You will see the monastery rise all around you like new grass in spring, and you will know that it is all My doing and the fruit of allowing My power to act through your stillness, your abandonment, and your quiet trust in Me.

You may think that there are not enough hours in the day to do all that needs to be done. I promise you that every hour given exclusively to Me will be like the seed of an abundant harvest. The fruit that you will reap will surpass beyond all imagining the little you will have given Me by abiding in My presence.

These are words that you can share with your sons. This is something that they can experience. They have only to give Me the little that I ask of you and I, for My part, will do all that I have promised.

There is more time in a day than what is measured by hours and minutes. I am the Lord of all time, and time given in tribute to Me is of greater worth than time invested in the most wearying labours. I do not ask that you stop doing the tasks that are before you, but only that you put Me before all else, giving the best of your time and the greater portion to Me alone.

Thursday, April 14, 2016

Consecrate yourself to My Mother, and lift your eyes to her all-pure countenance. She is the star whom I have set in the darkness of the firmament, lest those who belong to Me lose hope and perish in the tempest that threatens the very survival of all that I have done and of the works of My saints. Those who flee to My Immaculate Mother and cling to her mantle of protection will emerge from the sorrows of this time and, after the raging tempest, will rejoice in a peace that the world cannot give.

> *Amen, amen I say to you, that you shall lament and weep, but the world shall rejoice; and you shall be made sorrowful, but your sorrow shall be turned into joy.*
> JOHN 16:20

Pray close to My wounded Heart and abide in the radiance of My Eucharistic Face. Thus will you be sons of the Host for the Host and the seed of a new generation of adorers in spirit and in truth. Only remain with Me. Keep watch before My Face and listen to all that My Heart will say to you. I am here for you. Be here for Me, and so console My Heart, which so many of My own have forsaken.

Thursday, June 2, 2016

Convert Thou me entirely, O my beloved Jesus, that I may live every moment—up to and including the very moment of my death—with my eyes fixed on Thine adorable Face, and with my heart hidden in Thy piercèd Heart. Make me, I pray Thee, what Thou hast called me to be.[1]

Let me so love Thee and adore Thee that I may be for Thine afflicted Heart the consoling friend for whom Thou hast waited so long. Leave me not alone, never forsake me, so that I may never leave Thee alone, and never forsake Thee.[2] *Fix my vagrant heart before Thy tabernacle—before the one where Thou art least adored and most forgotten—that I may persevere in a watch of adoration, of reparation, and of love before Thy Eucharistic Face.*

What can I give Thee that Thou hast not given me?[3]

Give Thou, then, to me superabundantly, so that I may give back to Thee superabundantly.

Give Thou me, I beseech Thee, but a spark of Thine own blazing zeal for the glory of the Father; let it consume me entirely as a holocaust to the praise of His glory.[4]

Give Thou me, I beseech Thee, a share in Thy spousal love for the

---

[1] 1 Cor 1:26–30; Eph 2:10; 1 Thess 5:23–24; Jer 31:18; Lam 5:21.

[2] Ps 26(27):9; Ps 37:22 (38:21); Ps 70(71), vv. 9 and18; Ps 118(119):8; Ps 139:9 (140:8); Sir 51:14.

[3] 1 Cor 4:7; Rom 8:32; 2 Pet 1:3; 1 Chron 29:14.

[4] Eph 1, vv. 6, 12, and 14.

Church, Thy Bride in heaven and on earth.[1] *Like Thee, with Thee, in Thee, let me lay down my life for her.*[2]

Give Thou me, I beseech Thee, Thine own Heart's filial love for Thine Immaculate Mother, that I may love her as Thou wouldst have me love her; that I might serve her with a devotion that is true, and pure, and constant.

Give Thou me, I beseech Thee, the tender compassion with which Thou wouldst have me care for souls, that in my care for them they may experience the solicitude of Thy Sacred Heart.

Make me, if possible, more Thy priest today than I have ever been before. Ratify and confirm me in the ineffable grace of real participation in the Mystery of the Cross, where Thou art Priest and Victim. Burn more deeply into my soul the indelible character of Thy priesthood, and, in that same fire, consume and destroy all that dims, obstructs, or impedes its glorious radiance, so that the light of Thy sacrifice may shine before men, and its healing power go forth from me as it went forth from Thee, for Thou, O merciful Saviour, hast made me Thy priest forever.

A thousand, thousand lifetimes would be too little time to thank Thee, to bless Thee, to praise Thee for so immeasurable a gift. Give me then, when Thou callest me to Thyself, an eternity in which to praise Thee beyond the veil where, for the moment, Thou art hidden in the glory of the Father and in the brightness of the Holy Ghost.[3] *Amen.*

⊕

---

[1] John 3:29; 2 Cor 11:2; Eph 5:22–32; Rev 19:7, 21:2, 21:9.

[2] Eph 5:25.

[3] Cf. Heb 6:19-20, 9:24, 10:19-21; Phil 2:11; 1 Pet 4:14, 5:10; John 1:14, 17:24; 2 Cor 4:6; 2 Pet 1:17; Matt 17:2; Mark 9:1.

In the holy place, I contemplate Thee.
PSALM 62:3

Silence of the Sacred Host, pervade me.
Hiddenness of the Sacred Host, envelop me.
Humility of the Sacred Host, shield me.
Poverty of the Sacred Host, be all to me.
Purity of the Sacred Host, cleanse me.
Radiance of the Sacred Host, illumine me.
Countenance hidden in the Sacred Host,
    reveal Thyself to me.
Heart all afire in the Sacred Host,
    set me ablaze with Thy love.

O Sacred Host,
    living Flesh and Blood
        of the Immolated Lamb,
            I adore Thee.
O Sacred Host,
    living Flesh and Blood
        of the Immolated Lamb,
            I offer Thee to the Father.
O Sacred Host,
    living Flesh and Blood
        of the Immolated Lamb,
            I beseech Thee to unite me to Thyself
                now and at the hour of my death.
                Amen.

Appendix I

Prayers from *In Sinu Jesu*

⊕

THE CHAPLET OF REPARATION
or, Offering of the Precious Blood for Priests

This chaplet of reparation and intercession is meant to be prayed on an ordinary five decade rosary.

Incline (✝) unto my aid, O God; O Lord, make haste to help me.
Glory be to the Father, and to the Son, and to the Holy Spirit;
As it was in the beginning, is now, and ever shall be, world without end. Amen.
Alleluia. (*After Septuagesima*: Praise be to Thee, O Lord, King of eternal glory.)

On the Our Father beads:

Eternal Father, I offer Thee
the Precious Blood of Thy Beloved Son,
our Lord Jesus Christ,
the Lamb without blemish or spot,
in reparation for my sins
and for the sins of all Thy priests.

On the Hail Mary beads:

By Thy Precious Blood, O Jesus,
purify and sanctify Thy priests.

In place of the Glory be to the Father:

O Father, from whom all fatherhood in heaven and on earth
is named,
have mercy on all Thy priests, and wash them in the Blood of
the Lamb.

(see March 8, 2010)

✠

O Virgin Mary,
my Mother of Perpetual Help,
my hands are in thy hands,
and my heart is in thy heart,
and this forever.

(October 5, 2007)

✠

O my Jesus,
I place myself in spirit before Thy Eucharistic Face
to adore Thee,
to make reparation,
to say to Thee all that Thy Spirit of Love
    will cause to rise in my heart.
I come to look at Thee.
I come to listen to Thee.
I come to receive from Thee all that Thy open Heart
    desires to say to me and to give me today.
I thank Thee for having made Thyself close to me.
I praise Thy mercy.
I confess the redeeming power of Thy Precious Blood.
Amen.

(October 10, 2007)

✠

O sweet Virgin Mary,
I am thy child.
Keep my hands in thy hands
and my heart in thy heart
all throughout this day
and even during the night.
So do I want to live and die.
Amen.

(October 10, 2007)

✠

O Jesus,
I want to go in spirit to the tabernacle
   where Thou art most forsaken
   and most forgotten in the world.
I want to go where no one adores Thee,
   where no one bows before Thee,
   where Thou hast only Thy Angels
 to adore Thee and to keep Thee company.
    And still, it is a human heart that Thou desirest,
   and above all, the heart of a priest.
I give Thee mine
   in an offering of adoration and reparation.

(October 10, 2007)

✠

Lord Jesus,
I present myself before Thy Eucharistic Face today,
   placing myself in spirit close to that tabernacle in the world,
   where Thou art most forsaken,
   most ignored, and most forgotten.
Since Thou hast asked me for it,
   I offer Thee my heart, the heart of a priest,
   to keep company with Thy priestly and Eucharistic Sacred Heart.
I adore Thee in a spirit of reparation
   for all the priests of the Church,
   but especially for those who never, or hardly ever,
   stop in Thy presence,
   there to put down their burdens,
   and to receive from Thee new strength, new lights,
   new capacities to love, to pardon, and to bless.
I do not want to leave this tabernacle today.
I want, at every instant, to remain immersed in the adoration
   for which Thou waitest from Thy priests.

(October 11, 2007)

✠

I unite myself to the most holy Virgin Mary,
    Mediatrix of all graces
    and first adorer of Thy Eucharistic Face.
By her most pure Heart,
    may the prayers that rise from my heart
    reach Thy open Heart,
    hidden and, so often, left alone
    in the great Sacrament of Thy love.
        Amen.

(October 11, 2007)

✠

O my beloved Jesus,
I suffer that I cannot abide close to Thy tabernacle.
I feel deprived of Thy real presence
    and, nonetheless, I rejoice
    because this shows me well
    how much Thou hast attached me
    to the adorable Mystery of Thy Body and Blood.
Thou willest that I should be a priest adorer and reparator
    for Thy Eucharistic Heart,
    an adorer of Thy Face that,
    through the Host,
    shines for us.
Let this be done according to all the desires of Thy Heart.
    Amen.

(October 13, 2007)

✠

O my beloved Jesus,
    the efficacy and fruitfulness
    of this time of adoration
    comes not from me
    but from Thee.
It is all Thy doing.
I place myself before Thee
    as a vessel to be filled.

(April 10, 2008)

⊕

O my beloved Jesus,
    I come before Thy Eucharistic Face
    and I draw near to Thy open Heart
    in this the Sacrament of Thy love,
    to respond today to what Thou hast asked of me.
With trust in Thy infinite goodness,
    and fearing nothing apart from sin
    and the peril of separation from Thee,
    I say "yes" to all that Thy Sacred Heart desireth for me.
I want for myself only what Thou wantest for me.
I desire what Thou desirest for my life,
    and nothing else.

Making use of the free will that Thou hast given me,
    I give Thee, my Sovereign and all-powerful God,
    the freedom to sanctify me wholly in body, mind, and spirit.
I allow Thee, as of this feast of Thy Sacred Heart,
    to fashion and wound me into a living representation of Thyself
    before Thy Father and in the midst of Thy Church.

Wound me, that I may be another Thyself
    at the altar of Thy sacrifice.
Wound me with that love that is indescribable in earthly terms
    so as to heal all the wounds of my sins.
Penetrate my soul with Thy divine light.
Let no vestige of darkness remain within me.

I renew my total consecration
    to the pure and sinless Heart of Thy Immaculate Mother,
    and await from her maternal hands
    all that Thou willest to bestow upon me.
I thank Thee for Thy Mother's incomparable work
    in my soul and in the souls of all Thy priests.
Through her, I am entirely Thine.

Accomplish all the designs of Thy Sacred Heart upon my life.
Glory be to Thy Eucharistic Heart
    from my own heart
    and from the heart of every priest of Thine.
Amen.

(May 30, 2008)

✠

O my beloved and ever-merciful Jesus,
  I adore Thee and I offer Thee all the love and desire of my heart.
The desire I offer Thee is the very one Thou Thyself hast given me:
  the desire for holiness, that is, for union with Thee.
Unite me to Thyself:
  my heart to Thy Heart,
  my soul to Thy Soul,
  all that I am to all that Thou art.

(June 26, 2008)

✠

My beloved Jesus,
I thank Thee for having called me to a life of adoration.
I thank Thee that Thou wantest Me, unworthy as I am,
  to abide before Thy Eucharistic Face
  and to approach Thy open Heart
  in the Sacrament of Thy love.

I thank Thee that Thou hast called me to offer Thee reparation,
  first of all for my own sins,
  too many to be counted,
  and for all those offences
  by which I have grieved Thy most loving Heart
  and offended souls dear to Thee
  and purchased by Thy most precious Blood.

Thou callest me also to make reparation
  for all the sins of my brother priests,
  poor sinners like me,
  often caught in the snares of the Evil One,
  and insensible to the delights and peace
  that Thou desirest to give them in Thy presence.

I thank Thee that Thou hast chosen me to make reparation
  for the coldness, indifference, irreverence, and isolation
  that Thou receivest in the Sacrament of Thy love.

To Thy presence, let me offer my presence;
  to Thy pierced Heart, let me offer my heart;

to Thy divine friendship,
let me offer all the yearnings of My soul
for that companionship of Thine,
which surpasses every passing earthly love
and satisfies the deepest needs and desires of my heart.

(July 3, 2008)

✠

I beg Thee to keep me pure, transparent, humble, and free,
    that I may fulfil with integrity, detachment, and joy
    the spiritual paternity to which Thou hast called me.
I ask moreover for the grace to relate to all who will come to me
    as a father to a son, as a brother to a brother.
I beg Thee to purify and strengthen every bond of friendship
    in the fire of Thy Eucharistic Heart.

I surrender to Thee my humanity
    with its wounds, its brokenness, and its scars.
I give Thee my past in its entirety.
I beg Thee for the grace to walk in the newness of life
    that I know Thou desirest for me.

And that all of this may come to pass
    in the most efficacious and fruitful way,
    I abandon into the most pure hands of Thy Mother, my Mother,
    all that I am, all that I have been, and all that Thou,
    in the boundless mercy of Thy Eucharistic Heart,
    wouldst have me be for Thee, O my beloved Jesus,
    for Thy Mystical Body, Thy Bride, the Church,
    and for the glory of Thy Father.
Amen.

(July 3, 2008)

✠

Lord Jesus Christ, Priest and Victim,
　Lamb without stain or blemish,
　I come before Thy Face,
　　laden with the sins and betrayals of my brother priests
　　and with the burden of my own sins and infidelities.
Allow me to represent those priests
　who are most in need of Thy mercy.
For them, let me abide before Thy Eucharistic Face,
　close to Thy open Heart.
Through the Sorrowful and Immaculate Heart of Thy Mother,
　Advocate and Mediatrix of all graces,
　　pour forth upon all the priests of Thy Church
　　that torrent of mercy that ever flows from Thy Heart,
　　to purify and heal them,
　　to sanctify and refresh them,
　　and, at the hour of their death,
　　to make them worthy of joining Thee before the Father
　　in the heavenly Holy Place beyond the veil.
Amen.

(November 10, 2008)

✠

O my beloved Jesus, unite me to Thyself,
　my body to Thy Body,
　my blood to Thy Blood,
　my soul to Thy Soul,
　my heart to Thy Heart,
　all that I am to all that Thou art:
So as to make Me with Thyself, O Jesus,
　one priest and one victim
　offered to the glory of Thy Father,
　out of love for Thy spouse, the Church—
For the sanctification of Thy priests,
　the conversion of sinners,
　the intentions of the Pope,
　and in sorrowful reparation
　for my innumerable sins
　against Thee in Thy priesthood
　and in the Sacrament of Thy love.
Amen.

(April 15, 2009)

✠

My Jesus, only as Thou willest,
   when Thou willest,
   and in the way Thou willest.
To Thee be all glory and thanksgiving,
    Who rulest all things mightily and sweetly,
    and Who fillest the earth with Thy manifold mercies.
Amen.

                                      (January 8, 2010)

✠

Do Thou in me and through me, O my beloved Jesus,
all that Thou desirest to find in me and do through me,
so that, in spite of my miseries, my weaknesses,
   and even my sins,
my priesthood may be a radiance of Thine,
and my face reflect the merciful love that ever shines
   on Thy Holy Face
for souls who trust in Thee and abandon themselves
   to Thy divine action.

                                   (January 26, 2010)

✠

My Jesus, how can I refuse Thee anything?
All my trust is in Thee.
In Thee is all my hope.
I am all Thine,
   and Thy friendship is my assurance
   of happiness and of Thy unfailing grace.
I give Thee my heartfelt "yes."
I am all Thine, beloved Jesus:
   a priest in Thine own priesthood,
   and a victim with Thee in Thy pure, holy,
   and spotless oblation to the Father. Amen.

                                   (January 27, 2010)

✠

O my beloved Jesus,
I surrender to Thy Sacred Heart
all that I love.

                                   (February 9, 2010)

✠

My beloved Jesus,
I surrender to Thy Heart's love for me,
and I offer myself to Thee
   as a victim of adoration and reparation
for all whom I have hurt or offended,
   that they may be healed and restored
   to Thy friendship within Thy Church,
and for all Thy priests,
   especially for those who are still wallowing in sins
   and blind to the sweet light of Thy Countenance.
My Jesus, I give myself as a victim of love
   to Thee who gave Thyself as a victim of love for me.
I desire to have no will apart from Thy will,
   the perfect expression of Thy Heart's love for me
   and for all Thy priests.
I offer myself to Thee also for all the intentions of the Pope.
I ask Thee to strengthen him and to console him,
   and I consecrate him to Thy Mother's Immaculate Heart.

(March 20, 2010)

✠

Yes, Lord Jesus,
I consent to lose all save Thee,
for in possessing Thee,
   I will lose nothing,
and in loving Thee
   I will be loved by Thee,
and in that love find perfect happiness
   and the grace to love others
   as Thou hast loved me.

(September 22, 2011)

✠

Be it done unto me according to Thy word.
Lord Jesus, I accept Thy plan.
I give my free and full consent to Thy will.
I am willing to forsake all else and leave all else behind.
I am Thy servant and,
   by Thy infinite mercy,
   the friend of Thy Heart. Amen.

(September 25, 2011)

✛

O my beloved Lord Jesus, truly present here,
   I adore Thee with all the love of my heart.
It is for this and for no other thing
   that Thou has brought me here:
to adore Thee, to abide in Thy company,
   to seek Thy Face, and to rest upon Thy Heart.
Keep me faithful to the calling Thou hast given me,
   and let nothing distract me from Thee,
   who art the One Thing Necessary,
   and apart from Whom there is nothing in heaven or on earth
   to which I will give my heart.
To be near Thee is my happiness.
Hold me in Thy presence,
   and let me never depart from the radiance
   of Thy Eucharistic Face. Amen.

                        (January 27, 2012)

✛

Jesus, Jesus, Jesus,
   let nothing take me out of the radiance
   of Thy Eucharistic Face;
rather, let all things work together
   to compel me to seek Thy Face and to adore Thee.

                        (January 27, 2012)

✛

O strengthen my loving attention to Thee,
Thou who art lovingly attentive to me
in this the Sacrament of Thy love.

                        (January 28, 2012)

✠

Lord Jesus,
Thou askest not the impossible of me,
   for even when Thou askest what,
   to my eyes, appears impossible,
   Thou art already making it possible by Thy grace.
To Thee, and those who love Thee,
   nothing is impossible.
I can do all things in Thee
   who strengthenest me to do them.

(January 29, 2012)

✠

Lord Jesus Christ,
   although I cannot, during this hour,
   approach Thee physically in the Sacrament of Thy love,
   I would approach Thee by desire and by faith.
Transport me, I beseech Thee,
   by the lifting up of my mind and heart,
   to that tabernacle in the world where Thou art, at this hour,
   most forsaken, utterly forgotten, and without human company.

Let the radiance of Thy Eucharistic Face so penetrate my soul
   that by offering Thee adoration and reparation,
   even as I am busy doing ordinary things in an ordinary way,
I may obtain from Thy Sacred Heart
   the return of at least one priest to the Tabernacle
   where Thou waitest for him today. Amen.

(January 30, 2012)

IN SINU JESU

✠

O my beloved Jesus,
I am happy to be in Thy presence.
Thy psalmist said it: "To be near God is my happiness."
There are no words to describe what it is to have Thee—
    God from God, Light from Light, Very God from Very God—
    so close.

Thou art hidden, but I see Thee.
Thou art silent, but I hear Thee.
Thou art immobile, but Thou reachest out
    to draw me in and hold me against Thy Heart.
One who possesses Thee in the Sacrament of Thy love,
    possesses everything.

Because Thou art here, I lack nothing.
Because Thou art here, I have nothing to fear.
Because Thou art here, I cannot be lonely.
Because Thou art here, heaven itself is here,
    and myriads of angels adoring Thee
    and offering Thee their songs of praise.
Because Thou art here, I need not search for Thee anywhere else.
Because Thou art here, my faith possesses Thee,
    my hope is anchored to Thee,
    my love embraces Thee and will not let Thee go.
                       (March 10, 2012)

✠

Give to me, Lord Jesus,
    according to Thy Heart's desire.
I am an empty vessel waiting for Thee to fill me.
I would remain before Thee, silent and empty,
    and prepared to be filled
    with whatever it shall please Thee to pour into me.
Fill me according to Thy desire,
    not only for myself, but for others,
    for the souls whom Thou wilt send to me,
    that I may give them something pure,
    something divine to drink.
                       (March 10, 2012)

✠

Unite me, I beseech Thee,
  to Thy Eucharistic humility,
  to Thy silence, Thy hiddenness,
  and Thy ceaseless prayer to the Father.
Unite me to the uninterrupted oblation
  of Thyself to the Father
  in the Sacrament of Thy love.
There is no moment in which Thou art not offering Thyself,
  no moment in which Thy immolation on the Cross
  is not re-presented to the Father
  from the silence of Thy tabernacles.
Let nothing, then, separate me from Thyself,
  the Lamb of God by Whose Blood the world is redeemed,
  souls are washed clean of sin,
  and the Father's Heart is moved to pity
  for the most hardened sinners
  and for the very least of His creatures.
Amen.

(March 18, 2012)

IN SINU JESU

✠

O my beloved Jesus,
I adore Thy Eucharistic Face,
 the radiance of which is my unfailing light
 in the shadows of this earthly exile.
So long as Thou art with me, I will fear no evil.
Thou art here, close to me,
 and I am here, close to Thee,
 to believe in Thee, to hope in Thee,
 to love Thee, and to adore Thee.

Apart from Thee I desire nothing on earth,
 and without Thee, what is heaven?
Here in Thy Eucharistic presence is heaven on earth.
Here is the joy eternal of all the angels and blessed.
Here is the fulfilment of the longing in hope
 that burns like a fire in the souls of purgatory.
Here is the heart of the Church on earth
 and the glory of the Church in heaven.
Here is the stupendous miracle of Thy love for us:
Thy abiding presence as the Lamb who was slain,
 and the triumph of Thy Cross and Resurrection.

Why, then, art Thou left alone in this Most Holy Sacrament?
Why art Thou forsaken in Thy tabernacles?
Why are Thy churches empty or so rarely visited?
Reveal Thyself again in the Sacrament of Thy love!
Make known Thy presence here to those who doubt,
 to the ignorant, the indifferent, and the cold-hearted.
Draw all—baptized and unbaptized—
 into the radiance of Thy Eucharistic Face,
 and let not a single soul escape the embrace
 of Thy Eucharistic friendship.
Thus wilt Thou satisfy Thine own thirst
 for the faith and love of our souls;
and thus wilt Thou satisfy Thine own Heart's longing
 for the love of the hearts which Thou hast created
 for Thyself and no other. Amen.

(April 20, 2012)

IN SINU JESU

$\oplus$

Come, Holy Ghost!
Come, living Fire!
Come, Anointing from above!
Come, living Water!
Come, Breath of God!

Mark me with an incision of fire
    for the work to which I have been called.
Sign my soul deeply and indelibly
    for the adoration of the Eucharistic Face of the Son
    and for the consolation of His Eucharistic Heart.
So burn the mark of this vocation into me
    that I will suffer from every betrayal of it,
    and from every infidelity to it.
So seal me for this vocation
    that I will find Thee only in fulfilling it
    and in its perfection in the lasting adoration of heaven,
    where Thou livest and reignest with the Father and the Son.

Let the adoration of the Lamb
    begin for me here on earth today,
and let it increase and deepen in my life
    until it becomes ceaseless:
a spring of joy flowing from an inexhaustible source,
    Thine own indwelling presence in my soul,
to quench the thirst of the Bridegroom Christ,
    and to make fruitful His priesthood in the Church.
Amen.

(May 27, 2012)

IN SINU JESU

⊕

Convert Thou me entirely,
  O my beloved Jesus,
    that I may live every moment—
      up to and including the very moment of my death—
    with my eyes fixed on Thine adorable Face,
  and with my heart hidden in Thy piercèd Heart.

Make me, I pray Thee, what Thou hast called me to be.
  Let me so love Thee and adore Thee
    that I may be for Thine afflicted Heart
      the consoling friend for whom Thou hast waited so long.
    Leave me not alone, never forsake me,
  so that I may never leave Thee alone, and never forsake Thee.

Fix my vagrant heart before Thy tabernacle—
  before the one where Thou art least adored and most forgotten—
    that I may persevere
      in a watch of adoration,
    of reparation, and of love
  before Thy Eucharistic Face.

What can I give Thee that Thou hast not given me?
  Give Thou, then, to me superabundantly,
    so that I may give back to Thee superabundantly.
      Give Thou me, I beseech Thee, but a spark
    of Thine own blazing zeal for the glory of the Father;
  let it consume me entirely as a holocaust to the praise of His glory.

Give Thou me, I beseech Thee,
  a share in Thy spousal love for the Church,
    Thy Bride in heaven and on earth.
  Like Thee, with Thee, in Thee, let me lay down my life for her.

Give Thou me, I beseech Thee,
  Thine own Heart's filial love for Thine Immaculate Mother,
    that I may love her as Thou wouldst have me love her;
  that I might serve her with a devotion
that is true, and pure, and constant.

IN SINU JESU

Give Thou me, I beseech Thee,
  the tender compassion
    with which Thou wouldst have me care for souls,
  that in my care for them
they may experience the solicitude of Thy Sacred Heart.

Make me, if possible,
  more Thy priest today than I have ever been before.
    Ratify and confirm me in the ineffable grace
  of real participation in the Mystery of the Cross,
where Thou art Priest and Victim.

Burn more deeply into my soul
  the indelible character of Thy priesthood,
    and, in that same fire, consume and destroy
      all that dims, obstructs, or impedes its glorious radiance,
        so that the light of Thy sacrifice may shine before men,
      and its healing power go forth from me
    as it went forth from Thee,
  for Thou, O merciful Saviour,
hast made me Thy priest forever.

A thousand, thousand lifetimes would be too little time
  to thank Thee, to bless Thee, to praise Thee
    for so immeasurable a gift.
      Give me then, when Thou callest me to Thyself,
        an eternity in which to praise Thee beyond the veil
      where, for the moment, Thou art hidden
    in the glory of the Father
  and in the brightness of the Holy Ghost.
Amen.

(June 2, 2016)

Appendix II

Words about These Words: Excerpts from *In Sinu Jesu*

I SHALL speak to you, I shall speak to your heart, so that you may hear My voice for the joy of your heart. You will hear My voice especially when you will come before My Face, when you will adore My Eucharistic Face and draw near to My open Heart. I will speak to your heart as I spoke to the heart of My beloved disciple John, the friend of My Heart, the priest of My open Heart. (*October 8, 2007*)

If I am speaking to you in this way now, it is because you need to hear My voice. For too long you have been far from Me, without being able to keep Me company, without being able to hear all that I wished to say to you. But now, the moment has come. Now and henceforth, I am speaking to you, and I shall speak to you, so that many may be brought back to Me and, in Me, find healing and peace. (*October 11, 2007*)

Here in My presence I will fill you, not only for yourself, but also for all those to whom it will be given you to transmit My messages of love and of mercy.... What I want above all else is that My priests be saints, and for this, I offer them My presence in the Eucharist. Yes, this is the great secret of priestly holiness. You must tell them this, you must repeat what I am saying to you, so that souls may be comforted by it and stimulated to seek holiness. (*October 29, 2007*)

I want you to tell priests of the desires of My Heart. I will give you many opportunities to do this. Make known to them these things that I have made known to you.... The graces stored up in My Heart for priests are inexhaustible, but so few open themselves to receive them. You, My friend, My chosen priest, remain in My presence and open your soul to all that I desire to give you. Open the ear of your heart to all that I have to say to you. Listen to Me. Write what you hear. Soon I will let you share with others the things that I will have spoken to you in silence. (*January 17, 2008*)

My beloved friend, priest of My Heart, I want you to review the words that I have spoken to you. I ask you to keep them fresh in your mind and to store them up in your heart, for the day is coming, and it is coming soon, when I will ask you to share with your brothers the things that I will have made known to you. (*May 15, 2008*)

From the very beginning—from that night in the cenacle when I handed over the mysteries of My Body and Blood—My Face and My Heart have been present in the Most Holy Eucharist. But this is a true revelation in the sense that now, I desire to draw back the veil, and to do this I will use you. There is nothing new in what I am saying to you, but there is much that has been forgotten, cast aside, or even refused out of hardness of heart. I will use you to draw back the veil on what *is*, wheresoever I am sacramentally present: My Face shining with all the splendour of My divinity, and My pierced Heart, eternally open, a wellspring of healing mercy and of inexhaustible life for souls. (*June 26, 2008*)

I have much to say to you. Why do you hesitate? Why do you not take up your pen and write the words of My Heart to yours? I am faithful to you. I will not forsake you, nor will I go back on any of the promises I have made to you. (*August 24, 2008*)

Do not stop transcribing My words to you. I speak to you to comfort and enlighten you, to show you how much I love you and want you at every moment close to My open Heart, but I speak to you also for your brother priests and for those souls who would pray for them and who would offer themselves, that priests might be sanctified in truth. (*November 29, 2008*)

The purpose of any words that I speak to you is to unite you to Me in the silence of love. That is why friends and lovers speak one to the other: to express what they hold in their hearts. Once these things have been expressed, it is enough for them to remain united one to the other in the silence that is the more perfect expression of their love. ... There are times when words are useful and necessary to your human weakness and to the need you have to be reassured of My love for you, but in the end, silence is the purest expression of My love for you and of your love for Me. Little by little I will lead you into the silence of unitive love. I will not stop speaking to you altogether because you have need of My

288

words and also because they will be useful to other souls, but I will teach you to imitate John, My beloved disciple, by resting your head—so full of thoughts and cares and fears and words—upon My Most Sacred Heart. (*March 21, 2009*)

See the changes I have wrought in you, and know from these things the truth of our conversations, for My desire is, and remains, to speak to your heart, even as a man speaks to his friend. When doubts come, dismiss them. Know that I speak to you in a language drawn from your own experience and from the resources of your own imagination and mind. The message nonetheless is Mine. It is I who am communicating with you in this way to hold you fast in My divine friendship, and to draw you into the sanctuary of My Heart, there to worship and glorify with Me the Father Who is the Source of all heaven's gifts. ... Do not yield to fear, to doubt, and to a purely human scrutiny of something which is of Me, and which I freely communicate to you out of love. (*July 7, 2009*)

I desire that My words and those of My Mother should reach a great number of priestly souls to bring them comfort and courage and light. I have spoken to you not only to comfort you and give you the assurance of My merciful love and friendship, but also so that, through My words to you, other priests may come to know of My burning love for them and of My desire to welcome them into the embrace of My divine friendship. Offer the Mass of the Holy Spirit today for this intention. My words to you will continue because I desire to instruct you, to uphold you, and to unite you to Myself through them. Be not anxious when listening for the sound of My voice in your heart. You will recognize My words, and this will happen without anxiety or stress on your part. Be at peace. You will receive the words that I want you to hear and those that I give you for the comfort and upbuilding of your brother priests and of the sons that I am giving you. One of the signs that these words originate in My tender love for you, and not in your own thoughts, is that, when you re-read them and meditate them, you will experience the peace and joy of My presence. (*January 18, 2010*)

Yes, much of what I am saying to you needs to reach other souls. Go about this prudently and in obedience to your Father, the Bishop. He will read and understand that this little light should not be hidden under a bushel basket. It should be protected and carefully passed from hand to hand so that more souls may rejoice in My warmth and in the light of My Face. (*March 13, 2010*)

When I withdraw this grace of conversation with Me for a time, it is so that you will not mistake it for the product of your own imaginings, and also so that you will not grow accustomed to My words and so, little by little, fail to take them to heart and to treasure them. I speak to you so that you might share My words when the occasion arises to do so. Share My words humbly, with no thought for yourself. (*April 15, 2010*)

When I have something to say to you, nothing can interfere with the word that I would give you, apart from your own lack of preparation or refusal to hear My interior voice. This is the voice that is interior to you, but that comes from Me. It is the expression of My Heart's desire for you, and of the things that I would share with you, heart to heart, as a man speaks to his friend. Remain open, then, to the sound of My voice, and let nothing deceive you into thinking that I have forsaken you or that our conversations have come to an end. I have so much to say to you that the rest of your earthly life will not suffice to hear it all, but you will hear nonetheless all that I want you to hear, and all the rest will become clear for you in paradise. (*May 16, 2010*)

My Heart speaks to you so that you may speak My words to the hearts of many others, those whom I will send to you and those to whom I send you to preach. So long as you remain faithful to keeping watch before My Eucharistic Face, I will give you My words and see to it that they remain in the treasury of your soul, to be drawn out and offered to other souls on the day and the hour foreseen by My providence. (*May 29, 2010*)

I speak to you in this way not only for you, beloved friend of My Heart, but also for those who will receive these words, ponder them, and draw out of them the inspiration to love Me more generously, more fruitfully, and more joyfully. I speak to you for the sake of My priests. You will be astonished at the reception given to these words of Mine. Many souls of priests will be quickened and consoled by them. Many priests will be moved to spend time in the radiance of My Eucharistic Face, and to abide close to My pierced Heart. This is My desire for them. I want to draw all My priests into the radiance of My Face, and then into the sanctuary of My open Heart. (*August 26, 2010*)

If you remain close to Me, abiding in the light of My Eucharistic Face, and close to My Eucharistic Heart, I will not allow you to be deceived in the words you hear from Me, nor will I allow you to lead others astray. You have only to prefer My company to every other companionship, the love of My Heart to the love of every other heart, and the sound of My voice in the silence of your soul to every other voice. (*September 1, 2011*)

The words I give you are for your instruction, for your consolation, and for the conversion of your heart in love, but they are not for you alone. Others will read them and they too will be moved to repentance. They will be comforted, and begin to seek My Face and draw near to My Heart in the Sacrament of My love. (*September 23, 2011*)

I speak to you because you need the assurance of My friendship and the guidance that only I can give you in this way. You may not recall all that I say to you, but My words are not without a lasting effect, even if you forget them, or no longer read them. No word of Mine is vain. Every word that I utter is fruitful in the soul that offers no resistance to it. You have not resisted My words—quite the opposite: you have received them according to your ability, and so I am making them bear fruit in your soul, and in your preaching, and in your life as it unfolds. (*November 6, 2011*)

The vision has been shown to you; you have written it down. Now is the time to make it known. Hearts will be moved, and through the kindness of a multitude of little ones I will provide what is needed for My work to go forward. (*November 21, 2011*)

Live the message I have given you, and then make it known, for by means of it I will touch the hearts of many of My priests and bring them back to Myself. I wait for each one in the Sacrament of My love. (*January 30, 2012*)

Make these words known. They will touch many hearts and I will make them fruitful in the souls of those who will read them with simplicity and with faith. There is nothing new in the words that I speak to you; their newness is in the way I am expressing My Heart's desires and My abiding love for My priests, to you and through you, for the sake of many. Be simple, then; pass on what I say to you during these times of adoration, and trust Me to give growth to the seed thus scattered abroad. (*January 31, 2012*)

Come to Me in adoration, and I will make straight your path before you. I will remove the obstacles that loom in the distance, and I will provide for every need as it arises. Listen to Me and write My words, for I am speaking to you as I have done in the past and as I shall continue to do, for you are the friend of My Heart, and I have chosen you for this work which is Mine. (*March 6, 2012*)

I am speaking to you now as I have already spoken to you in the past, and as I will continue to speak to you for your own sake and for the sake of those who will read My words. . . . Listen closely to My inspirations and to the suggestions that I make through your guardian angel, through My Immaculate Mother, and through our friends, the saints whom I have charged to support you, to guide you, and to walk with you in this life. (*April 29, 2012*)

I am speaking to you now as I have in the past, from the depths of My Heart's love for you. Believe in My love for you, and I will protect you from the errors of your own imagination and from the deceits of the Evil One. . . . There are those who will not believe that I have spoken to you, or that I am speaking to you still. Do not allow this to trouble you. What I say to you will be recognized as coming from Me by the fruits it produces in your life. Do not dwell on apprehensions and fears of going astray. Trust in Me, and in the guidance of the Holy Ghost, who dwells within you, and rests upon you. So long as you hear in My words to you nothing that varies from the teaching of My Church, you can go forward in peace. (*June 22, 2012*)

The words that I have given you are given not for you alone, but for the priests whom I will send to you. Share with them this desire of My Heart for priests who will keep watch close to My altars and abide in My presence, even if this means forsaking things that are, in themselves, innocent, and good, and gratifying. (*March 28, 2013*)

My voice is always one of comfort and of love, producing peace in the soul—even when My words are cutting, even when they pierce the heart like the surgeon's scalpel. Trust, then, in My words to you, and close the ear of your imagination and heart to all else. (*November 28, 2014*)

Do not doubt that I have given you these words: I have prepared you over a lifetime to receive them and to transmit them. (*December 2, 2014*)

Index of Persons and Subjects

Subjects that arise on most pages of the book—such as adoration, reparation, friendship, the Most Holy Eucharist, and the Holy Face—are not included in this index. However, particular aspects of them are included, e.g., nocturnal adoration.

Index of Days and Dates

This index comprises the days, dates, feasts, and seasons that are mentioned in the boldface headings throughout the book. For mentions inside the body of the text, see the Index of Persons and Subjects *above.*

Days

Mondays, 4, 13, 18, 83, 88, 98, 107, 109, 119, 135, 144, 145, 150, 154, 158, 174, 177, 178, 180, 192, 198, 206, 219, 224, 230, 239, 242

Tuesdays, 19, 22, 34, 69, 95, 98, 100, 111, 115, 119, 120, 128, 136, 139, 145, 147, 155, 166, 168, 173, 178, 179, 182, 186, 208, 210, 221, 225, 228, 252

Wednesdays, 1, 6, 20, 36, 67, 90, 103, 109, 113, 116, 122, 139, 149, 160, 182, 193, 195, 203, 213, 222, 225, 253

Thursdays, 2, 7, 21, 24, 26, 30, 31, 42, 43, 45, 47, 48, 50, 56, 57, 58, 59, 61, 62, 63, 64, 68, 69, 70, 72, 75, 77, 79, 80, 83, 91, 97, 98, 103, 117, 123, 127, 131, 141, 160, 167, 169, 180, 183, 187, 196, 199, 224, 229, 232, 234, 236, 238, 240, 246, 248, 256, 257, 258, 259, 260, 262, 263, 264, 265

Fridays, 3, 10, 15, 33, 38, 47, 51, 66, 99, 103, 104, 105, 125, 131, 138, 150, 152, 163, 167, 174, 185, 189, 215, 223, 230, 235, 236, 245, 250

Saturdays, 4, 12, 16, 39, 53, 86, 106, 108, 125, 129, 132, 142, 143, 153, 156, 168, 171, 179, 194, 197, 198, 202, 205, 217, 227, 233, 234, 242, 244, 255

Sundays, 12, 16, 41, 54, 82, 84, 94, 100, 107, 126, 128, 134, 138, 144, 145, 159, 162, 164, 171, 172, 175, 177, 190, 196, 200, 212, 219, 229, 231, 232, 237, 247

Dates

YEAR	DATE	PAGE
2007	Wednesday, October 3	1
	Thursday, October 4	2
	Friday, October 5	3
	Saturday, October 6	4
	Monday, October 8	4
	Wednesday, October 10	6
	Thursday, October 11	7
	Friday, October 12	10
	Saturday, October 13	10
	Sunday, October 28	12
	Monday, October 29	13

Feasts & Seasons

Only those feasts, liturgical seasons, or special days that are expressly mentioned in the journal headings are listed below. (For internal or oblique references, see the Index of Persons and Subjects.*) As some of the dates correspond to the revised Roman calendar and others to the traditional Roman calendar, no attempt has been made to impose uniformity where it does not exist in the manuscript.*